DO YOU BELIEVE IN MAGIC?

ANNIE
GOTTLIEB

DO YOU BELIEVE
IN MAGIC?

THE
SECOND COMING
OF THE
SIXTIES GENERATION

Times
BOOKS

Grateful acknowledgment is made to the following for permission to reprint previously
published material:

Alkatraz Corner Music Co.: Excerpt from the lyrics to "I-Feel-Like-I'm-Fixin'-to-Die Rag,"
words and music by Joe McDonald. Copyright © 1965 by Alkatraz Corner Music Co. Used
by permission. All rights reserved.
Gold Hill Music, Inc.: Excerpt from the lyrics to "Wooden Ships" by Stephen Stills and
David Crosby. Copyright © 1969 by Gold Hill Music, Inc./Guerilla Music. Used by
permission. All rights reserved.
Ice Nine Publishing Co., Inc.: Excerpts from the lyrics to "Crazy Fingers," copyright ©
October 28, 1975, by Ice Nine Publishing Co., Inc.; "New Speedway Boogie," copyright
© September 4, 1970, by Ice Nine Publishing Co., Inc.; "Brokedown Palace," copyright
© January 8, 1971, by Ice Nine Publishing Co., Inc.; words and music by Jerry Garcia and
Robert Hunter.
Paul Simon Music: Excerpt from the lyrics to "American Tune" by Paul Simon. Copyright
© 1973 by Paul Simon. Used by permission.
Warner Bros. Music: Excerpt from the lyrics to "Ballad of a Thin Man" by Bob Dylan.
Copyright © 1965 by Warner Bros. Inc. Used by permission. All rights reserved.
W. D. Ehrhart: The poem "Guerilla Warfare," from *To Those Who Have Gone Home Tired:
New and Selected Poems*, by W. D. Ehrhart. Thunder's Mouth Press, New York, 1984. Used
by permission.
Hudson Bay Music Inc.: Excerpt from the lyrics to "Do You Believe In Magic" by John
Sebastian. Copyright © 1965 by Alley Music Corp./Trio Music Co., Inc. All rights adminis-
tered by Hudson Bay Music Inc. Used by permission. All rights reserved.

LIBRARY OF CONGRESS CATALOGING-IN-PUBLICATION DATA
Gottlieb, Annie.
Do You Believe in Magic?
1. United States—Social conditions—1945–
2. Middle age—United States. I. Title.
HN65.G68 1987 306'.0973 86–14390
ISBN 0–8129–1225–X

Manufactured in the United States of America
9 8 7 6 5 4 3 2
First Edition

Designed by Beth Tondreau

FOR THE FAMILY

AND FOR ROBERT J. MURPHY, M.D.

1948–1986

CONTENTS

C ONTENTS

ACKNOWLEDGMENTS

This book is a collective creation. Without the generosity and candor of the hundred or so people I interviewed in depth, it would not exist. Whether they appear in the book as themselves, or asked that their identities be protected (pseudonyms are marked with an asterisk the first time they occur), they gave of their thoughtfulness, their heart, their humor, and their stories more freely than I could have hoped. Many gave of their hospitality as well. They became not only my co-authors, but my "family" in the Sixties sense. The interpretations (or misinterpretations) and conclusions in this book are mine; the richness is all theirs.

I am grateful, also, to the magic that led me to so many of them, the inspired "chance" encounters that came to seem part of a larger design. Others who have been guided in this way will know what I mean. I often felt that I had been chosen to do this job and that I was receiving mysterious help with it. I felt inadequate, scared, and immensely privileged much of the time.

A note on the limitations of this enterprise. The Black, Native American, and Hispanic liberation movements were the leaders of the Sixties. It was their rediscovery of the varied heritages of America that inspired the rest of us to try to jump out of the mainstream. For the most part, those movements appear in this book through the admiring eyes of the white Sixties generation, rather than through the eyes of their participants, whose complex and distinctly different experience of the Sixties and Eighties requires a book of its own.

In addition to my interview subjects, I would like to thank the many people with whom I had unrecorded conversations that helped shape and confirm my sense of the "collective autobiography."

Thanks to Alison Friesinger for able research assistance, and to Donna Henes, Daile Kaplan, and Janet G. Nuñez for sensitive transcription of interview tapes.

The following were some of the crucial nodes on the "grapevine" that led me to my interviewees: Margot Adler, Apple Spa and Paddle Club (in the primal soup of whose whirlpool bath many friendships are engendered), Robert Campbell, Mary Christiansen, Gene DeFigueiredo, Amy Delson, Martha G. Ferguson, Paul Freundlich, Joan Giannecchini, Nancy Goodman, Donna Henes, Dalma Heyn, Wynston Jones, Jesse Kornbluth, Paul Levy, Jessica Lipnack, Jeffrey Maron, Donna Mildvan, Sara G. Monroe, Carl Nagin, Margaret and Warren Pearson, Joel Polis, Mark Satin, Gary Silverman, Charlene Spretnak, Jeffrey Stamps, Margaret Harris Straus, Phil Straus.

The following is a partial list of people who helped with information, ideas, or hospitality: Len Ackland, editor of *The Bulletin of Atomic Scientists;* the late Constance Ernst Bessie; Steve Cappell, Statistics, Vermont Department of Health; Barry Casselman; Catalyst, the research organization in New York City specializing in issues concerning women, family, and work; Diane Crispell, Research Department, *American Demographics;* Bob Draiss, Principal Stat Clerk, New York State Department of Health, Bureau of Biostatistics; Norma Durland, Locator, United States Bureau of the Census; Dr. Jay Harold Ellens; Leslye Noyes Faithfull; Darlene Stern Geis; Peter Geis; Robert Gilbert; Harry and Jean S. Gottlieb; Morning Glory and Otter G'Zell; Emil Hahn of Munich, West Germany; Geraldine Hanon; Barbara Hill, Office Manager, *The Mother Earth News,* Chicago; Perry Izenzon, Director, Potsmokers Anonymous; Chris Kalb of the Computer Factory; Jamie Katz, Editor, *Columbia College Today;* Kate McIntyre, Advertising Department, the Sierra Club; David and Marilyn Nasatir; the New York Public Library; Kenneth S. and Phyllis Norris; Margaret and Warren Pearson; Helen Powers, National Council of Jewish Women; Elizabeth Randall; Beverly Roets, Advertising Director, *The Mother Earth News;* Anne and Edwin Rothschild; Elodie Sanz de Santamaria; Paul Siegel, Chief of the Education and Stratification Branch, U.S. Bureau of the Census; Anne Smith, Coordinator, Women in Mission and Ministry, National Office of the Episcopal Church; Dr. Dorothy S. Zinberg, Lecturer on Public Policy, Kennedy School of Government, Harvard; Dr. Norman Zinberg.

I want to thank Clyde Taylor, my agent, of Curtis Brown, for his strong encouragement and representation; Hugh O'Neill, my editor, for his enthusiasm and patience, and for asking just the right fly-fisherman questions to bring up the book that was lurking; Jonathan Segal, editor in chief of Times Books, for his early and consistent support; and all those on the staff of Times Books, Random House, and Curtis Brown who "believed in magic."

Most of all, I want to thank Jacques Sandulescu, for both cherishing me and driving me past my limits, and for showing me how to write simply with his beautiful *Donbas.*

Others who provided vital sustenance during the writing of this book are Whitley Strieber, John W. Reckwerdt, Sensei Nobuyuki Kishi, and Eve DeFreitas.

Special thanks to the little giant, Georg Marzell.

INTRODUCTION: EXILES IN TIME (1980–86)

I don't know a soul who's not been battered,
I don't have a friend who feels at ease.
— PAUL SIMON
"American Tune"

"We're all in love with chaos, don't you see?"

It was 1980. I was trying to explain to my bewildered father, a product of the Depression and World War II, why at thirty-four I still didn't have a child, a house, or a financial plan for the future. I wanted my father to understand why my partner and I saw no reason to get married, preferring to renew our eight-year-old commitment from day to day; why we camped in our apartment like gypsies and spent most of our money on travel. I wanted him to understand why I was ambivalent about my thriving career as a free-lance writer, and still sometimes dreamed of chucking it to become a survivalist, a

3

mime, or a guru's devotee. Couldn't my dad see what we all saw so clearly? For the first time in history the continuity of life itself was threatened—and he wanted me to start an IRA!

I kept saying "we." Perhaps I was just seeking safety in numbers. But I think I was instinctively speaking as a representative of my generation. Certainly I wasn't alone in my oddness. Nearly every contemporary I knew had something a little *off* about his or her life. There was the dope-smoking banker who handled millions brilliantly by day and made fun of it at night. There was the diving teacher on a remote Caribbean island who had once been a scientist . . . and a Hare Krishna. There was the cabdriver who saw Vietnam visions on quiet Richmond streets. There seemed to be a lot of carpenters with college degrees and lawyers homesick for the Himalayas. And there were my four closest women friends: the professor and the executive, both (like me) childless and living with much older men; the attorney and the photographer/nurse, both soon to marry younger men at the eleventh hour for babies.

What was the trouble with us? Our life cycles were misshapen. Millions of us had never really entered the young-adult stage; instead, we'd dallied in a prolonged, nomadic adolescence that had engulfed our twenties and threatened to claim our thirties as well. "Remember Lauren Bacall in *To Have and Have Not*?" I asked my father in 1980. "Well, she was nineteen years old—and she was older than I'll ever be!"

Just as we reached adulthood, I explained, adulthood had ceased to exist. No coincidence: we'd done away with it, preferring to be, in Janis Ian's words, "aging children" rather than take on the responsibilities and restrictions, compromises and corruptions, we saw in our parents' lives (sorry, Dad). Now, though we were at last beginning to commit ourselves to love, work, and place, commitment had a foreign, disbelieving feel, as if the future were ice too thin to hold a promise. It might give way under our feet at any moment, as it did once before, just as we were coming of age . . . in the 1960s.

A T-shirt seen recently on the street provokes a rueful grin: STUNTED BY THE SIXTIES. Even those who feel enriched by that crazy decade know exactly what the T-shirt's author means. On the brink of adulthood, our lives were blown out of the water; as we stepped up to take our place in American culture, the culture was dynamited out from under us . . . by us, driven by imperatives we didn't fully understand. Between 1965 and 1970, all the mental and social structures we'd grown up with were trashed in an orgy of anguish and extravagance, political outrage and cosmic revelation, drugs 'n' sex 'n' rock 'n' roll. Whether we threw ourselves into the fray or watched from the sidelines, that time changed all of us, and scarred many.

But perhaps what had scarred us even more than the Sixties themselves was their failure . . . their disappearance into thin air.

Though we hadn't been sure of the details at the time, we knew we had a mission. We were to stop the death rampage of our dying civilization, join hands with our brothers and sisters of all colors, and begin healing the earth. Our experiments on ourselves had been meant to give birth to a new humanity. Instead, they had simply isolated us from the rest of our society. Older and younger generations had joined hands around us to carry on American culture much as it had been before (except that women now enjoyed equal stress with men).

"Sixties people are like an island, different from everyone around us," says a teacher of disturbed kids (born in 1954),† a veteran of the Earth People's Park commune in Berkeley. "Why don't people help each other more?" asks her sculptor husband (1949). "Having those values today makes me feel like a Martian." "The world has changed back," says a psychologist (1941), another daughter of Berkeley. "I'm afraid we were just an aberration." A poet disguised as a public defender (1947), who was at Columbia in 1968, says, "I feel like an exile in time."

Some Sixties veterans wore their exile with a tattered pride. Others opted back into "the System," cashing in on the deferred birthright of class and education. Graying men and women sat in law school and computer classes beside the sleek new kids. Therapists took courses

†Dates in parentheses are birthdates.

in real-estate investment or insurance sales. Hair fell to the floors of thousands of beauty parlors and barbershops. Credit cards bloomed in thirty-five-year-olds' pockets. In synch with siblings five to fifteen years younger, we bought our first houses and had our first babies . . . or our first babies by our second or third, *real* marriages. At the eleventh hour, we had knocked together a rough semblance of our parents' lives, lives we had once arrogantly despised. With this came a new respect for our parents and a late-mended generational bond where the gap had been.

How did we feel about all this? Humbled. We had been such a grandiose generation, buoyed on our youth and wealth. "We were wise guys, all of us," says Marc Barasch (1949), former editor of *New Age Journal*. "We thought we could get around gravity if we were clever enough or enlightened enough." It was a relief as well as a defeat to lay down that grandiosity and admit that we had ordinary human needs, like family and money, and ordinary human limitations as well. No, we could not utterly reinvent ourselves and human culture. Yes, we had some of the same dreams as our mothers or fathers. And it seemed we were too small to save the world . . .

Today the Sixties generation seems divided—at least in the self-image the media feed back to it—into two economic and moral classes, the poor-but-virtuous and the rich-but-compromised . . . both equally ineffectual. This, of course, is how we were portrayed in *The Big Chill,* a movie that made some people tearful (mostly because of its soundtrack) and a lot of people furious. There was the Vietnam vet, who had integrity but was impotent, literally and figuratively; then there were all the others, who had sold out for various versions of success. Finally, all they had left from the Sixties were their memories, their friendships, and their record albums.

With this dispiriting split in our generation's self-image has come a corresponding split in the way we view the Sixties. Some are frankly homesick for the easy sharing and passionate caring of those years. "It was a time of conscience, wasn't it?" says a male labor lawyer (1950). "Powerful nostalgia for that feeling of being on the right side," sighs a wealthy woman songwriter and filmmaker (1947). "We had fun then, and we also cared," sums up a black woman in her thirties reading Solzhenitsyn on a New York City bus.

Others have reacted against the Sixties, and now see them as excessive, deluded, and silly. Writer Stephen King (1947), revealing a talent for satire as well as horror, says, "I find it impossible to write about the Sixties. I can't write a sentence where somebody says 'Oh, wow,' or 'Power to the people,' without breakin' up. None of it seems real to me now, and I didn't believe half of it when it was going on. What comes up for me when I think about the Sixties is turning on 'The Tonight Show' and seeing Robert Culp in a Nehru jacket and a peace medallion. White go-go boots. It all seemed so surface, so Mylar. All reflection. A lot of dazzle and sizzle, and very little substance." For those who feel this way, even the soundtrack has soured. "I can't even listen to the music," says King. "Most of it really sucks."

Though former *New Age Journal* editor Marc Barasch disagrees about the music—the Beatles are "immortal"—he admits that a Sixties heritage can be "so embarrassing. Like, 'I did so many crazy things. I made such a fool of myself.' " Beneath this almost allergic aversion to the past, however, Barasch detects a current of deep disappointment. "When I took over the magazine, I went to Jerry Rubin's networking party in New York, and I started deliberately talking about the Sixties," he says. "This was in 1981, in the early yuppie days. Your badge was that you pooh-poohed the Sixties. It's gauche to remember that you were a part of it. I was going around challenging that, saying that the idealism was fine, and not to be embarrassed about it. I was amazed at how quickly people said, 'That isn't how the world is.' It's self-protection, like when you leave a love affair. What a fool, throwing yourself away on somebody. You're never going to be a fool again."

Both nostalgia and cynicism are fruitless relations to the past. Nostalgia can't bring the Sixties back even if we wanted them (and few of us do); cynicism denies their lasting lessons. Most of us are glad to be rid of the decade's arrogant naïveté, but even the most hard-boiled pragmatist wouldn't mind having back some of the freshness of vision, the moral energy, the sense of solidarity and hope. But throughout the Sixties generation, as we near forty, there is a feeling of, "Where did it all go?" Where are the millions of comrades in each other's arms, the warm bodies that packed every rock concert, college campus, and demonstration, the tattered and colorful armies of love? Forever dispersed into castles of bourgeois comfort and pockets of principled despair?

Haunted by these questions myself, I traveled around the United States talking to diverse survivors of the Sixties. I slept in elegant guest bedrooms with their own private baths, on sagging couches covered with worn quilts, and in an old purple school bus warmed by a wood stove. I was offered forty-dollar-a-bottle wine in crystal and Almaden in a cow's horn, sacramental dope and blade-on-mirror-squeaky coke. I held fragrant babies and read the shy poems of thirteen-year-olds. And I found that the reports of our death are not just exaggerated, but wrong.

Despite the sense of isolation almost everyone feels, despite the great differences and disagreements among us, we are still a generation far more united than divided. The forty-year-old corporate lawyer in the three-piece suit, the thirty-six-year-old social-service worker in the Volkswagen, and the graying hippie in the hills are brothers and sisters under their styles. And there is late, shamefaced, nearly universal admission of kinship with the Vietnam vet. Even our quarrels are family quarrels, aspects of an ongoing ethical debate among people who care about the same ends but disagree fiercely on how to achieve them. These quarrels—over the lure of technology, the morality of money, the shape of the family—are the heart of our generation's culture.

Sitting in an office in Washington or a yurt in Mendocino County, a kitchen in Boston or a family restaurant in St. Louis, I felt like nothing so much as an anthropologist visiting her own tribe. For the Sixties generation is a tribe with its roots in a time, rather than a place or a race. Like many human tribes, we were founded on a vision. We share a culture; we share a religion, though many would not call it that; and as we approach the "power age" of forty, and a second chance to make an impact on the world, we share a fascination with our origin myth, the experiences of the Sixties that, to a great extent, made us who we are.

First Wave, Second Wave

"Generations could be divided according to essential impressions around seventeen," a German emigré social scientist, Dr. Sigmund Neumann, said in a speech in 1939, "The Conflict of Generations in Contemporary Europe." "Modern psychology has proved that . . . impressions received in those years are deep and persistent. . . . This holds especially true of a generation of adolescents which went through experiences of weight. This gives them a unity, a common style, a new approach to life."

Dr. Neumann was speaking of the generation born between 1890 and 1900, whose impressionable late teens had taken the direct impact of World War I. But his description of that generation—and of its older and younger siblings, who received only glancing blows of the war—could almost be a description of the different sub-generations within the baby boom. The ways we were shaped by the Sixties depend on how old we were when they hit.

Neumann defines the vulnerable age as newly out in the world, but not yet established in it. "Not like a generation only ten years older had they already found a place in society," he says of the core World War I generation. "They had just left school, ready to carve out lives of their own," as the core Sixties group had just left home or gone to college between 1963 and 1968. It is the life stage of maximum idealism and susceptibility. The years just before World War I had seen "a unique youth movement . . . to fight the artificial and corrupt style of bourgeois life," as the early Sixties had seen folk music, the Civil Rights movement, and the Peace Corps.

Unlike Vietnam, World War I mobilized and decimated a whole generation. But like Vietnam, it was a bitterly disillusioning war. "Those who returned were cynics and skeptics," Neumann said. "They had lost connection with their profession, with their family,

with civil society. . . . Hopelessly worn out by this great ordeal
. . . they distrusted the noisy and petty world of busy people they
returned to. Those, in return, distrusted the strange fellows who had
seen a no-man's land, and had experiences which they could exchange only with their co-warriors."

Compare Marc Barasch, speaking of his contemporaries: "There's
a woundedness to this generation. You see it most clearly in the
people who went to Vietnam, but I see it in my friends, too. That time
was so painful, so difficult. It was our war." Of course that comparison can't be stretched too far without diminishing the experience of
Vietnam vets. The "war of values" most of us fought at home—
against our parents, our government, our whole cultural heritage—
may have been a "great ordeal," with its own body count of drug
burnouts and breakdowns, but let's face it—it was a great party, too.
And too many of us are making out too nicely now to be called a "lost
generation" (as Gertrude Stein called the post–World War I writers).
Nonetheless, those born between 1944 and 1949, who came of age
in the years 1965–70, are a special generation. Together with smaller
numbers born in the late 1930s and early 1940s, this "first wave"
was at the epicenter of the cultural earthquake. People now in their
late thirties and early forties met the Sixties tide at its flood in their
late teens and early twenties. They took the Sixties most seriously and
were the most traumatized and transformed.

Those born later, between 1950 and 1957—the "second wave" of
the Sixties generation—were old enough to be impressed and confused by the changes, but young enough to adapt to them. While
"first wave" people tend to be earnest, passionate, visionary, and
somewhat shell-shocked, "second-wavers" seem ironic and low-key,
with lower expectations, yet more resiliency. I think of them as the
"John Sayles–Anne Beattie generation," because those two artists so
perfectly epitomize their tone, compared to such apocalyptic fantasts
of the first wave as Jonathan Schell, Stephen King, and Steven
Spielberg. Second-wavers generally have achieved an easier blend of
pragmatism and idealism than their elders. Many cut their hair and

got back on the straight track sooner and with less conflict than their older siblings did.

Because the Sixties upheavals coincided with their teenage hijinks, not with their passage into adulthood, many second-wavers went through a turbulent, formless phase at the same time the culture did, and that, ironically, made it easier to assimilate and even to outgrow. Second-wavers were too young to see the wave of chaotic change as a threat or a revelation. It was simply their environment, and they swam in it like fish in the sea, adapting to its hazards and opportunities.

Even older second-wavers entered a counterculture already structured by traditions and rituals of its own. The first edge of shock and discovery had worn off drugs and unmarried sex. Drugs were more often for rebellion, adventure, and escape than for vision. Sexuality, no longer such a big deal, came earlier and easier to many second-wavers (too easily, some would now say). So did friendship between men and women and acceptance by both sexes of women's work aspirations. Feminism came early enough to be formative, instead of painful. (Many second-wave men are married to older, first-wave women.)

Despite these differences, the two "waves" of the Sixties generation are much more like each other than they are like the generations before and after them, who were too old or too young to be intimately shaped by the Sixties. "Their education was finished, their life was formed before the war started," Neumann said of the "pre-war generation" of 1914. Similarly, many of our older siblings were already on high ground when the wave of change hit—and they seem to have lived on another planet. An actor (1951) who has evaded emotional commitment describes his older brother (1941) who "bought into the Ozzie and Harriet thing and doesn't know how to get out of it"; an occupational therapist (1948) has to counsel her nephews about drugs because her sister-in-law (1941) "will take pills for a headache or have three cocktails, but does not understand smoking grass."

Even more striking is the contrast with those younger, those still in their twenties, who we had naïvely assumed would follow in our footsteps. "[E]ven if born before the war, [they were] not at all impressed by this paramount event," Neumann wrote of the generation shaped not by World War I but by its cynical aftermath. "They did not want to reform the world. They wanted to live." Does that sound like anyone you know? An editor (1955), who "caught the tail end of radicalism" from admired older siblings, is bewildered by her "preppy, conservative, conventional" youngest sister (1965). I can see the line drawn between my own brothers, just three years apart —the nomadic, anarchistic journalist (1956) and the serious, ambitious actor (1959).

The last members of "the Sixties generation" seem to have been born around 1958—the year, astrologers will tell you, that Pluto, the planet that demarcates generations, passed from revolutionary, self-centered Leo (where it had been since 1939) into conservative, materialistic Virgo. Did the Sixties really make us, or did we make them? Whichever, they were our time, and—first-wave or second-wave—we're suddenly eager to talk about them. Why precisely *now* is a mystery; perhaps enough time has finally passed to see it all in perspective and not feel threatened by it. Or perhaps it's just that, as Tabitha King says wryly, "We're middle-aged now, and middle-aged people talk about their youth." But I think there's more to it than that.

Everywhere I traveled, I sensed a wave gathering, a spring stirring. Once again, Buffalo Springfield could sing, "Somethin's happenin' here." Beneath the depression and self-interest which are our adaptations to Reagan America, the generation's real energies have begun to move again. As I say this, I get an unbidden satirical flash of Paul Henreid in the fog of Casablanca Airport, saying, "This time I know our side will win!" We know no such thing, but we are ready to try again. Consciences, long submerged in family life, have begun to lift their eyes from the changing table and to see as far as Ethiopia or El Salvador. Ideals, chastened and toughened by years of exile in Reality, seem poised to become practical, even profitable. Leadership is preparing itself, like crocuses under snow. In every dimension of

American life—in classrooms, governor's offices, nurseries, board-rooms, bedrooms—the seemingly ephemeral "flowers" of the Sixties are beginning to bear fruit.

This book is the saga of an evolutionary war, of a long night's journey to a new morning. It's about the scars, the delays, the defeats encountered within and without, the ways we went too far, the battles we won, the friends we made and lost, and above all, the stories we tell. It is a book full of voices and remembrances, of the Vietnam War and the anti-war movement, of restless travel and radical politics, of drugs and spiritual quests, of new forms of love and work. It's high time to tell our stories, and to say, if we can, what their moral is. For we are racing toward the confrontation for which the Sixties changed us, the showdown with our dark sibling, the Bomb.

PART ONE

RITES OF PASSAGE

The phenomenon we call "the Sixties" did not begin at 12:01 A.M. on January 1, 1960. It is not a chronological entity so much as a cultural or mythic one. Even if we identify the myth with the decade, it would be more accurate to say that it began on November 8, 1960, with the election of John F. Kennedy, and ended May 4, 1970, on the campus of Kent State.

Looked at this way, the theme of the Sixties is the alienation of generations. A typical family portrait from 1962 would show teenagers with short hair, neat clothes, and scrubbed, smiling faces, apparently on their way—despite a troubling fondness for rock 'n' roll—

to becoming replicas of their parents. Less than ten years later, the same young people, transformed into savages with Indian-warrior hair, tattered clothes, and contorted faces, would scream epithets at the armed representatives of authority, who would club and finally shoot them down.

That's the most literal way to demarcate the Sixties. But those who lived the decade in all its crazed intensity define it differently. Over and over, the people I interviewed said that what they think of as the Sixties began on November 22, 1963.

"When Kennedy was killed is when America changed," says ritual artist and healer Donna Henes (1945). "And that was freshman year in college, our beginning. Perfect timing." Tennessee-born photographer Jim Smith (1946), who describes his experience of the Sixties as "having my world view torn apart with nothing to replace it," says that "the Kennedy assassination really was the trigger." Even much younger people remember that day indelibly: the announcement over the school P.A. system, the teachers weeping, the stunned children sent home. Perhaps one badge of membership in the Sixties generation is an intelligible memory of the Kennedy assassination; those born in 1957 were in the first grade, six years old.

If the Sixties began in 1963, when did they end? Washington mortgage banker Rob Jacoby (1948) nominates 1973, the year the energy crisis triggered the contraction of the American economy. That would define the Sixties as a decade of *upheaval plus affluence* — the two ingredients that together account for the special character of the time. (Times of crisis without affluence, like the Great Depression, provoke a mood of desperate improvisation rather than reckless experimentation.) This definition of the Sixties also corresponds closely to the span of American involvement in Vietnam (the Tonkin Gulf Resolution was approved by Congress August 4, 1964; the Paris Peace Accords were signed in January 1973).

There is, however, a sense in which the Sixties began much earlier: on August 6, 1945, the day the first atomic bomb was dropped on Hiroshima. And in that sense, they have not ended yet. For the political, cultural, and spiritual revolution that erupted in the Sixties can be seen as a response to the challenge of the Atomic Age.

"The unleashed power of the atom has changed everything save our modes of thinking, and we thus drift toward unparalleled catastrophes," Albert Einstein said in 1946. The generation born right around the time the bomb fell—not only in America, but in Western and Eastern Europe and Japan—would, when they came of age, feel driven to search for new modes of thinking and living that might enable the natives of the planet to coexist rather than annihilate each other and their home.

A*CT I:*
1 9 4 5 – 6 3

Bomb Babies

Most of us trace our first conscious awareness of the nuclear threat back to grade-school air raid drills. But some of us who are truly of an age with the Nuclear Age—who were born between 1944 and 1946—feel so fatefully related to the Bomb that we wonder whether it may not have made itself known to us much earlier, in some way addressing our infant minds or cells.

It's striking how many of those responsible for bringing the nuclear threat into mass consciousness were born on the cusp of the Atomic Age: Jonathan Schell, author of *The Fate of the Earth* (1944);

Whitley Strieber (1945) and James Kunetka (1944), authors of *War-day*; Nicholas Meyer, director of *The Day After* (1946); Tim O'Brien, author of *The Nuclear Age* (1946). To suggest that we felt the presence of the Bomb is to enter into the realm of myth and fancy, but one of the lessons the Sixties taught us was that myth and fancy are a part of the whole truth.

It has always mattered to me that I already existed when the bomb fell on Hiroshima: I had been conceived in July 1945.

> I was the size of a thumb
> I shuddered in my mother's womb,

I wrote in a 1979 journal. "Already with one flipper on the bottom rung of the evolutionary ladder; too late to turn back." "You were in a prime biological receptor, your mother, in an amplifier, the fluid, in a total meditative state," muses photographer and astrologer Jim Smith. "You could very well have heard the shrieks." Even those who scorn this as New Age science fiction will admit that we who were very young on August 6, 1945, *were* in touch with "prime biological receptors": our parents. And our parents' reactions to America's use of the bomb ranged from unease to horror.

Looking back at Hiroshima's one "little" bomb, we can't imagine that our parents' generation could have grasped the full dimensions of what had happened. But listen to these editorials from *The New York Times,* August 7, 1945, the original "day after": "Its implications for good and evil are so tremendous in so many directions that it will take months before our minds can really begin to envision them. . . ." "With the horrible prospect of utter annihilation opened by the atomic bomb, it is hard to imagine how people of any nation on earth can possibly want another war. . . ." And on August 8: "The first reaction of the Allied world to this literally earth-shattering event was relief that this engine of immeasurable destruction was not in the hands of the enemy. . . . But in this relief was no elation; it was mixed with wonder, fear, and deep misgiving. . . . if it continues to be a weapon when this war is over, whoever uses it first will be the winner. But the winner will preside over a dust heap. . . ."

Instinctively, people's thoughts turned to their children.

"We felt a terrible guilt," says my aunt Darlene Geis, who had given birth to a son in 1944 and would have another in 1950. "Everyone hopes to bring their kids into a world that's a little better. We were just glad the Depression was over. And then this happened. We thought, 'What kind of world have we brought our babies into?' " Darlene believes that "the fears a child gets transmitted through its parents are much worse than its own fears," and that in the shadow of the Bomb, the parents, "those who were supposed to be strong and sure, to protect, were unsure, frightened, and vulnerable." For Sixties people, this tremor was built into the foundation. It made us susceptible, uncertain of the future.

But there was another level of response to the Bomb that was also an important part of the climate into which we were born. And that was the moral uneasiness many Americans felt at the fact that our country had been the first to use the new weapon. "It is a stain upon our national life," a reader wrote to *The New York Times* on August 8, 1945 (published August 11). "When the exhilaration of this wonderful discovery has passed, we will think with shame of the first use to which it was put." "It is simply mass murder," wrote another, "sheer terrorism on the greatest scale the world has yet seen." Even if you accepted the argument that Hiroshima was necessary to end the war and save American lives—and obviously not everyone did—how could we ever justify Nagasaki?

The sense of guilt was all the more dismaying because we had just come off such a high of good-guy heroism. Only three months after the defeat of the Nazis, Hiroshima and Nagasaki tarnished our shining white World Savior armor. The novel notion that Americans could be the bad guys—carried to hysterical extremes in the Sixties—was born with us in August 1945.

But the most paradoxical aspect of Hiroshima Day, and one that would prove especially fateful for our generation, is that in some way the Bomb blew open the barrier between East and West and began an almost genetic exchange of information. It's as if such a climax of violence fused the two countries together, all hatred spent. The relationship between America and Japan may be a marriage that began with rape, but a marriage of sorts it is, and many of us who came of age in the Sixties recognized ourselves as its children. My father fought against the Japanese; one of my closest friends and strongest influences has been a Japanese karate teacher (himself born in 1948). And many contemporaries have had similar experiences. This new sense of kinship with the Orient made the killing, past and present, vividly painful. The hybrid spirituality of our generation was conceived at Hiroshima; so was its anti-war passion.

The Time Between

In many ways, August 6, 1945, marked a great transition—most crucially to the Nuclear Age. But it also meant the end of the war and the beginning of a new era. Writer Don Robertson, at work on a novel set in 1945–49, describes those years as a kind of blackout period in American history. We know the identity of World War II, we can describe the Eisenhower Fifties, but the brief period in between remains strangely ill-defined. Into the unsettled climate of a country in transition, groping for its new identity, over sixteen million members of the "first wave" were born.

A few things we do know about the postwar years: Of the 15,707,167 American men who came home from World War II, about 1.7 million had some permanent disability. They had seen 405,399 of their comrades die. A record 2,291,045 marriages were recorded in 1946, a record that was not broken until 1979. (The record *rate* of marriage in 1946—16.4 per 1,000 population—has never been broken; the 1979 rate was only 10.6.) The number of births leaped from 2,873,000 in 1945 to almost 3.5 million in 1946 and about 3.75 million in 1947.

But if this was a time of hope and happiness, it was also a time of anticlimax and uneasiness. The relief of peace was almost immediately undermined by the metamorphosis of our wartime ally, Russia,

into a new enemy. The United States brandished its exclusive possession, the atom bomb, to keep the U.S.S.R. in line, and the Soviets
hurried to build a bomb of their own. By the fall of 1949 the arms
race was off and running.

Meanwhile, veterans went from the adrenaline high of war and the
dream of the girl in the snapshot to the low-grade stress of living with
a real woman and a screaming baby in cramped quarters. The middle
class among us see our parents preserved in the amber of the prosper-
ous Fifties; it's hard to imagine them starting out young and poor,
living in tiny apartments or trailers or with their parents. But that's
how it was for millions of couples while the husband went to school
on the GI Bill or worked at a low-paying job. Many young couples
took these stresses in a spirit of high hope and adventure, but some
new and reunited marriages were shaky during those early years.
Marital friction was part of the climate into which many "first-wavers" were born. Writer Stephen King was two in 1949, when his
ex-Merchant Marine father went out for a pack of cigarettes and never
came back.

Readjustment was tough on men, and it was also hard for women,
millions of whom had enjoyed independence and held down wartime
jobs before the men came home. My mother had left college to marry
my father at eighteen; while he was overseas, she lived alone for the
first and only time in her life, working in a machine shop and a
pants-pressing plant. Just twenty-two in 1946, she may have been
unready by today's standards to be a mother, but that was the urgent
ideology of the time. Betty Friedan documented in *The Feminine
Mystique* how the ideal of "woman in the home" was developed in
the major women's magazines after 1945, displacing the spirited
heroines of the Thirties and early Forties. In so many ways, the late
Sixties would be a reversed mirror image of the late Forties. Our
fathers came home from a glorious war; we refused to go to an
inglorious one. Our mothers poured into the home; we would pour
out of it. Our parents sacrificed personal dreams for family; we would
do just the opposite.

If the post-war period was stressful for whites, it was disillusioning for black Americans, for whom the wartime surge in employment opportunities dropped off. Japanese Americans were recovering from their internment in detention camps. Native Americans came home from doing the white man's killing and underwent ceremonies of purification. But the experiences of all these groups, their view of a very different America, went unheard, drowned out by the vigorous hymn of official America in 1950: a homogeneous white Protestant culture.

The Atomic Café

With the election of war hero Dwight D. Eisenhower in 1952, America had found its new identity. Ike's benign smile papered over the uneasiness of the postwar years with assurances of permanent prosperity, progress, and security. Despite the paranoia of the Cold War and the fanaticism of Joe McCarthy, despite the detonation of the immensely more powerful thermonuclear bomb on November 1, 1952, and the "police action" in Korea, white American family life in the Fifties proceeded on the premise that we were all safe and happy.

We kids knew better, at least in our dreams. Most of us remember crouching under desks or in the cloakroom, arms over our heads, while the alarm bells rang and rang. Many responded with nightmares of dying in a bomb blast. Older first-wavers from liberal families also remember the dissonant note of the Army-McCarthy hearings, the gray light of the first seven-inch television illuminating the dismay on our parents' faces. We were five or six, just old enough to understand that McCarthy was an American "bad guy." I got him mixed up with Charlie McCarthy, became frightened of ventriloquists' dummies, and had bad dreams about Mr. Bluster, the puppet villain on "The Howdy Doody Show."

From about the same age, six or seven, Marc Barasch had a prescient, recurring nightmare that could be the whole generation's: "I had this mission to save the world," he remembers. "I didn't think of it that way; I just knew the world was being destroyed. I was running away and I ended up in a clearing, and there was a spaceship. It was a UFO, even though I didn't know anything about UFOs then." ("Steven Spielberg was having the same dreams as you," I interrupted him.) "I got on with all these people I didn't even know. Some were children, and some were adults, though not like parents. The feeling was that we failed. It was a horrible feeling. It stuck with me. It was the only repetitive dream I've ever had in my life."

Our early fears of the Bomb were real. We felt dread when we were old enough to grasp the concept that a single H-bomb could vaporize a city; we would recognize that dread, like a recurring dream, when it flooded back during the Cuban missile crisis in 1962. But for much of our childhood, the fear stayed out of mind—in the subconscious. Consciously, "we had a sense of affluence without a sense of threat," says political activist and consultant Marc Sarkady (1949). "That threat grew up during our time of growing up, but we had a taste of peace."

If our confidence as a generation came from that taste of Fifties security and serenity, our sense of betrayal came from the realization that it had been a lie. In retrospect, the Fifties look like a decade of massive denial (not unlike the Eighties). The fear of atomic war and the doubt of American virtue weren't the only awkward truths we repressed. The myth of "togetherness" (a term Friedan found was coined by *McCall's* magazine in 1954) denied the real strains of family life and the malaise of many women. The national obsession with hygiene denied the natural life of the body. The standardization of suburban living denied the individuality of place and left little place for the individual. Ethnic differences were denied: Jews had Christmas trees, blacks ironed their hair, Indian children were punished for speaking their own language, and the kids in the *Dick and Jane* books were blond. The authority of nature was denied by the triumph of science, on every front from the wheat field to the delivery room. The danger of radiation was denied by those absurd information films the government produced after the dust cloud from an H-bomb test blew through St. George, Utah.

Some of this denial was simple ignorance; we really didn't suspect the harm that pesticides could do until Rachel Carson warned us. Some of it was willful ignorance, suppressing unwelcome truths to be happy or "normal." And some of it was barefaced lying. The Sixties generation would not make such subtle distinctions as we overturned it all in moral outrage. Journalist Nicholas von Hoffman titled his book on the generation after a piece of Haight-Ashbury coffeehouse graffiti: "We are the people our parents warned us against." It might be more accurate to say that we were the return of all that our parents repressed.

Hindsight is clairvoyant, of course. But some of us saw through the Fifties even while they were happening—though, like baby Superman discovering his x-ray vision, we thought at first that something was wrong with our eyes. It is striking how many people's early memories involve awareness of hypocrisy. "It started out as being a five-year-old in a Catholic church in the South," says photographer Jim Smith. "There was one black family in the church, and they were always seated in the last pew. I remember things going back that far, just little things that even at a very young age you start to think, 'It doesn't quite fit.' "

Leni Windle (1949), a nurse now staying home with two children, remembers, "As a kid I was always encouraged to hide my feelings. I remember people saying to me, 'You smile too much. A man isn't going to be attracted to you if you smile so much.' When I was depressed, I was supposed to hide that too. My father to this day will deny that he's ever angry. No wonder I was so confused. I felt one thing and was told that another thing was going on."

Of course, children have always been sensitive to adult hypocrisy. And individual children have grown up to be artists, satirists, or prophets, puncturing the lies of social life. But rarely, if ever, has the better part of a generation tried to hold on to that childhood sensitivity and make it into a principle of adult conduct. If there is one theme that runs like a red thread through the fabric of our generation, it is an obsession with truth: finding the truth, telling the truth, not lying to oneself or others, honesty, authenticity, integrity. If this is a part of our evolutionary task, it got its impetus from the decade of our childhood. "The most powerful resonances in my life are Fifties resonances," says Stephen King, "because of the big difference between what that surface was and what was going on underneath it."

Aliens

This uncomfortable awareness made many Fifties children feel like aliens in their own environment—one reason, perhaps, why the generation remains so fond of monster movies, Marvel Comics, and science fiction. "Since I was four or five years old I felt separated from the status quo," says Jim Smith. Leni Windle thought she was crazy. Stephen King "was at some pains not to let people know how really strange I was." Marc Barasch "never felt quite at home with my own family." Barasch calls this "the freak syndrome": "That's why the label 'freaks' was invented by freaks." Kids who felt this estrangement may not have been consciously searching for a lost home, but when they stumbled on a fragment of Kryptonite—in a movie, a book, a song, a friend—recognition was instantaneous, and the relief was fierce.

"I couldn't have been more than seven or eight years old when I saw *Rebel Without a Cause*," says Stephen King. "And I still remember the intense emotional reaction I had. This kid comes home, and he's been beaten up and treated badly, and Jim Backus, his father, says [simpering], 'Well, let's have some milk, and then we'll make a list. That always helps me.' And the kid says [screaming], 'YOU'RE TEARING ME APAAART!' And it was like somebody opened a window inside my own heart. Somebody had said the truth."

"Rebel" was an early clue. We couldn't have said that the "cause" was an emptiness at the heart of affluent America. But some of us began quite young to look for nourishment outside our own culture. "As a young person in grade school, in Rochester, I can remember looking at the books in the library, looking for the real books," says Ananda Saha (1942), poet, mother, meditator, and piano tuner. "That's how I thought of it: the real books. Where are they? And not finding them, and not knowing how to find them. But feeling that there was a clue to something that I couldn't get to."

Visionary architect Donna Goodman (1950), growing up in all-American Allentown, Pennsylvania, found her first "real book" at eleven: Nietzsche's *Thus Spake Zarathustra,* with its astonishing news that God the strict father might be dead. Ananda Saha, however, was not to find hers until after she graduated from college, in 1963: "I went into a bookstore in Aspen, and there was *The Sayings of the Buddha,* by the Peter Pauper Press. When I read the Four Noble Truths and the Doctrine of Reincarnation, it was *Aha! Okay!"* (At which point she stole the book, surprising herself: "I had the money, but I just took it. It was like a gift from the universe for me or something.") As the Sixties wore on, millions would meet Eastern mysticism with the same eerie sense of recognition. But some had already discovered it in childhood. Marc Sarkady recalls, "When I was a kid in New Haven, I used to go around on the Green with the *Tao Te Ching* by Lao Tzu, and I would just go up to people and ask if I could read them a verse."

Kids who had these interests managed to find each other, and they banded together in a sort of proto-counterculture. "I had weird friends," says Jim Smith, "guys I met as early as fifth or sixth grade. Gangs used to chase us in cars and try to beat us up, because we were just too weird for 'em. By the time we were fourteen we were reading books on Buddhism, we were into socialism, we were reading Jung, and my God, people in Tennessee didn't *do* that in 1962! We used to go to bookstores together and steal paperback books. I stole my education." (Sorry, booksellers, this seems to be a generational plague.) "I intend to pay them back one of these days, I really do," says Smith. "It's my student loan."

If we stole our spirituality from the East, courtesy of the Beat poets, Alan Watts, D. T. Suzuki, and the long-suffering local bookstore, our sensuality was borrowed from black America via Elvis Presley. And this was actually a much earlier and more widespread development. In the first wave, knowledge of Buddhism in high school was confined to a "weird" elite. (In the second wave, you could take a *course* on Buddhism in high school.) But by junior high, everybody loved rock 'n' roll. And almost everybody saw Elvis on "The Ed Sullivan Show."

Television was growing up with us, slowly gaining skill at delivering the images that would make us one organism with a mass memory and mythology. When Ed hosted Elvis in 1956, TV entered its inhibited, yearning puberty along with us. I was ten, and, watching the famed maneuvers of the Pelvis—primly censored just below the waist—I felt the first stirrings in my own. This was a subversive message from Elvis's mentors, much wilder performers like Little Richard and James Brown. Through him, we would gradually discover them, and the hot girl groups of Motown, and black music would start to pour into white guitars and white bodies in a torrent that has never stopped.

"Rock 'n' roll broke the color barrier," says fan Stephen King. Unlike the fine art of jazz, it did so on a mass scale, ultimately bringing dozens of black performers a level of visibility that only a few of the great jazz musicians had enjoyed. The Beatles, the Stones, Bob Dylan, and other white artists acknowledged their own apprenticeship to black rhythm 'n' blues. To white kids coming of age in a culture that sanitized sexuality, rock 'n' roll was another blast of the truth, and dancing was a revolution. Before we even knew where it was coming from, black culture was giving us vitality and—ironically—freedom.

The Dream and the Nightmare

"Free at last, free at last, great God Almighty, I'm free at last!" The voice of Martin Luther King trembled with power and passion. To black listeners, it was a familiar cadence in a new and daring arena. A Baptist preacher on national TV, King challenged the conscience of white America, not in polite pseudowhite accents, but in his own rolling black biblical thunder, making millions hear the music as well as the message. King confronted the indignity of racism with a dignified yet uncompromising demand for justice. His acts—and those of Fannie Lou Hamer, James Farmer, James Meredith, and others—made nineteen million black people visible and admirable to whites. In one great stride, 10.5 percent of the population had gone from the back of the bus to the moral leadership of the nation.

If the Civil Rights movement created a new black man and woman, it also created the possibility of a new America. Before 1960, America's culture and power structure had been monolithically white, Protestant, and patriarchal. The Civil Rights movement ended all that. As it turned out, black activists had opened the door for Native Americans, Asian-Americans, Latin Americans, students, women, gays, the disabled, the old—all those disenfranchised Americans who did not fit the standard of the adult white male property owner.

The new America implied by the early Civil Rights movement would be a radically different America. The voice of Martin Luther King and the voice of B. B. King would be heard throughout the land, loved and claimed as part of the American heritage. Buddhism, the Native American reverence for the earth, the Spanish language, would take their rightful places in American tradition alongside Yankee ingenuity. If this new, compassionate, and truly democratic America could prevail, it might be a prototype for a future world in which people of different races and cultures could coexist, drawing on the accumulated wisdoms of Europe, Asia, and Africa, women and men, the "primitive" and the high tech.

But from the moment it was born, the new America was under vicious attack by the old, as starkly exemplified by the police-sanctioned Klan beatings of Freedom Riders and by the nationally televised spectacle of "Bull" Connor and his bulls assaulting peaceful marchers in Birmingham with dogs, clubs, firehoses, and electric cattle prods. Time after time, the federal government, which early Civil Rights activists had believed would protect them, refused to send in troops until beatings and deaths had occurred. President Kennedy and his brother the attorney general were afraid that intervention would alienate both the powerful Dixiecrats and J. Edgar Hoover, who called Martin Luther King "the most dangerous man in

America." FBI agents in the South often cooperated with local police. The new America, with its uppity colored folks, was correctly perceived as a political and economic threat to the established order— and, of course, a sexual threat as well. To survive, it needed recruits from the majority. It found them here and there throughout white society, but it was to find them en masse in the Sixties generation.

We were young. We had, as yet, no great stake in the System whose apparent heirs we were. And we felt vaguely oppressed by it in many ways: the social and academic competition in high school, the anonymity of the great universities, the sense of hypocrisy and of sensual and spiritual poverty that had already sent some of us on a search with an unknown goal. When TV made us witness the oppression of southern blacks, and the brutality the System at its worst was willing to use against the gentlest challenge, our formless suspicions were suddenly, shockingly confirmed. "I don't believe you could watch a poor black being hit by a big fat southern cop and have it ever leave you," says New York editor Jonathan Segal (1946). "How could you not be moved by that image? How could you not keep it in your head?" And how could you not know which side you wanted to be on?

This posed a dilemma for young whites. If you were black, you were automatically on the right side (at last!), whether you joined the struggle or simply resonated with pride. But if you were white, like the guy swinging the club, you had to do something to dissociate yourself from him. Calling him a redneck was a start, but it wasn't enough. Only action could cleanse you. Only by taking the part of society's victim, and as far as possible sharing his fate, could you share his virtue. The Nazi camps had given us the concept of "identification with the oppressor"; out of the Civil Rights movement would grow a concept to dominate the Sixties: identification with the oppressed. Part guilt, part romance, part apprenticeship, it would drive the privileged young into an alliance with the poor against the conservative white working class.

This alliance began in the Civil Rights movement. At its beginning, the movement welcomed white participants, partly because its religious principles transcended race and denomination, and partly because of "the understood fact that deaths or beatings of whites would gain more attention than those of blacks,"[1] in the words of a white Movement historian. (This was proven during the Mississippi Freedom Summer of 1964, when the murder of a black CORE fieldworker together with two northern white volunteers provoked unprecedented national attention and government investigation. Unlike most of the blacks who had quietly given their lives for the cause, these three found their way into a white folksong: Goodman and Schwerner and Chaney, like the red rose and the briar.)

Early on, black leaders like John Lewis, national chairman of SNCC (Student Nonviolent Coordinating Committee) from 1963–66, distinguished between whites who took part "out of deep religious conviction" and those who did so "out of [a] social, do-good kind of feeling."[2] Only the former were welcomed as brothers and sisters; the latter, motivated by their own guilt or the Movement's glamor, were suspected of being in it for themselves, but were nonetheless put to work until SNCC and CORE ejected all whites in 1966.

The youngest whites who joined the early Freedom Rides and sit-ins were among the older members of the Sixties generation. Tom Hayden (1940), field secretary of a tiny new organization called Students for a Democratic Society, was one of them. But even those who were too young to go to the South watched the news from the front with yearning admiration, picketed their local Woolworth's, raised money for SNCC, and vowed to put their bodies on the line as soon as they got to college. Supporting the nonviolent black struggle was seen as heroic work, at once humble and dangerous, a "good war" for our generation.

In the early Sixties, we felt that the nation had awakened from its Fifties sleep. There was much to set right, but there was reason for pride as well. The ideals of the Founding Fathers were still alive, and the transition from the old to the new America might just be accomplished by moral force alone. An older generation of leaders seemed both responsive and protective, cautioning us against the impatience of youth as Martin Luther King sought to restrain angry young black leaders. The evil was "down there," in the South. (The Harlem riots of 1964 would begin to disabuse us of this notion.) Our ministers and rabbis marched with King, and most of our parents admired him. President Kennedy had created the Peace Corps as another outlet for our idealism. "The whole idea of that was that you can make a difference," says a woman born in 1945. "I was sixteen years old and I believed it. I really believed that I was going to be able to change the world." With an image of youthful activism at the helm, America was successfully socializing its white young.

We could not then have conceived of the Peace Corps as an arm of Yankee imperialism, any more than we could have dreamed that one or both of the Kennedy brothers were screwing Marilyn Monroe. We *believed.* "It was a feeling of being at the apogee of history," Marc Barasch remembers. "A godlike state, the Greco-Roman ideal flowering in some weird way. We had no sense of entropy. We were going to live forever." And so was our handsome young president, with his hero's backache, his two cute kids, his hair blowing in the breeze.

November 22, 1963.

That day, and the days that followed, television became our tribal bard, weaving an unforgettable visual ballad out of live coverage, news photos, the frames of Abraham Zapruder's home movie. The smiling, waving motorcade. JFK's elbows flying up as his hands clutch at his throat. Jackie crawling over the trunk of the car, reaching out for help in her blood-spattered pink suit and pillbox hat. Lyndon Johnson's stunned swearing-in. And then the drum taps, the riderless horse, "Hail to the Chief" played as a dirge. (I had never heard the song before, and I will forever hear it as a dirge.)

These were the images that finally fused us into one, even as they shattered our childhood innocence. We had watched events en masse before, but now for the first time we became conscious of our unity—and our vulnerability. After that day, as the world came apart, we began to come together, reaching out for the physical comfort and power of our numbers. In November 1963, we watched history together. By August 1968, we were making it together in the streets, while the whole world watched us.

ACT II: 1963–68

Things Fall Apart

Who can stop what must arrive now?
Something new is waiting to be born.
—THE GRATEFUL DEAD

"From the time John Kennedy was assassinated until a year after my graduation, I was in a process of total disintegration. Total," says photographer Jim Smith. "It was like my whole enculturation was falling apart with nothing to replace it. I don't feel that this was just a personal disintegration of my life. I feel that it was the disintegration of a culture.

"Basically, the enculturation that I went through, that we all went through, was that everything bad is in the past, everything good is in the future. That we're civilized now, that we're going towards a time when social justice is going to be the norm. I believed all of it. I believed everything. I was a devout Catholic growing up in a Southern Baptist town, which is doubly puritanical. And at the same time, I had this other part of me that was totally wild. All my life, one side of me has been apple pie, red-white-and-blue, Fourth of July, John Philip Sousa, all-American boy, and the other side has been a flaming radical, beat, hippie, alternate person. I was very schizophrenic. I think we all are.

"I was a senior in high school when John Kennedy was killed. And I think that really was the beginning of my disintegration. I was starting to have my world view torn apart. Realizing that, 'What they're saying is just not happening. It's *not* getting better.' And at the same time, the other side of me was saying, 'This was an aberration. It happened, but it's not the way things really are. It's not the norm.'

"Up to my last semester in high school, I didn't know what I wanted to do when I graduated. I finally decided that what I *thought* I wanted to do was go to the Air Force academy and become a pilot. I wanted to fly, and I had ideas of maybe being an astronaut. Somebody told me about this military academy in Alabama that had an academy prep program, high school and junior college. So I went there. Marion Military Institute, in Marion, Alabama. It was just fourteen miles from Selma. They wouldn't let us go near town on Freedom Day, but I had to go in the next day for a doctor's appointment, and I still remember the feeling. Like an armed camp.

"I didn't get an appointment to the Air Force Academy, but Senator Gore offered me an appointment to the U.S. Merchant Marine Academy at Kings Point. I'd never heard of it. I went to the library and looked it up. God, this is running away on a tramp steamer and traveling around the world!—something else I'd always wanted to do. So I said okay, I'll take it. That summer, listening to the radio, I heard the riots in Watts.

"As a plebe at Kings Point you're totally regimented. For the first six months you don't even get off the campus. *Short* hair. About seventy percent of the people there were flaming, flaming right-wing militarists. The other thirty percent of us were way out on a hippie limb, just closet hippies, smoking dope every night, and going to the West Village on weekends as soon as we could. A friend had showed me magazines on where to go when I got to the city. 'Look for the beatniks and the coffee shops on MacDougal Street,' he said. It was a wild thing to see, coming from 'Tinnissee,' but I was ready for it.

"I remember sitting across from my roommate in 1968, studying and listening to the radio, hearing the King assassination happen, the RFK assassination . . . and just looking up at this guy, looking into his eyes and him looking into mine, in *total futility*. And then seeing the Democratic convention on TV. Senior year, I started going to demonstrations. I wanted to be a street photographer. So I went to take pictures. And what I saw with my own eyes . . . well, that's really the only reality there is. Everything else is just hearsay. Whether you read it in a book or whether a friend tells it to you, it's all just hearsay unless you see it yourself. And I've seen a lot.

"The first demonstration I went to was against Nixon coming to the Waldorf-Hysteria, I mean Astoria, to accept a football award as Man of the Year, or some bullshit like that. They had all the demonstrators cordoned off about a block away, and it wasn't disorderly. But they had a big line of patrol cars on the street and a bunch of mounted police. And all of a sudden they would drive a patrol car up like a taxi, grab somebody under the barricades, beat 'em all the way to the car, throw 'em. in, and haul 'em off. Blew me away. Remember, all of this is building up while I'm cloistered, literally cloistered, in this incredibly right-wing thing. By the time I graduated from Kings Point, I was schizophrenic, I think, almost in the clinical sense.

"I graduated on June 5, 1969, and two days later I got married. I had met her freshman year through a computer, the first of its kind —Operation Match, masterminded by some undergraduates at Harvard. It was freaky how incredibly matched we were, to tiny idiosyncrasies, sexual things, everything. And then we were growing apart continuously for the next four years we knew each other. My marriage lasted a year and a month, and out of that time I was on ships for six months. Some marriage. But when it broke up, that was the last thing that totally wiped me out.

"I had taken a commission in the Navy reserve, which meant sailing in the Merchant Marine, and it put me on Vietnamese turf during the war. I took a load of beer and soda pop over to our boys, and then we stayed over there for a while taking damaged matériel to Okinawa, half tracks and small tanks and jeeps that had been blown up, and bringing loads of rebuilt stuff and ammunition back. I was over there for about five months. I never saw any real action, but I saw enough to see what an unbelievable profit scam it was, from the top on down. Saigon was one big black market, with the Americans playing a major role. The war seemed totally money-motivated to me. And it was the same thing that had separated me from society all my life: 'This is what's being said, and this is what I'm seeing.'

"The last straw was coming back from Vietnam, dropping mescaline for the first time in Berkeley, listening to a lot of talk there, getting on an airplane and flying back to New York, still tripping a little bit after about thirty hours, to lay eyes on my wife for the first time in six months and know *immediately,* upon eye contact, that it was over.

"It took six months for it to fall apart. But when it finally did, I flipped out. The end result was getting committed to Elmhurst General Hospital for seven days. It's a real horror story—Thorazine, Stelazine, the whole bit. It was a good and a bad thing. It was literally the death of my old self, and the beginning of something new."

Not everyone was as torn apart by the Sixties as Jim Smith. But in the years after that first assassination, we really did experience "the disintegration of a culture." As the war in Vietnam escalated, the alliance between blacks and whites broke down, and our leaders got picked off like ducks in a shooting gallery, the growing violence around us was matched by a growing bewilderment within. And as if to confirm our own half-formed apprehensions, strange omens and rumors were drifting to us on the winds of music.

Somethin's Happenin' Here

"The first intimation I had that something peculiar was going to happen was in the fall of '63, my senior year at Cornell," says New York artist Stan Kaplan (1944). "The Beatles' music had just become popular. Maybe a half dozen guys started to come to Cornell with 'long' hair, the early Beatle length. The girls liked these guys very much. I remember going to parties and listening to this new music. I would get drunk and listen and think: *The world is going to end. This is the end of the world.* Which was a presage of what, metaphorically, really was going to happen. A world *was* ending. But I didn't see it in those terms.

"After school I worked selling toys for a year. Very straight, nothing happened. Then I was going to be drafted, so I went into the service and spent six months in the reserves. When I got out, I decided to go back to grad school. I was utterly unaware of the war in Vietnam, unaware of any of that stuff. I was worried about me. Who am I? What am I going to do? Post-adolescent problems. I was living at my mom's house in Queens. And I remember going to bed one night and listening to the AM radio, and I heard this song at about two A.M.: 'Something is happening here/But you don't know what it is/Do you, Mr. Jones?'

"It was Bob Dylan, and I was listening to the words. And I remember thinking to myself, *What the fuck is this? What is this guy talking about?* It was absolutely hypnotic. It was as if I had just been changed to a different frequency, zapped right into the radio. I was listening with my ears the size of cauliflowers. I could not get enough of that song. But it ended, and I went back to school the next day . . ."

Something is happening. Something peculiar. What the fuck is this? The end of the world. And the beginning of something new. This was the current of feeling that ran and swelled under the distressing events of the Sixties. It was a sense that something primitive was forcing its way up from beneath, something destructive and creative that would not stop short of total transformation. In part it was the accumulated rage of blacks, racing through American streets in the form of fire. But it was more. It was the relentless removal of controls until, finally, all that the old America had repressed would erupt into the open—violence and chaos, femaleness and instinct, the irrational, the ecstatic, the sexual, the mystical. And the focal point of the eruption, the epicenter, would be us, the young. In the mid-Sixties, we felt the preliminary tremors; our stereos were our seismographs.

Rebirthdays

All we knew was that we felt driven, many of us, to seek out what Jim Smith called "the death of my old self, and the beginning of something new." Abbie Hoffman, asked his date of birth in the Chicago Seven trial, said, "Psychologically, 1960." It is that sense of a second birth that so many of us date back to some time in the Sixties, and we still remember the powerful feelings of destiny, discontinuity, and revelation. We didn't clearly understand what was driving us. Like birds seized by a migratory urge, we moved instinctively and en masse toward those places and influences that would change us. College campuses and "hip" neighborhoods vibrated with the excitement of a gathering flock, about to explode into flight.

"I remember, moving away to school in 1963, that I had a very strong understanding of transformation," says ritual artist Donna Henes. "Like, nobody knows me there. I can be anybody that I want to be. In high school I was very odd and very shy, because I'd had operations on my feet and needed crutches and wheelchairs. Braces, all the typical stuff plus a few extras. Fat. And how liberating that was, to be conscious that you had a second chance."

Arriving at Ohio State shortly before JFK's assassination, Henes discovered "drugs and Beat poetry, Bob Dylan, Lawrence Ferlinghetti, Zen Buddhism, *Siddhartha,* everything that first year." When Ohio State had its own free-speech strike in 1964, right after Berkeley's, shy Donna Henes became "the female Mario Savio." She was elected to the student senate, took part in voter registration of blacks and white miners, and was appointed the university's Human Rights Commissioner. As opposition to the Vietnam War geared up, Henes began using the student senate mimeograph machine to print anti-war leaflets. She was arrested, dropped out of school, moved into a commune on campus, and kept on getting arrested. "It wasn't like I walked into the middle of it all," she says. "It grew up around me. I think I'm really the perfect age."

That, strangely, is a sentiment shared by Sixties people of all ages, as if the call of destiny were so unmistakable that everyone must have heard it at once. "I think I went through the Sixties at exactly the right time," says occupational therapist Lynne Burbridge* (1950), who graduated from high school in 1967. "Because when I went to college, that's when everybody started being much more political." She has a point. Before 1967–68, getting radicalized in college was a minority experience. "In Ohio State we were probably the only ten people who were at that time political," Donna Henes says of her commune. Berkeley disabled-rights activist Kitty Cone (1944) recalls that at the University of Illinois in 1965–66, "there was a very small group of activists on the campus that included Rennie Davis and Roger Ebert. In 1966 we called an International Day of Protest at the same time as homecoming at the U. of I. We had an all-night vigil. I don't think there could have been more than twenty-five of us, professors and students. People went by and just screamed at us and spit and carried on."

Those who gravitated to early radical ideas and activities—folk music, Friends of SNCC, the Quakers, SDS—were often, like Donna Henes, the ones who had felt like "freaks" in high school. But not always. Kitty Cone had won two awards her senior year in high school: the Betty Crocker Homemaker's Award and the American Legion Essay Contest, on the topic, "What I Can Do to Help Fight Communism." Three years later, she dropped out of the University of Illinois to join the Young Socialists Alliance.

But you didn't have to be political to feel the ferment. Recruitment of minority students rose steadily throughout the Sixties, and college administrators made a point of putting people from varied backgrounds on the same dorm floor. "That was the first time I was exposed without parental limit to all different kinds of people," says Los Angeles health-care executive Jennifer Flinton Diener (1945), my college roommate. Pittsburgh contractor Jim Nathan* (1946), the first in his family to get a college degree, went to Hofstra University on Long Island. "He changed his life in so many ways," says his wife, Marian Goodman* (1948). "He met people from all over, instead of just the little enclave of the neighborhood." From quiet Ohio Wesleyan, Ananda Saha transferred to the University of Denver, "a larger school that drew on a wider range of people from all over the world. That was like a door opening for me."

It was a revelation, going from a homogeneous farm town, suburb, or ghetto to a dormitory that was a microcosm of the world. (I first heard the news that John Kennedy had been shot from a Chinese-American dormmate.) The mix could be volatile as politics heated it up, for the new proximity coincided with the new assertion of ethnic identity. Early in college, I read a short story about a black girl who was embarrassed when her white dormmates saw her straightening her hair. Within a few years, some of her sisters and brothers had turned the tables.

"My freshman year was the first year that Barnard decided to have integration," says Grace Parker Sannino (1947), director of public relations for the Calvert Group of Funds, who had come to Barnard from a farming town in New Hampshire. "They picked four blacks who could handle being with whites and four whites who could handle being with blacks, and I was one of those. I'd gone to this liberal summer camp, and there were two blacks that I met there, okay? Other than that, the only black person that I ever was exposed to was the minister of the local black church, who would come around and ask for donations. My grandfather always gave him money because the 'darkies' had rescued my great-grandfather from a southern Civil War prison camp, so 'darkies' were good, you know? But I was part of this experiment. And then my roommate discovered Black

Power, and she and I stopped being people to each other. Finally I went and slept on someone else's floor. It was awful." Another white student found bullet holes in the lid of his trunk in the dorm basement. His Panther roommate had been using it for target practice.

Even Alvin

It's hard to imagine that while all this was going on, some people spent four years in college drunk on beer or sunk in books, all but unaware that the world was changing. Boston banker Alvin Cohan* (1945) is exactly the same age as Donna Henes, yet he sums up his midwestern college career in two words: *"Animal House."* "The early Sixties had very little effect on me," says Cohan. "It was nothing more than an extension of the Eisenhower years. The emphasis was on having a good time. There was no awakening." When Cohan and a friend heard the news of JFK's assassination, "we looked at each other and went in and played basketball." His chief memory of anti-war politics is of passing by a modest demonstration in 1965 or 1966 and improvising a chant with some fraternity brothers: "Rah rah ring, drop it on Peking, rah rah roy, drop it on Hanoi." And yet, even Alvin Cohan was transformed by the Sixties—the *late* Sixties.

"I would count 1960 to 1967 as mindless, and then '67, '68, '69, those three years, as an awakening. That's when everybody started to think," he says, projecting his own "rebirth date" onto the generation. "Those three years and the early Seventies changed us all." What changed Alvin was, first of all, joining the Army reserves "to save my ass" and discovering that it was no surefire guarantee. "In basic training, they would all of a sudden blow whistles and call you into a room and tell you the Chinese had invaded and the president had activated the reserves. You had no access to any news. And I was *scared.* All of a sudden this wasn't a million miles away. It was there, and you were in it. And when you are going to go into a war, you suddenly realize that you damn well better understand what's going on. My first intellectual thought was in the Army. That was a very major advance."

By this time, Cohan had moved to New York City. "The media blast that hit you, being in the center of everything, had a tremendous effect on my psyche. I was meeting all these people who were *thinking*!" And they were thinking thoughts not native to small-town, short-hair America. "The president of the United States got on TV, and guys were dropping their pants and sticking their asses up! They were mooning the president! Well, I got to tell you, that had an impact. If the president was all fucked up, if Johnson and Nixon were killing people, it forced me to realize that the people who made decisions ain't so smart. That you can't respect somebody just because of their position. People are people. I guess that single thing changed me the most: seeing through authority." He was not alone.

Despite his Army haircut and bank job, Cohan began to feel friendly toward alternatives. "I could go to Greenwich Village and see real live hippies. I don't think I could have ever been a hippie—I was trying too hard to be a WASP—but I kind of understood what they were trying to say. It made a lot of sense." Perhaps that was because he had begun to smoke pot, another powerful transformer. "I hate to admit it," he says, "'cause you like to think that straight you have enough strength and ability to become a human being or a thinking person on your own . . . but ah, shit, if it hadn't been for drugs I'd still be back in Iowa, wearing a crewcut and saluting the American flag and not giving a shit about anything."

If the Village and pot could be such potent transformers, the Haight-Ashbury and acid packed an even bigger punch. From its origin in the early Sixties to its commercialization in 1967, the Haight was like that black slab on the moon in *2001,* emitting strange and irresistible signals, directing all who touched it to go even farther out. Marc Barasch picked up the signals in 1967.

"I had transferred high schools and moved out to California, but even in L.A., you didn't necessarily know that anything was going on. I remember driving up to the Monterey Pop Festival, and suddenly, about halfway up the coast, the music started to change. I started hearing things I had never heard, stuff from the San Francisco scene that was not played on L.A. radio. Jimi Hendrix, Moby Grape.

It was instant recognition. There was this strange metamessage. It was a high-context culture, meaning that there were so many shared nuances that you really didn't have to say that much.

"I was suddenly aware of this whole scene. Something was going on. I went back home and told my parents I wasn't going to go to college. They shamed me into going. But first I went to the Haight-Ashbury for about two months. The Summer of Love. I was younger than most in the Haight, crashing in a crash pad with twenty people. A lot of acid, though I waited till after getting back to take it. It was a complete change from how I had grown up. I felt I had fallen into some Utopia whose millennium had arrived. I was heedless of the future, and my past as well."

Barasch took some tabs of acid back to the East Coast at the end of the summer, "because my friends had only vaguely heard of this stuff that was going on. I just wanted to turn on a few people. I was never a Johnny Appleseed"—just one of thousands who made 1967 the year that the cultural revolution reached critical mass. The Haight had been acid-soaked for three years, and Leary and Ginsberg had been proselytizing for LSD on campuses, but it was only after the Human Be-In in Golden Gate Park in January 1967 that the zeal of the media and the pilgrimages of would-be hippies spread the psyche-delic movement and its sacrament throughout the land. A study conducted by Richard H. Blum in the school year 1966–67 showed that 21 percent of the students on one representative campus had smoked marijuana; 6 percent had tried LSD. In 1967–68, the year the second wave began to enter college, the figures had more than doubled: 57 percent had smoked pot, 17 percent had dropped acid.

A Radical Break

In 1967–68 political activism also took a quantum jump. In March 1966, twenty-two thousand people had marched down Fifth Avenue in New York City to protest the war in Vietnam. One year later, on April 15, 1967, ten times as many—over a quarter of a million—massed in Central Park to march to the United Nations. Draft-card burnings and turn-ins and campus demonstrations against recruiters from Dow troubled the spring of 1967. That summer, Newark and Detroit went up in flames. The ending of the graduate-student deferment in July helped bring the war home to more than the hardcore activists. Demonstrations that fall were more militant, attempting to disrupt "business as usual" in induction centers and the Pentagon. Over two hundred major demonstrations shook the school year 1967–68. One of them was the great Columbia University takeover, in which students occupied five buildings, seized files, and held a dean hostage. Public defender Bob Waldman (1947), who feels like "an exile in time," dates his exile from that time and place.

"My experiences were probably a lot more abrupt and less melliflu-ous than those of someone in the Haight," he says, evoking a widely sensed contrast between cultural and political revolution. "I entered Columbia in 1965 and was there till 1969, so I was in New York City during all that stuff. And it was all happening much too fast for me. I was this kid from the suburbs of Illinois who shows up, the first kid from my school to go to Columbia in anybody's memory. And I didn't know what was going on. Radicalism was in the air—radical behavior, radical possibilities. It was very intellectual and very politi-cal. And very violent.

"I remember one moment as almost an axis point in my life. We were occupying some building, up all night. There had been three or four years of speeches and marches and sit-ins, but nothing had really been done. What's next? Nobody knew. And then five or six crazies walked out and said, 'We're going to take over the president's office.' And a few of us followed.

"There was a cop there at the Administration Building, and we shoved this great big black cop aside. And broke the glass on that door. And for me, the sound of that glass breaking was the sound of history breaking. It was the sound of everything being let loose.

"Then began a year and a half, but especially two months, of insane energy. I know many people who went through extreme changes during that time. I think that in that class everybody was deeply affected, and that even though they may have gone off and done things which appear to be normal, they really aren't the same."

1968 was the second great turning point of the Sixties. With the assassinations of King and Robert Kennedy, we lost our last hope of combating racism or ending the war through the System, and the System lost our consent. Some simply gave up. "When RFK got assassinated, I didn't believe anymore," says a woman (1945) who had been an early peace marcher. "I dropped out because I thought it doesn't make a difference now. If you get someone who is good and really is committed, he'll get shot. So why try?" But many more of us took to the streets. After 1968, the anti-war demonstration was the standard adolescent rite of passage.

Leni Windle, who had been the only anti-war student in her conservative suburban Philadelphia high school, entered Boston University in 1969 and found that "everybody was against the war. At that point, politicking was almost no fun anymore, because I was no longer in the minority." Kitty Cone, who had taken part in a 1966 demonstration of twenty-five people at the University of Illinois, learned that in 1969 "they had a march of like ten thousand people, and all the fraternities and sororities did anti-war things for their big decorations for homecoming. And when they did the flash cards in the stadium they flashed peace symbols. It was an incredible change."

"Freaks" had become the norm. All-American boys and girls in the second wave left home and, unless they really fought the current, got swept up in the tide of demonstrations and drugs. There was less a sense of being out on the edge, more a sense of being carried along by the mass. Nonetheless, second-wave transformations could be dramatic, even if they followed a by-now familiar pattern.

Doug Weiner (1950), a "clean-cut high-school football player," arrived at Swarthmore in 1968 to play football. He read *Siddhartha,* and felt "like the caterpillar crawling out of the cocoon." A year later, with hair to his shoulders and a fast friendship with some Krishna devotees, he quit the team and joined a rock band. Getting number 363 in the draft lottery (on a day he remembers in vivid detail) canceled his anxious plans to apply for conscientious objector status.

His post-college passport sports a picture with a ponytail and entry stamps for India and Nepal. Today, he is a clean-cut labor lawyer of high ambitions and high ideals who studies karate and does volunteer work for Tibetan refugees. He is less scarred, he lost less time, than many. But he, too, is "really not the same."

Survivors of the "soft" war at home often gained more than they lost. But at the core of the Sixties generation are the real survivors, the ones most changed: the men who fought in Vietnam. It is striking how many of those who write about Vietnam vets use the language of transformation as well as of damage. Michael Herr, in *Dispatches,* wrote that they "had their lives cracked open for them";[1] psychiatrist Robert Jay Lifton wrote that "prior images of continuity are shattered in these men";[2] Steve Rees, a former underground GI newspaper staffer, writes of combat veterans being "robbed and then remade so basically that some could no longer talk with family or friends."[3] Vietnam vets did not choose their rude awakening, yet many of the transforming experiences the draft-exempt sought out—travel, drugs, exposure to other classes and cultures—had ironic, involuntary parallels in Vietnam (and in the journeys of draft evaders). It's as if the rest of the generation were compelled to live a less bloody equivalent of the rite of passage their brother grunts endured.

Exaggerating the genuine class differences for effect, you could say that, if the Sixties were the rich kids' war, the Vietnam War was the poor and working man's Sixties. The average Vietnam vet had his trust in his country torn apart much more brutally than the average anti-war demonstrator. He had a more traumatic and intimate encounter with the Orient. He was probably more deeply wounded in his ability to make a living and a family. He lost more time. Still, the experiences run parallel. Vets and non-vets did the same drugs, listened to the same music. They shared a culture—up to a point. Then we come to the unbridgeable gulf that divides the combat soldier in any war from the civilian—a gulf forced wider, in the Sixties, by the homefront generation's noisy non-support for those in the field.

And yet, for both those who fought in it and those who fought against it, the war made the Sixties real. It forced our transformation, made it a matter of life and death. War has traditionally been a rite of passage into manhood. Vietnam was a rite of passage into chaos, into the crack between worlds. The war shattered old images of manhood—shattered the old world built around Manhood. It left vets, non-vets, and women wounded and divided, holding different, jagged pieces of our puzzle: a new world.

THE
MOVEMENT

W*A R*

And it's one, two, three, what are we fighting for?
Don't ask me I don't give a damn
Next stop is Vietnam . . .
— COUNTRY JOE MACDONALD
"I-Feel-Like-I'm-Fixin'-to-Die Rag"

On Veterans Day, 1984, I went to see the Vietnam Veterans Memorial for the first time. The first thing that struck me about it was its placement: It is within sight of the Washington Monument, where hundreds of thousands of us gathered to protest the war almost a generation ago. You can see them both in one glance—what a postcard!—so that the memorial could almost be a shadow cast by the strict white finger of the monument, or a black scar burned into the ground. The thousands of people filing in and out of it on this day are slow and silent, in contrast to the shouting, chanting mobs of the past. Some of them are the same people, but the youthful rage that helped to end the war is long since spent. This grave, reflective mood is what is left.

That's the second strong impression made by the Vietnam Veterans Memorial at a distance: it's appropriate how sunken and somber it is, a dark defile, like the dark time that war was for this country. The memorial has been loudly criticized for just this effect, but most people feel that its dignity is in its truthfulness. Designed by a woman, and an Asian woman at that—Chinese-American architect Maya Ying Lin—the low black wall can be seen as feminine, a widow's or mourning mother's view of war. Instead of jutting proudly above the earth, like a normal war memorial, it leads down into it, like the entrance to Hades. But then, Vietnam wasn't a "normal" war, not by United States standards. We lost it.

Not far off, three heroic bronze figures of varied races have recently been added, just as we are only now granting Vietnam vets their share of conventional heroism. These three figures are not inappropriate. They look brave, alert, but slightly bewildered, as if they are watching out for an invisible enemy. But the Wall with its rank on rank of names remains the heart of the memorial.

People moving past the Wall reach out and touch certain names with their fingertips, the way they would touch a dear face, as if a dead or missing man's individuality now lived in the curves and angles of the letters. A heavyset man holds a piece of paper against the Wall, rubs over it with a pencil, and a Native American name appears, perhaps his son's. Guides in frayed combat fatigues stand on top of the wall with thick directories, calling out fallen soldiers' names to help friends and family find them, and handing out special sheets of paper so that people can take the names home.

Tokens are given as well as taken. Not only miniature flags and flowers, but intimate messages are left here, little notes and letters taped to the Wall or placed at the foot of a section: "We miss you & think of you all the time." "Billy, Though we didn't know each other long I felt as if I knew you all our life's. I will never forget you. Your friend forever . . ." Most remarkable of all, people have left *food*—a soldier's favorite chocolate roll, a can of sardines, bread—

as well as other offerings: tobacco, the Bible, the *Bhagavad-Gita,* a pair of boots, a can of beer.

This is extraordinary behavior for Americans, almost Oriental, like Chinese people offering food to their ancestors. It both responds and contributes to a powerful feeling that, wherever their bodies lie, the casualties of Vietnam live here, together, forever. Their restless spirits have found a home. And so have the pained spirits of living vets, who had to raise the money for their own memorial. For them, even more than for the families of the dead, the Wall is clearly a kindness and a mystery, a place to remember, a sheltering shadow where they can come to be with the shades of their friends.

On Veterans Day, about half the men in the crowd are wearing the faded green field jackets that set them apart as Vietnam vets. It is an anti-uniform that conveys both contempt for military exactitude and a sort of permanent weariness. It is often topped by a camouflage hat bearing a JANE'S FONDA COMMUNISM button. (Vets have not forgiven or forgotten Jane Fonda's starring role in the ranks of those who condemned them.) Some of the men are missing pieces of themselves. One big, black-bearded guy cruises the Wall in a wheelchair, both legs gone.

Most of the damage from the war is less blatant. Some vets stand around in small groups of two or three, talking quietly. One man in a torn plaid shirt turns to a gray-haired woman beside him, a stranger, and says, "I live here in town, and I still can't come near this without falling apart." His face is as wet as if he'd been in a hard rain. But more than anything, you see vets sitting and staring, or just walking. Their eyes are distant. They are alone, or if there is a woman behind or near them, they don't seem to be aware of her. One man's wife is wearing a field jacket of her own. She rubs her husband's neck while he stares at the three bronze soldiers and cries. There is no sign that he even feels her touch. He is lost in his own world, a world of memories where no one can follow except those who were there.

On my way out of the memorial, I pass a green wreath with yellow flowers and a black ribbon. It is one of hundreds from veterans' groups and families, but the legend on the ribbon catches my eye:

NEVER AGAIN. VIETNAM VETERANS PEACE ACTION NETWORK. In the center of the wreath is a poem or prayer:

> To the memory of those friends we have lost,
> with the pain which we will never forget,
> we dedicate our efforts.
> With the hope
> that the peace we build
> will be so strong and so long
> that war will become a dim reality
> for all of humanity.

The Vietnam War was the central event of our generation. Like a massive shock wave, it affected, in widening circles, the 58,022 lost in the war (eight of them women); the 100,000 or more who may have killed themselves since their return; the 153,329 severely wounded, and the 150,375 more lightly wounded; the estimated 250,000 victims of Agent Orange; the half million or more who still suffer from the nightmares and flashbacks of post-traumatic stress; the 3.78 million who saw duty in the war zone; the 11 million who served in the Armed Forces during that time of doubt, drugs, and rebellion; the 27 million men who were threatened by the draft and had to rearrange their lives around it; and all the lovers, wives, friends, brothers, and sisters, as well as the parents, grandparents, and children of those who served, died, vanished, protested, or fled. During the war the generation was divided, but with time its true shape has revealed itself: a set of concentric rings, with the Vietnam Veterans Memorial at dead center. The Wall is an enigmatic barrier between past and future; our reflections, trapped in the stone, could be our old selves, with their beliefs and illusions, as dead as the men and women whose names are inscribed there.

Every war transforms the men who fight it into killers and survivors. The intimacy with death separates veterans of all wars from the rest of us and welds them into a brotherhood that crosses generations, even centuries. Vietnam veterans are now belatedly being absorbed into that ancient brotherhood; their exile is coming to an end. With time, the most grotesque wounds of the war have healed. Of course, in many ways it was a war like any other—the same horror, the same high. Vietnam vets told me timeless war stories of duty, death, and friendship, luck, skill, and survival. It is this classic aspect of the war that is getting attention in the Eighties, as we scavenge our collective memory for fragments of patriotic pride.

Some Vietnam vets welcome their rehabilitation as traditional warrior heroes. Others, however, resist it, because it comes too late, and because it denies the unique and bitterly hard-won lessons of *this* war. The distinctive mark Vietnam left on our generation comes not from the ways in which it was like the "Good War" our fathers fought, but from the ways in which it—and the public response to it—was different from any war in our history. Two stories I heard from Bubba,* a Richmond, Virginia, cabdriver with a 30 percent disability, reveal the other face of Vietnam.

Atrocities

"This was about April," says Bubba. "We was sitting in camp around a small fire we had built in a can, thirty, maybe forty yards from a small village of South Vietnamese people. If I remember we were kinda just jawin', shootin' the time. It was about ten thirty A.M., a little early in the day for us to start anything.

"The Charlie that walked in the camp was about seven years old at the most. Just about her age." Bubba turned his head and I followed his gaze, through the cab window to a little blond girl skipping down the shade-dappled street. The chilling innocence of the juxtaposition made me see for a moment what it might be like to have nightmares in broad daylight.

"I noticed he had his hands in his pockets when he come into camp," Bubba went on. "One pocket bulged a little more than the other one. I figured he had some candy or somethin' that one of the other boys had give him. He walked into the circle, and stood there looking around for a minute. I took my eyes off of him to look at what the captain was telling me. I just happened to look back up. And his hand come out of his pocket with a grenade in it. I hollered for the guys to move, that it was a grenade, and the child dropped the grenade at his feet. It killed the child, two men, and put thirteen in the hospital.

"Most of our people have to live with things like that. And dream about 'em. I see 'em every now and then in the daytime as well as nighttime. Sometimes sittin' on a stand in the cab, I see that child I killed in August of '72. And all that child did was walk up to me and ask me for a piece of candy.

"My corporal and I was standin' drinkin' a beer. Standin' there runnin' our mouths when the kid come up and asked for a piece of candy. The corporal told him no. The child brought his hand from behind his back with a forty-five automatic in it. He shot my corporal in the face. I was standing right beside him. And the kid turned the gun on me. But before he could shoot me I shot and killed him. I fought the mother for ten minutes. She was like a wildcat. I ended up havin' to hit her with my fist to get her off me. The child was six years old, accordin' to his mother. She saw him shoot my corporal in the face.

"That was mainly some of the reasons why the Vietnamese people hated and despised us," Bubba concluded. " 'Cause we was killin' their children and their women, 'cause they were killin' us. Survival was the name of the game. You really never knew whether to trust them or not. It was that bad. 'Cause they had an enemy in their camp that they didn't like, and they didn't care whether they died or not."

These are not war stories. They are Vietnam War stories. "World War One, World War Two, I've heard stories and stories 'bout things that went on in both of those wars," says Bubba, who came from a military family as well as a storytelling one. "My stepfather was in World War Two, and he didn't see half as much as I did." Bubba was seventeen, the age of "essential impressions," when he went into the service. The war made him into a man, but a shattered man, survivor of two stomach wounds and a suicide attempt, gentle, capable, confused, full of tenderness and rage.

"I'm a pacifist, if you want to call it that," he said. "I'd rather talk to you than I would fight you. I'd rather love you than I would fight you." And yet, having killed a child, he was afraid of killing his own. "A few years ago I woke up in the middle of the night," he told me. "Sat bolt upright in bed, picked up my pistol, and fired. For no reason at all. I don't know why I done it. If one of my children had been walkin' through that house, I'd'a killed 'em. It scares me half to death."

No matter how we may try to sanitize or mythologize it now, Vietnam was a war of atrocities on both sides, and that is worth remembering, because it tells us something essential about what it did to so many of our generation. Vietnam was not a "normal" war, the kind of European land war our fathers fought in and most of our soldiers were trained for, in which the enemy is a male in uniform and certain "civilized" rules for killing are supposedly observed by both sides. By the time of Vietnam, that war was a thing of the past, although the U.S. command wasn't ready to admit it.

Guerrilla war, like the other two forms of late-twentieth-century warfare—terrorism and nuclear war—indiscriminately involves whole populations, men, women, and children. There are no rules. No one and nothing is off limits. The difference is that, unlike the terrorist who plants a bomb or the commander who "pushes the button," or even the pilot who sows napalm, the ground soldier in Vietnam had to administer this indiscriminate fate face to face, and witness it. More than that, he had to share it.

Hidden snipers were everywhere, and trees were hollowed out to serve as ambushes, giving many Americans "the feeling that they were making war against trees and bushes," as one Marine described it to writer Joe Klein in *Payback.* [1] Pit traps were dug, filled with sharpened bamboo stakes—the notorious "punji sticks"—and covered with leaves: "A guy would walk through and they'd pierce his leather boots, go right through his feet, up his leg, sometimes castrate him," says Margaret Pearson (1942), then an Army chief surgeon's wife who worked with the wounded in Japan. (Much of what I learned firsthand I heard from women to whom some of the most painful secrets of the war had been entrusted: nurses and physical therapists who cared for the newly wounded, and the fiercely protective inner ring of wives, lovers, sisters, and friends that surrounds the vets.) Mines were planted in feces for maximum contamination of wounds —guaranteed gangrene. Soldiers on patrol found mutilated American bodies, including severed heads hanging from trees. (In turn, some hardened Americans mutilated Vietcong bodies and collected trophy ears—a practice that horrified many a green eighteen-year-old.) But worse even than the treachery of the jungle was the hallucinatory paranoia of not knowing who was a friend and who an enemy.

Soldier after soldier wrote home from Vietnam that the people we'd been sent to protect didn't seem to want us there—an impression sometimes confirmed by sudden death. A smiling cleaning woman might be smuggling plastique onto a base; a child asking for candy might be hiding a grenade. Cruelest of all was this occasional use of children as weapons, subject of perhaps the worst Vietnam story I heard:

"I remember my brother's friend who went over there." (A woman is talking.) "He went over twice, had been injured and sent back. And he was on a road with his friend, and they were told, they were given strict orders—at that point they knew of all these terrible things with women and children." (This was after the 1968 My Lai massacre had been widely publicized in 1969.) "They saw a little three-year-old girl on the road. And his friend ran ahead, without thinking, to pick up the baby crying there on the road, all alone on the road. He picked up the child and she was wired. She exploded, he exploded.

"Jimmy* was only six or seven feet away. He lost part of his arm, his whole body was full of shrapnel. And he never was the same. Here was a guy that became so introverted, as far as I know he's not married or anything. It took him two or three years even to verbalize it. He told me not to tell my brother."

In such an environment, the real heroism of Vietnam combatants is that they held on to their sanity and humanity at all, that they were sometimes able to discriminate between friend and enemy and to suffer when they mistakenly killed the innocent. Total numbing was much safer, blind rage an understandable response. The massive

1981 government study *Legacies of Vietnam* suggested that up to 9 percent of Americans in combat may have committed "atrocities," while about 30 percent witnessed them. It is not surprising that incidents like My Lai occasionally happened, given the "body count" as the only measure of American progress, the zeal of some "lifers" to "kill all the gooks," the patent indifference of both sides to human life (the Army might speak of "winning hearts and minds," but grunts cynically called it "WHAM"), and the maddening difficulty of locating and identifying Vietcong. As W. D. Ehrhart (1948) wrote in his poem "Guerilla War":

> It's practically impossible
> to tell civilians
> from the Vietcong.
>
> Nobody wears uniforms.
> They all talk
> the same language
> (and you couldn't understand them
> even if they didn't).
>
> They tape grenades
> inside their clothes,
> and carry satchel charges
> in their market baskets.
>
> Even their women fight;
> and young boys,
> and girls.
>
> It's practically impossible
> to tell civilians
> from the Vietcong;
>
> after awhile,
> you quit trying.[2]

American soldiers did what their command structure encouraged them to do, what men in any war must do in order to kill and survive: they dehumanized the enemy. At times, this meant that they dehumanized all Vietnamese.

While their collegiate contemporaries back home were doing exactly the opposite.

The Americong

Ho! Ho! Ho Chi Minh!
The NLF is gonna win!

I can remember that chant being started at every major demonstration by a small, angry, tightly organized group flying the Vietcong flag —probably the U.S. Committee to Aid the NLF. (Sixties trivia question: Describe that flag.) What I can't remember is whether I joined in. Plenty of us did. Even those who would have felt foolish going so far, who stuck with the nonpartisan "Peace . . . NOW!," shared much of the sentiment. Sometimes we even shared the rhythm:

Hey! Hey! LBJ!
How many kids didja kill today?

The fact that the anti-war movement achieved its goal—America got out of Vietnam—seems to give our generation its clearest sense of power and achievement. "We stopped the war" is a statement often made to me with pride and satisfaction—at times prefaced by an unspoken, "If we didn't do anything else, at least . . ." There are dissenters. "Maybe I've become cynical, but I don't think we had that much of an effect on Vietnam," says Kathleen Brimlow (1948), former "flower child" and now nurse-midwife in training. "I would love to think we did. There was such a beautiful feeling of unity then." Most of her contemporaries, however, would still give the lion's share of the credit to those hundreds of thousands chanting in the street, who made their parents and their old Doc Spock and finally the U.S. government itself take another look at the war.

Not that we looked at it very closely ourselves. Editor Jonathan Segal remembers the moment when Kathy Brimlow's "beautiful feeling of unity" struck him as mass stupidity. "It must have been '68, '69. I was working for *The New York Times,* and I went out to a rally in Bryant Park. There must have been two hundred fifty people, all just about my age, and when I got there they were all chanting, 'Stop the war, kill a pig' and whatever else was in vogue at the moment. I was another one of them, one of the crowd. I think a folksinger was the speaker. Everybody was passing around joints. Nobody was listening to what anybody said. And every time there was a pause in the rally, they applauded and yelled, 'Stop the war, bring the boys home.'

"I was struck at that moment that here we are, all supposedly young, bright, thinking adults, and not listening or giving any thought. Maybe that's the way rallies are, the way groups are. But I said, Gee, what am I doing here? Does anybody know what they are doing here? Are issues defined? Are they debated? Are they discussed? Or is this just another excuse to pass the joints around? I knew I would agree with these people if push came to shove, but I wouldn't really like being in their company. There was not any wisdom or intelligence. And I just went home."

The embarrassing truth is that the anti-war movement's intellectual weakness may have been its strength. Simplicity and passion made it large and powerful, one big emotional *No* in which many voices could join. We hated the war, we hated our country—"It was so revolting, what the United States was doing," says a filmmaker turned lawyer (1946) who was then a conscientious objector—and we pitied, admired, and rooted for the tough, graceful little people whom we saw as fighting their war of independence, bamboo stakes against bombs. The more radical among us even identified with them, envisioning ourselves as revolutionary guerrillas attacking the evil American empire from within, fighting our own war of independence from our origins, casting our lot with the uprising oppressed all over the world. "We are the Americong," proclaimed underground journalist Raymond Mungo (1946).[3]

This romantic cult of the Third World victim-hero, which would ultimately lead white kids under cops' clubs for their baptism in blood, had its roots in the Civil Rights and Black Power movements. The Freedom Rides had given us the icon of good and evil for our era: "a poor black being hit by a big fat southern cop." That image, with its implicit challenge to choose power or virtue, became the model for all the polarized politics of the Sixties, both domestic and international. And black leaders traced explicit links and parallels between racist oppression at home and abroad. "The murder of Samuel Younge in Tuskegee, Alabama [the SNCC worker had tried to use a white restroom], is no different than the murder of people in Vietnam," SNCC chairman John Lewis said in January 1966. Lewis's successor, Stokely Carmichael, was even more emphatic in identifying Vietnam as a racist colonial war. Even Martin Luther King, in an April 1967 speech, had assailed "the greatest purveyor of violence in the world today—my own government."[4]

In short, the image of the Vietnam War the black movement taught its white apprentices was that of a big armed white country beating up on poor Asians, who were heroically resisting. It was a view diametrically opposed to the official one. The old America still presented us as world heroes, riding to the rescue of a defenseless democracy menaced by Communist tyranny. The emerging new America portrayed us as world bullies, who had been motivated by greed and racism from the moment we set foot on this continent. The slave ships. Wounded Knee. Hiroshima. Selma. And now Vietnam.

Thousands, then millions, of white students took this new American history to heart. Of course, it became easier to identify with the oppressed when, as Marc Barasch put it, "the same world view that was destroying Vietnam was trying to destroy me." But self-interest alone does not explain the idealistic, almost masochistic passion with which so many middle-class white kids rejected their own heritage. The uncovering of the fault of racism running through American life had caused a profound and traumatic revaluation (as the uncovering of sexism would a few years later). American history through dark or slanted eyes had the revelatory force of disillusion. Our parents had lied! Our trusted textbooks, our favorite Westerns, had lied! We felt betrayed, and worse, implicated without our consent. We were the heirs apparent of three centuries of genocide! And the people who had been killed and enslaved in our name were precisely those we wanted most to learn from: nature-loving Indians; gentle, mystical Asians; heart-and-soul blacks.

Cross-cultural empathy would certainly be vital for planetary survival. But ours didn't go far enough. We didn't really see "oppressed Third World peoples" as human, for we didn't see them as capable of human evil. Any atrocities they committed were innocent, cleansed by their oppression. We simply reversed the black-and-white values of the old culture, exchanging derogatory stereotypes for adulatory ones. Their bad guys became our good guys—and vice versa.

Bull Connor had his "niggers"; Medina and Calley had their "gooks"; we had our "pigs." The government saw Vietnam as a clear case of Communist aggression; we saw it as a "pure" war of national liberation. (In reality, it was some of both, with a dash of civil war thrown in.) We saw our leaders as racist, fascist imperialists; Nixon saw us as Communist dupes. (Again, there was some truth in both allegations.) If in our eyes the North Vietnamese and the Vietcong could do no wrong—an easy judgment to make from twelve thousand miles away—it followed that the Americans could do no right. Grotesquely, many of us extended our full empathy to the people who were blowing up our GIs, but not to the GIs themselves. They had no business being there, did they? "If you get shot, you will have deserved it," Boston writer Carl Nagin (1946) remembers saying to a friend, *Washington Post* heir apparent (now publisher) Donald Graham (1945), who had decided to enlist and fight in Vietnam. "It's a statement I'm not proud of," Nagin says today, "but it was indicative of a very unconscious, programmed response, an arrogance that was part of people's politics then." That arrogance was the first face of America that many returning veterans saw.

Hey! Hey! Green Beret!
How many kids didja kill today?

Special Forces Staff Sergeant John Armstrong* (1946) stepped off
the plane at Travis AFB, still wearing his camouflage "tigers,"
shortly after the shootings at Kent State. To Armstrong and his
buddies, the U.S. bombing and invasion of Cambodia that had so
scandalized American campuses had come as a long-withheld relief.
The VC would hit and kill, then slip over the border to safety, almost
thumbing their noses. The Green Berets had been at a frustrating,
sometimes fatal disadvantage until they were allowed to give chase.
The smells of the jungle and of blood still clung to Armstrong's brain.
The world he had just stepped out of and the one he was about to
step into had about as much in common as matter and anti-matter.
The explosion would happen in his head.

After taking the bus to Oakland, according to Army protocol,
Armstrong had to get out of his "tigers" and boots and into a clean
dress uniform with his decorations on the breast. The pettiness of the
Army bureaucracy grated on combat sensibilities, tuned to a total lack
of pretension. Armstrong's war had been stripped down to the compelling basics of fighting "with my buddies and for the country." He
had been wounded in the stomach, had sat with dying friends. He was
already edgy as he climbed into a crowded cab for San Francisco
Airport, gateway to the civilian world. As he walked into the terminal,
three long-haired young men started up the chant: *"How* many *kids*
didja *kill-to-day?"*

Armstrong's first reaction was blind rage. "I wanted to reach into
my jacket, pull out a gun, and say, 'None, sucker, but I'm gonna start
right now!' " He managed to suppress it and kept walking, feeling
eyes turn to follow him all the way down the corridor. Reliving that
walk gives him a bad case of the creeps. The main feeling he conveys
is not anger or hurt, but traumatic disorientation. "Thinking about
it on the plane home, the only thing that legitimated it for me was
that I had been protecting the freedoms that allowed them to say that

to me." Nonetheless, Armstrong thinks that "the problems I had for the next couple of years started then."

It was the archetypal experience of homecoming from Vietnam. Short-haired veterans who had struggled to survive in the jungle found themselves shunned as war criminals on the campus. Many of us now feel remorse for such acts even if we never personally committed them. Once so arrogant in our "non-violence," we have come to see the violence in our arrogance. "We contributed to Vietnam vets being so screwed up," says psychologist Marian Goodman, expressing both a sense of guilt and a stereotype of veterans that are widespread in the generation. "We just didn't *think* about it."

The Campus and the Battlefield

During the war, Goodman was a student at Tufts. Like surprisingly many college students, she didn't know anyone who served in Vietnam, so sharp was the class line separating the campus from the battlefield. The prevailing lack of contact between the two populations left most anti-war students ignorant of the forces that might send a young man to Vietnam and shape his actions once he got there. (Anti-war students who did have family or close friends in Vietnam felt more ambivalent about demonstrating. "My brother was over there, and even though I was against the war, I didn't protest it, because it was like protesting against him," says Massachusetts social worker Ellen Herman* [1947].) Many students assumed that if *they* could see the war was wrong, and find a way out of it, so could anyone, unless he was bloodthirsty or stupid. It was an extremely ethnocentric assumption.

On many campuses by the late Sixties, avoiding the draft by any means necessary—what Carl Nagin calls "a kind of domestic desertion"—was considered not only socially acceptable, but morally right. Even if you weren't going to turn in your draft card, or bend your life by becoming a teacher or fathering a child, you owed it to your ass and the Vietnamese to stay out of the war once your 2-S

expired. Convincing Army doctors and shrinks that you were anything but a red-blooded American male became a kind of subversive
art form. Many an anti-warrior of that era has his own "Alice's
Restaurant" saga, combining anxiety and absurdity.

Marc Barasch "went in and slightly exaggerated my normal neuro-
sis. A friend of mine gave me that tip. He said, 'Don't worry. Be
yourself, but a little bit more.' I also fasted so that I was quite thin."
"Some friends of mine were trying to figure out how to break each
other's kneecaps without it hurting," says North Carolina cartoonist
and triathlete Marc Dabagian (1953). A friend of Ananda Saha's
"took the last tab of acid that we had in the middle of the night before
going down to the induction center. He became quite catatonic when
he took acid, so that seemed a good way to go." A friend of Stephen
King's "painted his body with Day-glo slogans." King drove his high
blood pressure higher by downing a six-pack of Pepsi-Cola. Guys
went on two-week speed binges, deprived themselves of sleep, made
passes at the doctor. It was desperation theater, done with wit, nerve,
and no shame. And it depended on a supportive peer culture that
inverted old values with the liberal help of drugs, making fun of
authority and traditional masculinity.

The majority of Vietnam servicemen, by contrast, came from ethnic and economic subcultures that still upheld the old values. Theirs
was a world in which it was noble to fight for your country's ideals,
and more acceptable for a man to get shot at than to pretend to be
crazy or gay. For poor and minority men, getting drafted after high
school was not only inevitable, but an opportunity for training and
travel. Once a man was in Vietnam, by choice or conscription, he—
and his family—needed to go on believing that the war was right, to
justify his own risk and the deaths of friends. This need, plus the
natural antagonism of the battlefield, made most soldiers appear to
be pro-war on principle, further widening the gulf between them and
their anti-war peers.

Did the doubts of the war's rightness that began to creep into some
soldiers' and veterans' minds by 1967 originate in their own Vietnam

experience, or in the insistent voice of the anti-war movement? It is impossible to separate the two. It is probably most accurate to say that the existence of the movement gave form and meaning to doubts that were already there, offering an explanation that made new and terrible sense of the men's bewilderment. While the mass of the anti-war movement was either hostile to servicemen or "just didn't think about it," GI outreach programs approached them as victims and valued witnesses. Through off-base coffeehouses, underground papers, and Vietnam Veterans Against the War, activists offered troubled soldiers and vets a haven from the Army atmosphere, a persuasive reinterpretation of their experience, and an anti-military model of manhood. Feeling bitterly betrayed by their elders, some veterans grew their hair and drew together with their peers. In April 1971, over a thousand angrily hurled away their medals on the Capitol steps. Such veterans—and the soldiers who engaged in low-grade mutiny, refusing to go out on suicidal patrols—played a major part in ending the war.

There are moments when fighting men doubt every war, wondering whether any purpose on earth can justify such slaughter. And the Vietnam War was more dubious than most. Still, if the public had supported the war, and welcomed our men home with parades and kisses and jobs—the cleansing rituals that celebrate soldiers' sacrifices and absolve their guilt—most Vietnam vets might never have so deeply questioned what they saw and suffered and did. And a necessary wound in the national conscience would never have been opened—a wound that was, cruelly, inflicted first and worst on the veterans themselves.

Wounds of Understanding

We human beings have a unique capacity to slaughter our own kind. We do this by persuading ourselves that the enemy is *not* our own kind—that he is a "gook" or a "pig." But the capacity to recognize and respond to humanity is only repressed; it can break through differences of race, language, culture—even through the hate and fear of war. Some of the most poignant war stories record a meeting of eyes between male enemies, acknowledging each other's vulnerability and valor seconds before one kills the other.

Not even the crash course in dehumanization that is central to military training can completely shield a sensitive veteran from the knowledge that he has killed men like himself. Next to the death of friends and the loss of limbs, this is the wound of war that most needs soothing by the public's reassurance that the war was necessary. Vietnam veterans needed that balm more than most, because some had killed women or children face to face, acts that violated both instinct and training yet were in some cases necessary for survival.

Instead, they were called "baby-killers." But even if they had never heard that epithet, the homefront stress on the humanity and suffering of the Vietnamese, the images of screaming children, gouged into one of the deepest wounds of the war instead of letting it heal. Because their own generation had turned against a policy they had dutifully carried out, returning veterans were thrust from one pole of their human potential to the other, from desensitized killing to full awareness of the humanity of their victims. It was an unbearable transition, one that drove hundreds of thousands to alcohol or drugs, crime or suicide, and drove others to confess to family members or war crimes commissions. Anti-war students merely hated their country; Vietnam veterans hated themselves.

"My brother could be so dear," says social worker Ellen Herman of her veteran brother. "He's a big guy and very athletic, but also a heart. He could do all that macho stuff, but when he fell in love, he *fell in love*! Head over heels. He was like that.

"I didn't know how to say to him, 'Get out of here. Go to Canada.' Things happened too fast. He was sent to a camp in the South that was one of the best places to get trained for guerrilla war. And when he went over there, he was in an elite group up north that was notorious throughout the whole upper region. It was the real guerrilla stuff. My brother was given a lot of honors for rescuing people in his own crew.

"It wasn't till afterward, when my mother died . . . He said, 'Anyone who's really been in it, they don't talk about it. The ones who haven't seen it are the ones that are boasting. But the ones that have been in it only will say it to each other when they find out that they know.' But he told me. He was drunk that night, the night our mother died, and he said, 'I can't live with myself. These are the things I've done.' " (She is weeping as she tells me.) "Apparently he had tortured a lot of people, and killed a lot. He had to. It was so bad for him in terms of who he was—that wasn't him at all. And I thought, 'My God, what we've done to them!'

"He's still tortured by those memories. He still has nightmares of that war. He drinks too much, and I'm sure he's an alcoholic. And I've realized that in some fundamental way, he will never be healed of that. No matter how you were threatened, you just can't, I don't think, do those kinds of things and . . . you have to live with the fact that you were evil."

That was an agony, over and above the agonies of war, that no other Americans were asked to endure. Politicians and generals might repent of their early support of the war, but their responsibility for the horrors, so much greater than the vets', remained comfortably abstract. Anti-war students' sympathy for the Vietnamese may have been sincere, but it was cheap. Veterans like Ellen Herman's brother acknowledged the humanity of the enemy and the error of the war at the highest possible cost to themselves. And many accepted their guilt with the same innocence with which they had once accepted their duty. In doing so, they bravely—and sometimes suicidally—took on a task that should not have been theirs at all, yet for which they were uniquely qualified: the task of repenting, not just *this* war, but war itself. In declaring war as murder, and themselves as murderers, many Vietnam veterans became front-line casualties and heroes of the evolutionary war.

The wounds of understanding, for which there are no medals, were as honorable as any wound incurred in action. And they were arguably suffered in a better cause: the war against war, now approaching its decisive battle. But like all war wounds, they eventually had to heal to scar tissue—or kill. The suicide rate among Vietnam veterans is still 86 percent higher than that of their contemporaries. To survive, the majority of vets have had to outgrow the innocence that made them take a crushing double responsibility for the war. Many now feel that, having sincerely believed they should fight, they did not have to assume guilt for it as well, and having performed competently against great odds, they need not think of themselves as victims. In rap groups and vet centers across the country, vets have helped each other to survive psychologically, just as they did physically in Vietnam. Until the last few years, they have done it with little help or recognition from the rest of us.

Lesser Wounds

Meanwhile, lesser wounds of the battle against the war have healed as well, though they, too, leave scars: as small as a bald patch on the scalp from getting clubbed by a cop, as large as a prison record or severance from one's country. Thousands of men and women put their bodies on the line—or across it, into Canada. One who eventually returned, *New Options* newsletter editor Mark Satin (1946), is still bitter about the lost time—for himself and for the thousands of men he counseled. "I was an unbelievably young nineteen when I went to Canada in 1966," he says. "I was one of the first. There were only a couple hundred. In '67, I helped to start the group in Toronto that eventually brought up twenty thousand. I'd see these kids so strung out—terrified, on drugs, terribly confused, desperately needing counsel they could trust. Most of them were from small towns in the Midwest and the South; their heroes were people like Jerry Rubin and Joan Baez.

"I still feel a lot of resentment of those people who so blithely told us to drop out and live by our ideals. *They* never dropped out. They had lecture bureaus and major New York publishers! But I believed them. The most idealistic of us dropped out, wounded ourselves, and did irreparable damage to our lives and careers." Satin came home in 1978, a year after Jimmy Carter's amnesty, but it wasn't till after this book had been written that his wounds had healed enough to talk about them to me. At forty, he was putting out a highly regarded political newsletter with an all-volunteer staff, on a monk's salary—"my needs are minimal"—in Washington, D.C., the yuppie capital of the world.

Curiously, as the wounded heal, some of the most intact and successful members of the generation are discovering their guilt, or at least their chagrin. Many who didn't risk jail or exile, or struggle to prove pacifist convictions to a hostile draft board, now admit that staying out of the war and opposing it was less a hard moral choice than a perk of class or gender, a lucky confluence of peer pressure, self-interest, and ideals. "The war was wrong—just so wrong—but I must admit that demonstrating was a whole lot of fun," says Caroline Johnson* (1948), a former activist and drug counselor turned insurance salesperson. "The camaraderie, the social aspect—that was where it was happening!" Many people report meeting lovers, even future mates, at anti-war rallies. "If you weren't against the war," editor Jonathan Segal recalls, "you weren't going to get the good girls. It was a strong motivation." "If you weren't against the war you were like a pariah in society," says Los Angeles executive Jennifer Flinton Diener. "I think a lot of people were really doing it as a method of belonging."

Of course, the relative safety and popularity of anti-war views didn't make them wrong. Banker Alvin Cohan defends self-interest: "It was not a political issue. It was a save-your-ass issue. A far more important issue, I think, in retrospect. Our priorities were right. For the wrong reasons, but they were right. Choose life." Some vets retrospectively agree, despite their pride in their service. "I was *good,*" Bubba said—but he'd rather be well. Had he known what Vietnam would be like, he says, "I'd never have stayed in the U.S. I'd have been one of the many that took off to Canada that was considered criminals because they left the U.S. and would not enlist in the services. I'm talking about the draft dodgers. When I heard they were doing that, I felt they should be shot. I got to Vietnam and I wanted to find every one of them and kiss every one of them. And be one of 'em.''

It's a testament to the stubborn ambiguity of the Vietnam War that today, twenty years later, few men are entirely at peace about their decision. If some who served wish they hadn't, some who didn't now wish they had. Like women who have never given birth, they wonder whether they've missed an essential rite of initiation. "It was a blessing, then, to have escaped; it is a burden now," Edward Tick, an upstate New York psychotherapist, wrote in *The New York Times Magazine*'s About Men column. "Though still convinced the war was a mistake, I find there is something missing in me . . . I was, I came to feel, among those men of my generation who had never been tested. . . . We were never inducted, not merely into the Army, but into manhood."[5]

This form of self-doubt, which Esquire writer Christopher Buckley called "Viet Guilt," might more accurately be called "Viet Envy." Popular admiration has shifted away from the protester in favor of the vet, and it reveals how far the balance of the country has tipped back toward patriotism and power (and money and success: a kindred doubt nags the principled poor of our generation, many of whom now wonder if they just couldn't cut it). In the Sixties, we glorified the underdog, the martyr, the slender Vietnamese, Fred Hampton slain by the police. A "beautiful loser," in poet Leonard Cohen's term, was the thing to be. Today pop culture enshrines the superstar, the winner, the man and woman of action.

This shift is treacherous, but it is promising, too. The craving for confidence, action, and pride in America isn't bad in itself; it can lead forward as well as backward. But that depends urgently on the Sixties generation putting forth a positive new principle for action, one that does not shun power, but doesn't shut off compassion, either. While women are playing a major part in the development of such a principle, it won't happen without a strong role for men, because, without a way to challenge and dignify their strength, men are going to go back to war. We can see it happening already—*Rambo* was a top-grossing film of 1985—and it is very dangerous; a turning back to the easy, crazy sources of male and American pride.

John Wayne Lives!

The old America cheerfully and chillingly equated the aggressive use of power, masculinity, and virtue—call it the John Wayne syndrome. Action was straightforward for John Wayne and his sons, because morality was aligned with self-interest, and the world was black and white, a neat set of on/off switches. Friend or enemy. Good guy, bad guy. American or Commie. Fighting man or "pussy."

It was this gallant, malignant view of the world that killed—and finally died—in Vietnam. The hopeless confusion of friend and enemy, combatant and civilian, Communist and freedom fighter in that war shattered the John Wayne mind. So did a combat crucible in which a Klansman might owe his life to a black, or vice versa. At the end of the war we came staggering out of the dual world into a plural one, in which we had to learn how to think and act all over again. As the Grateful Dead sang, "It's got no signs or dividing lines/And very few rules to guide." No workable rationale for action had yet emerged to replace the clear, false Either/Or.

The counterculture had appeared at first to offer an alternative, but it was only a negative. We just said no to whatever the old America had said yes to: white skin, short hair, capitalism, success, sexual puritanism, soap and water, the American flag, the use of power ("the very existence of power is an evil," wrote Charles Reich in *The Greening of America*), active masculinity itself. Like all reactions, the anti-America drew its energy from that which it opposed. When the war ended, and Nixon resigned, its necessary destructive work was finished, and its energy ebbed. Constructive work would take much longer, and it could not be achieved by the mere massing of bodies. No can be shouted from a million throats; yes is said face to face, in response to love or reason.

When the war ended, we found that the power of sheer numbers, the only power we had ever possessed, had become irrelevant. Many of us would feel (and be) powerless for years—and some would conclude that our Sixties Samson strength (long hair?) had been an adolescent illusion. "I still think of myself as very idealistic," Ray Mungo told underground-press historian Abe Peck. "But I also feel very small. In the Sixties, I think we felt larger than we were. Because we were really united."[6] Only in the Eighties have we begun to discover an adult form of power that involves skill, influence, and a way of linking up other than linking arms in the street: "networking" (even those who hate the word practice the phenomenon).

The largely negative Carter administration marked an interim time in which the active power of the old America had been defeated and the active power of the new had not yet emerged. Jimmy Carter was an amazingly appropriate choice for a self-castrated America. His smile is the smile of a man who has said no to his dark side and, in doing so, has cut himself off from his own energy. *Star Trek* fans will remember the wonderful episode called "The Enemy Within," written by Richard Matheson, in which the transporter divides Captain Kirk in two, and he discovers that his decisiveness, his power of command, comes from his "bad," vital, animal side. Reason, compassion, and wisdom are on the "good" side, but without the "animal's" vitality, they are impotent. Jimmy Carter's human-rights stand was admirable, and he was a good reconciler at Camp David, but his niceness, and his weakness, was that of a man who has his animal firmly bound and gagged in the cellar. The drubbing America took under his presidency—symbolized by the taking of hostages in Iran and the bungled attempt to rescue them—was parallel to the drubbing men were taking from the women's movement. The two frustrations built up in parallel.

When the Iranian hostages finally came home to the cheers and ticker-tape parades Vietnam veterans had never gotten, the vets exploded. "Those people didn't *do* anything," Bubba says today, "and they were treated like heroes!" That was exactly the point. The only heroes America could unambivalently celebrate at that time were victim heroes. The only way you could be sure of virtue was not to do anything. It is a fact of mythic mischief that the Sixties repudiation of power reached its peak—or its nadir—on Inauguration Day, 1981. Enter Ronald Reagan to the rescue.

In a country sick of irresolution and humiliation, desperate to *act* and to *feel good,* John Wayne's old pal Ronnie made action look easy again. But he did it by turning back—by resurrecting the old black-and-white world view. *The Soviet Union is an evil empire. It's us against them all over the world. We are the good guys. Don't seven hundred thousand "boat people" prove it? Look at Vietnam and Cambodia now! And all because we lacked the will to win the war! Do we want that to happen on our doorsteps?* There is just enough truth in this, along with the blessed simplicity, to confuse and tempt.

The intense seductiveness of what Reagan offers can be seen in the delight with which the public welcomed the toy catharsis of Grenada. (Veterans of the Sixties alone were mostly appalled by it.) It can be seen, too, in the tenth-anniversary quarterbacking on the war: Were there, after all, in one formerly anti-war man's words, "worthy goals to achieve in Vietnam"? Given a unified national will, could we, should we, have won? Would winning early enough have held the national will together? Black-and-white thinking got us into that war —and out of it; ever since, we've been tormented by the shades of gray. What a relief it would be not to have to ask, "Is it right or wrong?" but only, "Can we win it without too great a cost?"

But as Reagan strenuously rows the national will toward the shores of Nicaragua, other currents flow the opposite way. The old anti-war movement—composed of many of the same people—is stirring, stretching, reawakening. A friend says, "I'm feeling political again"; she is studying Latin American history. Another sends me a "Pledge of Resistance" form: A national network of churches, synagogues, and activist and pacifist groups is gathering signatures of people who will commit themselves to non-violent civil disobedience should the U.S. intervene in Central America. Mingled with the sorrow and alarm, one senses a sharpening zeal for confrontation, a joy at once again having *something to oppose.* The military dreads fighting another war without substantial public support; the Movement vows to make sure they don't get it.

Both sides have valid points to make: the Reaganites, that America needs to be strong; the Movement, that that strength must never be used wantonly. But when the two sides confront each other, the result is a familiar stalemate—the paralyzing old Sixties polarization all over again. Once again, the militarists have the initiative; once again, our generation (minus defectors to the other side) is reacting. Once again, the stark alternatives offered are an imperial or an isolationist America; once again, the debate focuses negatively on whether we should use force. Reagan and the new warriors ache to say yes; the old anti-warriors say no.

Where is our generation's yes?

Power   and   Compassion

It may be in the tentative but growing exploration of ways that American and male power can be used *as forces for good.*

To much of our generation, that very thought is taboo ground, to be sown with penitent salt and avoided for a hundred years. The *Ugly American* era of missionary morality and imperial rape is still too recent. Perhaps a majority of Sixties survivors are "neo-isolationists," as one London-living American male (1948) expressed it: "Everybody could breathe a little easier if someone said it doesn't matter if we're number one anymore. We're who we are, America's America. We have a nice chunk of land and can grow a lot of corn and feed ourselves." Or we are one-sided interventionists, reversing Reagan and Kirkpatrick, agitating for action against South Africa and Chile while, in Mark Satin's words, "romanticizing the Sandinistas—just as we did the NLF."[7]

Lately, though, Reagan has been forced to abandon his double standard, and not only in words. We've seen our government compelled by the current of the times to align itself with "people power" against old cronies Marcos and Duvalier. We've been forced to recognize this as a positive (and overdue) use of American power, actually preventive of bloodshed. And it has made us question our own double standard. Slowly the alignment of the world struggle is shifting, from

Left against Right to what Czech novelist Milan Kundera has called "the struggle of man against power."[8] The paradoxical question for Americans is whether a great power can ever be a semi-disinterested ally in the struggle against power—and whether, without such an ally, that struggle can ever succeed.

Former "draft dodger" Mark Satin is one member of our generation who now believes that the United States can and should use its power "to foster the democratization and empowerment of the world's people."[9] "[T]he U.S. can't just 'get out' of Central America (or wherever)," he writes in *New Options.* "Getting out would just make it easier for other powerful nations to exercise their doleful influence. Far better that the U.S. begin to exercise its influence in ways that further humane values."[10] "Why make ourselves temptingly vulnerable? Why not, instead, make ourselves useful, with massive people-to-people diplomacy and assistance?"[11]

Satin calls this vision of an activist foreign policy "neo-interventionism," and names some other proponents, including New York Democratic Congressman Stephen Solarz (1940), who has played an active part in the Marcos investigation, and Central America lobbyist Bruce Cameron (1943), an advocate for the democratic "third force" in both Nicaragua and El Salvador. "[N]eo-interventionism does not include military intervention; and it is aimed not at protecting American power and privilege in the short term, but at encouraging humane and democratic values," Satin writes. Neo-interventionists may disagree on what groups to support and what tactics to use—citizen diplomacy, official diplomatic pressure, conditional aid and trade— "[b]ut they share one core conviction: the rights of individual people are more fundamental than the right of undemocratic nation-states to non-intervention."[12]

Satin would have us be rigorously consistent in our support of "people power" against oppressive power. "Is there a vital, non-Marxist-Leninist, democratic alternative [in Nicaragua]?"[13] he asks (and gives evidence that there is). "If Benigno Aquino . . . had been invited to the White House before his return to his home country— would he have been assassinated?"[14] And: "Literally millions of people [in America and Western Europe] demonstrated for peace in 1981–82 . . . Only a couple of thousand demonstrated on behalf of Solidarity. . . . Why . . . ?"[15]

In answer to *The New Republic*'s accusation that idealistic neo-interventionists "confuse foreign policy with philanthropy," Satin says that "we want democratic governments and an empowered world citizenry . . . because without them we cannot have world peace!"[16] He might have added that if we don't support people's legitimate aspirations for land, food, and liberation, the Soviet Union will. To avoid the pain of future Vietnams, rather than passively shrink from using force, we can actively prevent its becoming necessary, by sponsoring better revolutions than the Russians do. In this emerging view, altruism is the same as farsighted self-interest, and the future free world—to use *Star Trek* language again—looks more like a federation than an empire.

In the Sixties, scalded by the sight of a napalmed child, we said the United States was hypocritical. A fairer word would have been *schizophrenic.* From our beginnings, a genuine impulse to do good—to nurture human life as no country ever has before—has intertwined and conflicted with our more ordinary pursuit of wealth and power. The men who served in Vietnam may have been sent over for imperial aims, but most of them went over motivated by the impulse to do good. Those of us who opposed the war forgot that our brother grunts were as idealistic as we were; it was an American trait we shared. The first painful disillusionment for the GIs, long before coming home, was that the command didn't share their compassion, and the Vietnamese didn't want it.

"The village when we first come into it was worse than any slum I ever seen in the U.S.," Bubba recalled. "The people were walkin' around half naked or naked, no clothes at all. Some of 'em were walkin' around with fatigue shirts on full of bullet holes or a great big hole where someone had got blowed away with a mine. We got together, a bunch of us, and sent home for anything we could get, clothes and shoes and things like that, and had 'em sent back over there to us, and we just passed 'em out among the people." Despite the wounds it cost him, Bubba was respectful of the Vietnamese wish to be left alone. They, like him, were trying to survive. "We were in their way," he said. "As far as they were concerned, we were invading their privacy. But we fought for them trying to give them a free world, and they got nothing. As far as I know right now today, they still got nothing."

Bubba's remarks, and those of many other Vietnam vets, remind us that there can be a positive impulse behind war: an active protectiveness that is the male form of compassion. While some former anti-war protesters have come to realize that an adequate defense protects our freedom to protest, many Vietnam veterans came to realize—through the torment of destroying a village in order to save it, or saving a buddy's life only to come home to jeers—that war perverts prowess and protection into destruction. We have finally come out of the Vietnam experience with a determination to find active forms of compassion that can prevent war. And in answer to the neo-isolationists, the real fruit of our tragic "involvement" halfway around the globe is not the sense that we should stay home and mind our own business, but a permanent involvement in suffering and triumph everywhere—a vastly enlarged sense of what it means "to protect our own."

> You ask us why we're out here, carrying signs
> Out in this god-forsaken asphalt shopping center
> You who sent us to level the verdant jungles of Vietnam. . . .

wrote poet and veteran Michael Berkowitz.

> Go home, you shout.
> But we have none.
> You sent us abroad.
> And now the world is our home.

Now wherever you send us
We meet our brothers,
Not our enemy. . . .

We're here because it's the only way to reach you—
Before the next war.[17]

WANDERLUST

*When my brother and sister were my age, they had
already seen much more of the world than I will
probably ever see. They'd gone to India, Guatemala,
Cuba, Hong Kong . . . and driven across the country
half a dozen times each . . . And when, as a child, I'd
ask them about their lives, they'd tell me about the
movement. Movement. It seemed an appropriate word,
since they moved all the time . . .*
—DAVID LEAVITT (1961)
in *Esquire*

*Mama, mama, many worlds I've come
since I first left home . . .*
—THE GRATEFUL DEAD

The nomadic urge that seized our generation may have been the most
fabulous, fable-like, aspect of the Sixties. A long-haired kid with
backpack, thumb out, on the road to Kabul or Boulder—or just On
The Road—could be the emblem for the decade. (Poet Gary Snyder
compares the backpacker tootling on a recorder to the figure of a
humpbacked fluteplayer found in ancient Indian rock carvings all
over the Southwest.) The colorful tides of kids that swept back and
forth across the American continent and overflowed into Europe,
North Africa, the Middle East and Far East give the memory of that
time the storybook quality of a pilgrimage or crusade. We hit the road

barefoot, in hiking boots, in rubber sandals or Earth Shoes; with flutes and guitars strapped to our packs; in long purple velvet dresses and blue jeans with frayed-out knees. A Fellini circus parade. A gypsy caravan. A Tarot deck laid out in a line.

The imagery is mysterious, and so was the urge. While we made our share of true pilgrimages—seeking some swami, shaman, or sacred place—the quintessential Sixties journey was a search without a goal, what poet Roa Lynn (1937) has called an "open odyssey." America has always been synonymous with motion, but we moved as if moving itself was living, while Americans before us moved in search of a living. The prairie schooners, the underground railway, the Okie exodus to California, the black migration to the urban North —all had been quests for a better life, measured in liberty, land, and opportunity. We were the heirs of that "better life": a world at last made safe, sanitary, stable, respectable, comfortable, gleaming with "conveniences." It was all that our ancestors had sweated for. And all we wanted was out. We burst out as if a deeper ancestral momentum couldn't be dammed up, as if we knew that the task of discovering "the New World" was only half finished, and would not be done until it embraced the whole earth.

That urge for wholeness would drive us to discover and embrace everything our own culture had put down or ruled out. The children of security, we hankered for risk. Children of the "nice," the reasonable and rational, we wanted vision, passion, pain. Children of technology, we longed to get our hands in the dirt. Children of Lysol, Listerine, and Wonder Bread, we were starved for texture, taste, and smell. It was all "out there," outside those sterile space colonies, the suburbs; on the road, on the land, among people who had nothing much but life itself. They weren't far away.

Other Worlds

World-music scholar Anderson Duke Bakewell (1948) and his older brother (1946) were twelve and fourteen when they sneaked out of their handsome St. Louis suburban home and across the river to another world called East St. Louis. "It was our first introduction into a culture radically different from our own," says Duke. "No matter what they said, our neighbors—conservative, Republican—had more in common with the Russians than with the East St. Louis blacks. Most Americans have nothing in common with these people. They have an entirely alternate life.

"They were always our cooks and yardmen and gardeners, and we had that kind of relationship. As soon as we could get out alone, we used to go over there all the time. We had fake I.D.s, and they didn't care in East St. Louis. Now you can't go there at all. Then, it was a great feeling. Welcoming.

"They were the best musicians we'd ever heard. All the greats were there. We knew Howlin' Wolf and Muddy Waters and B. B. King and Albert King and Ike Turner and Chuck Berry. Miles Davis. We just happened to be in the right place at the right time. We started our own blues band, half black and half white. Played clubs. I was playing the drums and my brother was on the guitar. I think of my Eastern, non-European music interest as being a natural extension of that."

A few years later, St. John's College student Jonathan Segal would enter that same soon-to-be-forbidden world. "I used to go and listen to a lot of black music. Blues. I knew some of the black guys from the dining hall who washed dishes, and so forth. I was their main man, and they took me down to these little tiny clubs in town. I never had a problem being white. One day there was a group called the Vandykes, from Philadelphia. I went down there and drank beer out of the bottle. And there were a lot of funny things going on in the corners of the room. I felt more energy in that room, more basic life force, than I would very often feel at a political rally. And that stuck with me. Once you've had a tomato off a wild vine, why would you want one from the supermarket?"

It may be that the taste of another world within America awakened the hunger for other realities that would take us around the globe. For while East St. Louis might be right next door, it was as far—and as strangely familiar—as Tibet. The journey between cultures was the real distance, and the real homecoming to a lost part of oneself. In the new age of jet travel that began in 1958, it wasn't that much harder to cross an ocean than a street. The thousands of miles we traveled, after the black world closed to whites, only measured how far we needed to get away from ourselves and the world that made us.

There was another precedent for our wandering. While civil rights and the blues introduced us to another America, the Peace Corps was introducing the idea that a young American, alone, could travel to the heart of a Third World country—not as a tourist, but as an intimate emissary of modernity who would live among the people. (VISTA would soon reproduce this experience in Appalachia and Navaho-land.) The first volunteers were sent out in the old imperial mission-ary spirit, not to learn, but to teach and convert. That patronizing, one-way flow of information quickly broke down in the face of grind-ing poverty, gracious custom, and passive resistance to Yankee deliv-erance.

In his 1970 memoir *The Making of an Un-American*—"a sort of updated, radical's version of *The Ugly American*"—ex-volunteer Paul Cowan (1941) told how he and other volunteers, caught between the State Department and the *barrio,* underwent a disorienting shift in their perceptions and allegiances. Peace Corps psychologists, who had failed to prepare them, called it "culture shock." But the shock wasn't just the strangeness of another culture, it was the blindness of our own. It was the same awakening, the same deep questioning, that was coming out of Black Power and Vietnam.

Later Peace Corps volunteers were often "un-Americans" even before they left. Many joined the Corps to see the world while avoiding the draft (if their local draft board would buy it), and they served with an attitude of ill-concealed hostility toward the govern-ment they were supposed to represent. They were joined in remote parts of the world by legions seeking "culture shock" for its own sake, like a mind-expanding drug.

"I'd lived a sheltered little Jewish life in the Bronx," says Daya Goldschlag (1946), who crossed the Atlantic at nineteen. "I'd never spent a night away from home. When I got on the plane, all I could picture was black, blank. I had no preconception of my trip. I landed in Europe alone, slept in the airport, and went home with some Irish guys. From then on, it was one adventure after another. My parents got a postcard from Germany saying I was going to Persia. To travel in Arab countries, staying with Arab families . . . my whole head was just cracked open. I was never the same." That was the point.

America: Love It or Leave It

Goldschlag left in 1965, one drop in a steady trickle of student travelers and dropouts that would soon swell to a torrent. The tide of travel rose with the tides of dissent and drugs, driven by the same motives. From 1967 to 1973, the number of passports issued annually to students nearly doubled, from 292,000 to 559,000; in the summer of 1971, over 800,000 young Americans traveled to Europe. For many, the events of 1968 were final grounds for separation from America, the state and the state of mind. "I left right after Robert Kennedy was assassinated," says Francine Stone (1946), a playwright, mother, and expatriate now living in England. "I snapped. I went into physical shock and had to be slapped out of hysterics when the news was given to me. And I just left."

For second-wave lawyer Doug Weiner, then fresh out of college, the last straw came in November 1972. "Nixon versus McGovern. I traveled two hundred fifty miles that day to get to where I was a registered voter, to vote against Nixon. And of course it was a landslide for him. And the song 'Wooden Ships,' remember it? Crosby, Stills, Nash and Young. 'Wooden ships on the water, very free . . .' It goes toward the end, 'We are leaving, you don't need us.' And that was how I felt." Weiner got on a plane to India.

Whether the reasons were political or personal, most Sixties departures were precipitated by a sudden, overwhelming urge to *get out.* Like butterflies that must leave the chrysalis or die, we had to struggle free of the tight forms of the old society—school, marriage, family, job—and put protective distance between ourselves and those still-commanding guilts. "Out there" you could breathe, search, grow. "I got up in the middle of an economics class," recalls Duke Bakewell, "and I walked out and got on a plane and went to the Outer Hebrides. And I never looked back. Greatest thing I ever did in my life."

"My sense was that I needed to get away from all this," says Sy Safransky (1945), then a newly married reporter for the *Long Island Press,* now editor of *The Sun,* a spiritual-gadfly "magazine of ideas" published in Chapel Hill, North Carolina. "I needed to get away from New York, which was all I had known. I needed to get away from weekly visits to my family, from feeling discouraged about my work, and whatever else I couldn't put my finger on. I wanted to take a giant leap away from everything familiar. We'd saved up some money. We bought a van in England and for a year we traveled, '69 to '70."

Ananda Saha was feeling trapped in Denver by a dull job and a dying marriage when "four of us took an acid trip one night and decided to make a desert pilgrimage. We went to New Mexico and camped in a cave in a volcanic ridge that the Indians used as a prayer cave. We were there about a week, and three of us decided we should stay together. So we went back to Denver and I sold my upright piano and all my art books and got all the money together I could get. I had a VW, and the three of us decided what we would need for a longer voyage. We packed incense and paint, lots of journals, blankets, put them in the back of the VW, and took off. We drove to the Southwest and across to the East Coast, taking acid about every week. Took acid in New Orleans. Took acid in Jacksonville, Florida, during a hurricane."

New York artist Joan Giannecchini (1942) took off for Europe a few months after walking out on a stifling marriage—and a child. "I was twenty-three, twenty-four. Nobody in my family on either side would speak to me. I was completely ostracized. And I had this guilt to deal with about my daughter, and this man I had horribly failed after promising to fulfill him. All of that was weighing on me, and all of it was a struggle. So I went to Europe for a year. It was clearly just the right thing to do."

The irony was that the world we were so angrily leaving had richly provisioned us for the journey. We had lost our confidence in America, but not our American confidence, the imperial *chutzpah* that enabled us to walk in on a flamenco *fiesta* or a Hopi corn dance with no shame. "It was that feeling you grew up with that was part of the Fifties, that as an American you could do anything you wanted," says artist Stan Kaplan. "The world was an American sea. You could sail anywhere."

Likewise, our blithe lack of concern about funds and the future was rooted in the material security of the Fifties. When St. Louis restaurateur Karen Duffy (1945) and her first husband sold their house, packed up their two babies, and took off for Europe and Africa in a van, "people kept telling me it was a scary thing to do. 'How can you quit your job?' But we weren't scared. Our Depression parents couldn't understand. They had worked so hard to give their kids security, and their kids sought adventure." The security was parent to the adventure, in more ways than one.

A popular image of the traveling kids of the Sixties is that we all had American Express travelers checks in our pockets from Daddy, or at least that rescue was never more than a phone call away. Reach out and put the touch on someone. That image is partially true. Some of us traveled on graduation gifts or other family funds, like the friend who lured Doug Weiner to India: "His family was pretty well off. He purchased a Volkswagen van in Amsterdam and did the great magic-bus number." In other cases, the worldly goods we sold to buy that van had been a parental grubstake to start us out in life.

Most people I spoke to, though, were determined to make it on their own, on principle and/or because "Depression parents" disapproved of the wandering. Minneapolis architectural innovator Eddie Lilburn* would work for a while, sometimes for his realtor father, "save up, and then go off." His dad "realized it was something I had to do—he just couldn't wait for it to end." Doug Weiner drove a gypsy cab in Harlem and the Bronx for five months to finance his trip to India. Daya Goldschlag "never even considered sending home for money"; when she ran out, she sold her blood. While it would be wrong to underestimate our guts and resourcefulness, we shouldn't confuse them with heroism. As Karen Duffy points out, "You have to be raised secure to do that"—and most of us knew we had a strong, if grudging, safety net.

The El Cheapo Travel Company

Our chief protector, of course, was the pre–1973 dollar—like American confidence, riding rough but still high. Even in the pocket of the raggedest hippie, the dollar was emperor. Given its power and our equation of discomfort with adventure, the dollar would go very, very far indeed. At home, gas was forty-nine cents a gallon in 1972. We were delighted to drive a fifth-hand, hundred-dollar car, because when you're going nowhere in particular, engine failure is just another experience. We slept in cars, on friends' floors, in sleeping bags on beds of tree roots and cottonwood leaves.

Abroad, we went proudly third-class. "Remember that horrible place we stayed at in Calais?" Washington scientist Eve Mościcki (1948) asks her husband. "Oh God, it was an absolute rathole. But it served its purpose. It was cheap. You could really do Europe on two dollars a day." Add the smorgasbord of charters, hostels, rail passes, and discounts travel merchants lavished on the student market. "Air India had a tremendous bargain available," Doug Weiner recalls. "You could fly round trip from New York to Bombay or New Delhi for four hundred dollars!" (In 1980, it was $1,145; in April 1986, $976.) In 1971, thanks to an airline price war, you could fly Alitalia's New York–Rome round trip for $199, or Sabena's New York–Brussels round trip for $220. A student Eurailpass cost $125 for two months of unlimited travel, second class (one hundred four thousand were sold in the summer of 1970). In Amsterdam in the summer of '71, according to *Time,* "city-funded sleeping projects have been set up in abandoned factories and warehouses, offering foam-rubber mat beds, showers and rock music"—for eighty cents a night.[1]

New Jersey data-processing consultant Judy Goff (1947) "took off for Europe following graduation and spent sixteen or seventeen months sort of floating around with a backpack on my back. I spent six months in Israel, a summer along the coast of Spain traveling with this guy on a motorcycle, a month in Yugoslavia when my sister was there, and the rest was pretty much wherever your thumb would take you type thing. It was the best thing I've ever done in my life. I was staying in youth hostels, and they were a dollar a night. When I was in Israel I lived on a kibbutz for three months. A thousand dollars kept me going for almost an entire year."

The ultimate cheap-travel pass was the one you were born with, like birds are born with wings. Hitchhiking in the Sixties was more than a convenience; it was almost an ideology. Free, spontaneous, daring, sharing, democratic, ecological (saved gas), it summed up our credo in a single gesture: the cocked thumb. Above all, it was an act of faith in human nature. Blind faith, though it may have been: "I didn't have fear because I didn't know about the world," says Daya Goldschlag, who thumbed her way across Europe and the Middle East. "I was almost sold into slavery a few times, but I didn't know it. People tried to drug and kidnap me, and I'd sort of go, 'Oh, no thank you.' I must have had a guardian angel."

Despite the risks—in 1972, 33 percent of Boston's reported rapes occurred while hitchhiking, as did 70 percent of Boulder, Colorado's —it was such an *open* time. Borders were wide open between countries that are now at war or "closed and medievalized," in Bob Waldman's words. Doug Weiner's friend drove his magic bus "across Europe, through Turkey into Asia Minor, all the way through Iran, Afghanistan, Pakistan, India, Nepal, and back. You can't do that now." Nor can you (if you still dare) easily flag down a car; they whip by with tinted windows rolled up tight. But in the Sixties, barriers between strangers were down. Something about the gift of a ride— the chance and fate of meeting, the mutual vulnerability, the enclosure in space and time—made it intimate and mythic, like a shipboard romance. We heard great stories, had unforgettable peak experiences of generosity and even of love.

"The road took care of us," says Sy Safransky. "It involved trust, and things kept happening that would deepen that trust. Getting picked up and taken hundreds of miles, people going out of their way to carry you right to your destination. Taking you home and putting you up for the night. Feeding you. Good connections made along the way, heart to heart. It wasn't just hippies who would respond to us, but ordinary people."

"Old folks would pick you up and bring you home and play mom and dad for the evening," Kathy Brimlow confirms. "And there was an exchange. They were giving to you and that made them feel happy. But you were also bringing them idealism, new ideas and thoughts. It kind of renewed their dreams. It was a beautiful exchange. I don't see that happening much anymore."

Brimlow remembers one "beautiful exchange" in particular. She was hitching across New Mexico with a girlfriend, and they strayed into *Easy Rider* redneck territory. "We couldn't get a ride to Texas. The people were spitting on us, really doing a number. So the cops came, and they took us through the Texas border and dropped us off in Arizona. Here comes a little green Volkswagen. A man and woman are in there. They're a little older than us. They pick us up and bring us to their house, a cottage-type house.

"They were very quiet. They felt reverent but there was nothing phony about them. Very down-to-earth. We saw fruit being dried on the kitchen counter. They were vegetarians, but there was a strain between them. A loving strain. There was sadness. That we felt.

"We were sitting in the living room. I heard the girl crying. And I went to the bedroom and knocked on the door. They let me in. I said, 'I can't sleep. I feel that there's a lot of pain in here.' And they started talking.

"This was their last night together. He was going to Vietnam the next day. And he had the feeling—he just felt like he wasn't going to come back. It wasn't like being scared. He just had a feeling that this was it. And we all sat up talking about how we felt about dying, life, and loving and friends.

"I couldn't believe that they were sharing this with me, a complete stranger that they just picked up hitching on the road. I'm sitting in bed with two people who are not hippies in any sense of the word, who are going through one of the most difficult evenings of their life. He's going off to war and has a distinct feeling that he's never going to see her again. And they're sharing this with me. I said to them, 'I love you two so much. I feel like you're a part of my being.' And they said, 'We love you, too. You are a part of us.'

"I had two possessions that were precious to me. One was a set of glass wind chimes, and the other was Hans Christian Andersen's fairy tales. So I gave her the wind chimes, so she could hang them up, and any time she would hear them she would remember this evening. I gave him the book, so that he could take it with him and read the stories, which are so rich. And the place that he was going to be was so unrich. We just sat up until the sun came up, sunrise flooded into the window onto the three of us. And we held hands and cried and laughed. We were holy together and we were strangers. And the next morning we packed up all our gear and they put us in their Volkswagen and drove us to the side of the road. And we kissed and said good-bye.

"That was it. That was it. I hold those two with me through my whole life. I'm sure that they hold me too. This tiny little hippie girl that they shared so much with . . . I don't know whether he died or what. I don't know."

The Traveling Carnival

If our style of travel bred instant intimacy with people along the way, it also made for casual-intense bonds between wanderers. This was most true on the roads of Europe and Asia, where the thousands of voluntary exiles created a new nomadic culture. In the central square of Amsterdam, Mexico City, or Katmandu, you could contact the tribe and score good dope, good loving, conversation, or company for the road. "I wandered around smoking hash at every little town, every port, carrying it around in Campbell's soup cans, meeting freaks in the Balearic Islands," says Joan Giannecchini. "And I discovered that sex wasn't just something you do to keep the guys happy. I liked it too." "People sort of banded together," Judy Goff recalls. "There was a lot of traveling with one another. You'd meet someone at a youth hostel and travel to the next city together, and then you'd each go your own way."

This tribe of scholar-gypsy-lovers was international, for the same impulses that had moved us in America were stirring in postwar-born Germans, Dutch, Brits, French, Scandinavians, Mexicans, Aussies, Japanese. All over the world a generation was on the move, rioting in the universities, flowing together on the roads, reveling in commonalities and differences. "I went to France and formed friendships with Myriam and her friends who had manned the barricades," says Francine Stone. "And then I went to Czechoslovakia at the end of August '68, and I was with them right after the tanks rolled in. I watched the Chicago convention in Helsinki, wondering what on earth was going on. And I was in Sweden with the students there, who were very radical and wonderful. They were my education." Some are still her close friends.

Many Americans in Europe were fascinated by a radicalism more subtle and rooted than our own. "The conversations I had with European students came closer to the philosophical issues," says Jonathan Segal, who had been troubled by the anti-intellectualism of the American anti-war movement. "Europeans could be passionate on the Left and passionate on the Right, but there was a dialogue." (Not on one subject, though. We'd thought *we* hated our country, but Europeans' anti-Americanism stung—so much so that some of us pretended to be Canadian.) Francine Stone felt that "the texture of the late Sixties was quite different in Europe and England. Related, but different, probably because these kids came to radical politics from a dedication of generations." Intense conversations with contemporaries in the Netherlands, where socialism actually coexisted with freedom, transformed editor and chef Robert Gilbert (1950) from a Goldwater supporter to a liberal in two months.

Deeper transformations were also happening, drawing young travelers closer to each other and further from their cultures of origin.

"A German hippie who'd lived on the road for seven or eight years gave me my first hit of acid," says Sy Safransky. "He put it in my hand and said, 'Take this, it will make everything beautiful.' I was so terrified of it I carried it around with me for several months before I finally took it that winter in Spain. That first trip changed my life." Safransky took acid at intervals for the rest of his time in Europe, and found (like Ananda Saha and her friends dropping acid during a hurricane) that being on both kinds of trips at once greatly speeded up the work of wrenching loose from the old frame of reference.

Not that drug-related encounters were always enlightening. The international youth culture at its worst was a sleazy string of crash pads along the Hashish-Hepatitis Trail. But at its best it was the spawning stream of planetary culture, where ideas were exchanged, improbable friendships sealed, astonishments assimilated.

Funk Shock

Astonishment peaked in the Third World, where lowest-common-denominator travel maximized the impact on senses, mind, and guts. No air conditioning for us, no paper band across sterilized toilets. We wanted baptismal immersion in the film of dust, the press of flesh. Even dirt was spice to us; a world that *smelled* was as much of a revelation as a world that starved or meditated, danced to ecstasy or wailed in grief. "The search for funk," Francine Stone wryly calls it. And traveling outside Europe and North America by foot, thumb, bus, and third-class train, we found it—in sometimes overwhelming proportions.

"I was supposed to get a train from Patna to Benares," recalls Richmond, Virginia, gastroenterologist Paul Monroe (1949), who traveled around the world after his junior year at Amherst. "There were elephants in the streets, really strange. I had a backpack, a kazoo, and a Vietnamese coolie hat." Since Monroe is six feet four inches tall, gangly and blond, there was some disagreement about what was "really strange." "In India staring is not impolite. I sat down on this bench waiting for the train to come, and there were a crowd of twenty Indians standing around me staring. For hours they just stared. So I would entertain them every once in a while with the kazoo.

"I bought a third-class ticket. To go like a thousand miles would cost fifty cents. Third class means you have benches instead of seats, and animals. The train was supposed to leave at three P.M. Six P.M. passed, and still no train. About nine P.M. the platform was packed. The train pulls up and it's totally packed with people and that's our train. I take one step on the train and I couldn't get farther. So I got off, which was a big mistake because then there was no place to get back on. In all this hustle and bustle, someone picked my pocket and took all my cash. All my I.D. was stolen except my passport.

"I finally get on. All I could do is stand. The train goes about sixty miles an hour for about two minutes, then stops for about thirty minutes. Does this continually. A grandmother and I took turns sitting on the floor. At two A.M. one of the other people in the hallway was a Buddhist monk. And he wants to practice his English. He's going up to Kashmir. There was a wild monk up there who ran around without any clothes on, and the only language they could communicate in would be English. So he wanted to practice English on me.

"At three A.M. we get to Benares. The train stops at Old Benares and you have to catch a connecting train. So I asked the conductor when was the train to New Benares, and he laughed. Instant education on the train system in India. So I decided I'm not in any rush. Where am I going?

"I lay down for about an hour. I thought, This is stupid. It's the middle of the night. I'm lying on a stupid train platform in India. This guy from Australia had given me seven rupees, which was about seventy-five cents. I go trudging off to where the taxis are. First you negotiate. How much to get to town? They say twelve. I say four. We end up at eight and they refuse to come down. They're screaming at me, calling me names. I started to feel sick. I said forget it. I go back to the platform.

"I finally ask, Is there any other way to get to town? By now it's six A.M. There's a bus for three rupees. The bus stop is just a dirt thing with cowshit all over. After forty-five minutes of sitting there, it was the closest I'd ever come to breaking down. First I'd think of every beautiful woman I ever knew. Everything good that ever happened to me. Good food. Anything. And then I just started praying. It was that bad. It was the only time in my life I've ever prayed. Get me out of this.

"The bus pulls up. We jump on the bus, pushing people out of my way. I wasn't going to take any shit. This guy gives me this line in Hindu or something. Obviously this seat is saved. I said, 'Screw you, buddy, I'm sitting here.' The whole bus burst out laughing. We drive about a half mile. There's no way to collect tickets on the stupid train, but on the bus they stopped and they empty everyone sitting or standing, and they collect tickets. I got to the window seat and I'm vomiting out the window, the only time I ever got sick.

"I get off the bus and hire a rickshaw to take me to the tourist bungalow where I'm staying. A famous place among travelers in Asia 'cause it costs a dime a night, for a dorm. A room costs a dollar a night.

"The next day I go out sightseeing and go to one of the temples. To get into the temple you have to take your shoes off. There's no way I'm going to walk barefoot in there. Screw culture. I never saw a temple from the inside. So I hired a boat to go up and down the Ganges River. We saw people filling vials with holy water and bathing. There's a log with crows on it. The guy paddles me up to it. And it was a dead man. I got a first-class ticket to New Delhi and got out of India."

Monroe (who is my brother-in-law) offers a shrewd assessment of our mode of travel: "Your parents were saying it's silly to try to live on seven rupees, and your brother Alan [1956, a reporter and inveterate nomad] said it brings you closer to the people. I think it's halfway. By trying not to spend a lot of money you are forced to eat the food that's there. Take the trains that people take. That's what you are doing it for. You're not any less a tourist. You're not living their life, 'cause you can get out."

Through the Looking Glass

If these forays were stressful, they were magical, too. Like drug trips, they pushed us through the looking glass into realities so alien that the simplest transaction—like buying a piece of fruit—became enchanted. *"Dos pesitos, señora,"* said the fruit vendor in Mexico City's Chapultepec Park. The tender diminutive of "two little pesos," the fact that at twenty-five I was assumed to be a *"señora"* not a *"señorita,"* were a haiku-like glimpse into another world. The moment of arrival in a new culture always gave an addictive rush. We felt new, with a sense of infinite possibility. Perception was heightened, and memories are brilliant after fifteen years. No need for slides: we remember the exact color of the light, the noise of the marketplace, the moment when we pierced the veil of the exotic to make human contact.

Dawn in Mexico City, 1971. My college friend Judy and I have decided to take the bus to the pyramids of Teotihuacán, but not the cushy tourist bus—the city bus. In the dusky light we start walking deep into a gray, deserted neighborhood, following the instructions of an amused concierge. We are nervous, lost. An open-sided electric trolley full of crisply uniformed cops with rifles stops, picks us up, gallantly delivers the misplaced *gringas* to the bus stop.

We climb aboard a decrepit bus already half full of women going to market, men going to work. *"Buenos dias, señoras,"* one woman greets us graciously. We mumble a reply, almost struck dumb with shyness and shame, feeling so out of place in our old jeans among these full-bodied, full-skirted, calm women, the most regal people I have ever seen in my life.

The bus groans out along a straight road from the city, through the ring of *Nortéamericano* factories that encircles Mexico City and chokes off its air. Men are waiting by the side of the road, huddling near small fires they have built for warmth. They climb on the bus until it is packed, the aisle full. Judy and I slide down in our seats to be inconspicuous, and we listen to the racking coughs and the camaraderie, feeling like eavesdroppers or spies, thrilled and grieved by the poignancy of *other life*. Then we get off the bus and climb to the top of the Pyramid of the Sun and look out over the plains in the golden early morning light.

That was a taste. Bolder travelers dived deeper. Eddie Lilburn went to Morocco with two Scottish falconer friends in 1968. "I had the car, a VW station wagon, and they brought three falcons, two gyrfalcons and a goshawk. In retrospect, it was pretty clever to take the falcons with us. Because when we got off the boat we were immediately distinguished from all the other hippies who were getting off the boat. We had these exotic birds, and we had a vehicle. Most hippies didn't have vehicles.

"So we set off. Instead of going to Marrakesh, we headed for the hills. Up in the mountains we were greeted by the Berber falconers, who appreciated how beautiful these birds were. We were able to use the birds as an entrée to Berber culture that few people have ever had the opportunity to experience.

"We spent four months living with the Berbers in these incredible mountain villages. It was so exotic to be up there. I was just sick from the culture shock at first. One of the first nights I was there, I was a kid who was raised on hamburgers and all of a sudden I'm eating sheep's eyes, literally. We were given sheep's eyes and sheep's brains as the guests of honor. Unbelievable culture shock. It took me a month or two to realize how great it was. Not the food. Morocco."

Despite the widespread resentment of America and the bad behavior of some hippies, many young travelers were received with exquisite hospitality. And as strange as other cultures could be, it was even stranger to find one that seemed hauntingly familiar. Yet that was a common experience. "It felt like déja vu," Los Angeles-born filmmaker Cherel Ito (1947) says of arriving in Japan with her late husband, musician Teiji Ito, and living with a Buddhist priest in a room adjoining a temple. Duke Bakewell, who "never felt really at home in St. Louis," found his homecoming among the desert dwellers of Yemen, and has returned again and again to study their music, ecology, and architecture. My sister Janet Nuñez (1953), frozen in Chicago, flowered in Mexico.

Some of us thought these mysterious affinities must be evidence for reincarnation. Why else would, say, a WASP from suburban Philadelphia feel an overwhelming sense of homecoming in Nepal? Maybe the gods had decided it was time to shuffle the deck, to make Tibetan monks come back as New Jersey college dropouts and Nebraskan grain brokers as Tokyo businessmen. We might look like Archie and Veronica, but inside we were ancient seekers, temple priests. There's a less occult explanation; we may have recognized traditional cultures because they still spoke the language of archetypes, the psyche's mother tongue, while our Hollywood and Madison Avenue icons were only a badly degraded dialect. But reincarnation was, at least, a good metaphor for urgently accelerating cultural exchange. It was not a moment too soon to mix up timeless wisdom with technical savvy.

Novice Natives

Our number-one reincarnation fantasy, of course, was that we were the returning American Indians. This notion struck many Indians as the ultimate expropriation, but a few shrewd native spokespeople encouraged it, as a source of support and perhaps of real hope. Otter G'Zell (1942), self-described "old hippie," Neo-Pagan priest, and co-creator of the Ringling Brothers Circus's controversial Living Unicorn, narrates the myth as it entered our generation's folklore:

"As we've been told by many a medicine man, part of the Hopi prophecy is that in these times of the Great Purification, the spirits of all the Indians who were killed by the invaders would be born again in one generation. Those spirits would make themselves known by adopting a name that sounded similar to Hopi and that meant— like Hopi does—the peaceful ones. And they would take up the ways of the Indians: headbands and crystals and the philosophy and costumes of the Indians would seem natural to them. In 1975, Father

David Monongye had a vision that it was time to reveal the prophecy, because the hippie generation had come."

And come we had, by the hundreds and thousands, to camp on the Indians' land, pee in their streams, and invade their sacred ceremonies, as if the apocryphal claim of kinship gave us an open invitation. Not all pilgrims to the Indians were so insensitive. Some whites, wanting to give as well as take, participated in legal and illegal battles to reclaim tribal land, from Taos Blue Lake to Wounded Knee. But most of us were looking for a fantasy, not the hard reality, and our reluctant hosts knew it.

"The Indians didn't want any part of us," says New York special-education teacher Willa Barth (1954). "We weren't trying to take anything away from them; we were breaking with American traditions, trying to understand them. But they resented the fact that we would take their names. They were being stripped of their own culture, and we were catching a free ride on it." In 1971 Barth was invited to a Blackfoot ceremony in Montana by a little Indian girl. "When we got there there was a lot of hostility. We were asked to leave, because we were just hippies. They expressed the fact that they were trying to maintain their own identity, and we were trying to emulate it without really understanding it."

These forlorn visits to the reservation were clues to the real motive behind all our wandering. We weren't fleeing a home, we were seeking one. We were homesick for the earth, and for a way of life rooted in the earth. Hitchhiking across America, especially the vast spaces of the West, revealed that we didn't really belong on this continent yet, any more than we did in Morocco or Nepal. All the people we'd visited, even Europeans—even Mississippi blacks and their northern urban grandchildren—had roots in a place and a rich culture. They belonged. Only we seemed disembodied, ghosts in the machine that was relentlessly "developing" the earth. (We didn't know that our "nobodiness" was the price of our precious freedom; in the Sixties we thought we could get identity without giving up possibility.)

Our global travels were admiring apprenticeships to people who lived in place; our travels back and forth across America were a romance with the spirit of *this* place, where we hoped one day to belong. Of course, some Sixties travelers found roots ready-made, by grafting themselves onto another culture. Marc Barasch knew "a very committed radical who went to Costa Rica, married a Costa Rican, and aligned himself with the guerrillas there." Linguist Greg Paludis (1951), raised liberal Catholic in Michigan, went to Israel to study Hebrew, converted to Orthodox Judaism, married a Yemenite Jew, and is now an Israeli citizen. But most of us had fallen in love with the American land, and we wanted the Indians to teach us to be worthy of it—preferably in ten easy lessons.

Kathy Brimlow tells a story of reconciliation with the American earth, mediated by a native guide, that distills the guilt and longing —and the impatience—of a generation.

"A friend and I hitchhiked to New Mexico together," she recalls. "We got picked up by a girl named Blue in a Volkswagen van, who brought us to a village called Pilar. In the village there were some abandoned adobe huts, and the landlord said if the hippies wanted to come in and fix up the adobes, they could live there. So that's how we got our house.

"As soon as we'd fixed up the adobe, my friend said, 'I'm out of cigarettes. I think I'm going to hitchhike to San Francisco and get a few cartons.' I said, 'Okay. How long do you think it will take?' She said, 'A week or two.' I said, 'Okay. Bye.' And she left. So there I was, for the first time in my life, very alone.

"I'm telling you, this is alone. There was one girl way up the hill in an adobe. She left. Then there was this guy George who had a house there. He left to go on a trip. And there were two guys that lived in a house not too far away. But I never saw them. The nearest town was Taos, twenty miles north.

"I had no transportation. I had no running water. Four or five miles down the road was a pipe that came out of the mountain with spring water, and every now and then you'd wheel a cart down the road and fill up some garbage pails or old milk cans. I had no electricity. Two kerosene lanterns. A wood-burning stove and a pot-bellied stove. And that was it. I was a middle-class, suburban girl, alone in the middle of the mountains with none of the conveniences. And I was terrified, totally terrified.

"During the day and early evening I was afraid of real things. And at night I was afraid of . . . Oh my God, that place was so incredible. This is Indian country. And every night I would lie in bed and I would hear . . . it would start from way down in the canyon. [She makes the sound of wind blowing] This wind, this individual wind. It would sleek through, and as it would sleek through different areas you would hear clanging and noise. Then it would sleek through my village. And I would kind of feel like it was the Passover. The spirit of death. Like if I went out into the street I would be consumed by it.

"But I stayed there two weeks alone. And I finally made peace in a lot of ways. There was an Indian named John Comes Home.* I don't know how we communicated with each other. But he communicated to me that I had to make peace with the mountain. I was living at the foot of a mountain, and this mountain was very symbolic. It was full of piñon trees, and there were five little ponds, and from each pond a waterfall trickled down to the next one.

"So I decided to contact the spirit of the mountain if I was going to live in peace in the valley by myself. I stripped myself of all my clothing, took peyote. And I proceeded to climb the waterfall into the first pond to cleanse myself. Climbed the next waterfall into the next pond. That was the way I would climb the mountain, cleansing each of my senses. You see, there were five ponds . . . five senses.

"As I was climbing there was a guy, a bearded man, old, but young. Young but had an ancient face. Sitting against a tree and as I was ready to go into the pond he goes, 'There's a big old snake.' And he had a flute. 'There's a big old snake in that pond.' And I went into the pond. I bathed. And I climbed out. I was totally naked. I wondered, was that a real guy? Or was it an ally, you know, like in Carlos Castaneda, which I hadn't read at that time but I read afterwards.

"When I got to the top of the mountain I found a clearing at this cliff. So I went out and just stood there on that tiny triangular space, waiting to be confronted with the spirit of the mountain. I'd studied

Indian religion, and it occurred to me that the spirit of the mountain would come in the form of an animal. If that animal confronts you and you react with fear, then the spirit of the mountain can kill you. That animal will kill you. If it's a deer then you've already found a kind of grace. The deer could still kill you, but it's not as ferocious as a mountain lion or something else.

"I stood there on the cliff. And flying toward me I saw five big birds, flying in formation. My first reaction was terror. I thought they were vultures. Then I said, 'You have to have faith.' And I just closed my eyes and put my arms up. I justified in my mind that a vulture will not attack something living.

"So I stood there with my eyes closed, sun pouring on me. And then I just couldn't keep my eyes closed any longer. I opened up my eyes, and the five birds were suspended in front of me, at eye level. I looked at them, and it looked like they were looking at me. And then they went *whssssh!* [makes the sound of wind] and flew off. I just fell to my knees and thanked God. And I went home.

"John interpreted for me that I had favor with the mountain. That the spirit of the mountain was kind to me. That I didn't have to stay on that mountain for three days, that I was confronted favorably. When I described the birds, he said, 'Those were hawks, not vultures.' And hawks *will* attack a human, especially if there are a group of them. But I posed no threat. He said, 'You came to the mountain with respect. You were pure.'

"After that I slept peacefully in Pilar."

Back to the Land

Having fallen in love, it's natural to want to get married, with little or no inkling of the daily demands of your beloved. "We've got to get ourselves back to the Garden," Joni Mitchell sang. It was one of the most passionate and important dreams of our generation, even if most early forays ended, like Woodstock, in the mud. Thousands of visionary rural communes were founded during the Sixties and Seventies and, judging by the circulation of *The Mother Earth News*—

which climbed steadily through the Seventies to a peak of over a million in the early Eighties—hundreds of thousands of us tried some form of homesteading. The original back-to-the-land impulse, like the passage to India, was a headlong flight from modernity into what writer Carl Nagin calls "the romanticizing of the primitive." It's no coincidence that our first attempts to create a land-based culture of our own (just road-hippie culture with roots—we went right on living in the same old school buses) had all the charm and sanitation of a depressed Indian reservation or Third World slum.

"I traveled around the country looking for a commune to work on that had good design," says Eddie Lilburn. "I was appalled by most of those places. A lot of people got out there and found that they had no tools, no skills. The best they could do was re-create shantytowns, rather than build a really new vision.

"There was this whole idea that going back to nature you had to renounce technology, renounce the entire modern world, including hygiene. Go back to a primitive existence. So you had all these snotty-nosed little kids named Zeke and Clem, running around with no clothes on, eating razor blades—that commune-kid look. It was just filthy and natural."

It's not surprising that, in the words of Los Angeles screenwriter and actor Wynston Jones (1942), "most of those idealized little notions flowered and fell to ruin within two years." When blisters broke, rabbits ate the lettuce, pipes froze, tempers frayed, and the money ran out, those with a summer-camp conception of the country got weeded out. It was easiest to sustain a hippie hunter-gatherer fantasy in a relatively mild environment like northern California, where the Indians had had a good life before the missionaries came along. Add food stamps and marijuana culture to the piñon nuts, abalone, and wild pig, and you have an ecological niche capable of supporting a time warp. "You can go up there even today and find people living in caves and tepees and trailers, wearing long beards and robes, looking like gnomes," says Jones. "They're playing California Indian. That's what it was all about, being an Indian. And the redwoods were a perfect place to do that." Jones discovered one such lost tribe living on the Huber River near Reno in '78 or '79.

"I went up to visit this woman I knew in Nevada City, and she said come on down and meet the people in the commune. First we went to a guy's house who was a biker. All of his front teeth were rotted out, and he had boa constrictors for pets all around the house, carried all sorts of sharp knives in his belt, had very long hair and a beard and talked real tough about fuck this and fuck that. 'Fucking asshole, I'll kill the motherfucker'—stuff like that all the time.

"He took a four-wheel-drive truck to get us to this place. We had to go down an old stagecoach road. We pulled up to the place where you had to walk in, and we walked down about a hundred yards, and the biker stood up on a rock and gave a cry which echoed down the canyon. It was picked up by other people at various positions. They had this signal, which I assumed meant we were coming down now.

"There were a lot of people living along the river, and by the time we got there they had all gathered together in this community gathering area around some outdoor cabinets they had built. They were all nude. Everybody was nude all the time down there. So we all took our clothes off. It was only fair. I got my ass burned really bad in the sun.

"In any of the communes, there was always some central figure, some charismatic personality, whether he was a spiritual charismatic or a physical charismatic or whatever. Some kind of power. Down here was a guy who called himself Pan. About five foot six, wiry, had a glimmer in his eye. Long hair, long beard. The biker guy pulled out this big pouch and without saying a word to the Pan guy sat down and spread out a bunch of little feathered doodads he had made. They traded some items.

"We were welcome here. Sat around taking acid and then a girl named Kate showed me around. She showed me caves where people had built ladders made with boughs of trees and rawhide thongs with a crosspiece. You'd climb up the side of a cliff and there was a cave with a sort of loft in it, also made of thongs and branches. They had drilled holes through rock to make chimney escapes for smoke. And this is how they lived. The Pan guy lived in a house made out of beer cans. He'd found a cave and holed the entire front of the cave up with beer cans by pouring cement into them." The commune by the river broke up in another year, when the "Indians" finally wearied of roughing it.

Ananda Saha, too, tired of primitive living after a year at the Lama Foundation commune in New Mexico (which, like many spiritual communes, has survived storms of change to become a retreat and learning center). "My second husband and I lived in the community between children one and two," she says. "It was good because it was very hard, extremely physically hard. The year we were there a wing of the main building, which was the bathhouse and the living room, burned down. We were there during winter, forty degrees below zero. One week it never went above zero. We lived in a little A-frame with a tin stove. One morning we woke up and the kerosene was frozen in the lamp.

"We were almost all college graduates there. Extremely poor. Everyone was on spiritual paths. We had group meditation every morning. Every Tuesday we fasted and kept silence, continuing our regular work load. We planted and harvested the garden, milked the goats, made cheese, repaired the building, and mudded the adobe buildings. And we put Ram Dass's book together. We had meetings at night. Drove twenty-seven miles to town to get a shower. After the fire we instituted a night watch, so that every ten days we were doing a watch all night. I was nursing my first baby. It was a very hard life, but it was again that quest.

"I don't think I was ever happy there. It was astonishingly physically beautiful, that was what sustained me. We also had something we called glitch, like dysentery. We tested the water, couldn't figure out what caused it. One finally learned that if you didn't eat very much ever, you could keep it under control." Visiting teacher Hari Dass Baba wasn't kidding when, asked (as Saha tells it) "Should I go to India?" he answered, "India is coming here." Saha decided to leave Lama when she was pregnant with her second child. "I felt community pressure on me to be there and have the baby, but I decided that that was not where I wanted to be. I felt I needed to take what I learned on the mountain and go back to the outside world. I left and went to New Paltz."

On a round planet, journeys lead in a circle. The farthest point of flight into the past and the primitive—in a boat on the Ganges, by a tin stove near Taos—marked the beginning of a return. "It was a mind-expanding experience," says Doug Weiner of his seven months in India and Nepal, "but it was there that I realized I would never be fulfilled dropping out of twentieth-century America, because that's who I was." Similarly, the early communards and homesteaders had to admit that the primitive wasn't so romantic after all, and a twentieth-century American wasn't the worst thing in the world to be. Many threw down their hoes and came back to the city; most who stayed in the country let the twentieth century filter back into their lives. After several years of hoeing soybean fields by hand, the hippies of Stephen Gaskin's commune, The Farm, adopted tractors, and built a modern maternity clinic to back up "spiritual midwifery." Poet Gary Snyder, one of our foremost teachers of living lovingly in place, uses a chain saw.

But what's important is that none of us "came back" all the way —or we came back changed, wanting to change twentieth-century America. Getting off a plane from Old or New Mexico, we might be grateful for a vanilla milkshake and a hot bath, but we also suffered from reverse culture shock. My brother Alan returned from the Peace Corps in the lonely, foggy, muddy, macho Ecuadorean Andes, only to find that he had anxiety attacks in shopping malls. If there was such a thing as too little freedom from the rigors of mortality, tradition, and nature, there was definitely also such a thing as too much.

Traveling as we did had brought us into naked contact with humanity and the earth, and, like most people throughout recorded time, we'd found it beautiful and uncomfortable. Technology's job, we began to think, was to serve the living encounter, to make it more comfortable, but not less beautiful. This was tricky: the jet plane that had given us our favorite mountains and foreign friends, the car that stopped to offer that unforgettable ride, polluted the air. And we weren't about to give up those things. But we were convinced that the right way of life lay somewhere in between Calcutta and Levittown.

We had started traveling toward the future.

Like our Sixties exodus, this procession toward the future is a long and straggling line, its destination still uncertain. At one end are the remnant "old hippies": Luddites and localists, seemingly stubborn dropouts from the twentieth century, grimly, gleefully ready to be bombed back to the Stone Age—or ahead to what they call "the neo-Neolithic, the New Stoned Age." At the other end are the new yuppies: urbane, computerized condo-dwellers and business-class flyers, seemingly seduced by the high-tech vision of the twenty-first century. What on earth do these two groups have in common with each other, or with most of us in the middle? More than meets the eye. In every one of our lives, thanks to our travels, there is some combination of urban and rural, global and local, nature and technology (the cat on the computer), new roots and an old wanderlust that flares up as faithfully as malaria. It's these combinations that augur the future, and not just for ourselves.

To begin at one extreme:

The Loyal Opposition

Two hours north of San Francisco, I made a left turn off the Redwood Highway, drove through a commercial vineyard, and started up a steep, forested hill. It was December of '83, the rainy season; my knuckles were soon white as my rented car slewed perilously close to the dissolving edge of the one-lane mud road. Before long I was aghast to see another, decrepit car coming downhill toward me. We stopped, and the man and woman in the heap—Rip Van Winkle hippies frosted with gray—informed me that the etiquette of such meetings was for the car lower on the hill to back down. Since it was obvious that I couldn't do this and survive, they kindly offered to back uphill if their bald tires could hack it. They could, and I waved thanks and crept on, thinking that this whole crazy trip was like a reprise of the Sixties.

I felt even more that way when I saw the mailbox with the painted pig's skull and turned in to the "ranch" that Otter and Morning Glory (1948) G'Zell called the Magick Land. There was almost nothing there. It was just an open clearing, except for a 1940 milk van and two old school buses—one of them purple—sunk hock-deep in grass . . . and two white living unicorns, tethered to trees. (Asking "Is it a unicorn or is it a goat?" Morning Glory says, is like asking, "Is he a Negro or is he a human being?")

I was about to meet the clearing's other inhabitants: Otter, an intellectual hobbit; Morning Glory, a tart-tongued earth mother; their neighbor Lori Lobo* (1952), a wily coyote clown and philosopher, who lived in the van like a runaway child who never has to clean up her room; Forry, Lori's ferret friend; and Octobriana, a black-and-white cat. Off in the woods was the G'Zells' wooden yurt, a cozy eight-sided room with plastic skylights and a propane stove. I would sleep in the purple school bus, which had running water and a wood stove. The bathroom was a bucket full of sawdust, or a short walk to water a tree. For a shower, you had to drive down that horrible hill to town.

Otter, Morning Glory, and Lori explained to me that few of the 150 or so inhabitants of Greenfield Ranch—the back-to-the-land enclave of which the Magick Land is a part—still lived so primitively. (Mendocino County has several other such enclaves, described to me as "Mountain Ranch, strong Eastern spiritual thing; Running Springs, like Greenfield but not quite as coherent; McNab, almost like a straight subdivision but not quite; connected to us, another sister ranch of three thousand-plus acres called Round Mountain.") Greenfield began in 1972, when Berkeley realtor Tim Baker, unable to carry out his plan for developing the fifty-four-hundred-acre cattle ranch, sold off twenty-three large parcels of hilly, hard-to-get-to land, about two hundred acres each, at $125 an acre. "A lot of people worked a job in the city, saved up their life savings, sold their house, and took their nest egg and moved out here," says Morning Glory. By February 1974, over seventy back-to-the-landers were living on Greenfield, in tents, tepees, or the vehicles in which they'd driven up.

It was almost all unimproved land. "Everybody had to do every-thing from scratch," says Otter. Some found that their parcels lacked adequate water. "A lot of people succeeded in digging a well, and a lot of people got a dry hole and sank their life savings in it," says Morning Glory. The usual process of natural selection set in: some realized they "weren't cut out for country life"; others dug in and began to build.

Over the years, most Greenfield residents have built themselves permanent—and often quite elaborate—structures. "There's people out here whose homesteads and homes you wouldn't believe," says Otter. "Houses, gardens, barns." "Stained-glass windows," Morning Glory adds. "Beautiful stuff. Hot tubs. Solar cells." There is no electricity on Greenfield except what residents harvest from the sun, wind, or streams (though one couple did install a gasoline generator to run their washing machine), but thanks to some new technology —ironically invented for gas-guzzling Winnebagos—it's now possi-ble to run a stereo, computer, or TV on twelve volts, collected by solar panels and stored in marine batteries.

That sounds like good news, but purists like the G'Zells are wary of the corruptions of gadgetry. Morning Glory feels guilty about using bottled propane gas. Ace, the black-bearded "wrangler" who tends Greenfield's horses, 1947 fire engine, and 1928 road grader ("an honest machine, made to be maintained by its users and last sixty to eighty years"), speaks contemptuously of "the twelve-volt middle class." "The only thing that keeps them halfway honest," he snarls, "is that no one has yet invented a twelve-volt microwave."

The G'Zells and Lori live as simply as they do partly out of conviction—they are earth-reverencers for whom "taking our cans and bottles to the recycling center is as much a religious duty as meditation"—and partly out of preoccupation. "We haven't had a chance to get together the money for the building trip," says Otter. "We've been raising unicorns." They remind me of Australian abo-rigines, people who have a rudimentary material culture but an elaborate, invisible spiritual culture, including technologies of magic and dreaming by which they rediscovered the "lost art" of fusing two horn buds into one. (More on their Neo-Pagan religion in the section of this book called Spirit.) Television is not missed; many Greenfield denizens inhabit a rich world of thought and imagination, fed by books—especially science fiction and fantasy. "People up here don't watch TV," Lori told me. "They read." (And smoke dope.) I was reminded that while we are the first TV generation, we are also the last book generation, and even those of us who have television often prefer to entertain ourselves.

As conscientious objectors to techno-culture, the G'Zells, Lori, and their near neighbor Anodea Judith (1952), a massage therapist, persist in asking the disquieting question so many of us brought back from our travels: How much is enough? Sitting around the table in Anodea's two-story yurt, people keep referring to *"that* culture down there—*them."* ("It's not *my* culture," says Lori proudly. "I'm a barbarian.") "I visit friends in the city and their kitchen is a *separate room,"* Anodea marvels. "What an amazing waste! That culture is built on waste." Others join in: "Moonlight walks are more important to me than electricity." "The best things are those you can use for three or four purposes." "Entertainment is a cushion. It insulates and isolates." Thoughts we've all had, even as we succumbed to a "realistic" dependence on gadgetry.

But it would be wrong to see the G'Zells and their friends as independent or dismissive of modern technology. They exist in an intimate dialogue with "that culture," like prophets in the desert who'd be out of a job without the wicked city. Anodea commutes to San Francisco weekly to massage the tensions out of city dwellers. Otter and Morning Glory are leasing unicorns to the Ringling Brothers' Barnum & Bailey Circus, allowed one to appear on the TV show "Wish Upon a Star," and raised sixty thousand dollars through a limited partnership to fly to the Pacific island of New Ireland in search of mermaids. These are no new rubes, but cosmopolitan children of the twentieth century who can afford the luxury of living very simply in order to raise the consideration of technology from the level of unconscious addiction to the level of sacred dreaming. ("High" tech, indeed.)

"As a barbarian, I am not responsible for inventing that technology," says Lori. "I *am* responsible for deciding how much of it I will allow into my life." Two aspects this barbarian welcomes: gerontology and space travel. She'd like to live for six hundred years, and she says, "We're going to make it to the stars." (No doubt carrying *A Hitchhiker's Guide to the Galaxy.*)

The Twelve-Volt Middle Class

Even in its mid-Eighties slump, the circulation of *The Mother Earth News* is holding at over eight hundred thousand ("We're in an evolutionary period, waiting to see what the economy does," says advertising director Beverly Roets, confident that *Mother* will rise again), and copy-sharing may spread it to as many as three or four million readers. Who are these people *Mother*'s advertising brochure calls "The New Americans," who want to read practical articles on "gardening, crafts, alternative energy . . . self-reliance, outdoor living, and shelter"? In 1985, their median age was thirty-eight and a half—hard-core first wave. Their median household income was thirty-seven thousand dollars, 54 percent were college-educated, and 87 percent owned their own homes. Hardly typical hillbillies or hippies. In fact, 28 percent live in "metro centers"—big cities and their satellite suburbs—and another 31 percent live in small cities or substantial towns. Apparently quite a few urbanites are into gardening and carpentry—and/or the dream of going back to the land has never died.

I guess I'm living proof that it hasn't. A resident of Manhattan, I subscribe intermittently to *Mother,* read the classified land ads, flip through detailed diagrams for building a solar greenhouse, and put the issue away for the day when I'll have my house in the country and finally Learn Some Skills. What people like me really long for is the best of both worlds: the beauty of the country without the hardship and isolation, the excitement of the city without the stress. San Francisco computer programmer and comic Ron Bach* (1950) satirizes his own desire to have it all:

"The vision is this: I get up and I go out to my deck, and there's a lot of trees around. It's quiet and there's birds. This is the back-to-the-land aspect. And I get up when I want to—this is the independence. The me generation. Do whatever I damn well feel like. And I have some whole-grain cereal—that's the whole-grain movement. And there on the table is my terminal—this is the high-tech Eighties.

"I log on to my computer, and it might be attached to the one in the office. I do my work from the deck. There's rug rats around. Maybe I have an umbrella, I don't want to be too hot . . .

"I thought originally I'd like to do that all the time, but I don't think I could. Maybe do that three days a week and then two days go into the city center and do meetings. Have the contact with my peers as well as the privacy and independence. That's it. There's nothing about this vision that I don't like."

Of course, it leaves out a few things—like road maintenance, sewage disposal, zoning and building-code problems, fire, flood, snow, encroaching developers, logging companies spraying herbicides, termites, rabbits, rabies, cat-eating coyotes, and bubonic plague (carried by rodents in the glorious Southwest). But if you factor in the serious hassles—and most of us have moved enough times by now to know that one set of hassles is only traded for another—Bach's vision is not so far from reality. In Mendocino County, the Santa Cruz Mountains, southern Oregon, western Massachusetts, upstate New York—enclaves of beauty orbiting a major city or university within a three-hour radius—I found people who really *did* seem to have the best of both worlds . . . at a price.

David (1944) and Catherine (1946) Banghart live in a solar-powered house that they built themselves on eighteen acres with an ocean view in the Santa Cruz Mountains. Like most of their "rurban" neighbors—computer programmers, a formerly radical county official, a janitor, a housecleaner-florist, a couple who do carpentry and lead tours to Japan—the Bangharts are multi-skilled people who make their living partly from their land and partly from outside jobs. The result is enough cash to keep up land payments, and an enviable balance of rustic independence and engagement with the outside world. David worked for years as a construction superintendent and is now apprenticed to a fine metalworker; Catherine substitute-teaches three or four days a week. They keep eleven hives of bees, and Catherine molds, dips, and sells elegant candles; they make honey, grow some of their own vegetables, and gather wild mush-rooms in the woods.

Ironically, the Bangharts' land was once the site of Santa Cruz's biggest commune. "There's an old map of the county in the sheriff's office, and there's a big red circle on the map that says 'hippie commune,' so I guess it was notorious," says David. "The first be-ins in Santa Cruz happened right here." A tour of the land is haunting: It's an archaeological site, scattered with windblown ruins of the Sixties. A semicircular chamber cut out of rock, once a bedroom roofed with rafters and plastic, now flooded with water. Carved into the wall, a sculpture of a pregnant belly, which more than one hippie madonna touched as she gave birth. A lawn of startling velvet-green, now the Bangharts' dining room, formerly "the love garden." An octagonal wooden yurt, "the Cow Palace," featuring a wood stove made from the rear end of an old Ford (just open the trunk and pop in a log!) and a stall for the cow, as member of the family. All whimsical, fallen, empty.

Nothing could more vividly illustrate the difference between short-term and long-term "back to the land," between the ecstatic, no-tomorrow Sixties and the realistic, hard-working Eighties. The original commune left the land literally five feet deep in trash. "They never went to the dump," marvels David. That was why the Bang-harts could afford the ocean view. "We had to know that we could clean it up," says Catherine. "Some people can't, but that stuff is easy for us." David: "We were caretakers for wealthy people for a number of years, and that was a good experience." The Bangharts took out thirty-five truckloads of trash before they could begin to build their house.

That's the price: unflagging hard work and commitment. It sounds like the recipe for a lasting marriage, and it's interesting that the two capacities seem to go hand in hand: the Bangharts have been married since 1968. Catherine thinks "it takes a team" to live as they do. They worked on their house for almost a year before moving in. "We worked for a week or two on the framing, then we had a building bee one day and twenty-five people came out, and we raised the walls and put the roof on. We did the interior and the wiring." Catherine acquired carpentry skills on the job: "It was fun for me. And I got good muscles. I impress all the bodybuilders around town."

The job is not done, nor will it ever be. For the Bangharts and many like them, working on the house and land is the central act and pleasure of their lives. Catherine speaks of being in a "grounding cycle" after the "seeking cycle" of the Sixties. Once, moving was living; now, living is building, planting the seeds we brought home. "This structure is not going to be the eventual house," says David. "It will be on that flat where the view is. This will be our workshop and studio and honey house. We knew all along we weren't going to live here." Catherine: "We could end up having Salvadoran refugees in this house, for all we know." David: "The new house will be a project that will come over the next five years or so. I hope to do something on it this summer. Just ease into it."

Building the new house will mean expanding the solar system that makes the Bangharts' home independent in fact as well as spirit. "One of the decisions we made when we came up here was to use alternative energy," David says. "We have solar cells on the roof, marine batteries down here. All low-voltage. Our well uses twenty-four volts to pump our water. It's the only way we can get along without nuclear power, so it feels real good not to be supporting that, even though it's expensive at first. It cost three thousand dollars for everything—the well, the pump, and the house. But it's very cost-effective over the life of the equipment, and it works real nice."

While they are "conscious and careful of how much power we use," the Bangharts do not live primitively. They are, in fact, members of "the twelve-volt middle class." "We have a twelve-volt car stereo, a twelve-volt black-and-white TV. You can get color. There are twelve-volt toasters and irons and blenders and everything, but we haven't acquired all that. We've got a fan for summer, to keep the air moving—made in Mainland China. And we have an inverter for the vacuum and the Cuisinart. An inverter turns twelve volts to one hundred ten or whatever voltage you need. For a long time they were funky clunky things, but now somebody's made one that's great. I'm going to have a washer, a few things like that," Catherine says. Including, very possibly, a microwave—"one of those little teeny guys they're coming out with now. I could work it off the inverter. I consider microwaves to be very energy-efficient—they just run for a few seconds. I think anybody interested in conservation would be interested in them."

I told Catherine Ace's jibe. Her response: "I don't have anything against middle class. I don't see that as a term of derision. I'm a real fan of prosperity." Left-wing ideologues aside (and look how many of *them* ride in limousines), it's a safe bet that most people in the world would agree. Given the hunger for technology and the perils of fossil and nuclear energy, a global twelve-volt middle class may be a visionary goal.

"Our neighbors who go to Japan every year make a point of keeping up with the technical advances there," says David. "A year ago or so they learned that the electronics industry is now concentrating on twelve-volt power, because it's available to the entire world. Not just here, but in the Third World most people can get to a car battery and run something. Solar panels are the next step." Meanwhile, "New Americans" committed to solar and wind energy, do-it-yourself appropriate technology, and intensive organic gardening—still an elite—know they are testing a revolutionary way of life, one that combines the best of the First and Third Worlds and could ease the imbalance between them. Organizations like John and Nancy Jack Todd's New Alchemy Institute, John Jeavons's Ecology Action, and The Farm commune's Plenty are finding ways to share that way of life with Asians, Africans, and Latin Americans, people-to-people—our grassroots answer to the Peace Corps.

"You tell people in downtown Santa Cruz that you live with solar panels, and they'll say they thought it was something of the future," says Catherine Banghart. "Well, it may be smug of me, but I like to think that a whole bunch of us that did the Sixties had our minds consider a complete flip-flop of possibilities. And that, yeah, it *is* a thing of the future. And so are we."

Young, Untiringly Mobile
Urban Peasants

What about those of us who live in the city, drive newish cars, plug our VCRs and PCs into the local power plant, and have turned "the search for funk" over to a Third World cleaning woman whose job is to get it out of the corners? Did we bring *anything* back from the road?

A piece of fabric from Guatemala or a puppet from Indonesia on the wall; an Indian grass basket on the coffee table; a bleached cow's bone from Monument Valley, a shell from Baja, some river stones . . . things that bring comforting bits of earth texture into the high-tech slick of a modern apartment. Souvenirs. Touchstones. This is just taste, of course, but tastes are clues to allegiances, and Sixties-generation taste runs to lots of plants, Elliot Porter and Ansel Adams photographs, good maps of favorite places, political posters in Polish or Spanish, and folk art. The possession of such objects is usually accompanied by a deeper commitment to the world beyond the city.

Seventy percent of the Sierra Club's membership lives in the "top twenty-five markets"—large and medium-size cities and their suburbs. According to a good-news brief in the February/March 1986 *Utne Reader,* several major cities now recycle a substantial proportion of their trash, including Berkeley (40 percent) and Philadelphia (20 percent). Even wicked New York City plans to recycle 15 percent of its twenty-seven thousand tons a day by 1990.

While urban environmentalism may be more generic and romantic than that of people who pick ticks off their dogs every day, it is a real loyalty, rooted in powerful personal experiences, and expressed in our choices as consumers and voters. Sixties survivors buying cars are as conscious of gas mileage as of status or styling; we are staunch customers of "natural"-food stores and of the urban greenmarkets that have sprung up from Seattle to Manhattan. Wilderness protection, endangered species, and solar energy are permanent political priorities for millions of us whose immediate, daily lives aren't touched by any of them. But we remember; we were there.

We also remember Oaxaca, Bangkok, Prague, and having roots of personal feeling in those places—a special "heartplace" (Donna Henes's word), sensory memories, ongoing friendships—makes the world our home (as poet Michael Berkowitz put it) in more than the abstract, electronic sense. Watching news footage of the earthquake in Mexico City, there was a world of difference between "Oh God, another disaster" and "Is Jorge all right?" If this is our vivid advantage over the generations before and after us, who didn't inherit an open world and an explosion of affluence, it is also our responsibility. The woman who comes to clean may be an illegal refugee, paid in cash, whose family has become part of our own.

It's often easier for city people to think globally than to act locally —a problem that reflects both the nature of modern cities and the kind of people who choose to live in them. A piece of country land is exquisitely specific—the texture of the soil, the slope of the ground, the animals and plants, are as individual as a human face—and really living on it requires a physical intimacy and commitment (marriage again). Likewise, in the country, threats to one's well-being are direct and obvious: contamination of one's own stream is a more personal and traceable affront than chemicals in a city water system, and environmental concerns are a natural lead-in to local politics and community organizing. Cities, by contrast, are diffuse and anonymous, dispiritingly dependent on large systems; it's hard to pinpoint a threat, to rally neighbors, to feel that anything can be done. And cities, being man-made, are somewhat interchangeable—all the more so as they "gentrify" and natural neighborhoods are destroyed. For all these reasons, cities tend to attract the unreformed nomads among us, who aren't sure we've found the *right* place to live yet, or who want to be free to live in our heads.

Many of us have the habit of changing cities whenever we want to renew ourselves, the way a snake sheds skins. Travel always delivered that sense of glistening newness; we came to believe that moving was the way to leave behind an old self. Children's Television Workshop producer and astrologer Geraldine Hanon (1947) "grew up as a child in the Fifties in a rural farming town in Idaho, totally naïve about the world. When I was eighteen I went to school at the University of Washington in Seattle. I stayed there for twelve years —lived on a houseboat, hitchhiked around the state. And then along came the Saturn return, twenty-seven to thirty-two—the first adult identity crisis, when Saturn comes back to its natal position in your chart—and it was time not to be a hippie chick anymore.

"So, at thirty-one, I moved to Los Angeles, got involved in video art, started writing furiously, and just basically grew up. Then when I was thirty-five I had a terrific year, and I went to visit New York, and I said, 'Oh, I think I'd like living in this city.' Of course, I moved to New York. No job." Many women and men told me similar stories of a major relocation in their thirties, with evident pride in still being adventurous and free enough to start over from scratch.

While Lori Lobo and David and Catherine Banghart spoke of the kinds of trees they planned to plant on their land—olive, almond, Port Norfolk cedar—city people with jobs and mortgages day-dreamed of their next move. A New York veterinarian (1946) and a Baltimore public defender (1947) both talked of joining the Peace Corps in their forties. A San Francisco lawyer (1946) spoke of selling his new house and going with his banker wife (1954), a scholar of Chinese poetry, to live for a couple of years in Asia. "I'd like to do the Kyoto pilgrimage: three months on foot, eighty monasteries." A successful New York writer (1945) considered moving his wife and son to Texas for good or to the Soviet Union for a year's research. New York artists Joan Giannecchini and Stan Kaplan, stricken by wanderlust, "put a map of the world on the wall and went crazy. So many places to go!!"

While all these proposed moves have their positive side—an expansive sense of being at home in the world—they're also symptomatic of not being really at home anywhere, privileged vagrants. A fortieth birthday, or the birth of a child—somewhat hampering the nomadism—can provoke a new thoughtfulness about what we're really searching for . . . or running from. "We decided that if we get money from a film script, what we are going to do is go out and buy ourselves one of those Winnebagos, those giant things that have the car and the bed and the house all in one," Joan Giannecchini fantasizes. "And we are just going to drive around. We are going to change our names to Duke and Tina Tacky and we are going to live in Wyoming and get up with the prairie dogs and listen to country-and-western music and drink a lot of beer and watch TV in the afternoon." She sighs. "The intellectual and emotional baggage that you pack with yourself all the time—if you could only leave it somewhere for a while . . ."

Lynne Burbridge, now settled in a Philadelphia suburb, has lived in Rhode Island, Colorado, Boston, Ohio, Cape Cod, Connecticut, and New York, among other places. "It's very hard for me to even remember now where I lived when, what was the sequence of places, 'cause it was such a casual thing, like going to visit a neighbor," she says. "But I think that now I envy people who've lived in the same place all their lives. Because it's like we would always just get up and move when things weren't going the way we wanted them to. Dealing with things as they are and sticking it out is still hard for me to do."

Some of us woke up one day and realized that since we *shlepped* ourselves wherever we went, we might as well stay where we were. Home is where you make it. "I remember someone said, 'If it's not in your back yard, where are you looking?' " says Leni Windle. Only then did we look around and, in T. S. Eliot's words, begin "to know the place for the first time." "Just in the last year or two have I allowed myself to be permeated by California, and even to begin to like it," says Jennifer Flinton Diener, who has lived in Los Angeles for twelve years! Seduced by street music, subway graffiti, and the sleek new urban greenhouse architecture, I've come to feel the same way about New York, after a decade of being about to split for New Mexico.

Like building and planting in the country, the physical effort of renovating one's own old house or loft in the city can create a bond to place. In fact, the greatest division in the generation may not be between rural and urban, but between those who have manual skills —an ideal of the Sixties—and those who don't. (And many who don't still want to acquire them.) Knowing how to work with one's hands is like being a skilled lover of places, and as most of us have loved or married more than once, quite a few have put down roots in more than one place. One of the surviving Sixties communes provides an extreme—and attractive—example of such "multi-rootedness." The Lyman Family has *really* managed to have it all: this extended clan of about seventy-eight adults and thirty-nine children lives in the city *and* the country, on the East *and* West Coasts *and* in the heartland, in place *and* on the road.

In the mid-Sixties, a soon-to-be-controversial group of musicians and music lovers, gathered around a charismatic banjo player and "world savior" named Mel Lyman, took over a group of abandoned houses on Fort Hill in Boston's rough Roxbury ghetto. Rebuilding these houses, they taught themselves construction and carpentry skills—and kicked off a renovation boom in the neighborhood, now mostly black middle class. A house on Martha's Vineyard and a 280-acre farm in Kansas came into the Family through member Jessie Benton Lyman (1939), daughter of painter Thomas Hart Benton. The group also acquired a loft on the Lower East Side of Manhattan and a compound in the Hollywood Hills. Today, the Family (bereft of Mel Lyman, who died in the late Seventies) supports itself by fine carpentry and housecleaning, and provides a lot of its own food: bluefish and albacore caught off the Vineyard, carp, meat, cornmeal, and sorghum from the farm. These staples are carried back and forth across the country by Family members going to visit or to live for a while in another one of their homes. They usually travel in a large camper van, with banjos and guitars, kids, cats, and dogs.

Who wouldn't love to live like that?! Those of our generation who still live communally simply have the shared resources and the commitment to express impulses common to us all. Ask the average Sixties survivor what he or she would do with a financial windfall, and the answers "Buy land" and "Travel" will come with no hesitation and no sense of contradiction. None of us will ever entirely relinquish our mobility; in this "grounding cycle" of our middle age, the instinct is to work our way deeper into *all* the places we love.

It never occurred to us, in the great days of the Movement, that the real meaning of the word "radical" might be: someone with roots.

REVOLUTION

Jerry Garcia of the Grateful Dead said about fifteen years ago that the revolution is already over. This is just a cleanup action. It's going to take a long time.
— **DAVID BANGHART**

"I felt that there would be a revolution. I wanted to believe it would happen in my lifetime. And when the Kent State students were killed, and all the campuses all around the country went on strike, that's when I really thought it might happen. I was excited about it, but I was also scared, because I valued my life, and when you make a revolution, a lot of people are gonna sacrifice their lives. And I was worried that I couldn't stand up to the test."

Tina Ivans* (1949) laughs as she tells me this. Today, Ivans is working in a New York law office and finishing law school at night.

She plans to follow in her lawyer father's footsteps. And yet, from 1967 to 1975, Ivans was a full-time organizer for the Young Socialists Alliance, the youth group of the Trotskyist Socialist Workers Party and one of several far-left organizations—including Youth Against War and Fascism, the Maoist Progressive Labor Party, and the Weatherman faction of SDS—that drew their membership mostly from the alienated young white middle class. A few months after she joined the YSA, Ivans's distraught father shouted at her, "Comes the Revolution, you and I will be on different sides of the fence—and you will be the first one I'll shoot in the head!"

Ivans can laugh about it, if ruefully, today. Her life's tide of estrangement and reconciliation has been the political rhythm for most of the generation: we went way out, and then we came back in. Ivans's life is comfortable, the way it was always destined to be. There was no revolution. The impulse that drove us into bloody confrontation with the System subsided unfulfilled. Where did it come from? Where did it go? What was it really driving at? And what, if anything, did it change?

Apocalypse Now!

From 1968 to 1971, that impulse—to social justice, personal risk, and blinding transformation—was in full flood. "I wanted apocalypse, Utopia," underground veteran Jane Alpert (1947) recently told an interviewer.[1] So did we all, and we wanted it *now.* That apocalyptic impatience was the most striking characteristic of the Sixties. Sociologists traced it to the tantrums of spoiled children, or a TV-bred taste for instant gratification. Beleaguered college administrators blamed it on "outside agitators." But it was too strange and strong to be explained away so easily. It was the impatience of prophecy. We had *seen,* and the vision we'd had—of the terrible destructiveness of the present world order—made it unbearable that the status quo continue to exist for another minute.

"Revolution" was, at first, a metaphor. We longed to see a world transformed. Being young and American, with little sense of history, we knew nothing about the processes by which that might take place. All we had was that acute sense of emergency. "Revolution" came closest to expressing the totality and urgency of the needed change. But the concept ended up distorting the content, bringing in romantic and violent overtones of its own.

At least three white versions of "revolution" flourished in the Sixties, until violent confrontation won—and lost—at the decade's end. Most short-lived was the instant-consciousness revolution: Tim Leary and Allen Ginsberg urging everyone from the White House on down to drop acid. Put it in the water supply. The vision of peace, love, and oneness alone would change the world. That dream died in the speed spasms of the Haight.

One step leftward and earthward were the Yippies, the Diggers, and the White Panthers. These groups combined expanded consciousness with small-c communism, playfulness with disruption. "Everything free" was their main idea, as articulated by White Panther Party founder John Sinclair: free sex, free dope, free music, free schools, free land for all comers at Morningstar Ranch, free money fluttering from the balcony of the New York Stock Exchange, free food ladled out daily by the Diggers in Golden Gate Park, free political prisoners Huey Newton and Bobby Seale. Abbie Hoffman proclaimed "the birth of FREE AMERICA in our own time . . . We demand the Politics of Ecstasy!"[2]

The anarchism was sexy, the generosity was bold and sweet—a powerful symbol of love made material—but it had a fatal flaw. It depended unconsciously on the flood of affluence issuing from the warmaking capitalist machine. Yippies and Diggers played at the redistribution of wealth the way little kids play house with food from Mommy's kitchen; they never began to confront the realities of power. And that made their synthesis of culture and politics creative, but hopelessly romantic. In fact, it wasn't really politics at all; it was art.

Another step into the material world stood the New Left, potentially the Sixties' most substantial contribution to American politics, until it got sucked down the drain of hard-line Marxism. Students for a Democratic Society began in 1962 with a sober statement on participatory democracy, a vow to hold America to its own revolutionary promises. Even as SDS moved leftward, it distinguished itself by its more than material analysis, its attempt to fuse the traditions of Marx and Freud in the footsteps of Reich, Marcuse, and Norman O. Brown. Before its self-dismemberment in 1968–69, the New Left had been grappling with hard, real questions about the interaction of class structure and psychology. Its half-forged link between a transformed consciousness in the middle class and transformed circumstances for the poor is an unfinished task of our generation.

Black militants, meanwhile, had a harder view of "revolution," linked to the anti-colonial movements of the Third World. To them, the redistribution of power was a matter not only of justice but of survival, and with the pent-up impatience of centuries, they felt that the American system had been tried and had failed. "Picking up the gun" wouldn't overthrow the System, but it could shake it; it was a small but real redistribution of power that forced the bearer to be taken seriously. "[W]hen [the Black Panthers] marched into Sacramento with guns," says former Philadelphia Panther defense captain Reggie Schell, "they were telling America, 'This is it . . . Selma's gone, all that other, you forget that; this is the new human being, this is the new man and the new woman that's emerging.' "[3] Police heard that declaration as a threat, and "urban guerrilla war" was no fantasy.

Despite embarrassing attempts to portray "the student as nigger," there was almost no comparison between the situation of a ghetto black and that of a middle-class college student. Yet blacks were the single most powerful influence on the white movement. They built social justice, racial equality, and the ideal of "the community" permanently into the vision of a new America. And their proud and provocative impatience spurred ours. In emulation of these romantic outsiders, thousands of students would drop out of the System and go to war with it.

Peer Pressure

The more black militants rejected whites, the harder we strove for their approval. Frantic not to be "part of the problem," many of us would have sold our birthright for a soul-brother handshake. There are countless tales from the Sixties of eager white capitulation to the most extravagant black assertions and demands—behavior that might be called "panthering," since the Black Panthers were particularly adroit at evoking it. I heard a story about an Italian boy in Brooklyn who was allowed to join the Panther party, but only after swearing that he could "kill a pig." Stephen King remembers an incident at the University of Maine, Orono, in 1968:

"I went to a big assembly where three Panthers from Boston were talking about the war and racism and poverty and discrimination and how all these things tied together. They were talking about some kind of capitalist conspiracy that sounded more paranoid the more they went on. So finally I stood up in the question-and-answer period and said, 'Look. Are you really trying to say that Rockefeller, Dupont, and all these people have got some great underground cavern where they go to plan Vietnam and discrimination and all this other stuff?' —and this huge wave of BOOOOOS came from the audience! I immediately sat down. It was embarrassing! And this Panther said [softly, smugly], 'You got a surprise, didn't you, man?' "

A very potent kind of peer pressure, reinforced by moral pressure, was transmitted from blacks through the white student community, creating an atmosphere of challenge to be "more radical than thou." Those who resisted this pressure found it as tyrannical, in its way, as the authoritarianism of the System or the conformism of the Fifties. "The demands of the youth culture were almost like an equal and opposite set of demands to the demands of authority," says Sarah Weil* (1946), now a professor of English. "I found myself reacting against both of them, trying to protect myself from both and to maintain some kind of independence. There was a funny contradiction in the Sixties ethos, which was on the one hand, 'do your own thing' and, on the other hand, doing your own thing had to be acceptable to your contemporaries' idea of what was good. I approved of what my contemporaries thought was good, but I did not approve of group behavior. So I remained tangential to a lot of it in action, even though I did give in to the demands of the Sixties in my conscience."

This is not to imply that all radicalism was mindless. Wynston Jones believes that the natural idealism of adolescence was fueled by our generation's superb education, which gave students "the clarity of thought to examine things and come to their own conclusions. They found the social structure around them wanting." And Marxism, despite its stained record in reality, still offered the most impeccable radical credentials, the most objective analysis of our painful privilege, and a common enemy to reconcile us with our justly resentful brethren. The barricades were the one place where Martin Luther King's dream of "black and white together" still held.

We, the People

Artist Stan Kaplan's radical commitment, like that of so many in the Sixties, was born in the street. "A very straight, successful kid," who seemed destined to be a doctor or lawyer and "wasn't into anything political whatever," Kaplan decided to investigate Haight-Ashbury early in 1967, right after the Human Be-In in Golden Gate Park. He loved acid rock and acid sex, but a group of adults holding hands around a table in the I/Thou Coffeehouse, "trying to absorb the vibrations from a flower," did nothing for him. "I was carrying too much intellectual baggage. I approached the whole thing with a very critical eye." It wasn't until shortly before he left the Haight that Kaplan had his epiphany.

"It was a Sunday in June, and the street was jammed. It had become commercialized." (Thousands of aspiring hippies were flooding into the Haight for the Summer of Love.) "The police came down for some reason. I think the merchants had called them because the hippies and riffraff were blocking the streets, stopping traffic, and no one could get through to buy things. There was a lot of commotion, a lot of antagonism, and then the police started to yell. Not using their sticks or anything, just yelling. There was a jazz concert going on on a fire escape, and the police told them to stop playing. People got annoyed, and they came down the street yelling, 'Make way for the people!' And then somebody yelled out, *We are the people!*'

"And I realized that that was the end of my experience in Haight-Ashbury.

"It encapsulated the whole thing, because that was the place I had come to. I understood, when he yelled that, what that meant. I would not have understood five months before, but now I understood it exactly. I went back with this whole new set of values forming. Not formed but forming. That which I had always considered to be unquestionable, suddenly was all uncertain. I knew I had to undo all that."

Back at Columbia for graduate school, Stan found himself most impressed by "the people who were moving in a very political line. They were thinking about things, they were excited about what they were doing. They were committed in deed as well as in word. I didn't know a goddamn thing about any of it, and I said, 'I have to do something about this.' So I went out and simply read through all the books that I could find: the histories, the bios, the political theory, Marx, LeBlanc, Emma Goldman, Rosa Luxembourg." It was a kind of self-education very common in the Sixties. So far from being passive consumers of learning, we devoured our own homemade crash courses in our hunger to understand the world we wanted to remake.

"It was an eye-opener of the first magnitude," says Kaplan. "I was absolutely overwhelmed. For the first time history made sense to me. The world started to make sense. And the key to my understanding the world was to understand the notion of exploitation. I remember coming out of the psychology library on a gorgeous afternoon. The campus of Columbia was jammed with young, vital, attractive white kids, riding their bikes, playing ball, listening to radios, dancing. I was all of a sudden thunderstruck when I realized that these kids were all up at Columbia because someone else was fighting a war in Vietnam and someone else was pushing a rack in the garment district. It was *connected*! It wasn't random! Certain people, by virtue not of how smart they were, but of how much money they had or what their background was, went to college, while others went to work or to war. That's the whole notion of class. And I began to realize, this is terribly unfair. This is not right.

"That was the emotional basis of all the radicalism that I engaged in in the next four or five years: traditional left-wing intellectual activist work, anti-war activities, local activities. I moved up to Harlem with a woman and we were the only white people. We lived there four years, and we got along quite well with the people in the neighborhood. We didn't come on as reformers or Weathermen or anything. We were simply living there, and I got involved in utility fights, eviction proceedings, strikes. I remember even at the time thinking that nothing could be more American than trying to rectify the situation where some people were always on the bottom and other people were always on the top."

The Young Left

Like Tina Ivans's, Kaplan's radicalism remained disciplined and nonviolent because of his ties to the Old Left. Ironically, Old Left organizations were among the few places in the Sixties where the generation gap was bridged. "The Socialist Workers Party didn't get involved in the crazy Weatherman demonstrations," says Ivans. "They were even against civil disobedience. They stood for legal, peaceful demonstrations."

Young radicals whose circumstances or temperament led them into one of the splinters of SDS had a very different experience. These were all-peer groups, rejecting experienced patience and help, attempting to reinvent the revolutionary wheel from reading and all-night discussions. Adolescent absolutism is notorious; young people make the most lethal terrorists. Cut loose from any restraining influence, Weatherman and the Progressive Labor Party turned inward and fed on their own intensity. Peer pressure and the tyranny of the Dare became hopelessly entangled with "political correctness." Members were determined literally to brainwash themselves, to expunge "bourgeois" traits like monogamy, heterosexuality, personal ego, educated speech, and non-violence. The Weatherman "Days of Rage"; the Madison, Wisconsin, bombing in which a laboratory researcher was killed; the explosion on 11th Street in New York City that sent a naked Kathy Boudin fleeing underground—all were solipsistic attempts to live the revolution now, to prove to blacks and to ourselves that there were whites who would pay the price.

"There was a feeling that action was what gave moral credibility to words," recalls Carl Nagin, "and that people who weren't willing to act on things, take a stand and confront, were full of shit." In practice, the vast majority of the generation shunned acts of violence, especially against persons. (Property was less sacrosanct. Though I never did it myself, I thought blowing up an empty bank or ROTC building was fine.) Bombings and bank robberies were the work of a handful who carried the rhetoric of the Sixties to its logical conclusion. But they weren't qualitatively different from the rest of us. They were simply more extreme in their desire, if not to transform society, at least to transform themselves trying. Most of us had felt the pull of violence as a rite of passage. We wouldn't commit it first, but we would court it. We might not be willing to get blood on our hands, but blood on our heads was another matter. It could combine loss of innocence with proof of virtue, like blood on a virgin's sheets.

Am I saying that we went to demonstrations intending to get clubbed or Maced, to throw rocks and bottles? No, but we always knew it could happen, and that added to the angry thrill. Jim Smith, the photographer who had watched police beating demonstrators at the "Waldorf-Hysteria," "never missed another demonstration. And it wasn't just to take pictures, 'cause a lot of them I went *not* to take pictures. I went to trash. I never did, but I went expecting violence.

And I just went to be there, because I felt very much a part of it. That was the war. It *was* a war."

Our War

And so—seeking a test of courage parallel to Newark or Khe Sanh —we had our war. It was a war for the mythic territory of the streets between the System and the People, and noncombatant status was shameful, like being a pacifist in World War II. One had at least to be a witness, to bring back imagery that is still some of the most vivid in our generation's minds. Tina Ivans's brother David* (1951) remembers his astonishment at seeing submachine guns on tripods on street corners, ranks of jeeps armed with barbed-wire riot-control grilles, incongruously interspersed with red, white, and blue posters reading DEMOCRATS! WELCOME TO CHICAGO—MAYOR RICHARD J. DALEY. (David still has one of those posters.) Lynne Burbridge remembers "machine guns on top of the White House, tanks in the armory ready to come out, people sitting in a restaurant with tears streaming down their faces from the tear gas and Mace mixed together, flowing through the streets of Washington, D.C."

Armed, uniformed, regimented, and mechanized, the troops of "the enemy" seemed armored against their own humanity as well as ours. It was easy to see them as sadistic aliens. Wynston Jones recalls a Darth Vader–like presence at the San Francisco State student strike: "The Tac Squad were a special squad of San Francisco police assigned to deal with these problems. Very menacing figures. Enormous guys, most over six feet. They were chosen for size and clothed in black leather. Clubs. They would ride in gangs of ten and twenty on their motorcycles. It was totally terrifying to see these sharks.

"Several friends of mine were totally apolitical, completely innocent bystanders, and the Tac Squad like a grim reaper just mowed them down. Beat them senseless. One ended up in the hospital. They became quite political after that. That happened a lot. There was a day we all called Bloody Tuesday. I saw unconscious bodies being hauled off with white sheets over them so that the press couldn't take pictures of how bloody they were, but the blood was staining through the white sheets and the press got the pictures anyway." Not only the Tac Squad, but the Oakland and Berkeley police, the California Highway Patrol, the National Guard, and the Alameda County Sheriff's deputies converged on the People's Park demonstration. "They shot people over in Berkeley. They shot one guy in the stomach with a shotgun at People's Park, and killed him." The man was James Rector, a twenty-five-year-old carpenter from San José. Shot on May 15, 1969, he died of his wounds a few days later.

Police and FBI infiltrators were known to be among the most inflammatory "protesters." "There were a lot of *agents provocateurs* around then, and that wasn't just paranoid rhetoric," says Marc Barasch, who was in Yale SDS. David Ivans saw a young man in a white SDS motorcycle helmet smash a Chicago cop car's windshield with a baseball bat. Having heard reliable stories about police infiltration of radical groups, David was aware that the vandal might or might not be a real SDS member. The Left wasn't innocent of provoking violence, either.

"It was a lot of fun for a lot of people to do something that would cause the cops to lose it," recalls Wynston Jones, "calling them pigs, saying little things in their ear, giving them gestures. The cops had no training in resisting people taunting them like that. They would lose it entirely and start swinging their clubs, knocking people. There were enough clever people around who understood the media, and understood that you could get publicity by showing the cops out of control. We saw this at the Democratic Convention, too."

Leaders of the Chicago Seven have admitted that they deliberately planned a televised confrontation to discredit the authorities. Jerry Rubin recently told underground-press historian Abe Peck, "I felt that America had to have on national TV a violent purge in which it came to terms with its own violence. . . . police beating up kids in the streets . . . how does that relate to the Vietnamese violence? and the violence against black people who don't fit white middle-class standards?"[4] Many trusting demonstrators became, in effect, the

Yippies' cannon fodder. "We were midwestern college kids, earnest and utterly naïve," says one woman (1946) who was there. "Our model was Martin Luther King's 1963 Civil Rights march—giant and peaceful. And the Yippies had the first-aid stations all set up in advance! We didn't discover that till afterward, when we went there with our heads bloodied."

The Yippies were master media manipulators. And like the organizers of the Mississippi Freedom Summer, they understood that even moderate violence against white middle-class kids could open the public's eyes as routine violence against ghetto blacks would not. "The whole world is watching," the Chicago demonstrators chanted. Or, as Dylan had sung, "It's alright, Ma (I'm only bleeding)." "I think even my parents understood for just a split moment what it was that the young people were talking about," attorney Patricia Waldman (1952) says of the Chicago convention. And it was then that the anti-war movement really began to gather respectable support and momentum. Ironically, our most earnest effort to shed our class power had only confirmed it.

Capturing the Flag

For more radical demonstrators, the war in the streets was an inner war between the child of privilege and the would-be revolutionary. We wanted to be taken seriously as enemies of the System; we wanted to lose our telltale trust of the cops, our freedom to walk down the street unmolested. And so we dressed and talked in ways that made us walking provocations. When the cops' reactions were brutal, we were genuinely shocked and scared, but perhaps also secretly pleased. Five or more years earlier, we had turned on the TV and seen "a poor black being hit by a big fat southern cop." Now we ourselves had merged into that image—on the right side. We had been baptized. We were the People, with the People's mysterious power to menace the guardians of order. And some of us were getting a crash course in what it felt like to be an outsider.

Marc Sarkady had dropped out of Brown University to work on

a collectively run Rhode Island underground paper, the *Extra*. A natural leader, he found that he was "able to relate amicably to all different kinds of groups. I worked with SDS, Black Panthers, White Panthers, Yippies, socialists, Trotskyists, Leninists, women's groups, gay groups, community groups." Sarkady remembers the wonderful solidarity of the time. "For all the craziness, people cared. We were ready to do anything for each other, die for each other, just do whatever was needed to protect each other and protect this life culture we cared so much about, this new society we wanted to build.

"Many of us had pivotal experiences that really affected us, and one of those for me was getting arrested for my political beliefs. I was arrested at a Black Panther demonstration, where I had given a speech, for wearing an American flag around my head. At the time I saw wearing the flag as a symbol of my connection with our forefathers in the American Revolution, some of whom wore the flag around their heads at Valley Forge with George Washington. Being arrested for this was a very powerful, scary, moving, difficult experience. I went to jail for two days, the first time I was ever in jail, and during the whole process I was very much humiliated. I was beaten up. I was kicked around, physically kicked. I was hit and slapped. I remember thinking, How could these people do this to me? What did I do to them? There was a thirteen-year-old boy there, who had been arrested at the same demonstration, also being hit and hurt. It was really intense.

"At that time, there was no question that I would have called myself a pacifist. I would have said that I felt non-violent. But after my arrest my picture was put up in the police station, and it was passed around the entire police force that I had done terrible things to the flag. Then my life shifted. Because when I drove around town, I would be stopped. I was probably stopped once a week for a year and a half, never charged for anything—just harassed. Sometimes I was pushed around, brought down to the station, intimidated, and then released, but I repeat, never charged with anything.

"It was a confusing and debilitating situation, and very radicaliz-

ing. I started to strongly question my earlier pacifistic views. Maybe
it *was* important to push for revolution. Maybe armed struggle was
important. Armed self-defense. Protect your rights. I went through
a period of a few years very estranged from the System, and that
would be an understatement. I lived with a rifle next to my bed,
always loaded and ready, in direct response to my fear of the violence
that I felt coming toward me. I was prepared to defend myself to be
able to live. I thank God it never came to using that. I feel that I was
very luckily saved and guided through that time."

Not all were so lucky. On May 4, 1970, a handful of National
Guardsmen "lost it entirely" and opened fire on student demonstrators at Kent State, hitting thirteen people (including innocent pass-
ersby) and killing four. It was the climax of the "very confrontational,
hostile, dangerous relationship"—Sarkady's words—between the
two antithetical Americas. A spark of violence leapt the gap between
two groups that had come to embody each other's demons: the free-
flowing and foul-mouthed, the short-haired and repressed. Student
provocation and threats had played a major role. The ROTC building
had been burned down on May 2, SDS radicals had threatened to raze
the campus if their demands were not met, and (by James Michener's
well-researched account) some students threw rocks and chunks of
wood studded with nails at the Guardsmen. But hardest for the
National Guard to endure were the obscenities, especially from
women students. "I wouldn't dare to repeat what they said," one
sergeant told Michener's researchers. "I'd never heard such filth
from . . . truck drivers . . . A very pretty girl stuck her hand right
under my nose, gave me the finger, and uttered words I've never used
myself." According to a fellow Guardsman, the words were "mother-
fucking cocksucker."[5]

It *was* a war. We used the weapons we had, weapons trained
unerringly on the middle-American psyche—a middle finger jabbed
skyward, a flag as headband or crotch patch—and the cops and
the Guard used theirs. It was what psychoanalyst Rollo May calls
"pseudoinnocence" to pretend that, because we had no guns, we were
children playing. We were cultural guerrillas, adept in the jungles of

the mind, throwing psychic shock grenades that exploded in our opponents' vital sanctities. At Kent State, the student movement finally got its wish to be taken as seriously as blacks. Why were we so surprised? The horror and disbelief that swept the student community (over a million students on 448 campuses went on strike) were sadly amusing to many blacks, especially when the killing of two black students and the wounding of twelve at Jackson State ten days later got no such attention.

Retreat

If May 4, 1970, was the day that the war between the generations and classes of white America became a war in earnest, in retrospect it was also the day that war began to end. It was as if the rising tensions had needed to climax in the taking of life. After the strikes in the wake of Kent, the energy of confrontation began to ebb. There were many reasons, not just the fear of getting shot that had made Tina Ivans think twice.

The draft lottery had lifted the threat of Vietnam from most college men. The anti-war movement had become a broad-based, moderate movement that no longer needed its radical spearhead. And the increasing extremism of radicals generated more revulsion than inspiration. Some black leaders were beginning to deescalate the rhetoric, in the realistic recognition that the System was bigger and better armed. A new gap widened between the quixotic fragment of revolutionaries—many now armed and underground—and the mass of the generation.

What most of us were doing was retreating—onto communes, into consciousness-raising groups, into ourselves—in a state of "disorientation" and "demoralization." Like most wars, our "revolution" had lost touch with its original objectives—peace, justice, compassion, brother-and-sisterhood—and had come to be about itself, about confrontation and destruction. The New Left itself had been riven by "fraternal back-stabbing and throat-slashing," in Marc Barasch's words, "that soured me on any notion that left politics per se would be viable." "It got to a point where we had gone as far as we could go and had no idea what to do next," says Grace Parker Sannino, a founder of New England's anti-nuclear Clamshell Alliance. "Fortunately, we had the sense not to do anything." "I went through a whole summer when I didn't speak," says visionary architect Donna Goodman. "It was 1972, right after finishing Smith. I'd been in jail graduation day, for a protest against an air force base for sending planes to Cambodia. I wanted to do something constructive and positive. I didn't want to go on living as a kind of outlaw and protester. But I had no idea what to do with my life now that the Sixties were over." You could say that we all went underground in the Seventies—and it was hard to tell burial from planting.

"In 1971 there was a big demonstration in Washington on Mayday," says Marc Sarkady. "There were about fifteen thousand people there, and almost everybody was arrested and put into this big stadium. I was not arrested. I looked around at this very confrontational thing and I said, This isn't making sense. So I left all that and went out to live in the woods for three or four months. The first month I just had a sleeping bag, not even a tent. Except for my dog, I was by myself, living in nature." This was a remarkably common Sixties to Seventies rite of passage—the retreat from urban madness and mass action into nature and solitude. And, like others in a generation rediscovering the power of myth and symbol, Sarkady made a ritual for himself.

"I decided what I needed to do was to somehow get out of the cycle of violence—to lay down the gun. This meant laying down the actual physical gun and the psychological gun of interpersonal violence. I took two bullets with me to a stone quarry where I love to go swimming and camping. I decided I would symbolically bury these bullets. I buried one at this place as a symbol of me burying the gun. Then I worked for the next five years to lay down the emotional gun. After five years, I went back and buried the second bullet in the same place, rededicating myself to live by my principles in the world."

While he worked to lay down the psychological gun, Sarkady, who had left Brown University after one year to get involved in politics, decided he wanted to understand for himself where oppression in the world came from. "On some very deep level I wanted to understand the historical roots of what I was working to change. So I studied for two years. I read history, anthropology, psychology, history of religion, economics. I read Marx, Engels, Freud, Feuerbach, Hegel, all the originals. Plato. The direct stuff, so that I could make up my own mind.

"My original hypothesis—and I think a lot of people had and still have this hypothesis—was that the problem was the people in charge. The problem is THEM. If only we could get rid of them, then we will be the people, and everything's great. I came out of this studying period with a very different sense that the leaders, and the structure of society, came out of the dynamics of how people were. Society will not be truly transformed by a *coup d'état.* What's going to give us the new kind of society we want is people changing together, growing together, learning how to be in a new way.

"So it wasn't important to complain anymore. It wasn't important to look at 'them' and 'us,' the way we did in the Sixties. What was important was to combine internal and external change, spiritual and political work, personal and social work. So I started a center in New Hampshire, Another Place, based on those principles. It was a conference center and also a utopian community, an incredible laboratory. We would meet every weekend to discuss a particular sector of society —schools, business, right livelihood, politics, health and medicine— and in the way we lived, we tried to practice what we were preaching. I spent six years doing that."

A Matter of Class

While Marc Sarkady was burying the bullet, others were burying their Marxism. Stan Kaplan had always had his doubts about his "very political, ultra-left view of the world. It was very narrow, very bigoted, a view in which politics was the whole world. I don't think I ever totally accepted it. At the same time, I also felt that the fault was mine, that I was simply not understanding properly. That if I continued to study, thought and action would meld and I would become the perfect radical."

Kaplan's "political crisis" came during the years 1974–77. "I found myself speaking and the crowds dwindling. Everybody around me had stopped being interested. Not that they disbelieved it, but they were getting a little older, moving up. They were starting the yuppie class. A lot of the people I had been radicals with were intellectuals and professionals, and they were like, 'I can't come out and discuss the dialectic tonight because I have to watch Channel Thirteen.'

"I was still very much wedded to the ideas and the activism, but the Marxist style was beginning to wear on me. I had written many plays, and all but one were quite political, about strikes and the Depression. Agitprop. I decided that I wanted to do more personal things. That was a big break for me."

At about the same time Stan Kaplan began to seek the political in the personal, Tina Ivans, by now a branch organizer for the Socialist Workers Party, was "losing faith." "Breaking away from the Party was a four-year process. That was probably the most painful time in my life," she says. "I felt like a traitor. I actually got physically sick. But a lot of disorientation had started to creep in. Talk about the revolution and the working classes was great when we were all on the campuses organizing anti-war demonstrations, but after the war ended, it became a different question." It became a question of class.

During the war, the Young Socialists Alliance had recruited many young, middle-class people who were attracted by its organized and persuasive approach to the anti-war movement. "We had some working-class people," Ivans remembers, "and we all tried to absorb working-class ways—the way you talk and all." But when the war was over, and the party returned to its traditional focus on the industrial proletariat, the middle-class students stuck out like sore thumbs, fake hardhat accents and all. The party's solution was to turn them into authentic blue-collar workers. For most, this self-transformation was all too drearily real.

"I left around the time they talked about the 'turn,' where they were taking everybody and putting them into unions and factories," says Ivans. "A lot of people balked at that and left. I was working in immigration law then. They wanted me to leave and get a job in the post office. There was no way. Because I had lost the ideological commitment. I had become disillusioned with socialism; looking at socialist countries, I just hadn't seen it work anywhere. I worked every day with people who were clamoring from all over the world to get here. And I couldn't say that I wanted the System to change."

Other middle-class radicals met their limits in dealing with black militants. Many Panther supporters, black as well as white, who had admired the party's community commitment were ultimately turned off by its armed theatrics. "Some of it was just absolutely silly," says John Niles* (1947), a soft-spoken black realtor who, in college, had donated "bourgeois skills" to Panther community programs. Joan Giannecchini got scared silly as the producer of a documentary-in-progress on Bobby Seale's 1973 campaign for mayor of Oakland. "For a white, middle-class kid going to UCLA film school, it was an eye-opener beyond eye-openers. My picture of the Black Panthers changed from being the avant-garde of the black people to being absolutely terrorists, black mafiosi. These were people who would throw an event and use guns to bully people into cooperating.

"Before that I espoused anything that was ultra-radical, but it turned me off that kind of politics. It also made me understand I have no business working for blacks. I can't express their feelings. I don't know what the fuck they're talking about. My experience is not theirs."

The war for the streets was over. The fragile alliances disbanded. The ghettoes were quiet. The armies dispersed. The scorecard on our "revolution" was humbling. We had changed the world less than we had changed ourselves, and we had changed ourselves less than we thought. Our biggest impact had been on the colleges and universities, which had yielded to most of our demands for minority recruitment, "relevance," and student participation. These were no small victories, and they would mean much to minority students, who could now get a mainstream education in an atmosphere of respect for their own traditions. But the gains were accompanied by a loss in educational standards—and inherited by a generation of students who saw education as a pipeline to security, not a door flung wide on the world.

In the matter of class, the only victories were individual. The class structure remained unshaken, but there were more "crossovers" in the Sixties than ever before or since. Many middle-class kids at least spent time in the worlds of the working class and the poor, and some chose to stay—or got stuck. Some minority activists found that activism gave them an entrée into the middle class, and occasionally even into celebrity—developments that tended to make them less hostile to capitalism. (As I write, Bobby Seale is once again harassing the pigs . . . with a book and videocassette on barbecuing.) Though the crossing of class boundaries has had its casualties—among whom some would include black yuppies, as well as the college-educated homeless—it was essentially a positive process. It made people of different races and classes real to each other, so that "We are the people" became less of a fantasy. "Crossing over" shaped a generation of future leaders and voters potentially capable of identifying beyond their own narrow interest groups.

A Fractious Rainbow

At first, though, the disintegration of the New Left produced neither national leaders nor a coherent bloc of voters. Instead, it spawned a clutch of special-interest groups: women, gays, the old, the disabled, the ethnic rainbow. The metaphor is apt: it was as if the white heat of confrontation passed through a prism and split into many colors, each for itself. The most vigorous people in the Seventies were those who had realized that they themselves belonged to an oppressed group.

Oppressed-group politics at their worst could be querulous, claiming entitlement by powerlessness. But at their best, they were models of democratic self-empowerment. Through a shrewd combination of organization, demonstration, and negotiation, and through alliances with mainstream lawyers and legislators, women won back pay from

AT&T, the Taos Pueblo Indians regained title to their sacred Blue Lake, and gays got housing and job discrimination banned in fifty cities. These victories, won by the effective use of modest power, brought their victors *more* power, more equality, a lessening of dependency and bitterness. And they were victories that proved the grudging but real responsiveness of the System.

Kitty Cone, who came from a political family, had been fascinated with politics all her life. From high-school conservatism, her politics had marched leftward throughout the Sixties: the NAACP, Friends of SNCC, SDS ("a very typical chapter in that the men tended to dominate all the discussions and the women tended to run the mimeograph machine, and would sort of be expected to screw and make meals"), the Young Socialists Alliance and the Socialist Workers Party. Had she not been confined to a wheelchair by muscular dystrophy, Cone probably would have become a feminist activist when the tide of revolution ebbed. Instead, she went to work for the Center for Independent Living, the Berkeley, California, disabled-rights organization that pioneered the national independent-living movement, winning attendant-care money from the State of California and curb ramps for wheelchairs in Berkeley and Oakland.

Cone's most dramatic encounter with the System came over Section 504, a set of federal regulations that would require such institutions as universities and hospitals to provide wheelchair accessibility, sign-language interpreters for the deaf, and Braille or recording facilities for the blind as a matter of civil rights. "When Carter came into office, the Secretary of HEW, Califano, decided that he would put together a task force and rewrite the regulations. We got word from the inside that they were totally watering them down. So the American Coalition of Citizens with Disabilities organized a big demonstration and sit-ins at all the regional headquarters of HEW. In San Francisco, I and several other people were given the job.

"I have to say it was a masterful job of organizing. We built a coalition of people with all different disabilities. We had a big rally outside, and then we just opened the doors of HEW and ran inside as fast as we could and ran up to the fourth floor to meet with the director. And we took over the offices, and started calling up the other HEW regional office rallies and Washington to find out what kind of success they were having. It took place in seven cities, but the only place we weren't forced out was in San Francisco. And so San Francisco became the focus for the whole issue. It was on the national news every night.

"We occupied those offices for twenty-eight days! It was amazing. Committees would meet several times a day, and most nights we'd go to sleep about three and get up at six. We were all exhausted. There are people whose physical condition has never been the same. I don't know how we survived. But we had a lot of local support. Food was donated by the Black Panther Party and the Glide Memorial Church. Mayor Moscone brought us a shower, and the head of the Department of Health sent mattresses.

"Finally, they sent a contingent of about twenty of us, a cross-section of different disabilities from different regions, to Washington to try to make an impact there. We had tremendous labor support. The International Association of Machinists turned over their offices to us, found us a place to stay, fed us, rented trucks to transport us, let us use their phones. A few things we didn't get, but for the most part, we won! It was a big victory. In the areas of employment, education, transportation, housing, and health, fifty million Americans had civil rights protection for the first time."

It Works!...?

Such victories—like the legislative gains of the environmental movement—gave weight to a new suspicion: maybe the despised System could be made to work for our vision after all. There were actually levers built into the government by which "the power of the people" could be brought to bear. We first discovered this elementary fact of high-school civics (a class that I, for one, slept through) during Watergate—a crisis that cut both ways. While it finished off our last shreds of respect for American leadership, it kindled a new respect for the design of the American government. The "system of checks and balances" *worked*! Activated by vigilant journalists, judges, and legislators—most of them, to our chagrin, well over thirty—it had corrected its own excesses. Watergate awakened many of us to the fact that America had already had a revolution, and that it had given us a form of government that could serve idealism precisely because (unlike Marxism) it had built into it a certain cynicism about human nature.

Environmental activist and author Jeremy Rifkin (1945), David to the Goliath of genetic engineering, traveled a typical Sixties route. In 1966, he was "a part of the established order"—senior-class president and fraternity council vice president at the University of Pennsylvania. Then he saw some of his fraternity brothers "beating the living crap" out of demonstrators against chemical and biological warfare, and "things started to change." By 1969, he was involved in "some very heavy radical stuff" in the East Village.

With Todd Ensign (1940), later a prime mover of the Agent Orange lawsuit, and Michael Uhl (1944), who went on to organize the Safe Return amnesty movement, Rifkin set up the Citizens' Commission of Inquiry into U.S. War Crimes, which had Vietnam veterans testify at hearings all around the country and in Washington under the auspices of freshman congressman Ron Dellums. At his angriest, Rifkin had been "pretty far left," but "my politics had always differed substantially from a lot of the Left in a lot of ways," and by 1975 he was organizing the People's Bicentennial Commission, "the alternative to the government's bicentennial. It was an attempt to reclaim America's revolutionary tradition.

"We did a whole bunch of paperback books. We had five thousand school systems buying our materials, five or six thousand libraries. We did programming. We introduced a new concept called 'economic democracy.' I wrote two paperback books on it for Bantam. It's now been picked up by Tom Hayden. Those were the first books to actually explain what it is, how we can achieve worker ownership and community control of production. We did big rallies, demonstrations against the big corporations. For the two hundredth anniversary of the Boston Tea Party, we had twenty thousand people in a blizzard at Boston Harbor. For the shot heard round the world at Concord, we had fifty thousand people show up to meet Ford when he came over the bridge."

Like the disabled sit-in at HEW, such creative blends of confrontation and reconciliation were one of the best legacies of the Sixties. They were, after all, a form of "participatory democracy"—"the only thing we really learned" from Sixties politics, in Marc Barasch's opinion. Veteran organizers like Rifkin and Cone had invented a way to put hundreds or thousands of citizens in direct contact with their leaders, while millions more took part through the media. It evoked "the power of the people" more vividly than voting, bringing the idea of democracy alive in an age of dispiriting anonymity.

But the very idea of a "demonstration" implies that someone in power will respond, as we knew in our bones even in the angriest anti-war rallies of the Sixties. It is, finally, only the power to persuade. As such, it is fragile, as we found out when Ronald Reagan was elected. Suddenly, the relative responsiveness of the Carter and Jerry Brown administrations (in which such Sixties activists as Sam Brown had held appointive office) was gone. Worse yet, a tide of counter-revolution was threatening to sweep away the gains that women, minorities, environmentalists, and the disabled had made. The defeat of the ERA was a pail of cold water in the face. It forced us to confront the hard meaning of a word we'd been poetically fooling around with for fifteen years: power.

In the Sixties, many of us who were middle class and college-educated had disempowered ourselves to share the experience and the innocence of the poor. Feeling our birthright as a burden, we laid it down. That fateful act left us with radical new understandings and alliances—and without the kind of money, connections, and skills that the organized right wing was now wielding so effectively. Too many of the idealists among us had joined the ranks of the powerless instead of helping to empower them, while the more pragmatic—the "young urban professionals"—had empowered only themselves. The fusion of ideas and resources that had made the Right so strong was lamentably lacking in our generation between 1980 and 1984.

The Darkest Hour

1984, fittingly, was our political dark night of the soul. As I traveled around the country shortly before the Reagan-Mondale election, unable to decide whether to vote, I found my own ambivalence reflected in my generation. "I probably won't vote, 'cause I decided that the only way I'm going to vote is to vote *for* somebody," Wynston Jones said in L.A. "I'm not going to vote for Mondale because he's less of an asshole than the other guy. I'm still voting for assholes. I'm not going to do it." Jones's feelings were shared by about a third of the people I spoke to. The other two thirds felt strongly that, even though there was no one to vote for, it was important to vote against Ronald Reagan, with his heartless economics and itchy trigger finger. "Of *course* I'm going to vote," said Zazel Lovén (1945), fashion editor of *McCall's* magazine in New York. "I don't know what's wrong with people. If everyone who had a social conscience voted according to it, we'd get rid of him."

Intriguingly, it proved impossible to predict voting behavior from political views or lifestyle. In Cambridge, Massachusetts, tentatively tweedy writer-teacher Carl Nagin, pro-Israel and suspicious of the Soviet-Sandinista connection, said, "I can't bring myself to vote"— unless perhaps to write in Mario Cuomo. In New York City, budding lawyer and ex-Trotskyist Tina Ivans, now pro–nuclear energy, anti–welfare fraud, anti–Yanqui imperialism ("I still think we're the biggest aggressors in the world"), said, "I have never yet been able to vote for a Democrat or a Republican." In Redwood Valley, California, some of the more surprising voters I met were Otter and Morning Glory G'Zell. "Old hippies" and priests in an anarchistic religion, who'd have to wind their way down that mud mountain road in an old car stuck together with wire and Band-Aids to vote, the G'Zells had learned their political lesson locally. "When Morning Glory and I first moved out here, the county supervisor for our district was an old son-of-a-bitch," Otter told me. "We were pained greatly to discover that he had been elected by eighteen votes the previous year. And that previous year, most of the back-to-the-land people out here just didn't bother to vote. *Eighteen votes* was all it would have taken to elect a liberal candidate and a neat person."

Eighteen votes, or even eighteen thousand, was an order of magnitude we could grasp. We had begun to win local elections here and there, and to put bits of our vision into action on the city and county level. But this huge generation that had once mounted a successful mass movement was unable to muster millions for Mondale. We tried. We even acquired some media savvy. "Feel the power," said an MTV ad that urged viewers to vote, while the camera panned the crowds at Woodstock and Jimi Hendrix played his warped yet loyal "Star-Spangled Banner"—scoring a direct hit on our old, physical sense of numbers and our rock 'n' roll patriotism. In a Mondale ad, which seemed more manipulative, Crosby, Stills & Nash sang "Teach Your Children" while the missiles arched away à la *The Day After.* Nothing availed. Reagan won by a landslide. "I didn't feel bad," says Stephen King, who had campaigned for Gary Hart in the primaries. "I felt like I'd been totally blown out of the water."

So did a lot of us. The sense of defeat that settled over Sixties veterans after Reagan's reelection was almost melodramatic. There was a general mood of "It's over. We've lost." Old radicals and hippies withdrew into an "ark mentality," waiting for apocalypse or fascism to fulfill their direst prophecies. Moderates felt justified in withdrawing into self-interest. It struck me that many people were acting, quite irrationally, as if Ronald Reagan had been elected president forever. When I pointed out that 1988 was a whole new ball game, and that we'd better be ready for it, the response was listless. It was as if many of us wanted to give up.

Fortunately, there are strong exceptions to despair, undaunted political activists of our generation who see 1984 not as the end but as just the beginning, and the ascendancy of the right wing not as a defeat but as a challenge to the bearers of the new world view to start taking power in earnest (one that ERA supporters were the first to take to heart). Right after the election, Carl Nagin predicted that Reagan "will provide the kind of discipline that will mobilize those who want a real alternative—who want to complete that unrealized, ambitious agenda of the Sixties." One of "those" is Marc Sarkady.

Second Chance

"Part of what happened to people was the intense feeling of being let down. Being built up and then let down," Sarkady says. "The idea that we would change the world and then it didn't change. I remember in 1969 thinking that there would be a revolution in six months. Well, obviously, that didn't happen the way we thought it would. But with hindsight I see that changes did happen. The fact that environmental concerns are part of reality now—that came out of the Sixties. Women's issues are just part of life now. Issues of color and class and race, all these things are part of life now. South Africa can't go on being the way it is. The world is pressuring it. It cannot maintain it for very much longer. So really, things are different. And yet, there is so much more to do. I think it's important to see the successes if you're going to go on.

"There's a piece of work that I believe is in the world for us to do. I believe that piece of work will take shape politically over the next fifteen years. It has already begun to take shape socially and culturally in a number of changes in people's minds and attitudes and values, about war and peace, about caring about people, relationships, women and men. Everybody's worth something. Everybody has dignity. We don't want to have war anymore. We don't want to have racism anymore. We want to stop destroying the earth. We want to have a fairer distribution of wealth. Now it remains for us to effect those changes politically. No one's yet come forth with a simple but workable synthesis of all these things in a political framework. But I know in my heart and my cells that it can be done."

Sarkady argues that the constituency exists to enact our agenda through the System—to bring about a second American revolution with the peaceful democratic tools bequeathed by the first. "Between the ages of twenty-nine and forty-five right now there are sixty-six million people," he says. "Between the ages of twenty-one and twenty-nine are another thirty million people; ninety-six million people between twenty-one and forty-five. It's the largest American generation ever in history"—all of voting age.

An observer in his sixties, Horace Busby, former secretary to the Cabinet and special assistant to President Lyndon Johnson, seconds Sarkady's view of the baby boom as a gathering tidal wave of political power. "There is no older bloc or combination of blocs capable of standing against the electoral force these potential voters now constitute," Busby wrote in 1985 in his political newsletter, *The Busby Papers.* "The total population between ages 45 and 73 is less than 70 million. What it means . . . is that the generations which regard themselves as in charge . . . are, in fact, on borrowed time. The younger hordes can take control any time they feel like it."[6]

The problem is that no one in politics has yet quite figured out how to awaken this sleeping giant. It is far from a uniform group. Few of those under twenty-seven or twenty-eight were significantly influenced by the Sixties, and 59 percent of them voted for Reagan in 1984. Even most bona-fide Sixties survivors now patch some traditionally conservative views—on crime, or jobs, or Soviet imperialism, or big government, or the destructiveness of the welfare system, or even abortion—into personal political philosophies descended straight from the streets of our youth. As witness Tina Ivans and Carl Nagin, this makes for a welter of contradictory hybrids: there are now pro-life feminists, pro-choice Catholics, pro-Israel leftists, domestic conservatives who are foreign-policy radicals, and vice versa. How do you get such a generation to agree on *anything*?

Back to the Future

There is one thing that we all plainly do agree on: rejection of the politics of the past. The really depressing thing about the 1984 election was being offered a choice between the Republican past and the Democratic past. Many recognized that even Jesse Jackson embodied a past—our own. "He's a throwback," says Carl Nagin. "He represented the style of the Sixties. It's very outmoded." "I think guys like Jesse have become captives of their own rhetoric," says realtor and former Panther volunteer John Niles. Today, minorities themselves have outgrown the politics of militant powerlessness for the politics of self-empowerment. Under the leadership of St. Louis "tenant empowerment" activist Bertha Gilkey, tenants of the once-notorious Cochran Gardens housing project have taken over the management and maintenance of their own project. Chicago consultant Gail Christopher heads a program to teach welfare recipients stress management techniques, exercise, and nutrition in preparation for job training.

The brief surge of primary votes for Gary Hart reflected our generation's hope that he might be the candidate of the future. But the candidate himself disappointed. "Hart did not have the personal qualities to match his 'new ideas,'" writes futurist political pundit and playwright Barry Casselman (1942), editor and publisher of *Many Corners* newspaper in Minneapolis, and the first writer to spot Hart, in November 1982. Casselman's early pick for the 1988 Democratic nomination is Delaware Senator Joseph Biden (1942): charismatic, close to our generation in age, but also a "tough," "ambitious," and seasoned politician who was sitting in the Senate when many of us were still sitting in the streets (he was elected in 1972). In Casselman's view, Biden is the likeliest heir to "the pragmatic-yet-idealistic center of the Democratic party" last occupied by John F. Kennedy. After watching the young senator's shrewdness, candor, and charm dominate the Rehnquist confirmation hearings, I thought that this time Casselman might be right.

It sometimes seems that 1960 is the one moment in the political past that we *do* feel nostalgia for. Columnist Bob Greene (1949) reports having a recurring dream of late that JFK is alive again. But I think that reflects a longing for Kennedy style—a sense that idealism, pragmatism, and charisma are the right recipe for a politician —rather than any wish to roll back the revolution in understanding of the last twenty-five years. With John Kennedy, our parents' generation took power, embodied in a man who had been through their great formative crucible, World War II, and shared their world view. I still remember my father's awed delight that "one of *us*" had become President. In 1988, oddly, I'll be exactly the age my dad was in 1960. It's our generation that now stands on that threshold of power. But 1988 is too soon to elect "one of us" president, for the far-flung outward and inward journeys that shaped our world view have not been compatible with a straight political career.

In the mid-Eighties, the real political creativity of our generation is focused in the struggle to move our most visionary ideas in from the fringe toward the practical political center. This struggle is still in its early stages, yet it is infused with an urgency such as we haven't felt since the Sixties. One of the best places to watch it unfold—and to take part—is in the pages of *New Options*, the eight-page monthly newsletter published and edited in Washington, D.C., since February 1984 by Mark Satin. For an explosive short course in political possibility, try ordering (as I did) a full set of back issues of *New Options* and reading one a day. (The address is in the Access section at the end of this book.) What are the best books and groups in the consumer empowerment (not "protection") and neighborhood self-reliance movements? Who is working on practical, compassionate, populist alternatives to the welfare state and the big-business state? What's the best way to cut the budget deficit? What lessons can we learn from the Sri Lankan Sarvodaya (local self-help) and Polish Solidarity movements? Each issue presents ideas, names and addresses, and a crossfire of reader debate.

Satin's is another archetypal generational journey. In 1967, in exile in Vancouver, he was "an angry radical Marxist." In 1978, the year he came home, he published the reconciliatory *New Age Politics*, which embarrasses him today because "it made ideas I believe in sound easy and simplistic." In 1980, he joined Marc Sarkady and others in an attempt (in Sarkady's words) "to embody a new holistic vision of politics in America": the New World Alliance, a political network that Sarkady feels "was still too rooted in the New Age countercultural movement."

Satin apparently absorbed that lesson, for every bright idea presented in *New Options*—from Earth First!'s libertarian eco-sabotage, to Robin Morgan's global feminism, to St. Paul, Minnesota's "Homegrown Economy"—is gut-checked for practicality and potential breadth of impact or appeal. "Fifteen years ago the burning question was, How radical are you?" the editor concluded a January 1986 issue on terrorism. "Hopefully someday soon the question will be, 'How much can you synthesize? How much do you dare to take in?' "[7] Some of the newsletter's severest self-criticisms are "too counter-cultural, Utopian, marginal," "a pipe dream for the 'happy few,' " "a soft blanket for 1960s-era activists."[8] (Since letter-writers from the left routinely snipe at Satin for "selling out" and "kissing ass," it makes for lively reading.) But *New Options* maintains that most "too-Utopian" proposals need to be sharpened up, not watered down. The tension between vision and pragmatism is kept keen and challenging.

New Options has made some preliminary stabs at naming the emergent politics of our generation. "Post-liberal, post-conservative, post-socialist" expresses only our disaffection with received ideologies, including that of the Left. Alternatively, the newsletter has tried "decentralist/globally responsible," just "responsible," "Third Force," "Third Way," "future focused," "Jeffersonian," "transformative populist," "New Age," and "light Green" or "Greenish." The German Greens, who ironically have roots in our Sixties—cofounder Petra Kelly (1947) went to high school and college in the United States—have reinspired American activists with their fusion of ecology, feminism, peace, and social justice. But they are widely perceived here as being too soft on the Soviet Union and too hard on mainstream sensibilities. Unilaterally reviling the United States and breastfeeding babies in the Bundestag (the German Parliament) are the kinds of things we were doing fifteen years ago. *New Options* suggests that the New Age/New Left has to continue to evolve into the "New Center"—or fail, for real this time, to change the world.

But how will a visionary new center—*Aquarian Conspiracy* author Marilyn Ferguson (1938) calls it "the radical center"—empower itself politically? Can it merge into the Democratic party without fatal compromise? Can it found a new party without fatal irrelevance? In the political realignment now taking place, *New Options* identifies no less than seven ideological stations within the Democratic party: "conservatives, 'realists,' moderates, liberals, but also 'economic democrats,' 'neoliberals,' 'postliberals.' " To make matters more confusing, some of the ideas put forth by Gary Hart, Bill Bradley, Missouri Representative Richard Gephardt, and others of the "new generation of Democrats" overlap with those of the "Kemp-Rumsfeld-Gingrich wing" of the Republican party. A new center is clearly emerging out of both political parties, one concerned with fiscal responsibility in government and the military, the service economy, high technology, family values, and decentralization. But is this streamlined new center as concerned about the poor and the environment, and about placing limits on technology and growth, as most of the Sixties generation still is?

"In my opinion," Democratic party consultant Ralph Whitehead (1943) told *New Options,* "[most 'new Democrats']—though they don't *offend* generational sensibilities—don't begin to engage the generational energies. The moment a more authentic generational view begins to emerge, things will happen very fast—very fast."9 "It may happen still through the Democratic Party in the course of the next fifteen years," says Marc Sarkady. "That's one possibility. But all you have to do is go to a Democratic convention and you know that that's not where it's happening right now." "I keep waiting for a new party," says Kenneth Guentert (1948), self-styled "Coyote Christian" and editor of *Festivals,* a magazine of intercultural celebration published in San Jose, California. But two new parties—Barry Commoner's Citizens Party and the New World Alliance—have already come and gone.

A New Party?

If we *were* to found a new party, one obvious choice would be Green. Loosely allied Green "Committees of Correspondence" (after those set up prior to the *first* American revolution) already exist in dozens of places, including New York, Pittsburgh, and Minneapolis, Kentucky, Kansas, and Colorado, at least eight in the Pacific Northwest, ten in California, seventeen in New England, and eighteen in British Columbia. An argument for "going Green" is that the movement is international: five European countries had Green representatives in Parliament as of April 1986.

But other colors have been proposed. Owen DeLong (1939), once a Harvard student of Henry Kissinger, speechwriter for Eugene McCarthy, and researcher for Bobby Kennedy, gave it all up in disgust after Watergate. But politics is still "a private passion," and DeLong is now considering founding a new party with fellow members of the Lyman Family. "It is called the Blue Party, in honor of everyone who has the blues about what's going on in this country and in the world right now," DeLong wrote in the second issue of the Lyman Family's magazine *U and I,* which focused on the farm crisis. "It's blue like the sky when it's clear and blue like the water when it's clean. It's the party of everyone who ever deeply believed in the power of the people to shape and reshape this great experiment in human affairs called America."[10]

As long as we're splashing colors around, my own choice would be the Rainbow Party (or if that sounds *too* childish, the New Spectrum), named not so much for Jesse Jackson's Rainbow Coalition as for "the rainbow banner of Terra" in Robert Heinlein's homesick space story, "The Cool Green Hills of Earth." An American flag with rainbow stripes has already appeared at Columbia University's 1985 anti-apartheid demonstrations, and the Rainbow Party even has an emblematic animal to compete with the elephant and donkey: the Living Unicorn. The rainbow as a political symbol for the Eighties is a far cry from the red fist of the Sixties. It suggests unity in diversity, hope, a bridge to the visionary future, and the fragile but persistent beauty of the earth. It figures both in the Old Testament and in Native American myth.

But a new political party—or a strong movement within the Democratic Party—would need much more than good symbols. "To organize a party to embody and represent these feelings, you need to be able to consider raising millions of dollars a year, not only from individuals who can contribute $25 or $50, but from people in business and with inherited wealth," says Marc Sarkady. "You need to be able to consider having a membership of between twenty and forty million people. You need to deal with the real, practical things that are going on in our world. That's the kind of political movement that's needed right now, not a fringe sort of cliquish countercultural thing over to the side" (Sarkady's criticism of the Green movement so far).

To help build that kind of political movement, Sarkady is starting a project to be called "Dialogues for the Second American Revolution," or "The Great American Transformation." He hopes to apply to political life a fivefold model of transformation that he has used successfully within large corporations. Its elements: vision, urgency, empowerment, trust, and personal responsibility. *"Vision* means seeing and shaping as precisely as possible where we need to go," he says. "We need to inspire, but also to distill our ideas into a usable form. What *would* be a sane energy policy? What would we really do about acid rain? Jobs? The economy?" To involve as many people as possible in the platform process, he would like to follow the Citizens Party precedent of holding town meetings, bringing together specialists and citizens in detailed dialogues on issues and potential solutions.

"Urgency isn't only something that's around us," Sarkady says. "We've known there was that kind of emergency for twenty years. Urgency is also something we create—a positive enthusiasm, an urge to move forward and do something *and* a sense that we can. And that leads to *empowerment*—creating a context where people feel their own power, our own power. I think there's a real despair in this country, a sense that we're losing ground. We all need to know that there *is* something we can do, and that it will make a difference. And we need some social architecture that helps us build together.

"Trust is about relationship-building. Our personal relationships really are the foundation of culture, the glue that holds us together

as we move forward. We need to integrate the intimate process, how people are and how small groups work, with the larger public process —how politics and society work." In other words, as we used to say in consciousness-raising groups, the personal is political—and politics has to be personal.

"Personal responsibility, finally, is about taking it into yourself— embodying it, this new politics, in me, myself, in you, yourself. Not blaming others, but each of us saying, What am *I* going to do about it? It must rest on the individual. That's the only way to make it real in the world."

Sarkady believes that these five elements, plus organizational savvy and money, could add up to the one quality that the progressive wing of American politics has lacked for the last two decades: sustainability. "We need something that builds for the next fifteen or twenty years. We've often thought from a crisis mentality: How can we respond to the crises around us *now*? That's led to a lot of one-time efforts: McCarthy's candidacy, McGovern's, Anderson's. We need to be in many state and federal elections, but we also need to build— gradually, slowly—a good foundation that really does change the climate of politics in this country. We can learn a lot from the conservative movement. In 1964 they started out with a vision, called Mandate for Leadership, and they built for sixteen years.

"Are we equal to this?" Sarkady wonders. "I just pray that we are. It's an amazing, wondrous, wonderful opportunity." And it will require a virtue still new to our generation: *patience*—the opposite of our youth's apocalyptic demand.

A New Spirit

But it will require even more. To truly rouse our forlorn idealism— equally turned off by power-broker cynicism, Maoist rhetoric, countercultural pipe dreams, and tepid compromise—it will be necessary to change more than the content and even the form of politics. We have to deepen the *ground* of politics, bring it down from the platforms of ideology and ego and into the heart. A broad-based visionary politics needs three things that are conspicuously missing from politics as it has been practiced so far.

1) *Reconciliation.* Our Sixties politics died of two diseases—confrontation and factionalism—which are really one. Our joy in sticking it to Middle America helped elect Reagan president; our ideological squabbles with each other tore our movement apart. In both cases, being right (or Left) became an end and a pleasure in itself, better served by making others wrong (or Right) than by winning them over. Our second and last chance to change the world will depend on our willingness to sacrifice self-righteousness for common ground, both with our former antagonists ("straight" workers, warriors, farmers, business people, politicians) and with each other.

Nothing is more disheartening than going, as I did, to a meeting of people interested in starting an American Green Party (at the New York Open Center in April 1985) and hearing the adversarial habit of mind that shredded the New Left break out before the moderators had finished their introduction. A woman stood up and made an aggrieved five-minute speech about the fact that there were no women on the panel. Panelists waited till she was finished, thanked her obsequiously—and then explained that both Petra Kelly and Charlene Spretnak (1946), co-author of *Green Politics,* had been invited, but were unable to attend (an important point that could have been handled in fifteen seconds). A man in a plaid shirt with a graying ponytail and an air of self-satisfied paranoia objected to the dialogue that was developing with panelist Dennis Kucinich (1946), city councilman and former mayor of Cleveland: "Why talk to politicians?" Street actions, the man argued, were the only way to go. (Who, then, will respond to them?) These characters and incidents will be all too familiar to anyone who has dealt with "Left-overs." As Pittsburgh's Carol Wolshin, another shade of Green, told the same meeting, "In Pittsburgh, economically depressed by the loss of the steel industry, the banks are working with unemployed people; the Left is throwing stink bombs, and it isn't working."

Some effective overtures of reconciliation aren't coming from the Left at all, but from what might be called deep center field. Once too far out even for *Rolling Stone*, the Lyman Family has proven that a coalition can be formed across class lines to achieve environmental and populist goals. Their alliance with East Coast fishermen was influential in pushing through a 1984 moratorium on Atlantic striped-bass fishing (a triumph chronicled in the first issue of *U and I*). Now they hope friendships with farmer neighbors in Kansas will give them a base to promote a return to labor-intensive, low-debt organic farming.

One advantage the Lymans have over the Left is a high degree of commitment to and consensus with each other, worked out through years of communal living—in a community that, significantly, formed around making music, and still has music as its heart. (Family member Jim Kweskin of Jug Band fame is now featured in the Family's new U and I Band.) In the words of lawyer Doug Weiner, who once left his college football team to join a rock band: "The kind of cooperation that a band exemplified is almost a model for society. These were people exerting their full capacity for energy, and it had to be in harmony, literally."

Today, our musicians are way ahead of our politicians in figuring out how to combine a compassionate vision with a common touch, how to make special interests universal. Springsteen, Mellencamp, "We Are the World," and "Farm Aid" are the only real heirs so far to JFK's blend of "idealism, pragmatism, and charisma" and Martin Luther King's gentle command of conscience. In the Sixties, people may have needed to be shocked; in the Eighties, they are ready to be moved. Professional politicians may be the last to notice, but the political language of confrontation and compromise—the demand and the deal—has begun to be infiltrated by the spiritual (and often musical) language of empathy and communion. Marc Sarkady thinks we may be metamorphosing into "the We Generation."

2) *Philosophy*. After reorganizing the People's Bicentennial Commission in 1976, activist Jeremy Rifkin turned inward to ask himself, Where do we go from here? "I thought that the basic principles of social and economic justice that the New Left espoused were obviously still valid," he says, "but that we had never worked out a

philosophy. We had never worked out an intellectual foundation for our world view. We had a few mentors—Lewis Mumford, Jacques Ellul, Wilhelm Reich, DeBeauvoir, Sartre—but it was very sketchy. That's why the New Left collapsed, in my opinion." Rifkin set himself and his associates the formidable task of "developing the foundations for a new *Weltanschauung* in a new world. We started on this series of books [*The Emerging Order,* with Ted Howard, 1979; *Entropy,* with Ted Howard, 1980; *Algeny,* with Nicanor Perlas, 1983]. I had no idea where it was going." It went in an unexpected direction. When Rifkin finally did articulate the essence of a "new *Weltanschauung*" in *Declaration of a Heretic* (1985), it sounded neither political nor intellectual, but explicitly religious: "the resacralizing of life."

3) *Leadership.* "Leaders suck," White Panther Party leader John Sinclair declared in 1969,[11] expressing a principle as native to our generation as "Don't Tread on Me" was to the newborn state of Vermont. It's still on our flag. "I guess I'm totally cynical about the people in power," *McCall's* fashion editor Zazel Lovén said in 1984. "I think politicians are the ultimate greed mongers," said photographer Jim Smith. It's a generational article of lost faith that whenever anyone—from Richard Nixon to Huey Newton to Gerry Ferraro to thee and me—gets a taste of power, integrity has faltered or fled. Honed on adult disappointments, our childhood hypersensitivity to hypocrisy has grown keen enough to pierce Madison Avenue shielding. We saw the raw ambition in Gary Hart's and Jesse Jackson's eyes, and we will see it in any New Age huckster who speaks our language with forked tongue. We demand of our politicians an almost impossible combination of purity and drive; may we ask as much of ourselves.

Yet with our cynicism coexists a deep longing to be inspired and led. Barry Casselman, impressed by Senator Joseph Biden's comment that "I think the American people should get goose bumps when we talk about government," coined the name "the Goose Bump Democrats" for some of the key contenders in the 1988 presidential race. "I can remember Martin Luther King's speeches like they were yesterday," says editor Jonathan Segal. "It doesn't mean he wasn't a manipulator. Anyone in power tries to manipulate in some way. But where is the magic? Where's the thrill? Where is the magic that uses the language so beautifully that even though he probably is manipulating you, you like him?" It's significant that Segal mentions King; his memory now looms larger for us than any Kennedy's. That may be because twenty years ago King stood at the meeting point of politics and spirituality, where we are just beginning to arrive.

During those twenty years, the political and spiritual revolutions went their separate ways and took opposite approaches to the dilemma of leadership. Some of us struggled to "undo the hierarchy" (Marc Sarkady's words) in our political enterprises, while others "surrendered" to gurus presumed to be above the corruptions of power. Neither worked. The ideal of the collective ended in hopeless inefficiency, while the dream of the enlightened leader died with Jonestown and Rajneeshpuram.

"There's no question in my mind that there needs to be leadership," Sarkady says today. "We really wrestled with that in the Sixties, and part of what we learned was that the hierarchy arises out of a needed function, not just out of some sort of power basis or corruption. We have to transform leadership, not abolish it." While Sarkady and friends were learning that lesson, ex-disciples of this or that perfect master were reclaiming their democratic autonomy. Only joining these two pieces of the puzzle—real spiritual humility in a leader, stubborn personal sovereignty in the led—would make politics possible for our generation, a politics of inspiration and consent.

The real revolution of the Eighties may be that the outer and inner revolutions are finally becoming one.

PART THREE

THE METAMORPHOSIS

Can you metamorphose?
Can you pass the twentieth century?
—THE ACID TESTS

DOPE

Do the drugs a generation uses shape its sensibility, or reflect it? The music of our parents' youth sounds boozy—the woozy cooing of a muted trumpet, the ice-cube tinkling, the sentimentality. Whereas a middle Beatles song is either a blatant acid trip or a slice of aural baklava, oozing heavy, stoned humor, its many paper-thin layers indistinguishable to the straight ear. So our drugs made a lot of our music, but did they make us? Or does a generation choose the drugs it needs to achieve the sensibility that is needed at a particular point in history? Did we discover marijuana and LSD by chance or evolutionary destiny?

There's no question that the shift from alcohol to grass and acid manifested an enormous break in sensibility between us and our parents. And it greatly facilitated the other changes that were taking place—the opening up to other cultures and to continents of the psyche that had been *terra incognita* to Westerners. Four hundred years after discovering the other side of the globe, we were finally tiptoeing into the other side of the brain, and drugs helped unlock the Doors. Pot, an inheritance from black musicians, gave white kids a new sensuous attentiveness to music and the body (never mind the mind). The hallucinogens were our legacy from Aldous Huxley, Western pioneer of Eastern mysticism. One man described acid to me as a "carrier wave" that spread certain changes in consciousness through the culture much farther and faster than spiritual organizations and teachers alone ever could have.

Of late, cocaine has been the carrier wave for a new and sinister shift in sensibility. But it's surprising how many Sixties veterans give little thought to drugs anymore, except as an occasional social diversion—or a worry about our kids. According to Marcelle Clements (1947) in *The Dog Is Us,* a survey by the National Institute of Drug Abuse found that half of our generation's marijuana smokers had stopped by 1979. And many former daily smokers say that they now use it only a few times a year. Hallucinogen use is even rarer. Joan Giannecchini and Stan Kaplan like to take psilocybin and go to horror movies—*Alien* was a favorite—but only one other woman I talked to had tripped in the last several years. ("I keep thinkin' I oughta go back and trip again," says former frequent flyer Stephen King, then shakes his head: "Nope. Too old.")

At the other end of the age spectrum, nearly half of American high schoolers have used marijuana, and in their case, the charge we hotly denied is true—it *does* lead to harder drugs, including cocaine, downers, heroin, PCP . . . and alcohol. From a parent's point of view, drugs look like just one more of those Sixties excesses—perhaps the worst —that have shredded the fabric of society.

It can't be denied that Sixties freedoms opened a Pandora's box of drug abuse and drug traffic. We knew that very quickly: drugs destroyed some of our friends and half our heroes before the Sixties were even over. Zazel Lovén, who appeared on the cover of the Doors' album *Strange Days,* remembers the good old days on the music scene: "A lot of people that we knew died. Janis, Jimi Hendrix, Mama Cass. Jim Morrison was completely gone. He just drowned in the bathtub or something. We weren't surprised. These people really lived hard. I think it was amazing that they lived as long as they did."

Maybe a cruel kind of natural selection was at work, for those who survived the new chemical environment can't deny that drugs helped form and transform us. They were an evolutionary tool that many of us used very deliberately on ourselves. "If it hadn't been for grass I'd still be wearing a crewcut and saluting the flag." "If it wasn't for those experiences I might have ended up in the suburbs. LSD changed my life."

P o t

"The first time I got stoned on marijuana I thought that I had died and gone to heaven," says Boston banker Alvin Cohan. "It was wonderful. It made me hungry. It made me laugh. My mind was bizarre. It opened me up intellectually. 'Cause when you're stoned, even though you make no sense and you are not productive, you think about things. You focus a little bit. I had never focused on anything. Grass was an awakening.

"You got stoned and there were parts of your body that you never knew existed, that you could suddenly concentrate on for hours. You could listen to yourself breathe for an hour, and it was a major event. It was a discovery. I was working in a bank and would get stoned with friends at night. You'd pull the shades down and shut the door and have a marijuana cigarette and giggle and laugh and go get stuff to eat, and then you'd talk a little bit and then you'd go to sleep. We did that a lot. It was the late Sixties, early Seventies. It was a felony."

And it was a communion. The illegality of pot alone would have made it the perfect symbol of our secession from the straight world and our guerrilla bond with each other. Turning on was the initiation rite into the youth culture. We instinctively knew how to do it: in a ritual circle, like Indians sharing the peace pipe, the only sounds the hissing sips of smoke and the occasional implosive giggle. In Vietnam, getting stoned bonded grunts together against the alien command that had dropped them into the madness. The famous film clip of GIs smoking dope out of a rifle barrel is our version of beating swords into plowshares.

But the nature of the drug made it even more Masonic. It was (and is) impossible to explain its effects to the uninitiated; you hadda be there. Of course, it also depended on who "you" were. One of the mysteries of drugs is how they interact with individual psychology and metabolism. Some people used marijuana as a tranquilizer, an exit from aggression and ambition; they seem to have been the ones most likely to end up in a dependent daily haze. Others used it in almost the opposite way, as a narrow-beam, high-intensity flashlight for exploring the interior.

The two groups overlapped; rapt spelunkers of the skull could look pretty tranquil and unambitious. (*Reefer Madness* was so ludicrous; who'd want to go on a rampage when you could barely make it to the refrigerator?) But "explorers" tended to cut back when the drug began to dull the mind. What we liked was the way it sharpened it. Stoned, you could focus your whole attention, like a laser, on one phenomenon, which became the whole world: a lightning train of thought, cut loose from logic; the texture and architecture of music; the taste of Häagen-Dazs vanilla ice cream.

Did marijuana make us more intelligent? That's a heretical question to ask, when studies show that the drug impairs mental and physical performance, and chronic users report an alarming memory loss. But we *know,* especially those who used it moderately, that pot changed our minds for good, and in some ways for the better. It made them more complex and creative and funny, probably in ways no intelligence test can measure, perhaps even in ways that only another altered mind can appreciate. Marcelle Clements writes that friends who'd long since stopped smoking "still had in common a strange, enticing quality that I can only describe as the ability to disturb

. . . that old insistence on maintaining a special attitude toward their environment."[1] "It gives you a sense of displacement, a sense of distance from the main cultural stream," says screenwriter and actor Wynston Jones, who plays monsters in horror movies.

Marijuana may in fact have been a sort of Einsteinian sextant— a navigational aid to the complex new world of relativity and multiple points of view. "Drugs and the Sixties increased my tolerance for ambiguity," says Jones. "There is no one true reality." The only problem is that a hypertrophied sense of ambiguity and absurdity makes it hard to decide and act. To ask a question that would have been heretical in the Sixties: What has the marijuana culture produced? Bittersweet commentaries on the bad old world, from jazz to comedy to the fine art of bullshit. "I became quite a connoisseur of bullshit," says Jones. "It helped me a lot when I was a college teacher." He still talks a vastly entertaining line, like so many of our generation's observer-philosopher-humorists. Is pot a sideliner's drug, a consolation for the powerless? It *can* be quite literally counterproductive, which is why the counterculture loved it—and why some people avoided it, or quit.

"Sure, I did my share of pot smoking," says airline purser Gloria Benedetta* (1946). "But the problem I found, being achievement-oriented, is that it really cuts down on your productivity." Some former users lament the lost years. "I'm doing what I knew I was going to do when I was twelve years old," says Jay Newman* (1953), in a doctoral program in psychology at age thirty. "But it took me all these years to get my act together. And I really think that it took me as long as it did because I was getting high. Mainly on pot, but also hallucinogenics, mescaline. It was definitely not a loss, but I wouldn't want to make too big a deal of how valuable it was. I think the experience in and of itself was valuable. It's very non–goal oriented; it helps you become more attuned to process. But I probably could have gotten that in a year. I didn't have to do it for six or seven years." Newman and I agreed that this gave a whole new dimension to the word *wasted*.

He quit smoking because he began to get paranoid. "It might be an internal way of our body and mind telling us, 'Look, you've gotta stop doing this if you're going to get on with your life.' Drugs seem foreign to me now. I can't imagine getting high nearly as much as I used to. And I'm curious about the people who still do smoke pot regularly. I wonder how their lives look different. Because something about responsibility—for me it's so tied in with that. It's no coincidence that I started being more responsible when I stopped doing drugs."

What about the people who still do smoke pot regularly? Potsmokers Anonymous, a small New York organization that only advertises in *The Village Voice,* sees several hundred people a year—some from as far afield as California or Alaska—who've been smoking for an average of eight to ten years and complain that "my life's not moving." But I encountered two kinds of people who, like Rastafarians, have made cannabis a part of the rhythm of their lives—virtually a part of their metabolism—and whose functioning is altered, but not exactly impaired. These people may be addicted or habituated, but most of them don't light up a joint first thing in the morning, or freak out if they can't get it. One group uses pot as a social sacrament, the other "to relax."

The first group is the "old hippies." "I have friends who became hash smokers because they traveled in India," says Zazel Lovén. "And they are still hash smokers. They don't do anything else. They don't even smoke cigarettes. They eat health foods. They're working people; they're a little bit beatniky, but they function in society. But they smoke hash all the time. They believe in it. They're just devotees, the way, I guess, the Afghanis are." Marian Goodman has vegetarian friends who practice yoga and "use grass to get into heavy discussions."

Everybody knows someone like that, just as everybody knows somebody who went down in acid flames. Whether their cannabis intake is cause or effect, old hippies seem to exist in a different time frame. Unlike most of your harassed friends, they are always free to sit down over a cooling cup of tea and philosophize (a.k.a. "bullshit") for hours. Even when they live in the city, they move in the long-wave rhythms of the country. But the majority of them do live in the country, in counterculture enclaves like those in northern California, southern Oregon, and New England.

My hosts in one such enclave explained to me that when friends get together, it's the convivial custom to alter consciousness. "Stunk and droned is the way we usually refer to it," said one. Sure enough, a glowing pipe made the rounds, followed by a polished cow's horn full of mild wine. We played a ruminative, goalless game called "Elvish Chess": a little pouch of shells, seeds, stones, bone bits, and beach glass is dumped out, and participants patiently arrange them into a design, three moves at a time, then deconstruct it just as slowly. It was dreamy and nice, lit by flashes of my urban panic: "Aren't we supposed to *do* something?"

In old-hippieland, I learned, dope is not only smoked as a friendly sacrament, it's grown that way. After years without a hit, I'd been stunned by the strength of Eighties *sinsemilla* (as much as twenty-five times stronger than Sixties grass, according to the American Council on Marijuana), and had heard rumors from a Washington friend about "botany students from the Sixties who've made a science out of breeding better dope." Now, at the source, I was told that they've also made an art of it. "The best dope is grown in very small quantities by small numbers of people," said an informant. "When it gets bigger than that, you can't keep out the males and keep the plants from getting seeds. [*Sinsemilla* means "without seeds."] It's just the females. Virgins.

"There's all kinds of very sophisticated horticultural techniques, a lot of new strains—Southeast Asian, Indian, Caribbean, Mexican, Colombian—that are being bred specifically for this climate, altitude, and soil type. And the plants get attention all the time. People will sit in the garden and play music to their plants. They're often given goddess names. It depends on who's growing it, but by and large, most people have their plants named, because plants have different personalities." Next time you take a toke, you might wonder *whom* you're smoking.

In old-hippieland, pot is part of a dissident subculture (and small, sacramental growers are constantly harassed by state troopers, free-lance rip-offs, and organized crime). The other group of regular pot-smokers is superficially quite different: urban high achievers who come home and bust a joint at night to unwind. A corporate executive, a wine salesman, an international banker, they are part of the big world, even very successful in it. But on closer inspection, they're in it but not of it. They are "playing the game," much more consciously and cynically than most players, and their inner alienation gives them an ironic competitive edge.

"It doesn't have any effect at all like it did," says Alvin Cohan, who still smokes almost every night. "It's no different for me than having a cocktail. I like the feeling. It's relaxing. There's a lot of pressure at work. Then I come home and take off my clothes and roll a joint and get stoned and eat salami and white bread and lettuce, 'cause I still get the munchies. It calms me down. I wouldn't think of having one during the day or in the morning, 'cause I don't think I could function very well. Some guy needs thirty-five million dollars, right, and there is some pothead on the other end of the phone giggling. This is not good. But to the extent that I find my workday bizarre, I think it has to do with the fact that I smoke a lot. And I kind of have a twisted sense of reality.

"You got to think about what I do. I work in a bank. Major money bank. A very powerful organization. And to me it's funny. I listen to these guys, and they really take themselves seriously. Like it's really important. I think what we do is bizarre. I'm very good at it, and I like it, but it's crazy. It sure does make it fun when a Jewish kid from Iowa can walk into a room with the largest shipowners in the world, the central bankers, and they are afraid of me, 'cause they don't know what I am going to say or do.

"I wield the hand of God. I carry a lot of influence internationally. I don't believe it myself. It's funny. These people take me seriously and I'm nuts. I'm not dealing with a full deck. It's a wonderful, wonderful game. Sure, I get wrapped up in my job. The power is nice. You want to be an expert. There is competitiveness. But I laugh at myself when I can't sleep at night and toss and turn. I say, What am

I, crazy? I think drugs saved me," Cohan concludes. "Without them, clearly, I'd be exactly like everybody else." He points out a key effect drugs have had on most of us, whether we still do them or not: "We live in both worlds. We are a generation of AC/DC bi-intellectuals."

Smoking pot, however, widens the gap between the worlds rather than bridging it. Most old hippies have no interest in taking the controls of the dominant culture and trying to turn its course; they're simply standing back to watch the crash. Alvin Cohan, with his hands on the wheel, watches just as bemusedly; his power is the power of indifference, not the power of vision. For all its mind-enhancing properties, marijuana isn't an empowering drug. It taught us to "go with the flow" and enjoy the process—fuck the result. At best, it could be described as passive-subversive.

LSD was another story.

A c i d

"That first trip changed my life," says Sy Safransky. "It stopped me dead in my tracks, turned me around a hundred and eighty degrees. What I remember most vividly is . . . literally, seeing the earth breathing. What I became aware of was a whole sense of life around me rather than something that was background to my process of categorization. It was ecstatic. I started believing in God."

"The first time I took a mind-expanding drug, it became very clear to me why it was called mind-expanding," says Ananda Saha. "I was no longer limited to my old perceptions. I could see I was connected in essence to all around me, not separate. With that realization I felt a flood of love, as if I were in a sea of love, and there were no boundaries. My hand and the tree it was touching were the same. And afterward not being able to recapture that realization, but still knowing."

"I definitely think that basically I was in a coma, and LSD awakened me," says sculptor Jeffrey Maron. "In high school, I was asleep. My intuition was lying dormant. I was living the life that was prescribed for me, externally. With LSD, I had a revelation that there was a whole lot more to who I was than that. My drug experiences taught me what my intuition was. Now my life is guided by my intuition."

These are not so much stories of a drug as of a moment. "In 1965 to '66, there was a Uranus-Pluto conjunction at seventeen degrees in Virgo," an astrologer told me. "Uranus is drastic change. Pluto is death and rebirth. LSD came right out of that energy change on the planet." That's one way to explain it. There was also a conjunction of another kind. At that critical, alchemical moment in history, three ingredients came together in just the right way to cause an explosion.

The first ingredient was the late-adolescent first-waver: literate, cerebral, idealistic, inhibited, vaguely alienated, full of trapped energy. Literacy may be especially important. When the first wave was young, TV was small and black-and-white, poor competition for books, and "grammar school" meant just that. We read a lot, and the reader's well-developed power to create mental imagery may have been one reason why we experienced hallucinogenic drugs (and marijuana) so much more vividly than most of our younger siblings.

The second ingredient was the Asian mind—both Oriental and Native American. It was in those cultures that we would find our lost sense of mystery and power. Many of us had felt drawn to Indians or India or Japan years before discovering drugs. But for a lot of us, drugs helped, especially at first. They didn't give us visionary experience so much as destroy our resistance to it. "My wife at that time was equally into the spirit, but I think she's one of those people who just didn't need the drugs," Sy Safransky says. "I did. I needed some dynamite shoved up my ass. Tight-assed."

So call it dynamite: the third ingredient—LSD-25, mescaline, or psilocybin. Powerful drugs, but without ingredient number 2, they would have been merely fun or frightening. Much was said at the time about "set" and "setting," and acid came to the first wave wrapped in a spiritual mystique, deliberately derived from Eastern and native practice, handed down from Huxley to Leary to Kesey to the Haight. Until things got out of control—along about the 1967 Summer of Love—most people received some sort of sacramental suggestion with their sugar cube or blotting paper. "The friend who gave it to me dressed me in white and sat me down in front of the Buddha and read me the Tibetan Book of the Dead," says Cherel Ito. "I was at the Fillmore East," Kathy Brimlow remembers, "and somebody just came up to me and said, 'Are you searching?' I said, 'Yeah.' He said, 'Here's something to help you.' And he put it in my mouth. I kept it in there, and I was very happy I did. Because it gave me the vision and the courage to actually go after what I had been longing for my whole life, and that was a spiritual quest."

The image of the quest—combining serious inquiry with high adventure—sums up first-wave hallucinogen use. For the most part, it was, in the words of poet and dancer Bonnie Wolf* (1950), "deliberate" and "responsible." The paradox is that we knew we needed the "dynamite" of drugs to break out of our structured character, yet that very structure enabled us to use the drug as a tool—a measured madness, a controlled burn. Once you dropped acid, it was anything-can-happen day—that was the point—but before lighting the fuse, you could at least point yourself in the right direction.

Studying: "I started reading those books with the unpronounceable titles: *I Ching, Bhagavad-Gita,* Alan Watts books, the usual primers. Trungpa and Ram Dass" (Sy Safransky). *Cleansing:* "I became vegetarian, dropping coffee and sugar. Started doing yoga" (Safransky). "While I was doing all the psychedelic drugs I was also meditating" (Ananda Saha). *Setting,* preferably natural: "We went all over Denver tripping, to the parks, the zoo, the mountains. I had a rule that I wasn't going to take LSD unless I was outside" (Ananda Saha). *Rationing:* "One of my big questions was, if LSD was an ecstatic experience, why wouldn't I be doing it all the time? I knew that that was something I wasn't supposed to do" (Safransky). "I didn't do a lot of tripping. I did it metered. With several mescaline trips, I did one a week, and nothing else for the week. No grass. Nothing. I tried to digest and then go to the next one, to continue the quest" (Bonnie Wolf). Since spontaneity and risk were key values, all these rules were made to be broken at least once or twice. The results usually confirmed the wisdom of the rules.

"I think I took LSD eight times, mescaline about eight times, peyote about three times," says Jeff Maron. "Only once or twice did I use it indiscriminately, and that was peer pressure. Otherwise, I never abused it. So I never felt in any way guilty about it. To me taking drugs was not just a recreational thing. It was something that I did for a purpose. I did it to see its effect on me, to understand a greater part of myself. And it worked." Kathy Brimlow puts her finger on the difference between use and abuse: "I was not into taking drugs. I was into learning."

Everything we learned from the "non-ordinary reality" of acid was something we needed to know to take the next evolutionary step. Theoretically, we could have learned all the important stuff without drugs. And we might have. (Some did.) But we might not have, too, and it's as if earth couldn't take the chance. Acid was a catalyst in the strict chemical sense: a substance that accelerates a naturally occurring process. It knocked down the barriers and let the vision through—in the most dramatic and unforgettable forms.

Here is some of what we saw.

ONENESS   "All of a sudden, the people I was with, we were one," says Jeff Maron. "We shared, you know, whatever; we're humans. We shared everything." On acid, normal barriers and distinctions between "you" and "I" could break down. Some people experienced a vulnerability and intimacy far beyond the ordinary meanings of those words. "It has really affected the way I feel about human communication," says Bonnie Wolf. "It's one of the things that really changed me. I used to feel that we have to talk to each other from outside of each other. On acid I realized that you can jump those boundaries without intruding. You can enter someone else's sphere, and they can enter yours. I know I have literally gone into bad trips that people were having and guided them through. 'Okay, now you are on fire and the fire is getting worse.' But you have to feel the fire. You can't stand outside and talk them down."

The bliss of oneness, if it went too far, could turn to terror. An LSD "overdose" threatened to annihilate individual identity. "My quintessential experience was when I accidentally took too much acid in Chicago," says Jeff Maron. "I went into the bedroom with my girlfriend, and I was lying on the bed, and I looked at the wall and I saw through the wall. I saw the people who were in the next room, and they started to expand into the face of every single person I had ever known in my life. And they all started to come toward me, and as they came toward me they started to congeal into this ball of white light. And I knew that the minute it would touch me I would be absorbed by it, and I'd become light. And I said, 'Fuck, I'm not ready for this.'

"I jumped out of bed and ran down the stairs out into the street. I had no clothes on. I was running down the streets of Evanston, Illinois, in Cook County, a suburb of Chicago. Someone called the police. They came, and apparently I punched one of the policemen, of which I have no memory. They broke three of my ribs and put me in the hospital. I woke up and the first thing I saw was all white, all white. And just these two eyes, just two eyes looking at me. And they said, 'What are you doing here?' I thought, This is it. I've gone too far. And it was this guy I knew who became a paramedic. I was in the emergency room. He was looking down at me."

Stan Kaplan had a similar experience with an unknown drug in the Haight, the summer of "We are the people." "I was sitting in a room with four or five friends, and someone else came into the room. It was a guy about sixteen or seventeen, wearing an alligator shirt and chinos and sneakers, a crewcut. He said hello to everybody in the room, and they said hello back. I said hello to him, and he said hello to me. And then I looked at him and he was me.

"I was so scared that the top of my head felt like it had a hinge in the back and a beam of white light shot out, blew the top of the head off. My persona was on the beam of white light and we went all the way up into the sky, out of house, out of body, up into the stratosphere with the stars and everything. 'Blow your mind.' I got utterly petrified. I said, Get yourself together, man, you are going crazy. And I tried to talk, and I couldn't. So I started to crawl around the room.

"My buddies were all zonked out. 'What are you doing?' I said, 'I have to go down to Haight Street.' 'Why?' 'I have to tell everybody that there is a God. And that there is an objective reality. I have to spread the message.' I'm crawling around on all fours. These guys popped up and grabbed me by my feet and pulled me back. 'You go out to Haight Street like that and we're going to have to come get you out of the ward tomorrow.' "

"Some of it got scary," Sy Safransky admits. "The scariness didn't stop me. I've seen my greatest hells and my greatest heaven with LSD."

NATURE   Safransky also saw the earth breathing. (So did I, on my first mescaline trip, but since I'd already seen my purse breathing, I was less impressed.) Walking through the woods, actor and makeup artist Dean Katsaras (1950) felt the ferns reach out and caress him with aggressive little kissing, plucking motions. Ananda Saha and her road companions "took acid during a hurricane, listening to the heavens singing and the stars moving."

Despite the scare when Saha's companions wandered off into the storm, outside in nature was known to be the safest place to trip, where you had the fewest bummers and the least perceptual distortion. There was great harmony in the world if you got away from people. To children of the city and the scientific age, acid or mescaline could restore the old knowledge that nature is alive, akin to us, and full of intelligent power.

"I was on Mesa Verde with a friend, walking the petroglyph trail," says Jeff Maron of his last trip. "There had been a tremendous drought that summer, to the point where people were very concerned, animals were dying. So we were walking on the trail. At one point we passed a rock, and on this rock was sitting a lizard. And the lizard spoke to me. 'Hello.' He didn't say, 'Hi, Jeff.' He was talking to me in my head, communicating to me. He said, 'I'm your ally.' [Maron had read the Castaneda books.]

"I said, 'Bullshit. I don't believe that.'

"He said, 'I can prove it. Ask me to do something.'

"I said, 'Okay. Make it rain.'

"And I kid you not, this cloud came. The sky was total blue, not a cloud in sight. This one black cloud rolled over Mesa Verde. It rained for a minute and a half. The cloud consumed itself in the rain, it consumed itself totally in the rain. And that was it. And then the lizard ran off.

"It leaves me with a tremendous sense of awe for the spiritual powers and for the power of life."

ESP   And for the powers of the mind. "I had a similar experience once with a frog," says Maron. "I took peyote and I saw a frog across the lake and we talked. And I said, 'No, I want to see that frog closer.' And the frog was brought right in to within that far of me, as if I was wearing binoculars. We have a lot of powers that we don't use."

The discovery of unused powers of the mind—not just the enhanced power to observe, as with marijuana, but power to transcend the laws of matter—was what made LSD an empowering drug. If grass gave us "go with the flow," acid's gift was "create your own reality." Jeff Maron remembers "really feeling that your capacity was unlimited, limitless, that you were what you wanted to be, and whatever you could conceive of you could probably be. Those concepts were always espoused by great people in the past, but societal pressures inhibit that so much. And yet, with acid or peyote, you see clearly that you can overcome, that anything is possible." Even after coming down, with those powers locked back inside, you knew they were there. The sense of possibility stayed. It is with us still.

MAGIC   And so is the sense of mystery. "I came out of high school with a nice suit of shiny psychological armor," says Marc Barasch. "I thought I knew which way was up, which way was down. It was a false sense of security. The one good thing that acid did was say *Forget it!* The world is vast and serious and terrifying and totally beyond your systematizing as a rational being. You better get used to it. I was not glad. I was scared. It was a lot to handle."

But the mystery wasn't alien, a meaningless Existentialist universe. It could be eerily helpful. "I was in San Francisco and I was walking down the street," Kathy Brimlow recalls. "It was nighttime. And this guy asked me for a match. He was standing in a doorway. I gave him a match. And I said, 'Is something going on at your house?'

"He said, 'Yeah, I've got these two kids that just came in from New York. They're on LSD and they're both freaking out."

"I said, 'Can I go up? I'm looking for them.' Now, I had no idea that my best friend and her lover had come from New York. I had no idea that they were *in* New York. This guy had just asked me for a match. And I walked in there and I called my friend's name.

"She said, 'She's come to us! Kath, we're in a psychedelic dungeon!'

"I said, 'Don't worry. I know the way out.' [Laughs] You know, it was a psychedelic dungeon. Oh, I don't know if you were ever in there, but it's horrible. There're all these little people, all these little gremlins, knotted-up, twisted, demonic-type characters that crawl all over the space. And many people have had the same experience. It seems to be a real place, because you could find somebody on the East Coast, the West Coast, the North or the South that had had that experience. It's some kind of psychic plane where you can get stuck. I said, 'Don't worry, I know the way out.'

"I took each one of them by the hand, and I had a Corvair car. And I just happened to be dressed that night in this long, flowing pink chiffon . . . I was the good witch Glinda, from *The Wizard of Oz*! And they were like two children, they totally put their trust in me. I put them in the car and drove them up and down the hills with all the lights. And I said, 'This is a wonderfully magic land.' And then we went down to Ghirardelli Square, and the pier, and I said, 'There's the ship.' Everything was lit up beautifully. It looked like a wonderland, it really did.

"That was magic. It was magic that they were in trouble, and someone they believed in found them. Oh yes, and how, we had holy experiences!"

OTHER CULTURES   Gremlins, goblins, good witches, and talking lizards aren't exactly "holy" in the conventional Western sense. Reading fantasy fiction, Tibetan Buddhism, and *The Teachings of Don Juan* undoubtedly helped shape our trips; reciprocally, taking drugs helped us understand other cultures that had given a place of honor to visionary experience. "Acid was just a tool at the beginning," says Jeff Maron. "Then I went to Japan, and what I saw there *really* changed my life. Because I saw people live with a spiritual consciousness in a contemporary society." The day after my first mescaline trip, still in a strange, sensitized state, I went to the Museum of Natural History, saw the awestruck faces of the Mayan figurines, and understood.

MELTING WATCHES, MAGIC MIRRORS   "When I was in New Orleans on acid, I remember someone saying, 'I dreamt this in Paris,' " says Ananda Saha. "There was a certain fluidity of time." Time and form could actually melt before your eyes, a time-lapse lesson on mortality and mutability.

"The first time I did it I had no idea what I was getting into," says computer programmer Ron Bach. "I was at a coffeehouse, and it was on postage stamps, and it got wet. And somebody said, 'Well, if it gets wet it ruins it. It's not powerful at all.' There were two postage stamps, and since they'd gotten wet, the glue stuck together. So I just ate the whole thing.

"It was about midnight when I took them. After the coffeehouse closed, there was a group of performers that stayed after hours, and there was a girl singing folksongs. And as I watched her she kept getting younger and younger. She started out in her twenties and went through like teenager, and then down to a child—and it just happened in a few minutes as I stared at her. And there were some plastic miniature roses in the front window that had melted from the sun's heat. And as I watched them the leaves started to grow, and the flowers started to bud and open up."

"They said don't look in a mirror," says Bonnie Wolf. To do so was to risk being told, "Behold your many forms." Jeff Maron looked in the mirror "and saw myself go from puberty to old age instantly. I saw myself completely go through my life." Bonnie Wolf looked, too, and saw many lives. "I looked at my face. And first one layer would peel, and there would be another face. And it went animal, skeletal, tree, human, young, old, me, animal, all these evolutions of face and of identity. And I think I started to open to the vastness of ourselves."

SELF   Acid could also be a guide to more personal dimensions of the self, a kind of accelerated introduction to therapy. "One day I was doing some acid with a friend," says Sy Safransky. "The guy said, 'Have you heard the album that John Lennon just made? Would you like to?' He went out to buy it! It was the one he did just after doing Primal Therapy with Janov. The screaming.

"I had never touched that stuff inside myself. It was one of the most profound and moving experiences of my life. I went home that night and realized that pretending to be a novelist was performing to my father. I said, Fuck this. I stopped doing the writing."

"I think that these hallucinatory drugs were truly self-exploratory if you wanted to use them that way," says Bonnie Wolf. "It didn't matter whether the trip was good or bad. You learned yourself. I never really had horrible trips, but I had one where I was very, very cold. I was just freezing. I had to be under blankets and blankets and blankets. And I was learning my fears. I was learning my isolation. I was learning my sadness. And I was learning my pain in life.

"You discover that you can trust yourself on a drug. You can trust yourself in whatever state you are in. You are still you. If you'll remember, the Art Linkletters of the world were saying, 'If you take this drug you are not still you. You have given up control. You are somebody else.' No. You let go the reins, and this *is* you. I don't use any drugs now. I don't smoke cigarettes. I'm real health-conscious. But I think these drugs were healthy.

"If you did them responsibly."

CHEMICAL CASUALTIES   Of course, not everybody did use mind-expanding drugs "responsibly." "In some cases they were mind-destroying," says Sy Safransky. "I would see people clearly destroyed by them. Drugs became the agency by which they punished themselves. The same people might have done it in souped-up cars, or by drinking a pint of whiskey every day."

Marc Barasch has a different theory. "Looking at friends who took too many drugs, I know why they were doing it. They were trying to break through. They were resonating with this enormous duty with which they were charged: 'We're going to make the new man.' It was their own distorted version of being heroic. Some romantic, sacrificial-lamb quality. I had a friend who had come to Yale to study the Latin classics. He took about three hundred LSD trips, and finally he started to break through so fast, get so far out so quickly, he lost his natural reference points. He sort of made his way back in time." There could be a fine line between trying to transform and to destroy oneself. Like Weathermen, some acid kamikazes demonstrated a fanatical hatred for the earthbound, culture-bound self.

It's hard to say whether too much LSD could make almost anyone schizophrenic, or whether even a few trips could trigger the disease in someone predisposed to it. But another name for the hallucinogenic drugs was "psychotomimetic," and some trippers became psychotic. "I know three guys, brilliant straight-A students, who dropped acid like it was going out of style," says nurse Anne Bach* (1954). "They dropped it three hundred times. They were just totally destroyed. They had to be hospitalized. We're talking Thorazine. One guy recovered. One killed himself. The third guy lives with his parents and manages his schizophrenia pretty much around diet right now. Last time I saw him, he was holding down a job."

"It has messed up a lot of people that I know tremendously," says Alvin Cohan. "Some of my friends and frat brothers became vegetables. One guy, a Polish kid, who would have been a great football player, is still rewiring his parents' house, and he is thirty-nine years old. He was in a nut house for a while." As Marc Barasch says, "Everyone has these stories." A recurrent and ironic feature of them is that the worst chemical casualties always wind up living with their parents, dependent on the code of devotion and duty of the very culture they sought to destroy.

On the other hand, it was possible to do quite a bit of acid and remain unscathed—and unsaved. In between the ten-trip mystics and the three-hundred-trip kamikazes, Stephen King, who logged about sixty trips, is more casual than casualty: "I suspected then that a lot of things that had been said about acid were blown up. I really enjoyed it most times. I never had a bad trip, and I never had a real cosmic trip, either. Whenever they ended I always felt like somebody had taken a dump truck and unloaded my head.

"You see things you never want to see again. I always used to get the feeling when I was on acid, maybe because it was cut with speed, that there were so many things I had to do, and it just seemed so *hard* to get goin', y'know, you sweep the floor, and, oh shit, I gotta get the broom out of the closet, God, it's on the other side of the room, man, gotta turn the knob—ah, *God*! But finally you do it. I remember plunging the sink once in our apartment, and plunging a hand out of it—and quite a hand, all covered with coffee grounds and everything. That was about the worst it ever got."

It's a curious fact about LSD that at about the same time it began to be widely known and used, it began to lose its spiritual clout. The 1967 Summer of Love, when seventy-five thousand aspiring hippies flooded the Haight-Ashbury, was probably the turning point. At summer's end, eighteen-year-old Marc Barasch brought a few tabs of acid back east from the Haight and dropped it with high expectations. "I was very disappointed," he says. "I wanted to see God. I remember looking at the sky expecting to see God's face, like I was promised. What I saw was a bunch of Fillmore posters plastered on the sky." It was the beginning of the end.

Why acid gradually lost its transforming power is a fascinating question. The fact that it did demonstrates that any drug experience is determined far less by the drug than by what we bring to it. As dealers flooded the Haight to prey on the hippies, the quality of the drugs declined, but so did the maturity and motivation of the drug takers. Many summer visitors to the Haight were high-school age, not pioneers but passengers on a bandwagon. A complex visionary experience had been boiled down to "Love and Peace," and kids were eagerly swallowing drugs—any drugs—with little or no preparation.

"This is a little metaphor for what was going on," says Wynston Jones. "I'd gone to a rock concert over at Santa Clara. All the big groups were there: Janis Joplin, Jimi Hendrix, Country Joe, Jefferson Airplane. And in the middle of the concert some guy leapt on stage with a five-gallon bucket filled with pills. He said, 'These are the best pills I've ever taken,' and he hurled them out into the audience. People were gulping them down, not knowing what they were. A kid came running by, about fourteen, and he had a little handful of these pills, and he said, 'Do you know what these are?'

"I said, 'No, I don't have any idea.'

"He said, 'Well, I'll find out,' and he swallows them all. By the end of the day, thirty-six people were in a coma, and there was a line of ambulances there. They were PCP tablets."

But even under far more controlled conditions, spiritual experience is notoriously perverse. As if to underscore the point that it's a gift, not a commodity, it never comes when it's expected, and it never comes the same way twice. Even those who'd had revelatory acid trips eventually stopped having them. The wave of transformation had moved on, into other vehicles: meditation, diet, mantras, scriptures, gurus. Those who were "into learning," like Kathy Brimlow, went with the wave, leaving drugs behind for the amusement and self-destruction of those who were "into taking drugs."

First-wave questers are bewildered by acid's devolution from a sacrament into a second-wave party drug. "Later, I saw people just taking it for fun, at parties, going to school stoned," says Ananda Saha. "It was incomprehensible to me how it could be used like that." Second-wave trippers could almost be talking about a different drug.

Their travelogues tend to be cheerful and stereotyped, without the awe or the original detail. "I thought it was great," Lynne Burbridge says simply. "Watching the wallpaper drip. Laughing uncontrollably." Dropping acid had become an entertainment. "Now, taking it is like having a VCR," says Bob Waldman.

But even as fun, acid was more adventure than anodyne. Hallucinogens were too unpredictable to appeal to seekers of reliable chemical confidence or oblivion. The acid visionary and the speed freak or junkie both put psychoactive substances into their bodies; that's where the resemblance ends. Vision and addiction are as far apart as God and the Devil. The comparison may not be whimsical.

Speed, or the Death of the Haight

The Haight-Ashbury always had its dark side, literally. "All the flower children stayed on the sunny side of Haight Street," says Kathy Brimlow. "I don't know if it was ever a conscious choice, but all the lovely shops were on that side. On the shady side were a lot of hotels. I wouldn't call them flophouses, but they weren't homey residences. More transient-type. And the people on that side of the street wore leather and chains and walked fast and stiff. And the people on the sunny side of the street all wore flowing clothing and they walked slow. It may not have been so cut-and-dried; certainly we both walked on the other sides of the street. But it was really predominantly the speed-type people who were on the one side of the street and the psychedelic flower children on the other."

The shadow would grow, crawling across the street until it engulfed the Haight—and the whole drug subculture. Speed *was* the shadow, and heroin stole after it, a shadow's shadow. "Speed killed the Haight," asserts Richard Leonard (1928), then proprietor of the Art Owl Store at 1369 Haight Street and one of those tolerant older eccentrics who served the hippie community as alternative parent figures. He explains speed's diabolical appeal to the lost and empty: "It's the ideal hippie drug. It makes you feel *wanted,* and it gives you a purpose, fills up your day with something to do." It took more and more speed to get that rush of busy self-esteem—and more and more heroin to come down. While sleazy dealers fattened off the need, Leonard says, kids "fixed closer and closer together" till they became psychotic or comatose—or joined a religious cult, or went home.

In many ways, speed and heroin were evil drugs—consciousness-destroying, counter-evolutionary. Their promise was effortless power and pleasure; their fruits were death and money. The Maysles Brothers, making *Gimme Shelter,* didn't imagine the bestial and demonic overtones at Altamont. The kingdom of speed and heroin was hell.

"When I returned to the Haight in the early Seventies, the streets shined with slime from garbage and were actually slippery," says Wynston Jones. "A bunch of speed freaks hanging out in alleyways. In the first seven months of 1970, there were fourteen murders there, usually by crazed people. Someone whips out a shotgun from under his coat, blows away the first seven people he meets, then blows his own brains out." Richard Leonard recalls one girl "killed by a biker. She shot up his part of the dope, so he beat her to death. He lived two weeks longer, then OD'd. Someone had dumped one-hundred-percent heroin on the street instead of forty percent." A friend of Stan Kaplan's lived downstairs from the scene of the famous Super-Spade murder. "The guy upstairs was a black drug dealer who had sold some bad stuff to somebody. These guys heard the cat mewing for days on end. They went up and opened the door and found the body, stabbed to death with its arm hacked off.

"A younger friend of mine, who did not graduate from high school, knows many people who committed suicide, all drug-related," says Kaplan. "I was at the front of the generation and he was at the back. We did all the same things, but he did it years later. He went to the Haight-Ashbury, but it was a totally different experience for him, because while I was going on the upswing, the idealistic side, he was going on the downswing, the burnout cruise. My message was love and giving and sharing and communication and optimism and idealism and possibilities. His was drugs, how to sell it, how to make money, how to keep the pigs out of your house. His stories all have to do with bad news: money and drugs, rip-off and death.

"My friend came out okay. Today he's a businessman and makes a lot of money. He's thirty-two. He's very cynical. That's what they saw: who got. Who made out. He said when he lived in Haight-Ashbury he was a schmuck. He belonged to a commune which was a political power in San Francisco. He went out and organized and did the work, and meanwhile the guys who were running the commune were taking in ten thousand dollars a week in drugs and putting it in the bank."

The early acid vision had been one of trust and generosity: the Diggers dishing up free stew in Golden Gate Park. With speed came greed, violence, and paranoia. In the Sixties, drugs drew the battle lines and defined the antagonists for the prolonged struggle to come.

Coke: the Devil in a Three-Piece Suit

"Cocaine reappeared as a significant recreational drug in the late 1960s and early 1970s," James Lieber wrote in early 1986. "It did so at least in part because of a successful crackdown by police on amphetamine laboratories and the trafficking networks sustaining them, which created a place in the market for a new stimulant. But cocaine was given a better press than amphetamines, probably because it was far more expensive and thus kept better company."[2] In other words, the devil learned to dress up, talk smooth, dangle his bait on a golden hook, and practice much subtler forms of violence. He was no longer a hairy biker. He was a Hollywood producer. And he offered a grown-up, glamorous version of the amphetamine rush: the illusion of success.

"More people in their thirties use cocaine than any other age group," says Dr. Arnold Washton (1947), director of the 1-800-COCAINE hotline and of addiction research and treatment at the Regent Hospital in Manhattan. "At least two-thirds of users are between twenty-five and forty"—a precise definition of the Sixties generation. (These figures were obtained just before the craze for cheap "crack" triggered a teenage cocaine epidemic, but one subsequent 800-COCAINE survey showed that half the callers to the hotline who had smoked crack were twenty-six to thirty-five years old. Ninety-eight percent said they "became rapidly addicted after switching to crack.") Coke has a powerful physiological appeal. It's the one drug lab monkeys will mainline till they die; the only other stimulus animals prefer to food, water, sex, and sleep is an electrode planted in the brain's pleasure center. To the human brain, cocaine offers the classic devil's bargain: a short circuit to feelings of power and fulfillment. It's not hard to understand its appeal for our generation. Grass and acid had slowed us down, made us reflective rather than productive. Now, suddenly, we found ourselves in an accelerating society that measured worth by money and success. Once again, many of us looked to a drug to transform us—this time, from idealistic "schmucks" into confident winners.

"If ever there was a drug that fit the tenor of the times, it's this one," says Dr. Washton, "just as marijuana, in its pharmacological effects, filled the needs of the Sixties for a laid-back, narcissistic, inward drug. This is a generation that swore they'd never grow old, never have to deal with mundane, stressful tasks or limits. In the Eighties, they suddenly got the idea that time was running out for them. Cocaine reinforces the Eighties spirit. It makes you feel in charge, stimulated, outgoing, a superman or superwoman. Its main purpose is performance enhancement—sexual performance as well as the drive to succeed. But this is a time-limited effect. You get tolerant and have to increase the dose. Cocaine sets a trap for unsuspecting baby boomers, whose previous experience with light drugs tells them they can control it. They've never been addicted before."

If the late Sixties were a time of vision and hope, the Eighties so far have been a time of addiction, which is despair. Writing in the August 1985 *Vogue*, Jane O'Reilly put her finger on the connection between cocaine and conspicuous consumption. " '*I want, I want, I want*' is the mantra of the 'eighties," she wrote. "Spending frenzy is part of the short-circuited sensibility of the cocaine age. . . . Even earning money is addictive. . . . The one sure thing is that none of these fixes satisfies our undefined longings. Whatever it is we want, we cannot name it, and we cannot buy it."

All the Eighties addictions—cocaine, money, material possessions, entertainment, pornography—are interchangeable symptoms of one disease. They offer fake power, fake pleasure, fake energy, fake fulfillment, the show of success without substance or soul: the hollow shell of the American Dream. In the Sixties, we knew, the old American Dream had died, and a new dream had been born—or had it been stillborn? In the Eighties it is hard to tell, and those who despair of the new vision have joined those who have never seen it in a conspiracy to reanimate the corpse of the Dream. Cocaine is the stuff that animates zombies.

To me, chronic cocaine users have an odd insubstantiality and hollowness. Like the humans in the new *Invasion of the Body Snatchers* who are about to collapse inward and disappear, they've had their souls stolen. Perhaps the most frightening person I met in my travels was a drug dealer and coke user (1942) who was also a red-clad disciple of Bhagwan Shree Rajneesh. He asked me not to identify him, because he would be expelled from the Rajneesh organization for dealing. Yet he used the "go deeply into all that life offers" philosophy of his guru to justify his cocaine abuse. What was scary about him was that he had no center at all. He was utterly mutable, a moral (amoral) chameleon. He told me cheerfully that cocaine had initiated him into "the connection between sex and violence, the erotic charge that came out in *A Clockwork Orange.* The way I've experienced it is as a sensory overload. It's like you have to keep doing harder and harder things to feel what you normally feel. The stimulation has to be more intense."

In 1984, Americans used an estimated sixty-one to eighty-four tons of cocaine (up from thirty-six to sixty-six tons in 1981). Twenty-two million of us are thought to have tried it, perhaps as many as five million to use it at least once a month, a quarter of a million or more to be desperately dependent. The price has plummeted, purity has skyrocketed, and two thirds of cocaine users who seek treatment are now smoking crack, freebasing, or mainlining (compared to a quarter in the late Seventies)—the most potent ways to take the drug. "[A] public-health problem of major proportions," James Lieber calls it. Some old hippies have another way of putting it. They call it voting for death—by a generation that should know better.

"If you want the name of a villain that has co-opted a lot of money and energy and power . . ." says Morning Glory G'Zell.

"Cocaine is really an incredible curse," says Otter. "It's totally diverted the resources and energy."

"If the money that's gone into cocaine had gone into solar research . . ." adds Lori Lobo.

"Never mind the defense budget," I interject.

"We can't control the defense budget," says Morning Glory. "We *can* control what we put in our own bodies. I mean, really."

"It's just like alcohol in that it affects certain people," says Otter. "There's a lot of people it doesn't, though. Most of the people we know are not interested in it at all."

Lately, some of the people Otter knows have been very interested in a new, already-illegal drug called MDMA, ADAM (the new man?), or, most alluringly, Ecstasy.

Ecstasy: A Drug for "Our Side"?

MDMA is a laboratory-made "designer drug" that combines—chemically and psychologically—features of methamphetamine and mescaline. That would seem, on the face of it, to make it an ironically perfect "carrier wave" for the emerging "Live Aid" sensibility, which reconciles compassion and success. People who have taken Ecstasy describe its effects in words like "insight," "vulnerability," "trust," "openness," "empathy." Without the melting faces of acid, the drug is reputed to remove the barriers of fear that block intimacy and communication. According to University of Chicago researchers, it could also cause "long-term damage to central nervous system structures."[3] But MDMA showed promise as a catalyst in therapy, and therapists who had used it were dismayed by its 1985 Drug Enforcement Administration classification as a Schedule 1 controlled substance, like heroin . . . and LSD.

"I remember listening to the Beatles, *Sergeant Pepper's Lonely Hearts Club Band,*" Jeff Maron says of his first acid trip. "They were talking about the same things I was experiencing and communicating it. That was the whole thing, communicating. People don't communicate today. They antagonize, they control, they project." Is yet another drug the answer? "The articles never mention the down side," says an acquaintance who reluctantly gave up Ecstasy. "There's a speediness to the drug." (The "initial side effects," according to one science writer: "15 minutes or so of sweating, rapid eye oscillation and an increase of blood pressure and heart rate.")[4] "And, well . . . I found that I had to take it twice a week to stay up there" (after what the writer describes as "24-hour aftereffects of exhaustion and appetite loss").[5]

It is drugs' most bittersweet legacy to our generation: the desire "to stay up there" in a life made of ups and downs. Drugs were like a helicopter that dropped us off on a peak in the Himalayas to enjoy the view without the climb. That experience, like other Sixties epiphanies—the weekend singing in jail, that night on the beach in Greece—gave us, for years after, a greed for ecstasy, an impatience with the mundane, a mistrust of the efficacy of effort. For those who took a shortcut to magic, it's been hard to learn patience, persistence, discipline, to endure exile in the ordinary. Like Adam and Eve kicked out of Paradise to till hard soil, many Sixties survivors seem faded, wry, nostalgic, resigned.

Maybe a truly wise culture would provide for the periodic use of drugs in a ritual context, to refresh the vision. Some old hippies still use grass and hallucinogens that way. But without that ceremonial restraint, drugs proved as treacherous as they were easy, and our culture's own native wisdom gradually reasserted itself. After all is said and done, most of us put our trust in work.

"Drugs are too easy," Jay Newman says firmly. "There's no work involved." And that seems to be the generational consensus. Yes, LSD catalyzed the vision of the Sixties. But the fact that so much of that vision came rushing through a drug may well have been the cause of its rapid evaporation, the widespread feeling that it was all a mirage. Paradoxically, those of us who used them most sparingly, and now use them rarely or not at all, are the most grateful to drugs. Grass enhanced our minds and senses (and senses of humor). Even more important, acid awakened our spirituality. It freed us for good from the evil spell of the mechanistic world view. And it started some of us on a lifelong journey called, simply and enigmatically, the Path.

SPIRIT

Social justice and peace will only come as the fruits of spiritual transformation.
—JIM WALLIS
Sojourners Community

That power which exists in all beings, known as Truth, Reverence to Her.
—EIGHTH-CENTURY TIBETAN CHANT

Here is a curious fact. For those who experienced the Sixties as a war, or a party, or a trip, they ended. For those who experienced them as a spiritual awakening, they were only the beginning. Of the spiritual path we can truly say, with Frodo, that "the road goes ever on." The question that has split us since the Sixties is whether that road leads anywhere but into one's own navel.

The "flower children" of the Sixties and the burnt-out politicos who turned inward after 1970 argued that they were burrowing deeper into society's problems to change them from within. Critics countered that the inward turn marked the beginning of the "Me

Decade," and that spirituality, especially the quasi-Eastern brand, was the reemergent selfishness of the middle class, no longer radicalized by the personal threat of the war. Malon Wilkus (1951), president of the Working Assets social investment fund and an advocate of economic democracy, expresses this point of view:

"Hundreds of thousands of people directed themselves inward and thus away from political and economic issues, which I think are much more fundamental in our country. That's what's sad to me about how things developed. I think that basically we lost a decade. I think Reagan is a result of that. I think that even Nixon's election was actually the first result of that. People failed to see that their actions represented the same old American 'me first' approach that has been the bane of our body politic for years.

"I'm not necessarily anti-religion. I think individuals choose their religion based on very personal values and considerations, and that's fine. It's a private matter. But it can also be a distracting matter. Don't get me wrong. All people in social change have very clear moral positions; we always have had. But many people that have those values are finding that they can be dealt with quite nicely in more traditional religious forms, like Quaker, Protestant, and others. There's no need to come up with a new religion, a new everything, which is what a lot of young people tried to do at that time. They thought they could come up with something better. And what they came up with is spiritualism—a self-indulging ethic that turns people in and away from society at large."

Whether or not one agrees with Wilkus, he has an important point. Those of us who turned toward Eastern religions in the Sixties turned away not only from the rote religion of our childhood, but from the possibility represented by Martin Luther King, the rabbis who marched with him, the Berrigan brothers, and Vatican II. The link between traditional religion and social activism had been revived in the early Sixties. Those who were looking for justice, brotherhood, compassion, conscience, witness, often needed to look no further than their own corner church, temple, or meeting house.

Obviously, we were looking for something else. It was something that many of us had tasted as children, stirred by nature, music, or religious ritual. "I can remember when I was in sixth grade, going to a church camp and experiencing Jesus," says Ananda Saha. "It was a very real thing. We went and meditated in the trees where nobody else was around, and I could really feel that that being was with me." But as we grew older, the hypocrisy, half-heartedness, or rigidity of so much institutionalized religion contradicted the sense of those early experiences and turned us away in disenchantment. "My family was half-assed Jewish." "My parents were religious just in name. They weren't Christians, they were bigots." The upsurge of religious activism in the early Sixties challenged our low opinion of church and temple as social institutions, but many of us had already given up on them as spiritual sources. Saha's next major religious experience was stealing the Buddha from an Aspen bookstore.

It was real religious or mystical experience we were after, undiminished by Sunday-school platitudes, deeper than the ethical Judaeo-Christian platform of shalts and shalt nots. Ironically, what we sought was far more like what Jesus offered his disciples than what most Christian ministers dispensed in his name. Transfiguration. *Re-ligio* (reconnection to the cosmos). Life Everlasting. There is an apocryphal story that during his lost twelve years, Jesus went as far east as India to escape the limits of his own tradition. And so did we.

Breakdown and Breakthrough

Why did the Sixties see such a spasm of spiritual longing, such an epidemic of *satori*? It would be wrong to attribute it to drugs. LSD facilitated it but did not cause it. In fact, many of us "caught" it without drugs.

At least a year before my first mescaline trip, I was two thirds of the way through Alan Watts's *The Way of Zen* when one innocuous paragraph tripped me into another state. Suddenly I was looking at life from the inside instead of the outside. Everything was seamless, fluent, unspeakably right. It lasted a while. I rode the New York subway and saw that everyone had a second, glowing heart behind their heart, which was all they really wanted, only they were unaware of it. I read Idries Shah's *The Way of the Sufi,* and every word had been written directly to me. I explained earnestly to a friend that "as long as we're alive, we're immortal!" She looked at me as if I were crazy. I knew I had never been so sane.

And then, of course, it faded. It always did, leaving us cold to old pleasures and desperate to find the door again, which, like a door in a fairy tale or dream, was no longer in the same place. Mystics in all times and places have said that that state is our home. Freud said it was a memory of the womb. It does seem to be the source we come from and go back to, and—unless we're willing to give up everything else to stay there—only visit briefly in between. The intriguing question is why, at certain moments in history—and the Sixties were one of them—the door cracks open and summons so many to the source.

The answer may be that cultures, too, die and are born. And in the Sixties—perhaps ever since World War II—a "body" of ideas, values, and beliefs was on its deathbed. At such a time, the collective consciousness returns to the source before being reborn in a new cultural body. The Sixties cult of the Tibetan Book of the Dead, that guide for souls between bodies, may have reflected our awareness of this journey. At such a time, diabolical, or destructive, forces, from war to hard drugs to Satanism, act as agents of decay, hastening the breakdown of the old cultural body and of the individual personality structures that are its "cells." And, much as the joy of sex makes us reproduce, the bliss of *satori,* stronger than the fear of the void, drives us out of our old minds in obedience to the will of evolution.

In the Sixties, two kinds of people were drawn to meditation or mystical training: those who wanted help in breaking down imprisoning ego structures, and those who had already broken down and needed shelter, a simple structure to support without reimprisoning them. The glamorization of madness in books like R. D. Laing's *The Politics of Experience,* the reckless way we courted it with too many drugs and overwhelming experiences, the number of us who did time in mental hospitals show that in the Western countercultural tradition, with its Romantic roots, perilously little distinction was made between breakdown and breakthrough. What Eastern culture offered that the West did not was a tradition of honoring breakthrough and a science for achieving it and living to tell the tale. Many of us sensed that learning to meditate, seeking a teacher's or guru's guidance, could transform us more radically and reliably than storming the gates of heaven alone.

Finding one's particular path, however, was rarely a rational choice. It was more like falling in love: the inexplicable pull, the eerie, knowing intervention of chance. "When the student is ready, the teacher will appear," went the ancient saying. For many children of science, being led through a maze of significant coincidence to the right book or school or teacher at the right moment was the first undeniable sign of life from what Alcoholics Anonymous calls "a higher power."

The Teacher Appears

"I remember feeling that I needed to find a teacher," says Marc Barasch, who had read Suzuki Roshi and Hesse's *Journey to the East* at Yale. "It began to become a very important thing for me. I dropped out of school. I was living with my parents, working in a stockroom. I happened to go to the local countercultural don, who ran a health-food store. I mentioned my interest in Eastern teachings. He said, 'I have a teacher. His name is Rinpoche. He's a Tibetan and he'll be back in a couple of days.' Of all the paths I felt that Tibetan Buddhism is much too crazy. It's rococo, like Roman Catholicism. Obviously not for me.

"About a year later, all of a sudden all these people passed through my parents' living room and said, 'We're going to Boulder. Do you want to come?' I had been to Boulder before, and it had no meaning to me. Nice town. But now every time they said 'Boulder' I felt this sort of recognition. This urge to just jump in the car with them. But I was a rock musician at that time, and I had a recording deal. I was working in the studio and I felt, 'I can't drop this.'

"The last ride left, and I had a literal vision of these people going across a vast desert on camels. Some were walking. It was like a corny calendar, like the Wise Men. I felt absolutely devastated. I knew I should have gone to Boulder, but I didn't know why. I had a friend who was a professional psychic. She used to pick horses for the Mafia. They paid her a hundred dollars a week. She said, 'The reason you were seeing this is because you were going to meet your guru. Don't worry, a year from now you'll meet up with him.' I didn't believe her. I felt I had really blown it. Lost it. I felt a sense of despair.

"I had gotten a letter from a friend who had joined this other religious group. I got very excited about that. I needed to talk to him. I wanted to know, What is the path? How do you find it? Are there any teachers? I flew out to California and started hitchhiking up and down the coast. Aimless. Longing to find a teacher. It was very romantic. At one point I vowed that I wouldn't eat until I found my teacher. The point was that the Buddha sat under a bodhi tree and all of a sudden he saw things as they were. There was no one to tell you what that meant, so we did these ridiculous little ad hoc things. I was just a long-haired, emaciated freak, wandering around California waiting for the moment when I might look at a tree and see its treeness.

"I finally wound up in Oregon, at Julian Beck's son's commune, called the Rainbow Farm. Eugene was and still is a nexus of the counterculture. It's sort of stale and grungy now, but then it was a wonderful place. I figured maybe this is where I should just stay. Then I met this quite daft, crazy couple who thought they had discovered an organic enzyme cure for heroin addiction. The CIA had gotten wind of that and was chasing them around the country. They were classic paranoids. I didn't laugh at them. I showed the least bit of interest and was receptive. So they said that I was one of them and should go with them.

"I was willing to believe that my fate had taken its own course, so I just said fine. Okay. And I got in the car. I got a fever in Reno. They nursed me back. I was delirious. I seem always to get fevers when there is a life change. Wound up, of all places, in Boulder! Slept in the car. Wandered around wondering whether whatever was here for me would still be here. Wandered into a bookstore. I saw Trungpa's book. I was browsing and it came into my hand. I'd been told about him, that he was a sort of defrocked lama living in the canyons outside Boulder. The minute I read it, I became very excited. I just resonated.

"I went up to his house, and someone met me at the door. I said, 'I have to see Trungpa.' They turned me away. 'No, he's leaving. You are too late,' they said. 'You can't see him.' And I started to cry. I hadn't wept in years. I do it quite easily now, but I didn't then. It was such a strong reaction, I realized this is an important person. When I met him I just instantly swooned. I just felt, This is my teacher. That's that." Barasch stayed in Boulder for the next ten years.

Daya Goldschlag was involved for over ten years with an American Zen Center, after being blessedly guided there in a time of need. "It was an accident," she says. "I'd spent a year in Europe and the Middle East, Persia, Iraq, and I'd hitched across the States with a man for four months, visited Esalen, dropped acid a few times. I was living in L.A., working at an antique doll and toy museum, and I couldn't understand or speak English too well. People would talk to me and I wouldn't always understand, and when I tried to talk I couldn't always. People were a little concerned about me.

"I was going to get up the next morning and hitchhike to Mexico. Thank God I didn't. I went for a walk without any preconception, went into a phone booth, and called a friend. 'How are you?' I said, 'I can't talk well.' He said, 'Don't go to Mexico. Go to this Zen monastery. Tell them you know me, you're a little confused, and you'll work and need a place to stay.' So the next morning, instead of hitchhiking to Mexico, I hitchhiked to the monastery. I say it was an accident, but it wasn't. I arrived in my weird state, and the first person I met turned out to be my husband and the father of my child.

"There were a lot of crazy people at Zen Centers, people who'd been out in the drug world. Or if you go and start sitting, it brings a lot to the surface. After a week I was able to talk, because there was silence. When people passed each other they bowed. The constant ritual gestures took care of interactions, made them very clean, simple, and clear. My only desire was to go back and live there, and I did, six months later.

"I lived at the monastery for five or so years altogether, and at the Zen Center for even longer. For years and years I got up at three forty every morning in very cold weather and went and sat in an unheated meditation hall, worked in the rain. Ate with our bowls in front of us, formal, in the meditation hall. Very ordered. That was my identity for well over a decade. It was a great treasure in my life."

While only a small minority of the generation became as committed to a spiritual school as Barasch and Goldschlag—or even more so (for both ultimately left)—the vast majority of us were acquainted with the basics of Eastern religion through reading. And millions practiced some form of meditation, be it ever so humble as TM, or experienced some form of spiritual training, from yoga to est. There was, and is, disagreement about the right way to go. Free-lancers directing their own spiritual growth—which is most of us—tend to regard disciples of a guru or members of a movement as brainwashed cult zombies. They, in turn, tend to see us as deluded dilettantes, dabbling in the harmless and useless shallows of transformation, too chicken to plunge in. Since spiritual devotees, like Weathermen in the political realm, ventured furthest toward the generational ambition of "creating the New Man," it's worth taking a closer look at the results.

Surrender and Betrayal

It's a common belief, in our individualistic democracy, that submitting to a "master" or a hierarchical discipline is a criminal abdication of the sovereign self. As proof, we hold up the Moonies, that Venus's-flytrap luring lost hippies with love and cookies; or Jim Jones, with his electric Kool-Aid cyanide test; or Rajneeshpuram, paranoid Eden of free love and machine guns. We conclude that all gurus are power-tripping con men, and all followers are cop-outs who let their personal power and judgment be taken from them. It's hard to conceive that in some cases, at least in the beginning, "surrender" could have been an act of the greatest courage—not the courage of one's convictions, but the courage to let one's convictions be radically questioned, on the grounds that they might be part of the problem.

The thrill of *satori* is seeing the world and oneself made new. While it lasts, one's old mind-set is laughably irrelevant. When it fades, one's old mind-set comes back with a vengeance—and a sense of loss. It appears that one's safe set of habits and beliefs is the barrier to the blissful state. But trying to break out of that stubborn prison alone is a bootstrap operation. Gurus and masters of all kinds say that they are outside the prison and know how to get you out, and their uncanny power and perception make that plausible. Some, like Muktananda and Rajneesh, could reportedly deliver a blast of bliss more mind-blowing than any chemical. But for their power to transform you, you must trust them, no matter what strange things they tell you to do: sit *zazen* till gangrene sets in, work from before dawn to after dusk, clean toilets with your Ph.D., give up your money, sleep with no one, or that one, or the master himself.

Obviously, this is a situation with enormous potential for abuse. The problem is how to distinguish abuse from outrageous acts committed in your own best interests, to shock you into glimpses of enlightenment. In an evolved being, Rajneesh's Rolls-Royces, Trungpa's rumored drinking and womanizing, might not be what they seemed. Christ shocked by consorting with thieves and whores; two thousand years later, Rajneesh shocked Christian sanctimony by consorting with the rich. In short, once you'd learned to mistrust your own judgment, your teacher could be the Son of Man or Charlie Manson, savior or opportunist (Lori Lobo's "Swami Snatchabuck" or "Guru Tukargaraji"), and how would you know the difference?

Through the heart, the masters said. Trust the heart. "Nothing to lose but your head,"[1] said Bhagwan Shree Rajneesh, who cheerfully promised new disciples to cut theirs off for them. "The heart is never untrue and the head is never true. The head lives in lies. . . . The heart is authentic."[2] This was a consistent feature of "hot" spiritual groups (as opposed to "cool" ones, like Zen Centers, which would dismiss both head and heart with "Watch the breath"). "On Fort Hill it was good to operate from what they described as your 'heart,' but not good to operate from the mind," says one man who was briefly involved with the group around homegrown musician-messiah Mel Lyman. "The intellect is what screws everything up. You should turn off that part of yourself that objects to things and thinks about things and is critical, and you should only listen to the voice of this ill-defined notion of 'the feeling mind.' " Tactics used on "the Hill" to break down resistance, he says, included "very serious, personal, intense confrontation. Groups would gang up on one or two people and utterly humiliate them."

This man backed off with aspersions of "fascism"—a charge repeated in the two-part *Rolling Stone* cover story that precipitated the Lyman Family's ten-year withdrawal from the world. To this day, the Lymans say the stories were grossly distorted; writer David Felton says they weren't. There is this ambiguity to many stories about spiritual groups. On the one hand, their tactics often violated democratic ethics and "personal space." ("There was a woman follower, a professor, who wasn't developed sufficiently to have any direct dealings with Trungpa," says Al Belasco, another Boulder visitor. "She was a servant in the house. Her job was to present bones on a silver platter to the dogs. But she wasn't high enough to actually serve the dogs. Someone else used silver tongs to give the dogs a bone.") On the other hand, democracy admittedly includes the sovereign right to stay as fucked up as you are. And while some group members were traumatized, others benefited from the battering of their egos.

Today, the Lyman Family, minus Mel, is a close, creative community of warm, intense, and open people. They've come through the fire more human than they were. So have many Rajneesh disciples I've met, men and women with glowing eyes and a tender tolerance. On a much lesser level, people who managed not to storm out of the est training when the trainer called them "assholes" often burst out laughing later in the training when they realized that it was true.

Apparently, there's something to be said for letting go of your

self-will. But when, if ever, do you take it back? (I took mine back
from est when they tried to slip a seminar sales pitch past *satori*-
lowered defenses. I thought that was brainwashing for bucks. They
said I was choosing mind over "aliveness.") Apparently, too, there
are people who "know better" and have much to convey. But how
omniscient are they, and how omnipotent do you make them? True
spiritual teachers aim to empower their students, not exploit them.
"[I]f am really a guide to you, all my guidance will be to lead you
to your inner guide," said Bhagwan Shree Rajneesh. "Once you are
in contact with the inner guide, I am no longer needed. Now you can
move alone."[3] But Rajneesh also invited close disciples to be with
him "forever, so nothing can hold you back from dissolving . . . to
be with me, to be *really* with me means to be anonymous, to lose
yourself so totally that you have no will of your own."[4] The guru-
disciple bond seems to be a relation of love and liberation that uses
the forms of dominance and dependence—and sometimes gets caught
in them.

Some spiritual groups, like Scientology and Synanon, devolved
into a horrifying paranoia in which members were terrorized and
driven to escape. Sometimes, as in Jonestown, the leader himself
proved too human to handle all the power projected onto him; it
intoxicated him to madness. In other cases, like Rajneeshpuram, the
problem may have been less the guru's than that of his lieutenants.
There is no greater power in the world than spiritual power, and every
saint has attracted an inner circle of devoted power addicts, eager to
monopolize his favor and dole it out to the plebes. As spiritual groups
like Rajneeshism grew large, the rank and file often found themselves
being manipulated by the elite, who could give or withhold "official"
approval and access to the overstressed guru. To get your dwindling
"fix" of bliss, you had to toe the party line. Disciples became even
more estranged from their own judgment, for less gain. Eventually,
many reached a breaking point and left. (And, of course, the diseased
power structure of Rajneeshism ultimately collapsed, leaving the
guru himself, perhaps justly, perhaps tragically, discredited.)

But perhaps the most common reason for leaving a serious spiritual group, or moving to its less demanding fringe, was the decision not to "go all the way." Some forms of Eastern religion are quite absolute in their insistence that all else be given up for "enlightenment." If you really want to be liberated from delusion, every attachment, sentiment, idea, pleasure, and aversion—most of what we call "life" —will get in your way. Stories of spiritual groups are rife with small, grim sacrifices to the greater glory. Donna Henes got a two-week-old kitten from a friend at Muktananda's ashram: "They were trying to kill all the stray cats. The mother of my kitten, they tried to poison her. They tried to shoot her. This is an ashram! My friend who found homes for the kittens didn't even tell me this terrible thing. And she was a real animal person."

Daya Goldschlag observed of her Zen Center that "family was secondary. Relationships were secondary. *Zazen* was the most important—and work. Your emphasis had to be on your sitting meditation, yourself, and your community. At the most you got six hours' sleep. There was very little free time or energy for relationships, and not much privacy either. When I left the Zen Center I didn't have any communication skills. I had to learn how to express my inner self outwardly."

There is a strange ambivalence in the statements of many Eastern-style teachers. On the one hand, they say that enlightenment is the next step in evolution, the only way to save the earth. "Now the time has come that if the Buddhas are not tried then there is no future: man is doomed," said Bhagwan Shree Rajneesh. "Each person is born to be a Buddha: less than that is not going to fulfill you. I declare to you your Buddhahood. . . . [But] Buddha is not whole, neither is Zorba the Greek. . . . I teach *Zorba the Buddha*—a new synthesis. . . . The world has not to be renounced, because God has not renounced it—why should you? Live it in its totality—and [that] brings transcendence."[5] Lee Lozowick, a self-described "weird Jewish guru" and "Godman" with his main community, Hohm, in Arizona, has also said, "[T]his work . . . *has* to be done, or the world dies."[6]

On the other hand, here is Rajneesh again a few years later: "There will be wars which are bound to end in nuclear explosions.

. . . Tokyo, New York, San Francisco, Los Angeles, Bombay, etc.— all these cities are going to disappear. . . . It is going to be global so no escape will be possible. You can only escape within and that's what I teach."[7] And Lozowick: "It just doesn't seem like life is that big a deal over and against the afterlife."[8]

There is a world-hating, life-negating strain in the Hindu-Buddhist tradition—the doctrine that life is "illusion" and "suffering"—just as there is in the Judaeo-Christian tradition. The West has taken this as an injunction to dominate the world, the East to withdraw from it, but today the endpoint of both is the same: the abandonment and destruction of the planet. Psychiatrist Robert Jay Lifton, author of *Hiroshima* and advocate of "the embodied self," has noted that in "nuclearism," "bodies and persons are absent."[9] He could almost have been describing the far reaches of meditation mania. It's from this quality of abstraction that so many of us have retreated. We know we need a religion of life.

S c r e w   Y o u   T o o ,   G u r u

It's significant that the concept of one transcendent God, separate from the world and superior to it, is a male problem. Many spiritual groups have been plagued by more mundane male problems as well. To put it bluntly, most gurus are men, and most of them screw around —not just the self-styled pseudogurus, the carny swamis, but some Zen masters, yogis, and lamas with impeccable spiritual pedigrees, too.

In so-called "crazy wisdom" schools, at least no pretense is made of conventional morality; the guru's shocking behavior is supposed to be part of a strategy to liberate students from the prison of mind. Tibetan teacher Chögyam Trungpa, Rinpoche, is particularly notorious—no doubt just being "meek, perky, outrageous, and inscrutable," the "four dignities of the warrior" in his book *Shambhala*. "At this point we are estranged," Marc Barasch said of his guru in 1984. "I'm a very bad student of his. I haven't been able to hear what he said very clearly, because of my own obstinacy. He is a rather unorthodox, difficult teacher, and I don't approve of him. That was the problem."

When a teacher professes probity or celibacy, the shock that alienates his students is not amorality, but hypocrisy. Scandal hit Swami Muktananda's ashram in 1982, when the late saint was credibly accused of messing around with pubescent girls. Daya Goldschlag left her Zen Center over the indiscretions of its American master, who has since stepped down.

"I found out about an affair that he'd had while his wife was pregnant," says Goldschlag. "It wasn't so much that he had the affair. He's only a human being, and everybody has passions. Everybody is learning. But he had been very, *very* hard on a number of my friends who had had affairs outside their marriages. And I felt like he was just a total hypocritical, manipulative bastard. I was so angry I couldn't believe it, because of the double standard, the hurt and pain that these people had gone through because of what he'd said."

Goldschlag recounts the painful reawakening of private judgment and the panic of the group mind. "I'd lost all respect at that point. I was involved in a women's Buddhist group, and I tried to bring this up in our meeting, because I felt that people were having hard times and not realizing who their teacher was. And people didn't want to hear it. It's real hard to have your father, your God, knocked off the pedestal and be left on your own to ask the questions. It was very painful for me, because I had nothing saying to me, 'What you're feeling is so. It's *not* because you're a bad student and undisciplined and uncommitted. There are things here that aren't okay.' When I left, there were friends who didn't have much to do with me. They've since come up and apologized."

Goldschlag evaluates the phenomenon of surrender: "People give themselves completely, which is not so healthy. I think what happened at the Zen Center is very healthy, even though it has put people through immense suffering. It means that people are having to really look to themselves, and now I understand how important that is. It's a very difficult balance between surrendering yourself to someone who has really developed himself or herself and practiced hard for this understanding, and trusting your inner self. A true teacher will constantly keep you on that edge and help you." Goldschlag has since found a new teacher—a woman. "At some point in my life it won't matter anymore if someone is a man or a woman, but not now. Right now I don't want *any* men teachers."

Despite the risk of rape, the aggressive transforming power of a male teacher, the experience of spiritual seduction and surrender, was an important stage on some people's paths. Those who have doggedly stayed with it, like Lee Lozowick's inner circle, deserve respect for the special courage to keep on letting go. They may well go further than the rest of us. But the fact is that most of us didn't want to go so far. We wanted to let go of the old world, but then come back and embrace the new. Those who accepted a good teacher's ruthless help in letting go have brought valuable qualities back with them: a flexibility, a humorous honesty about themselves, an ability (in est-ese) to "get off it" and to inhabit different points of view. They are more able than the average stubborn individualist to surrender temporarily to a group pursuing a goal. And they have an awareness of the ultimate transiency of all attachments without the ascetic's fear of making them.

The practice of meditation, too, has left its mark on those who no longer do it formally or regularly. "I don't do daily meditation as much as I used to," says Lori Lobo. "It's more like little prayers, little tunings-in." "I do sit from time to time, but I've really been able to understand the concept of meditation in action," says Ananda Saha. "Working on musicians' pianos is a meditation." "It's just being quiet, silencing yourself and becoming reverential," says David Banghart. "I think it's like any skill: you pursue it intensely until you find its essence, or what you need from it." Veteran meditators have a subtle spaciousness, a calm in storms. "It's given me the ability to welcome changes, to go through them and to keep a sense of being able to go through them," says Saha. "Not that I don't get bowled over at times, but I think that we have more perspective, an ability to see a wider dimension, so that whatever is going on isn't so all-consuming." These are all qualities of a new human being, adapted to the new world realities of diversity, crisis, and change.

But this supple equanimity is only one aspect of what I think of as our generation's religion. In a sense, we *have* "come up with a new religion," as Malon Wilkus said, though he and others might not like to call it that. For me, the root meaning of the word, "reconnection," is stronger than its negative connotations. Rather than replace it, I'll put it in quotes.

Our emerging "religion" is not borrowed, but homegrown—and potentially planetary. Buddhism, Native American religion, various forms of psychotherapy (especially Gestalt and Jungian), Jewish, Christian, and Islamic mysticism, have all poured into it and fused into a new brew, alive, nameless, and endlessly mutating.

This new "religion" is so adaptable that it can thrive among atheists and in the Catholic Church. In fact, there are as many versions of it as there are individuals—and more, for yours keeps changing with your life. But all its forms share certain constant characteristics, which reveal it to be the antithesis of fundamentalism—its antagonist in the evolutionary struggle of the millennium. Insofar as Christianity and Judaism dare to merge with this new "religion," it is revitalizing them (and making them more appealing to us). But fundamentalists of all kinds fear and hate it, because they perceive—rightly—that it involves a blurring of tribal boundaries, a softening of special identities and of the old feuds that kept them firm.

Our "religion" is life-positive, eclectic, feminist, decentralized, anti-authoritarian, compassionate, individualistic, communitarian, and passionately attached to this earth.

In other words, it's the same as our politics. Or rather, it's the deeper dimension of our politics.

Politics of the Flower

"Spiritualism is the highest form of political consciousness," declared a Hau de no Sau nee (Six Nations Iroquois) position paper presented to the United Nations Non-Governmental Organizations in 1977. Much of our generation, at least as influenced by American Indian as by "Indian Indian" spirituality, would agree. Traditional radicals like Malon Wilkus think our "spiritualism" is narcissistic, and it has had that aspect to it. In the Sixties, many of us were playing Indian of one kind or the other; in the Seventies, we may have studied the sacred texts of our own *chakras* and star charts a bit too reverently. But what is emerging in the Eighties, now that the infatuations have worn off, is a basic spiritual orientation that embraces everything we call "politics" and will transform it. "It's a mystical presence that is beginning just now to have a political expression," says Whitley Strieber, co-author of *Warday* and *Nature's End*. "It's not ideological at all."

Here are some of the ways the spiritual awakening that began in the Sixties is revitalizing both politics and traditional religion.

MEDITATION AND JUSTICE   Sitting in meditation, "turned inward and away from political issues," we were doing something that would have profound political consequences. For, as Al Belasco says, "Yourself is not just yourself. We are all connected in some way." Once you've discovered your identity with the consciousness at the core of everything, you begin to recognize that same consciousness in others, however unlike you they appear. That's the difference between the Sixties politics of guilt and rage and the coming politics of love. It's one thing to say you *should* feel for your fellow human, to make him into an object of pity and romance. It's another thing to actually feel for him, to look into her eyes and see yourself.

As a motive for activism, abstract, mathematical "equality" can't touch spiritual communion. Martin Luther King knew that way back in the Sixties. So did the Catholic activists who went to jail for their anti-war convictions. Most of us couldn't break through to that living core in Christianity or Judaism. We found it through yoga or Buddhist meditation, but it's the same core.

Though he no longer meditated regularly after leaving his guru, "the idea of compassion really stuck with me," says Marc Barasch. "It's not as simple as just good works. It's a commitment to opening yourself up with a can opener, making yourself vulnerable. It's painful. Allowing pain to touch you. It's feeling other people." Al Belasco, who grew up Catholic and meditated with the Tibetan Buddhists in Boulder, says, "I believe that only when you can see the poorest of the poor, the most outcast of the outcast, that smelly, filthy person hanging out on the street corner *as yourself*, are you reaching the highest level of awareness and compassion."

This is not so very different from the Christian compassion expressed in Latin American liberation theology, in the U.S. bishops' pastoral letters on nuclear arms and economic justice, in the activism of the Sojourners community in Washington, and in the sanctuary movement. Some prodigals have returned to Christianity with a new appreciation of its radicalism. (Judaism has retrieved fewer strays because, with notable exceptions—such as Arthur Waskow's Shalom Center for the prevention of nuclear holocaust, the national progressive and feminist organization New Jewish Agenda, and the new quarterly *Tikkun* magazine, whose name means "To mend, repair and transform the world"—it has focused more on the survival of Israel than on the survival of humanity. One woman I spoke to feels "Jewish in my bones," but goes to church with a friend for the activism.) But those who prefer their secular meditativeness to any organized religion feel the same raw responsibility for the homeless and the oppressed.

A "RELIGION" OF LIFE   To make our earthly priorities clear, we don't call the quality we all have in common "spirit" or "soul" or "consciousness." We call it *"life."* That has the added advantage of broadening it beyond the human. Meditators and acid trippers felt, as St. Francis did, kinship with animals and trees and the ocean, as well as other people. Meditation, the discovery of universal subjectivity, transformed both social justice and ecology from ideologies into empathies—and fused them into one. The basis of our "religion" is the oneness of human beings with each other and with all life.

It is also, in Jeremy Rifkin's view, the basis of our politics, and the potential for unity both among various progressive movements and between Left and Right. "I think that the politics of the coming era do not deal with Right and Left distinctions," says Rifkin. "I think they deal with a different spectrum. I would put on one side of the spectrum the sacredness of life: plant life, animal life, human life. And on the other end of the spectrum, I would put efficiency. Benthamite utilitarianism. Productivity. Profit. Wealth. In socialist states it's the same. All values are instrumental to production.

"I keynoted the National Right to Life convention a few years ago, talking about genetic engineering. And I said to them, 'Look. I go to a feminist convention, and they say they're for the rights of fifty percent of the human race that has been powerless to speak for themselves. I go to an environmental convention, they say they're speaking up for the rights of animals and plants and trees that are powerless to speak for themselves. I go to your convention, and you say you're for the rights of the unborn who are powerless to speak for themselves. I go to a liberal convention, and they're speaking for the disenfranchised who are powerless to speak for themselves.

" 'It seems to me that all your movements are talking about the same thing: the sacredness of life. You may disagree on where to put your energies [and on how to resolve conflicts of interest—A.G.], but you're all saying that there is a part of life that is sacred, and should be honored and respected *beyond* whether it is instrumental to any productive end.' I think that we can start to develop a new world view based on the resacralization of life."

DISORGANIZED RELIGION   Another quality our "religion" and politics share is a mistrust of centralized structures, a conviction that father figures, fixed hierarchies, and institutions inevitably become corrupt. For many of us, it's a conviction based on bitter experience.

Writer Whitley Strieber thinks that the powerful transforming energies today are working *outside* of institutions, even alternative institutions. "What's really happening in the radical movement in the United States right now is never even talked about," he says. "The people doing it don't want [the media] to know. They're not interested. They're anti-hierarchical. It's becoming very mystical, very individualistic. These are people who believe that structure is itself the problem, that political structure expresses an aspect of the human psyche that must be overcome. We must evolve beyond this, because if we can't we're going to destroy ourselves. And that *any* structure is to some degree bad, and antithetical to what I've heard called 'the perpetually opening flower,' which is what some people in this movement call themselves.

"The idea is of something that has no hierarchy, that's always creating itself. Like nature itself, where life is always flowing out of some unknown mystery. The nature of that flower is, it's always changing. It has no organization; it doesn't even have a name. And the reporters on *The New York Times* and the academics who write for *The Nation* and *The New Republic* can't write about it, because it has no form. A great lesson was learned just recently from what is happening to the Green Party in Germany, and that is: As soon as the political expression of this way is institutionalized, it's destroyed. And that's exactly what the Green movement is. It is a broken-off limb. And that limb is now, by the people who are really involved in this, considered dead.

"Direct transmission is the only way. One to one. And you would be amazed at how many people there are, how *many* people. You look and you'll find them, when you find the place in yourself that wants this. You have to think of it as a perpetually opening flower. That's what it is."

It's very likely that some of the mysterious people Strieber alludes to are in institutions, but not of them. What he describes sounds a little like the Sufi movement of medieval Persia. To the uninitiated eye, some great Sufi masters were ordinary shoemakers, doctors, or merchants. "The real masters in this world, in order to succeed, must remain invisible even to their own students," says Strieber. "I think the greatest teachers are probably the ones who don't call themselves and are not called teachers," says Sy Safransky. And, in a sense, we are all each other's teachers. It's unlikely that the institutions of politics, business, and religion will soon wither away. What's more likely to happen—what's already happening—is that they're gradually being infiltrated by people who don't identify with their roles, but are using the encounters of work or worship as opportunities for "direct, one-to-one transmission." (Ram Dass and Paul Gorman's book, *How Can I Help?,* is a superb handbook for spiritual subversives in the "helping professions.")

Large institutions are also losing ground to much smaller, livelier, more informal ones. In politics, the block, the neighborhood, and the region are the vital units of action, not the city or the nation. And as some of us warily reapproach traditional religion, seeking a thread of continuity with the past, we're bringing in the future by replacing hierarchy with community and formal ritual with creativity, commitment, and play.

"Small worship groups are forming around the country to unite people looking for a sense of liturgical participation and Gospel-based social action—precisely what they often find missing from large and often-impersonal parishes and synagogues," Norman Boucher reported recently in *New Age Journal.* "Faith communities like Father [John] Giuliani's Benedictine Grange [in West Redding, Connecticut] . . . The Vineyard in western Massachusetts . . . or Havurat Shalom [Fellowship of Peace, founded in 1968], which has inspired hundreds of similar *havurah* in synagogues around the country, are formed to satisfy this need."[10] Protestant friends of mine have "shopped around" among different denominations for a small church with an independent pastor and a warm sense of community. In such a setting, people feel free to improvise on themes from tradition. At The Vineyard, Boucher writes, "one Sunday the Gospel reading dealt with the need to be a fool for Christ, so the mass was celebrated in clown costumes."[11]

INTUITION AS DIVINE REVELATION   With the centralized structure of both traditional religions and guru movements comes reliance on a single, divinely empowered authority that "knows better" how we should live our lives, whether it's the pope, Master Da Free John, or the Bible according to Jerry Falwell. Almost half a millennium ago, Martin Luther made a revolution against the centralized authority of the Catholic Church, insisting that the individual soul could contact Christ without "help" from a hierarchy of middlemen (who got rich in the process). An even more sweeping revolution is now going on against *all* forms of centralized spiritual authority. Most of our generation seems to believe that, while large blasts of "divine revelation" have come through scriptures and masters, little glimpses of revelation and guidance are available to everyone every day. The "authority" that gives us these glimpses is called intuition.

"Now my life is guided by my intuition," sculptor Jeff Maron said of his acid awakening. He speaks for all of us who have learned to question our "judgment," but to trust our gut feelings and our dreams. Our generation's fondness for ancient forms of divination—astrology, tarot, the *I Ching*—comes not from some craze for the occult, but from their great usefulness as aids to intuition. "My favorite guru," Lori Lobo calls the *I Ching*. "When he gets too uppity, I just close him." These are the tools of a democratic spirituality.

So, for some of us, are the late Jane Roberts's *Seth* books—Sy Safransky's "main sources of inspiration now spiritually"—other "channeled" material, like "A Course in Miracles," a series of lessons on love and forgiveness supposedly dictated by Christ, and courses in "channeling your own spirit guide." Though there's a certain amount of flakiness and imposture in the "spirit guide" game, the belief that anyone can learn to tune in to higher wisdom, as well as Seth's (and est's) teaching that (in the words of enthusiast Ron Bach) "there is no external reality, it's created by your beliefs," have the effect of empowering some people to direct their own lives.

In one form or another, intuition is the antidote to fascism in a chaotic, changing world where the real Satanic temptation may be the comfort of absolute authority. It's worth noting that non-authoritarian evangelical Christians have their own forms of intuitional divination: prayer and Bible study. They trust that Jesus' mysterious intent can be read as well by the "saved" individual and community as by any charismatic preacher on TV.

THE ASSEMBLE-YOUR-OWN-RELIGION KIT   In the future, everyone should have his or her own religion, said Bhagwan Shree Rajneesh (shortly before allowing one to be founded in his name). In a time when information and transportation technology offers access to the spirituality of many cultures past and present, one's own "religion" is apt to be assembled out of those pieces of the global heritage that strike a personal chord.

Our casual sense of entitlement to all the religions of the planet enrages fundamentalists, with their need for boundaries, and offends some traditionalists of cultures we "raid," like the Native American. But most patrons of the "spiritual cafeteria" have matured since the Sixties; we're generally respectful of original sources, and cheerfully admit to being beginners, borrowers, and bastardizers. Still, our sense of entitlement is real, and it comes from two levels.

At the deepest, "spirit" level, those who've had a mystical experience often feel that the core of all religions is the same. This has had the effect of reconciling some of us to our birth religion—quite a few Jewish Buddhists have come home through the Kabbala or Hasidism —and freeing others to cross over into a form of mysticism that feels more like home. Gymnastic dancer and choreographer Toby Towson (1948) has the Sufi name of Zahir; Bernard Glassman (1939), a Brooklyn Jew, is now Zen master Tetsugen Glassman-Sensei. Then there are a lot of people, like me, who belong to no tradition in particular but have been moved by many. Some modern spiritual teachers, including Rajneesh, Lee Lozowick, and Da Free John, have encouraged the concept of a global spiritual heritage and ventured to interpret or organize it.

At the "soul" level, where the one white light of spirit is refracted into many images, symbols, myths, stories, rituals, heroes, gods, and goddesses (a valuable distinction made by Jungian psychologist James Hillman), Jung's theory of archetypes in the collective unconscious has encouraged us to regard all pantheons and mythologies as texts written in the native language of our dreams. Thus, you don't have to be a Hopi to relate to Spider Woman weaving the world, or an ancient Greek to appreciate Hermes, the quicksilver messenger. Sculptor Jeffrey Maron has been influenced by the imagery of the Hopi Indians, pre-Columbian Mesoamerica, ancient Greece, India,

and Japan. His bronzes look like abstract, organic archetypes—
sacred objects for a planetary culture.

Filmmaker and world traveler Cherel Ito, who shaped Maya
Deren's footage on Haitian voodoo into the film *Divine Horseman*,
talks about how different cultures connect to each other and to her:

"My husband Teiji and I went to Haiti together. He had been
initiated by Maya [his former wife], and he introduced me to it. I
hadn't been aware of voodoo before; I was more aware of Oriental
philosophy. But it made sense to me. It was just logical. After being
in Bali, you see what trance is, first of all. You see how the body can
become ecstatic. The ego departs and the god takes over. The American Indian ghost dancers did that too.

"If you take every mythology from all over the world and break
it down into cosmic elements, you'll find so many consistent similarities. The Chinese goddess of love, Kuan Yin, is the same as Erzulie
Freda in Haiti. Ofudosan, the guy that brandishes the sword in Japan,
is the same as Mars and Ogun, the Haitian god of war. It's these
cosmic powers that are all similar. And in places like Haiti, Nepal,
South Dakota, people are constantly serving the gods. A bowl of rice,
a few flowers—it seems so civilized. Just little thank-yous every once
in a while. Native Americans won't pick a leaf of tobacco without
leaving an offering. There's spirit in everything."

I asked Ito whether she identified particularly with one culture.
"No, I feel more universal than that. I feel that I can't pray in another
man's language. That wouldn't be true to myself. I believe in the
powers, though, I believe in all those forces. I've experienced them.
I've always believed in ritual, in ceremony. Ever since I can remember, I've had a little altar—a little Buddha, a little candle, a little
something. A little incense. And it's just personal, without being
according to the law."

"I was always doing rituals," says "urban shaman" Donna Henes,
who now performs them in public places at the solstices and equi-
noxes. "In my dorm at Ohio State I had an altar. I always had a
candle lit, and I used to stare into it. I remember breaking up with
this guy, and I wrote his name and everything I didn't like about him

on a piece of paper and burned it. I put it in a salt shaker and I hung it upside down over my bed, so that the ashes . . . I was always compelled to do this weird stuff." An attraction to ritual is common in our generation, as if it were some kind of soul food we'd been starved for. The hunger has led some of us back to traditional religion, others to assemble or invent rituals of our own. Henes teaches a course called "Altared Sensibilities," in which she points out that our displays of favorite pictures, *chatchkis,* mementos, shells, and stones are our personal "altars." Marian Goodman has friends who are "into yoga, became vegetarians, have a little altar to Buddha in their home, and are also practicing Jews."

Sam Mackintosh (1939) founded, and Kenneth Guentert edits, a magazine called *Festivals,* which offers an international smorgasbord of customs, rituals, and holidays, and invites readers to draw on them to create family celebrations. The result is a satisfying blend of continuity and innovation. Among the goodies in a recent issue (April/May 1986): "How to Make a Maypole;" "The Chinese Way of Death;" "Peyote Piety;" "A *Koi* for Every Boy" (how to make a paper carp for the Japanese Boy's Day); a letter pointing out that the Vietnam Veterans Memorial is a "cenotaph" or empty tomb, like those in Hebron, Israel, a goal of pilgrimage; and the editor telling why "the real sacred space in our house is the bed."

One intriguing effect of all this planetary perspective has been a growing realization that Judaism and Christianity—and, alas, Islam —are in fact one tradition (rather like going up into space and seeing that Canada, the U.S., and Mexico are one continent). On every level, from an intermarriage rate two to three times that of the Fifties (half of Catholics and one third of Jews now marry outside the fold) to the founding of an Interfaith Seminary, Christians and Jews are getting together with a strange sense of reunion. (The small but growing numbers of Israelis and Palestinians who are meeting and talking seem to feel the same way.) In my own family of six siblings, *not one* has paired off with a fellow Jew. My reporter brother, Alan, married an Episcopal theology student, Elizabeth Randall (1957). My brother David (1959) and his wife, Shelley Williams (1959), both actors, were married by a Congregationalist minister under a homemade Jewish canopy. Working out the details can be tricky, but tasty. "I'm not willing to make the commitment of going to a synagogue, and Phil couldn't join in bread-and-wine communion," says my old high-school buddy Margaret Harris (1946), married to fellow photographer Phil Straus (1951). "So we always have bagels and lox after church. It sort of balances things out."

Jews for Jesus is only the most extreme expression of a bashful new Jewish respect for that outcast son. "I have found myself over the last couple of years becoming more open to Christ, whatever that is, whoever that is," says Sy Safransky, who came to it through "A Course in Miracles." The woman who told me she "feels Jewish in my bones" still does—and has been baptized Episcopalian. Other Jewish seekers were sensitized by Buddhist training to the poetry of the Sermon on the Mount. Safransky calls people like us "wondering Jews." And Christian fundamentalists rejoice, for the return of the Jews to Israel, and our conversion, are supposed to be signs of the Last Days . . .

But the current flows both ways. How do you explain linguist Greg Paludis, who grew up liberal Catholic and is now an Orthodox Jew? And how do you explain "Coyote Christian" Ken Guentert, certainly one of the wildest examples of Sixties-generation spiritual improvisation, who says, "I really consider myself a Jewish Catholic"?

Guentert attended seminary at Notre Dame during the Vatican II revolution. ("My consciousness was formed by that radical change that happened during the summer between my sophomore and junior years in high school, from the closed system where we had silence in the halls and a schedule so rigid that we could only have visitors once a month for an hour, to an open system where we could go home on weekends and there was no silence in the halls.") In college he was "much affected" by the anti-war movement and the *I Ching;* he remembers putting down "Abraxas, Jesus, and some others" as "my gods" on an application for conscientious-objector status. Those were his only real ventures outside the Judaeo-Christian tradition. His real adventures have been within it.

They began with meeting a man he calls "the Gonzo Exegete": Stan Bomgarden (1947), "a Reformed Church of America minister with a doctorate in scripture from theological seminary. He taught me the Bible, and the way he taught it, he somehow got me interested in Judaism. He told me if I wanted to talk to God I should learn Hebrew. So I started taking Hebrew, and coincidentally I had an opportunity to go to Israel on an archaeological dig. That was really important for my Christianity, to see the places where Jesus walked and lived, but it didn't hurt my relationship to Judaism.

"I found that Judaism didn't seem to conflict with Catholicism, it complemented it. When I was free-lancing, I found that I needed a day when I refused to write. So I made that day the Jewish Sabbath. On Saturday I would play or go fishing. Then I started going back to the Catholic custom of not eating meat on Friday. I'm not sure why I did that. It's obviously connected. Then I would go to church on Sunday.

"I have a *tallis* which I pray with. It really confirmed me, because I feel like I'm in a real tradition when I wear it. As soon as I put it on I pray in it. It's just a body style. I didn't like to kneel. I couldn't get into the lotus position for very long. And I'm a fairly nervous person, so I stand up. So I put this *tallis* on and I could walk around and *doven,* although I don't think I do it correctly. You're not supposed to make the shape of the cross. But I find the bobbing up and down very helpful.

"I'd been to a meditation class with a friend, and we'd practiced some sort of Sanskrit mantra. It was very colorful, but it scared me. I didn't know anything about that tradition. I didn't know a thing about Shiva. But I knew a mantra was a powerful thing, so I used the *sh'ma.* All of those things sort of rooted me into a tradition, and they helped better than anything I've ever felt in terms of what was right. Feeling your way."

Guentert now attends a synagogue where he likes the rabbi's homily, as well as church, where he teaches scripture in the Rite of Christian Initiation for Adults: "I've started thinking of myself as a rabbi. Jesus was a rabbi." He has become involved in the sanctuary movement, "an old tradition that comes out of Hebrew scripture. You could grab a corner of the altar and they couldn't kill you. There's nothing more powerful than this religion when it gets connected up to prophecy standing for justice." And he has a long-range dream of starting "a Torah community that would be composed of Talmudic Jews and Messianic Jews and Christians and Muslims. At the *minyan* discussions on Saturday nights, people would bring their various traditions and work out the community laws on the basis of Torah, by arguing. I guess you could say I'm a Messianic Jew. I know I'm pretty different, but a lot of people respond to me when I talk about it."

Guentert is "pretty different," not only from most Christians and Jews, but from the typical planetary eclectic of his generation. "Sam Mackintosh is wider ranging than I am," he says. "He's interested in the unity of all the different traditions, whereas I am much more interested in attaching to Hebrew roots. There is a school of thought that says all gods are one. I think Sam will say that Allah is Yahweh, Krishna is Wotan. But I won't say that. I will say that Yahweh is unique, and that's a different perspective. I'm more into storytelling, angers, the kind of lively relationship with God that the Jews have, as opposed to the light, the divine—though I'm still kind of Taoistic about flowing with the river. But I'm not really comfortable with saying that all religions are one anymore, because I've read too much of the Old Testament to think that way. The story is very particularistic. 'I am the Lord who led you out of the land of Egypt.' So was I Krishna? I don't know." What marks Guentert as one of us is his creativity, that sense of entitlement to "feel your way" across boundaries to spiritual renewal.

The political dimension of this aspect of our "religion" is the potential for tolerance, respect, and reconciliation among widely differing paths. Eclectic improvisers must defend strict traditionalists, because they keep the original stock—the "gene pool" of human religion—from extinction. Armageddon aside, our only real beef with fundamentalists is their insistence that they know the right way for everybody.

WOMAN AND NATURE   The theological center of our "religion," and the real revolution, is the restoration to equality or supremacy of the female principle: the divine creativity of the earth. In politics, the feminist movement and the environmental movement have been separate. In spirituality, they are increasingly understood to be inseparable.

For many of us who didn't much care for "God," nature was the refuge of religious feeling from childhood on. Feelings first experienced as a child in the woods were rekindled in the Sixties when, somewhere in our brains, LSD met *Silent Spring* and ecological consciousness was born. Ecology, earth passion, is our real "religion," shared even by those who don't think it's a spiritual concern. But many of us knew before 1970 that visiting the vast Southwest—"the spiritual center of our continent," according to Hopi traditional leaders—was a pilgrimage to our Mecca. And astronaut Edgar Mitchell told us that seeing the earth from space was a religious revelation.

It now seems like a short step to seeing that blue mandala as the living goddess suggested by scientist James Lovelock's "Gaia Hypothesis."[12] But that step probably wouldn't have been made without the work of feminist "thealogians" like Mary Daly *(Gyn/Ecology)* and Susan Griffin *(Woman and Nature)*, who saw the intimate connections among the oppression of women, the exploitation of nature, and the rule of a transcendent father God. Many of the first women to topple that idol and unearth the pre-Christian Great Mother were lesbians. Only their eyes were clear enough of the need to appease the male.

Since then, not only gay and straight women, but many men have come to affirm the words of Donna Henes's favorite tantric Tibetan chant: "Reverence to Her."

That power which exists in all beings, known
as Truth, Reverence to Her.

That power which exists in all beings known
    as universe, Reverence to Her.
That power which exists in all beings known
    as suffering, serving, Reverence to Her.[13]

"We've lived with a bachelor God," says Jeff Maron. "The whole concept of the earth as a mother is essential." The movement to restore the female principle to religion ranges from all-woman Goddess worship at one pole to women's attempts to crash the Catholic priesthood at the other. In between are some fascinating experiments in balancing the female and male principles.

Some "Goddess people," like the contemporary witch Starhawk (author of *Dreaming the Dark*), are reinvestigating the role of the natural male principle, depicted in pagan religions as the Goddess's consort, the Green Man (spirit of vegetation), or the animal Horned God—images of maleness that are fleshy, feeling, mortal, rather than "above it all." Meanwhile, some "God people," like Elaine Pagels (1943), author of *The Gnostic Gospels*, are reinvestigating esoteric Judaeo-Christian traditions that, like those of India and Tibet, honored a female principle as the equal and essential "bride" of God.

Just how "equal and essential" do the traditional religions think women are? Resistance and relenting—and the determination of women—are evident in the tiny but rapidly growing numbers of female clergy. As of May 1986: over one hundred women Reform Jewish rabbis, nineteen Reconstructionist rabbis (with four or five more ready to graduate), two Conservative rabbis, over six hundred Episcopal priests and over three hundred deacons, more than 7 percent of the clergy (but no rectors yet); over four hundred Lutheran and three hundred Baptist ministers. The Jewish Theological Seminary (Conservative) first accepted women students for ordination in 1984; in 1986, 30 percent of its rabbinical classes were women. Thirty-five to 50 percent of Episcopal theology students, and over half the class of 1988 at Union Theological Seminary, are female. At Union, "perhaps the most discussed question [is] how to . . . [find] a way of recognizing God's female attributes."[14] One of the most crucial of these, it seems, is *immanence:* the full presence of divinity in nature, the Creator alive in the Creation.

Our generational "religion" of ecology finds its purest expression in the "deep ecology" movement and its purist political activism in the non-violent confrontations of Greenpeace, the animal-rights movement, and Earth First! But just as environmental concerns are now a congressional priority, ecology has also burrowed its way into traditional religion, especially Christianity. In Catholicism it is called "Creation-Centered Spirituality" and led by author Matthew Fox, who has been inspired by the life-affirming vision of such medieval women mystics as Julian of Norwich. In evangelical Protestantism, it is called "the Christian stewardship movement."

"It's a redefining of the Book of Genesis, and it's very profound," says Jeremy Rifkin, a Jew whose 1980 book *The Emerging Order* was chosen as one of the ten best books on the evangelical movement. "They're saying that God's big instruction, his mandate, his covenant about dominion—we got it wrong! Dominion did not mean subdue nature, it means *stewardship.* God created this whole thing and called it good, so any time we despoil it or manipulate it, we are in rebellion to our covenant. Our job is to take care of it. To my mind, the stewardship vision is very much a vision to bring the feminine side of our psyche back into play."

BODY AND COMMUNITY

With the affirmation of nature comes affirmation of the body, with all its needs, flaws, and pleasures. This is not so surprising out among the hippies, but it's a real change for Catholics. Ken Guentert, who was asked to leave the Notre Dame seminary "for writing a poem about masturbation" (and including it in a "one-person newsletter" he sent to a friend in the mission), went on to publish a delightful newsletter, *Body & Soul,* on themes of spirit incarnate: "Eyes," "Guts," "Tongues," "Bones," "Bellies," "Hair," "Sweat," "Scars," "Bathrooms," "Glands & Grace," "The Sensual Jesus." (It has now been folded into *Festivals.*) In faith communities like the Benedictine

Grange and The Vineyard, Holy Communion has been made very physical, with rough homemade bread replacing the ethereal Communion wafer. Norman Boucher quotes Father John Giuliani: " 'Take this bread and eat it,' Jesus said. . . . Having to chew, getting your face, your jaw into motion, having to swallow—that's the experience of eating; that's as much in touch with the substance of the symbol as anything can be."[15] "One of my favorite lectures when I'm teaching natural law is that God made the clitoris," writes Patricia Ferris McGinn, a former nun, wife, mother, and therapist, in *Spice: The newsletter for women whose husbands are ministers.* "And it is not needed to make babies. It is for one reason—erotic pleasure. . . . that is part of the plan."[16]

Outside religion, the fitness movement has a spiritual dimension for many people. "Running is a meditation for me," says Sy Safransky. "To ignore the physical, at least for me, is perilous. Running, exercises, yoga, stretching, t'ai chi—I don't think it matters so much what the form is as long as we acknowledge we are in bodies. We are physical beings." For survivors of Fifties puberty, that is still a luxurious surprise. We revel in sports and dancing and massage, and hug and touch our families and friends a lot more than we used to. The body has become our medium of celebration, compassion, and community.

Physical movement can be a form of spiritual communion, bonding a group of people very deeply. "Society is falling apart. People need connection," says Philadelphia lawyer Stacey Meadows Adels (1958). "I think it's very important to work toward feelings of connectedness. I know that, for some of our friends, church is the place where they find their community, but Peter [1957] and I don't believe in practicing Judaism. One way we've done it has been by our participation in a dance workshop. It's not about structured dancing, learning steps. It's dancing in a free style, dancing with other people from your soul. So it's really expressive, and very liberating. We did it religiously, every Friday night for a year and a half" (until the "time crunch" of two careers and a baby made it impossible).

"Religiously" was an interesting choice of word, I thought. "It was!" Stacey said. "It was very spiritual." I told her that my community—my "church," in a sense—is a karate school. There, the movements are much more formal, but it's moving and fighting with other people from your soul. Sweating and shouting together in unison has made people of all different sizes, shapes, ages, sexes, and colors conscious of what we have in common, creating a calm, elated comradeship that none of us has ever felt before. Unable to explain it, we call it "magic."

Do You Believe in Magic?

"You know, there's a legend in history that magic occurs at certain times," says Otter. "In the time of Arthur, magic was stronger. The magic times are coming back again." We are sitting around the G'Zells' yurt, cozily cluttered with books, papers, plans for the mermaid-seeking expedition, Otter's sculptures of mythic animals, and Morning Glory's fantastically decorated "medicine skulls" (wild pig, not human). There's that sense of being outside of time, and of all the time in the world. It's winter, the season when Native American tribes got together inside and told stories. Rain patters comfortingly on the plastic skylight.

Otter has been telling me about Neo-Paganism, the religion in which he and Morning Glory are priest and priestess (and which they helped to found back in the Sixties in St. Louis, as publishers of the seminal journal *Green Egg*). Neo-Paganism—or the G'Zelis' current version, for it seems to be a stubbornly individual, mercurial religion—is a blend of Native American nature mysticism, the G'Zells' pre-Christian tribal roots (she's Irish and Choctaw, he's Scots and German Swiss), and whatever else works: folk magic, tarot, directed dreaming, shamanic totemism (everyone knows his or her animal: Morning Glory's a possum, Lori a coyote), science fiction/fantasy, and global myth ("A major part of our lives is our personal mythologies. Find out who your archetype is and scramble like hell to get there"). All this and more is set forth in Margot Adler's definitive book on Neo-Paganism, *Drawing Down the Moon*.

The G'Zells and Lori have their own core coven, the Holy Order of Mother Earth (H.O.M.E.), and they conduct larger ceremonies for their neighbors: "sweats, and Native American chants, and an annual tree planting, and the biggest one, the summer solstice. It usually involves getting totally zonkered, having an amazing feast, and watching everybody try new tricks off the rope swing, and everybody running around naked ("Not *everybody*," Lori objects) and having a wonderful time. And in the middle of this is a big circle right in the magical center of the place. It's a perfect formation—a stone and tree circle. A kind of altar. And we'll have a ceremony there that's designed to send out a protective umbrella over the Magick Land. To invoke the elements and ask them to grant us their blessings instead of their furies. To keep it safe from harm and from people who shouldn't be here."†

This "religion" has its politics, too—a tough, tribal resistance and friendly anarchism. "Basically, we come from a long history of people who fought the Romans," says Otter. "We never thought of Rome as our government, whether it's in Washington, D.C., whether they call him Caesar or President. This is not our government. Our government is the tribal council, and it always has been and always will be. As far as we're concerned, if you can't get everybody right there in the same place to talk about what you've got to talk about, forget it."

As I listened to the G'Zells, and looked around at the carved staffs and embroidered robes of their calling, I thought, This is very Sixties. If you've really grown up and left the Sixties behind—God help you—it might seem merely quaint. The casual nudity, the moon rituals and magic spells, might amuse or offend. The connotations of "witchcraft" can arouse hostilities and fears as old as the Inquisition. (Neo-Pagans say the word *wicca* means "flexible," like "wicker": The witch can bend or change reality and herself). Still, I thought, if you look underneath the Sunday-school-pageant costumes and the Sixties sexual customs (all optional anyway), this is very, very close to the

†In 1986, unfortunately, the G'Zells' landlady decided that *they* shouldn't be there. Pending resolution of their dispute, they are cheerful exiles in the valley, running a "fantasy, nature, and science" store called Between the Worlds.

"religion" of our generation. I think that many of us who call ourselves non-religious, or Christians or Buddhists or Jews, are in fact
(small-letter) neo-pagans. *Pagan*, after all, means "of the earth."

See if these excerpts from a summary of Neo-Pagan values, by
Isaac Bonewits of the New Reformed Druids of North America, seem
as familiar, as *homey*, to you as they do to me:

> 1. *The idea that divinity is immanent (internal) as well as transcen-
> dent (external).* This is often phrased as "Thou art God" and "Thou
> art Goddess." [As in Heinlein's *Stranger in a Strange Land*, or the
> Hindu *namaste.*]
>
> 2. *The belief that divinity is just as likely to manifest itself as female
> . . . .* There is a very strong gender equality running throughout the
> Neopagan Druid worldview.
>
> 3. *A belief in a multiplicity of "gods" and "goddesses,"* whether as
> individual deities or as facets of . . . archetypes. [Otter, in another
> pamphlet, includes "tribal deities such as Jahveh (the collective con-
> sciousness of the Hebrew people)"—which I guess makes Ken Guen-
> tert a neo-pagan.] This leads to multivalued logic systems and
> increased tolerance toward other religions.
>
> 4. *A respect and love for Nature as divine in Her own right* . . . makes
> ecological awareness and activity a religious duty.
>
> 5. *A distaste for monolithic religious organizations and a distrust of
> would-be messiahs and gurus* . . . makes Neopagans hard to organize,
> even for "their own good."
>
> 6. *The firm conviction that human beings were meant to lead lives
> filled with joy, love, pleasure, and humor.* The traditional western
> concepts of sin, guilt, and divine retribution are seen as sad misunder-
> standings of natural growth experiences. [Otter decides that "sin" is
> "synonymous with hypocrisy," and "crime" with "rape."]
>
> 7. *A simple set of ethics and morality based on the avoidance of actual
> harm to other people* (and some extend this to some or all living beings
> and the planet as a whole).
>
> 8. *The knowledge that with proper training and intent, human minds
> and hearts are fully capable of performing all the magic and miracles
> they are ever likely to need,* through the use of natural psychic powers.

9. *A belief in the importance of celebrating the solar, lunar, and other cycles of our lives* [in old and new ways].

10. *A minimum amount of dogma and a maximum amount of eclecticism.* Neopagans are reluctant to accept any idea without personally investigating it, and are willing to use any concept they find useful, regardless of its origins. . . .

14. *The knowledge that human interdependence implies community cooperation.* Neopagans are encouraged to use their talents to . . . help each other as well as the community. . . .

15. *An awareness that if they are to achieve any of their goals, they must practice what they preach* . . . a concern with making one's lifestyle consistent with one's proclaimed beliefs.[17]

Our generation's "religion," then, is a sophisticated return to precivilized wisdom, informed by modern psychology and science.

One aspect of that wisdom is what Otter calls "believing is seeing": A yearning belief in the possibility of something, be it Jesus or unicorns, can call it into your life. In the Sixties, our collective sense of possibility created a tremendous energy field, in which many strange things could, and did, happen. For most of us, that power has retreated. I found it intensely alive in the Magick Land, a piece of ground lovingly cultivated by ritual. Things *happened* to me there.

The rainbow didn't strike me as odd until I put it all together afterward. Otter had given me a complicated set of instructions for finding them, which involved driving about two hours north from San Francisco and looking for a particular left turn. It was a partly cloudy day, and just as I saw the turnoff, *just* as I saw it, there was a full rainbow over the road. I thought, Gee, pretty rainbow, made the turn, stopped the car, and got out and looked at it. Then I set forth on my initiation ordeal, up that horrible road. Only much later did I remember the corny, greeting-card association of the unicorn and the rainbow—and realize that I had passed through a gateway.

Before I left the next day, Lori and Anodea and Gary and I were strolling through the muddy hills. Whenever I'm in the country, I pick up a stick or a stone, something to take back to New York to remind myself that the whole world isn't concrete. Passing a puddle, I saw a stick that had an interesting bend in it. I walked past, stopped as if I'd been jerked by a leash, went back, and picked up the stick. Fifteen minutes later, we were sitting in Anodea's yurt, drinking herb tea and talking about the collapse of Western civilization while I turned the stick idly around in my fingers. Suddenly I saw that, on the side that had been face down in the puddle, it had two little knobs that looked exactly like breasts. It was, obviously, a long, lithe, and very sensuous goddess figurine.

"Well, you witches better decorate this for me," I said. Anodea rummaged around in a cupboard and came back to the table, saying, "We found this buried with a little pile of bones. Must have been around someone's pet cat's neck or something." It was a rainbow ribbon. Lori and Anodea tied it around her waist. And that's how she lies on my mantel, pillowed on a river stone from Transylvania.

Down from the Mountain

"There are countless stories like that," says Kathy Brimlow. "But interpreting them in this day and age, what's the practicality?" Brimlow, now a registered nurse approaching midwife training, is one of many seekers who have trouble integrating their spiritual vision with life—and making a living—in Eighties America. Every visionary ultimately has to come down from the mountain. Whether you live in an ashram or an apartment, "the Path" leads back into the valley of ordinary life—where it encounters its greatest challenges, disguised as daily annoyances. Relationships dredge up old structures in the psyche. Earning a living entangles us in the old structures of society.

What good is a gender-balanced universe if we can't work it out in our own households and workplaces?

What good, as we make our first mortgage payments, is all that painful compassion for the homeless in the street?

"It's just surface show unless you're living it," says Lori Lobo. Amen.

BRINGING IT ALL BACK HOME

L*OV E*

I get by with a little help from my friends . . .
— R I N G O   S T A R R

"The Love Generation." We never could call ourselves that with a straight face, but it was our media tag. It went with the summer-of-'67 image of a girl with flowers in her hair, giving it innocently away to guys who looked like her and made love or music, not war.

The image may have been trivialized and exploitative, but it had its roots in our own belief that we could recapture the animal innocence of the body and replace the neurotic nuclear family with the Family of Man (or better yet, the Family of Woman). In our brave new world, we would abolish all that had oppressed in the name of love: inhibition, shame, jealousy, possessiveness, domination, dishonesty, sex roles, even sex differences. That was the dream. There were moments—often stoned moments—when it seemed within reach. But the reality of love in our generation has been somewhat different. It has had its dark side.

It's the young man who didn't speak to his mother for years, then cut his hair for her funeral.

It's the sincere spiritual seeker whose first sexual experience was getting raped by a Hell's Angel in the Haight.

It's the twenty-three-year-old suburban housewife who heard the siren song of acid rock and left her husband and small daughter to go live on a commune.

It's the principled young academic couple who broke up after bitter fights over housework.

It's the thirty-four-year-old actor who's not ready for a commitment; the thirty-nine-year-old therapist who can't find a man quite good enough; the women who put off childbearing till their late thirties, only to find that they can't conceive.

It's a million new children of divorce every year.

It's a struggle—between "programming" and principle, love and freedom, "growth" and commitment, others and self.

If the right wing gets to write history, they will put us down not as the "Love Generation," but as the generation that destroyed the American family. They will point to the soaring rates of divorce, venereal disease, teen pregnancy, and abortion as sequelae of the Sixties. If they are right in their attribution of blame, then, ironically, the Sixties generation achieved one of our main objectives.

We might not have been able to tear down the state, but the family was closer. We could get our hands on it. And, like the Confucian Chinese, we believed that the family was the foundation of the state, as well as the collective state of mind. To us, its children, the Fifties nuclear family—with its hypocrisies, its covert power struggles, its substitution of materialism for love—was the cornerstone of the Nuclear Age. We truly believed that the family had to be torn apart to free love, which alone could heal the damage done when the atom was split to release energy.

And the first step was to tear ourselves free from our parents.

Parents: Bringing the Revolution Home

"Bring the revolution home—kill your parents!" Today, that smugly hysterical slogan makes us cringe. But locked in the ordinary adolescent struggle to separate as well as the extraordinary struggle to bring forth a new world, we thought our mothers and fathers were enemy agents, planted in our homes to socialize us in the bad old mold. Their natural, if unenlightened, desire to see us follow in their footsteps took on a sinister cast. Many of us considered it our revolutionary duty to offend them, break their hearts, and scare them half to death.

We brought the revolution home, accusing our parents of collaboration or complacency. We brought our boyfriends home, and sneaked noisily into their rooms at night when our parents wouldn't let us sleep with them. (By the time second-wave siblings came of age, they'd given up on decorum.) We smoked dope at home. "I was sitting in front of the speakers with the stereo blasting," Jeffrey Maron recalls, "and my mother said, 'Jeff, you must be stoned.'" Eddie Lilburn came home at fifteen with an earring in one pierced ear; his father ripped it out. Many of us scorned our parents' world view—their values, their sacrifices, their cherished hopes for us—not only in word but in deed, by becoming artists instead of lawyers (if male) or lawyers instead of housewives (if female). The parent-child bond became the intimate battleground of two warring paradigms, with each side holding the other personally responsible for the sins of their generation.

The period of acute estrangement could last from a few hours to forever. "They were fairly strict," recalls Zazel Lovén. "When I was home from college I had to be home by a certain time, and they had to know where I was. Once they told me to come home for dinner and I arrived hours late. My father threw me out of the house. My mother sobbed. My sister, who was ten, ran around emptying the change from everyone's pockets so that she could give me money. It was a real high-drama scene, but it blew over very quickly." So did "revolutionary" Tina Ivans's father's threat to shoot her across the barricades. "Of course, that was in temper," she says now. "One thing about my parents—through all this, no matter what crazy things we were all doing, they would never disown their kids." Ivans's parents wound up keeping a scrapbook of her Young Socialist speechmaking. "They saw that it was developing me as a person, and they were kind of proud."

At the other extreme were prolonged, profound estrangements that ended when a parent died before reconciliation could take place. "One time I really cut my hair short was for my mom's funeral," says San Diego accountant Alex Weiss* (1950), who had alienated his conventional Catholic parents by dropping out of college, dropping into drugs and music, and growing his hair to his waist. "It was a symbolic gesture. Now that the battle was over, since she had conceded her life, I could concede my hair." There is bitterness in his voice—at himself, at his times. He lives across the country from his father, and when I interviewed him, he had not been home for three years.

"I think if there had been more of a family atmosphere in the country, maybe I wouldn't have rejected my parents so strongly," he says today. "The baby boom was so much bigger than the previous generation, it sort of developed its own momentum. A lot of the ideas that influenced me weren't my own. If there hadn't been that cluster of ideas, like anti-war, free love, the generation gap, I might not have rebelled so much."

In between the two extremes, most of us endured rough or distant times with our parents, but never completely broke off. "We went through eight or ten years of really hard stuff," says Marc Sarkady. "Yet my family was the kind of people who always spoke with each other, so even though in a way we weren't speaking, we were still speaking."

Underneath the hostility and pain ran a powerful current of appeal:

by violating our parents' expectations and proprieties, cutting all the strings they had attached to their approval, we hoped to discover their unconditional love. And we often found it, like striking bedrock, at just the moment when our explorations had gone too far, when they could have said, "I told you so."

"While I was in jail for wearing the flag around my head, the police broke into my apartment with sledgehammers, rummaged through my belongings and my friends', threw food and flour all over, and left the place in a wreck," says Marc Sarkady. "After I called my father from jail, he came and stayed in the apartment, because we were concerned that the police would break in again." I know a mother who flew across the country to be with her daughter during an abortion. And how many parents picked up young Icaruses who'd crashed on drugs?

That was the most common family profile: a foreground of bewildered or bitter disapproval, a deep background of inalienable support. Underneath all the excess, we were trying to teach our parents urgent and healing new values: that truth was more important than appearances, that there was more than one right way to live, that love should not bind but set free. In return, they were teaching us a lesson in loyalty. Despite all the abuse they took—and gave—when our communes and marriages broke up and our movements and gurus failed us, they were still there. Tied to us by the heartstrings, they had lived through the whole roller-coaster ride with us. We would not fully understand that till many years had passed—until, in some cases, we had children ourselves.

Lovers

Yeats might have called America in the Sixties "no country for old men." It was a time of "the young in one another's arms," frequently and often flagrantly. In the compressed lexicon of the Sixties, lovemaking was like hitchhiking, one of those all-purpose gestures: a politico-sensual act fusing defiance and delight. "Make love, not war." "The more I make love/The more I make revolution" (Paris,

1968). (The spirit of the slogan still lives: "Petting not Pershing," West Germany, 1984.) The slogans declared that the sexual revolution *was* the revolution, and that getting laid a lot would help save the world.

We may have been right at least about the revolutionary part. No aspect of our assault on the old order was more upsetting to our elders, or more indicative that we meant to destroy *their* world. But what the slogans reveal now more than anything else is what an adolescent uprising it was. It's not for nothing that Eros is portrayed as a boy. The simple, driving equation of Sex with Life—in terms of ecstasies, not consequences—is the symbolism of youth. What was unique about the Sixties was that it became the dominant symbolism. Several things had happened to overturn the normal rule of the reality principle over the pleasure principle, the old over the young.

One, of course, was our numbers. Young people in most times and places have had to conform to the values of their elders in return for an eventual share of power. But the baby-boom generation had power just by virtue of its size—and its position at the center of a youth-centered culture. With the avid collaboration of TV and the music industry, we wrote our own values, along classically adolescent lines: Sex, ¡si! work and war, ¡no!

We weren't just having fun, though. We were engaged in a historic experiment. Our culture had repressed sex and enshrined work and war. The result was a planet menaced by power-mad overachievers. You could read Freud and Reich a bit simplistically to suggest that taking the lid off sex was the solution to all of Western civilization's problems. In our cosmology, "natural" was good, so what could be better than doin' what comes naturally? We were blessed by the perfect convergence of a life stage and a mission: horny adolescence and the resurrection of the body.

Another factor that freed us to take on that mission, however, was not so natural: the Pill. The "sexual revolution" followed very quickly in the wake of its wide availability, as if we sensed that premarital chastity was really only a crude form of birth control.

Enovid was put on the market at the end of 1960. In 1965, an estimated 25 percent of women graduating from college were not virgins. In 1969, 55 percent were not. (By 1980, 25 percent of the graduating class in one Seven Sisters school had had at least one abortion during college.)

In theory, the Pill would make women free at last to enjoy their sexuality without fear of consequences. In practice, the Pill had consequences of its own—from bloating and depression to strokes—and it "freed" women largely to imitate some of the lousier behavior of men. Still, the idea that women had an equal right to sexual pleasure for its own sake was a truly revolutionary one. And with *Roe* v. *Wade* in 1973, pleasure was even further separated from its sobering reproductive risks.

The final precondition for "sexual revolution" was affluence. "There weren't the economic imperatives. You couldn't focus on those," says Seattle attorney Laura Cargill* (1946). "You were really left naked. You could do anything, be anything." Cargill was one who found the obligatory sexual experimentation of the Sixties "very damaging. I didn't become a person till I was twenty-seven or twenty-eight. I needed that numb time to heal. It was too much."

"Too much" for a lot of first-wavers, who entered college in a demure era and left it four years later in a resolutely scandalous one. Mores were overturned so fast that we suffered sexual culture shock. Looking back from the far shore, the old world of dress codes and dorm rules is as quaint as a daguerreotype. "Men could visit you in your room, but three of your four feet had to be on the floor," Grace Sannino recalls of Barnard, 1964.

Like smoking a joint when you could go to jail for it, sex against the rules had an edge of danger and defiance that is unimaginable today. Health-care executive Jennifer Flinton Diener, my college roommate, recalls that in our sophomore year, 1964–65, "someone had been showering with his girlfriend at night, and the plumbing was bad, and the water ran down into the tutor's room, and the guy was suspended! And so was the girl! Four years later tutors were living together in sin in the dorms as role models for the kids." In 1970, as the second wave flooded into college, the Harvard and Radcliffe dorms themselves went coed.

But fences that tumbled in the outside world only reflected battles already hard-won in individual bodies and minds. First-wavers left home with considerable sexual ignorance and timidity, the baggage of the middle-class Fifties. We were the last group to grow up under the strong influence of older people, the last to grow up with sex roles and sex segregation—in dorms, school, and sports—that made boys and girls strange and intimidating to each other. But in college, proximity and peer pressure overwhelmed parental restraint.

On liberal campuses, 1965 was the year the balance tipped; on conservative and Catholic campuses, 1970–72. Before that, if a girl slept with guys she was "fast"; after that, if she didn't she was "frigid" (mid-Sixties) or "uptight" (late Sixties). What was surprising was not the pressure from men (our mamas done told us about that), but the pressure from other women. "I can remember being a sophomore in a dorm with a group of girls that had already slept with boys, and they really wanted everybody else to do that," says New York art historian Carolyn Treat Davidson (1946). The pressure could be traumatic for both sexes as we forced ourselves over the hurdles of our inhibitions, driven not only by the heat of desire but by the desire to be cool.

"I had my first drink and my first kiss when I was eighteen years old," says Atlanta fashion buyer Dianne Henson* (1945). "I remember the date clearly: January 18, 1964. I remember what I *wore*. And I remember having a gin and tonic, literally the first time I'd tasted liquor—aside from communion wine—in my life. I remember becoming *very* drunk. And I remember that he took me outside—it was very cold—to kiss me. And he gave me a French kiss right away, and I had not even *touched* a man. I found it revolting.

"The next year, my sophomore year, I tried to sleep with someone. It was horrible. We got into bed together. I didn't know about men. I remember feeling this wad down in his nether regions. I was very turned on. But I had my legs together; I didn't know what to *do*. And he said, 'You're a virgin, aren't you?' And I said, 'Yes.' And he said, 'Well, then, I'm sorry but I can't do it.'

"I was upset, and he said, 'How does that make you feel?' And I said, 'Oh, oh, no problem,' which was a total lie. But I was so scared to admit that I wasn't sophisticated, that I didn't know what I was doing. I don't know how I lived through those days, really. I ate a lot of candy bars."

For many, virginity became an embarrassing burden, to be concealed—or left on someone's doorstep. "I was pretty innocent, but my poor friend Vicky* thought I wasn't a virgin," says Zazel Lovén. "I never had the heart to tell her—I lied. She went out and got herself deflowered just so that she could keep up with the crowd." "I had a choice of who I was going to lose my virginity to," says Donna Henes. "That, too, wasn't by accident. It was like, Who wants to be a virgin? You go to Planned Parenthood and you take the pills for six weeks, or whatever. And then it was, All right, who?"

What a contrast between those resolute initiations and the experience of a younger woman I know (1951) who lost her virginity at fifteen, fooling around with a friend on the living-room rug. Casual sex never came naturally to most first-wavers; we tended to be either monogamous or grimly promiscuous, as if taking a bitter pill for inhibition. Most second-wavers started younger and were easier with sex, and with the opposite sex. Their sexuality budded in a balmier climate than the winter night of Dianne Henson's first kiss.

The second wave was still in its malleable mid-teens when both Puritan prohibitions and sex-role distinctions began to break down. In the anti-war counterculture, membership in a gender mattered less than membership in a generation. Activities that had separated the sexes—like sports and war—had given way to shared, androgynous pursuits like demonstrations, drugs, and dancing. But underneath a surface androgyny, sensuality, and "liberation," differences between the agendas of the two sexes ran deeper than ever in the late Sixties. It was from that painful gap that feminism would be born. But first there was a sort of false spring, when the sexes seemed to be getting along just because they were so busy getting it on.

"I'd gone to an all-boys' public school in Philadelphia," says actor Joel Polis (1951). "Then I get to college, and it's 1969, and suddenly for the first time I've left home, I'm in Los Angeles, and there are all these women—girls, eighteen, nineteen. And there was such a revolution at that time; I remember a commune near USC where I'd walk in to visit my friend, and there were people making love in front of me, on the floor. And you would just step over them. It was not something that was private. And you'd just incorporate, integrate it into your whole mind-set."

The spectrum of sexual revolution ranged from high-school kids sleeping together and college kids living together to "free love communes," love with the nearest stranger, and public sex at mass gatherings. Like the rites of Dionysus, the more spontaneous and orgiastic aspects of Sixties sex were inseparable from drugs. Our parents' alcohol had merely loosened inhibitions; grass and acid dissolved interpersonal boundaries. Without drugs, the farther reaches of "free love" would never have been reached.

In 1968, NYU student and aspiring actress Bonnie Wolf was a sort of mascot to East Village luminaries like Abbie Hoffman and Paul Krassner. Bob Fass of WBAI's "Radio Unnameable" rechristened her "Bonnie Free" on the air. She staged a memorable happening called "Meet the Pudding" at NYU's Loeb Student Center. "It was in a geodesic dome in Eisner and Lubin Auditorium. We had a thousand pounds of chocolate pudding in a vat, and games, and free things. I was into that people could all get into a room together and it's all for free. Money doesn't matter. Peace for everybody.

"The Yippie pig was there, Pigasus—actually it was a sow, but they were very chauvinistic, 'cause they never admitted it was a she. I guess you couldn't run a woman for president at that time. And the Hog Farm commune, Hugh Romney, later Wavy Gravy, who took credit for the whole thing in *The Realist* even though Paul Krassner knew better. I remember there was a line of people around the block waiting to get in, and a line of tactical police force. It had been announced the night before on ABC-TV News. Seven thousand people came.

"The chocolate pudding was in a huge vat, and people ate it and dipped into it. They didn't know that it was laced with acid. I wasn't aware of that either. Somebody from the Hog Farm, the woman who was mixing the pudding, had put it in. But everybody was very happy. Eventually one guy got in and came back up in the center of the pudding, saying, 'I have been redeemed!' So then many people started jumping into it. People started taking their clothes off and filled another vat with water and were bathing in the water. All this freedom! Thousands of bodies! People were fornicating on the stairs of NYU Loeb Student Center.

"The police couldn't care less. There was no violence. But the alumni got very upset that people were fucking in the halls. I was called to the dean's office." "Bonnie Free" dropped out of NYU soon after: "Let's say they wished me a bon voyage."

Bon voyage indeed to another East Village tripper, Karen Goldin* (1949), now a Los Angeles screenwriter, who recalls taking acid for the first time from "an ex-Hell's Angel plus five people from Peru who spoke no English, all of whom I had met that night on the street." At the peak of the trip, Goldin and the biker were having sex, "and my body disappeared. It just rolled up from the toes and it went out my head in a gray tornado. And I was gone. And I had an orgasm with no body. It was absolutely one of the freest experiences."

No wonder our mothers worried about us. There was often a fine line between adventure and abuse—a line crossed in the presence of force, but also in the absence of pleasure. Weaver and fabric artist Janette Price* (1949) was "an eighteen-year-old virgin in the Haight, studying to be a kind of alternative nun. I'd already been living running around naked, but totally untouched. And I got raped by a Hell's Angel. From there it was downhill. I had a series of sexual encounters that I had no desire for and did not enjoy."

Looking back, the gap between the "sexual revolution" and feminism—from about 1965 to 1970—was a bad time for women, despite some good times. Even men, who shake their heads with fond amazement remembering Sixties sex, admit that women got the short end.

The clothing says it all. "Those were the days of miniskirts and short shorts and hot pants," Anne Strieber (1946) recalls. "Of course, you had to be fashionable. But it was like walking down the street naked. You had people grabbing at your body all the time, because you were sending out all these signals that you'd never meant to. And we were unprotected. You went out on dates alone to bars. You brought men home.

"I went out with this one fellow who gave me the willies, because he had dark eyes and you couldn't tell the difference between the pupil and the iris. He was a psychologist or a psychiatrist, and I remember he came home with me. Now, if a man was squeezing your thigh under the table and you *didn't* want to have sex with him, you *should not* invite him home, *right*? But we never learned in those days. He got so fresh I threw a chair at him." In similar circumstances, how many of us just gave in? "I found myself in a situation many times where either I'd have to get into a heavy-duty argument or let it happen," says Janette Price. "I'd say to myself, 'Okay, it's not gonna kill me.' "

We would have scorned the idea that we needed protection. "We wanted to be just like guys, taste everything," says Price. But we *weren't* just like guys. And, pre-feminism at least, most of us *were* looking for protection in the form of a relationship, whether we admitted it or not. We were a generation of women brought up with the primary goal of love and marriage. Straight, radical, or hip, our self-esteem still depended on pleasing men—and the way to please men in the late Sixties was to go to bed with them. We tried to buy love with sex. Our mothers had warned us that it wouldn't work.

"My mother would say things to the effect of, 'If you sleep with them before you marry them, they will have no reason to marry you,' " says Karen Goldin. "That was her upbringing and her idea of what pulls the man over that hump where he will commit. No humping." That attitude was everything our generation despised: dishonest, manipulative, crass. Love should be freely given. We knew our mothers had had no choice, economically or morally. They'd lived in the era of the double standard, of "good" girls and "bad" girls.

But now that we were enlightened, and sex was good and natural, there *were* no bad girls. Right?

In theory, yes. In practice, Janette Price heard guys introduce their girlfriends as "my slut." Most men didn't blame women for sleeping with them. But they might back away from a woman who had—if only because she might start to expect a commitment before the man even knew her . . . or himself. There was a painful grain of truth in our mothers' folk wisdom, and it was around that grain that the protective pearl of feminism formed.

In his theory of "the eight ages of man," psychoanalyst Erik H. Erikson says that identity precedes intimacy—that a young person needs to know who "he" is before "he" can really love. Erikson uses the masculine pronoun for both sexes, but it was observed early on that his theory didn't fit women. Pre-feminism, we seemed to find identity *through* intimacy—by becoming someone's girlfriend, wife, mother.

In the late Sixties, many men, at least middle-class men, were thrown into great identity confusion. Working-class men, on the whole, were not (yet), and those who adhered to traditional codes of manhood—like military service and romantic respect for "good" women—were as likely as ever to marry early. But counterculture men, devaluing work and war, lost the old reliable yardsticks for measuring themselves as men. Adolescence continued into the twenties; men uncertain of their identity shrank from intimacy like half-developed photographs from the light. At the same time, sex in delicious variety was suddenly available without consequences or guilt: women didn't have to get pregnant, and men didn't have to get caught. Try to get a kid with free run of a candy store to sit down to a square meal! The result: many men avoided intimate commitment —and women lost their traditional route to identity.

It hurt, but it was a blessing in disguise. The failure of intimacy forced women to grow up, to create independent sources of identity, self-esteem, and income. But first we created the women's movement, a chrysalis in which to re-create ourselves. Within its shelter, we began to examine the role we had lost, to see that in its present form it might not be worth having, and to feed subversive questions back to women who still lived in it. If the price of "love" was emotional and economic dependency—a kind of permanent childhood—then it wasn't love. (And it certainly wasn't security.) If men used our bodies, ignored our hearts, or disrespected our minds, in or out of marriage, that wasn't love either. It was fuck. Having Wavy Gravy take credit for your work—one of the straws that made "Bonnie Free" a feminist —was getting fucked. Making coffee while the men made speeches was getting fucked. Making fifty-nine cents to the dollar was getting royally fucked. And getting fucked was getting fucked, and no more.

The angry pride of early feminism finally gave women some of the sexual "protection" we had lacked. With a source of self-esteem outside the approval of men, we didn't have to throw chairs to say no. With our new self-respect, we had a reason to. Some women became celibate for a while. Others had a revelation that the soul brother they'd been so forlornly looking for was really a sister. Kinsey and other researchers have estimated that 2–5 percent of American women have an exclusive homosexual orientation. In the early Seventies, like their male counterparts, they went public, joined by thousands of other "woman-identified women" who had a choice —and chose to be gay.

With the birth of feminism, gay and straight, women took the sexual initiative away from men. The ideology that "sex is good and more sex is better" showed no signs of waning, but now such books as Lonnie Barbach's *For Yourself* appeared, teaching women how to masturbate, celebrating the beauty and individuality of female genitals in drawings more explicit than any *Penthouse* photograph. Mary Jane Sherfey published her treatise on women's near-infinite capacity for orgasms. We were instructed to go for our own pleasure, to tell our lovers how we liked it in bed (sunny side up or over easy?). On the positive side, we had finally learned to *distinguish* sex from love, and to know and like our bodies.

On the negative side, we'd learned to *separate* sex from love almost as cheerfully as men. Women became tough and invulnerable, or tried to. Severing the emotions from the genitals got rid of pain; the trouble was, sensitivity went with it. We hadn't discovered our own sexuality so much as trained ourselves to mimic men's. And we hadn't resurrected the body so much as objectified it. The search for spontaneity and ecstasy had ended in performance and technique.

The irony of the successful "sexual revolution" was that neither the impersonal fertility rites of the Sixties nor the bedroom aerobics of the Seventies had the awful magic of those first gropings in a dark car. Sexual veterans of both genders became nostalgic for the days of their blundering innocence, before heart, soul, and body parted company. Women were no longer "frigid"—the "big O" had become a skill at least as mandatory as the Three R's—but men were increasingly impotent, and therapists reported a puzzling new epidemic: "lack of desire." By 1982, herpes type II was reported to have infected twenty million Americans, the great majority of them white, middle class, and twenty to thirty-nine years old. It began to seem that no-holds-barred sex was not so "natural" for humans as it was for various hitchhiking microorganisms. As we wilted, they throve. ("AIDS, to me, is a metaphor for liberalism run amok," says *Festivals* editor Ken Guentert. "It's the body's refusal to attack anything. It's sort of the ultimate tolerance.")

The question has to be asked. Was the "sexual revolution" our one serious mistake? Certainly it did more than any other aspect of our behavior—even our anti-Americanism, the runner-up—to alienate the majority and get the rest of our vision condemned. As such, it hardly helped to save the world. "I think the reason that Reagan is getting such good play right now is that we were a little extreme in the Sixties," Farm founder Stephen Gaskin told an interviewer for *The Sun.* "And now we're being paid back for fucking in the streets. Next time, I'm not interested so much in that as I am in making real solid social changes that last for decades."[1]

One regrettable social change we *did* make, which has already lasted two decades, is that children are now exposed to sexuality before they're ready for it—or for its consequences. At the extreme, I heard stories of a kind of hippie child abuse. "I have friends who were quite radical with their kids," says Marc Barasch. "They're a little older than me, had kids a little earlier. They would have the kid in bed. The husband would be making love to the wife and the little kid would be riding the pony." "I've seen some really fucked-up kids from flower-child marriages," says Kathy Brimlow, who also knows some wonderful kids from flower-child marriages. The difference: "Some parents didn't have the ideals to back up their lifestyle. So the kids are seeing cheap drugs, sex, oblivious parents, parents who condoned sexual activity in the house for kids with everybody. And the kids are just lost. Some of them have been smoking pot since they were two."

Such stories are mercifully rare. But even the most protected kids are now routinely exposed to sexual pressures by age ten or eleven, through the media, music, and peer culture. And despite the increased availability of information on birth control, there are more than a million teenage pregnancies every year. Researchers estimate that 40 percent of today's fourteen-year-old girls will be pregnant at least once by age twenty. "I've talked to many women who are glad they don't have daughters," says Anne Strieber. "They wouldn't know what to say to them. What are you supposed to say? So far and no further?"

The Christian far right's remedy for these excesses is to try to turn back the clock, restore the Puritan patriarchy, and lock Pandora, the sexual woman, back in her box. That effort is probably doomed, but if it were to succeed, it would be a disaster. The triumph of the Sixties is that the cruel old controls on sexuality—fear and shame—were abolished; the problem is that new controls have been slow to evolve. We've had an anarchic interregnum, with the danger of a counter-revolutionary coup if the "new order" doesn't start to generate an organic order of its own.

Fortunately, our generation is finally beginning to thrash out a post-revolutionary morality. Activists like Andrea Dworkin (1946) of Women Against Pornography and Juli Loesch (1951) of Feminists for Life may not be typical—the new controls are far more likely to be voluntary than mandatory—but they herald a recoil from excess in precisely the age group that once called for total liberation. They suggest a desire, not only to protect the helpless, but once again to make special, even sacred, a life force that has been cheapened and commercialized.

Now the "free love" experiment has been tried. No one need wonder anymore whether it's the answer. And there is a world of difference between obeying moral strictures out of fear and observing self-imposed restraints out of understanding. Like Adam and Eve, we ate from the tree of knowledge and paid for it. We learned by exile that Paradise is a place defined and protected by walls; we learned by spillage that pleasure is like water, deeper when contained within forms—though forms are many. We learned that love for the body is sometimes expressed by *not* making love; that privacy isn't prudery, and is probably "natural." And like a child allowed to touch a hot stove, we learned it all for ourselves. Now we are beginning to combine the new freedoms of the sexual revolution with new restraints that can protect and enhance them.

Between friends of different sexual preferences, for instance, there is now ease and understanding—a major advance over ten years ago, when a friend's coming out could be an occasion of awkwardness and pain. Despite the growing hysteria over AIDS, in 1985 53 percent of the American public believed that "homosexuals as a group are becoming more accepted by society," while 34 percent thought "less accepted." In 1983, the figures were 46 percent and 43 percent, respectively. Sexually transmitted diseases are curing us of "ultimate tolerance"—even the gay male community is trying to reintegrate sex with love—but only a minority of Americans have reacted to the other extreme. The majority seems to be evolving toward a new ethic in which self-respecting sexual conduct is more important than the gender of one's partner(s).

According to emerging post-Puritan mores, the problem of teenage pregnancy has to be fought with information and incentives, not with a fire extinguisher of fear and shame. A *Time* magazine poll, taken in 1985 by Yankelovich, Skelly and White, Inc., found that 78 percent of Americans "favor sex education in the schools, including information about birth control."[2] In St. Paul, Chicago, and other

cities, high-school health clinics that dispense contraceptive prescrip-
tions (with parental permission) have drawn fire from conservative
groups—and cut the pregnancy rate in half. The most effective programs couple a positive attitude toward sex with positive reasons to
be responsible: health and hope for the future. Recognizing that poor
teenagers need goals, skills, and self-respect as much as they need
sex education, Janice Anderson (1949), a successful black business-
woman in Milwaukee, founded Reach for the Stars, "a volunteer
program that pairs inner-city adolescents with black role models who
are successful achievers."[3]

The sexuality of young adults is another place where we are finding
a badly needed balance of freedom and discretion. Here, our role
model is the generation after us—the later second wave and those
born after 1958. These younger people grew up without either the
inhibitions of their older siblings or the desperation to break through
them. They had a chance to observe our excesses and mistakes and
to learn from them. And they grew up with feminism, in a climate
of friendship, equality, and respect between the sexes. Eros takes a
natural and proportionate place in their lives. Both my brothers (born
in 1956 and 1959) discovered sex at their own pace, with lovers who
were friends first. And both lived with best-friend lovers for a few
years before deciding to get married. Their older siblings had to labor
through twenty years of changes to reach the same point.

Yet even many first-wavers benefited from the "revolution."
"Someone asked me about my childhood, and I said, 'Oh, I was very
shy,'" says New Jersey psychologist Margie White (1946). "'I was
a very repressed and inhibited child.' And she said, 'But you're not
like that now!' And I said, 'Well, I grew up in the Sixties!' That was
a terrific period for me, because there were no boundaries. I guess
it would have been more traumatic for someone who needed boundaries, but for me it was a very constructive thing. Very free."

Like White, those who benefited (like those who got the most out
of drugs) were those who could control the flow of change, who had
enough inner-direction to use freedom rather than be used by it.
White America was a culture that had been deeply afraid of sex, and

in the Sixties we went into the dragon's lair to confront that fear. The confrontation freed many people to find their natural level of loving and their unblocked creative springs. These real victors in the sexual revolution are hard to pick out, because they don't make a display or a profession of sexuality. They're not the aggressively "liberated," still busy trading insults with Puritanism. They're just clear-eyed and easy-bodied, a subtly new kind of American. They have that discreet yet uninhibited sensuality that has always intrigued us in French films. And they have a lot of energy free for other things.

There's no question that these new post-Puritans enjoy life on earth. But are they going to save the world? Not necessarily. The failed experiment at Rajneeshpuram suggests that Reich was wrong: freeing sex doesn't automatically banish the pathology of power. One can be orgasmic and a paranoiac leader (like Rajneesh's regent, Ma Anand Sheela), or a cowed follower, or an ardent materialist. Only the sexually repressed could have believed so fervently in the re- deeming power of sex. When the forbidden fruit is a bowl of apples on the table, the difficulty of being human just moves on. There are other things to long for and be afraid of.

Like love.

Mates

. . . Till life do us part.
— H O M E M A D E   M A R R I A G E   V O W S ,   1 9 8 3

Statistics tell the toll. While the national divorce rate doubled during the Seventies, it tripled among the Sixties generation—we accounted for three of every four divorces in that decade—and it "has quadru- pled for couples under thirty since 1960,"[4] according to Landon Jones, author of *Great Expectations: America and the Baby Boom Generation.* Barely half our early marriages are still standing, and their inhabitants have the superstitious humility of dwellers in an earthquake zone. "Eighteen years is just eighteen years," says Catherine Banghart. "You do it while it works. And you feel really lucky. And that's all you can know."

Dramatic as the divorce figures are, they don't tell half the story. Millions of unrecorded unions were as momentous as marriages, and ended, if they ended, with as much pain. The change in one generation is striking. While our parents tried for one lifelong partnership, first- and early second-wavers have normally had three or four major loves in twenty years. (Later second-wavers, more efficient, tend toward two: one for practice and heartbreak, one for real.) Those now settled with someone express the cautious hope, rather than the intent, that it will last, as if self and other were incalculable natural forces needing propitiation. "I've recently been married for the third time," *Sun* editor Sy Safransky told me. "I hope this is the last time. But it's always dangerous to feel you understand too much about this."

Others are still searching. Survivors of emotional fission approach each other warily, uncertain whether they'll find comfort or a fresh battle. The happiest, most hopeful new couples I know resemble weary veterans, leaning fraternally together as they limp down the road. And six million of us, by choice or default, live alone.

Men and women, paired or single, straight or gay, we're all veterans of this most intimate battlefront. It is probably accurate to say that facing one's lover, naked, took more courage than facing a squad of cops in full riot gear. "We, the New Age culture or counterculture, did know some things that were better," Marc Sarkady says confidently. "It was clear that there would be no racism if people lived the way we lived. There would be no classism. We didn't want wars, and we weren't going to make war. It didn't mean that there would be no misunderstandings between men and women, because . . ." The certainty fades from his voice. "There were things we didn't understand yet." We still don't. Our biggest gain from twenty years of struggle has been a genuine respect for our opponents—and the realization that some things pass understanding.

"The war between the sexes" was a Fifties joke. Blondie and Dagwood, Ralph and Alice Kramden, Thurber's sneaking husbands and nagging wives, acted out broad parodies of the conflicts between our parents. This was cold war, held in check by necessity. Men and women were assumed to be irreconcilably different and mutually incomplete, unable to get along with or without each other, designed to lock together in the economic and emotional symbiosis of traditional marriage. Our generation split that social atom, throwing all assumptions about men and women to the winds, and releasing elemental forces of longing and rage. "Hot" war broke out between the sexes around 1970, and it was declared by women.

One of the forces that freed female energy was education. We were the most educated generation of American women in history. Only 8 percent of our mothers had graduated from college; 20 percent of us did. The results were not what our parents or professors had intended. Most first-wave women were sent to college, like Gloria Benedetta, "to marry a doctor, an engineer, or a scientist, to be a good wife and an educated mother." If we did use our education in the marketplace, it would be as a stopgap: "I was supposed to marry a doctor and be a teacher until I married him," says Donna Henes.

But as the number of women in school reached critical mass, the power of education was not so easily contained. College bestowed two crucial gifts: the potential to survive financially on our own, and a taste of being whole. As students, women got to use mind, soul, and curiosity in direct encounter with the world. We found that we weren't as different from men as we'd been led to believe. And if that was the case, maybe we didn't need them to complete us.

But between the first insight and the second, years could pass. It was a gradual process, the coming to wholeness of women that would revolutionize the basis of love as well as the gender of work. Education had planted a time bomb, but in the late Sixties, most first-wave women went ahead with the old program. Though we did go to work in record numbers—as psychologist Marian Goodman says, "I had a college education, and I was going to use it"—by twenty-one or twenty-two most of us were either married or, in Anne Strieber's words, "looking rather desperately for a man." The belief was still deeply ingrained that "you couldn't really *be* anybody without one."

Some first-wave women may have had the sense of self to fall in love at twenty, but more of us fell into something else and called it love. *Sex:* My own first "serious relationship" was a case of belated teenage lust. *Convention:* "I had this strong feeling that I had to get married when I finished college. If you didn't get married and have children, what would you do with your life?" (Marian Goodman). *Rebellion:* "I was seeing two guys, and they were like God and the Devil. One had been in the Peace Corps. And look who I chose: the first punk of the world. He sharpened his belt buckle to go out on demonstrations. He told me I was the smartest woman he'd ever met" (Donna Henes). *Projection:* "I think I married Jim* because of his devotion to his music. He did practice every day, and that's what I was looking for in myself. Clarity of purpose" (Ananda Saha).

Lousy reasons to get married? Maybe, but probably not much different from the range of our mothers' reasons. The difference is that our mothers had regarded the married state as an end in itself. Economically and morally, it was hard for a woman of their generation to live outside it. But by the late Sixties to early Seventies, women had multiplying options—economic, sexual, emotional, spiritual. Those options not only consoled and engrossed women who had failed to marry early, they also began to attract women who *had* married early. Growth, exploration, and authenticity were becoming the leading values of our generation. They were values that did not fit very well inside the fixed structure of traditional marriage. They especially did not fit very well inside the traditional wife.

"I was always too loud, too *boom* for a female," says artist Joan Giannecchini. "Growing up I'd been pretty much of a misfit, too inclined to do what I damn well pleased instead of what I was supposed to do. Marrying this nice person was about acquiescing and saying I'll try. It was a ghastly mistake. I was twenty when I married, and I had a kid right away.

"My husband didn't want me to work. He wanted me to stay home and take care of the little one. But I took a job working part time for a very radical and politically involved lawyer. One of the young women who did filing in this law firm had the long hair, braids. She was probably no more than two years younger than I was. She was always talking about turning on with her friends. And so she gave me a joint. And I took it home.

"I will never forget this night. We had a fireplace, we lived in the burbs—a little two-story house and a Porsche, all the trappings. It was perfect. My husband had an airplane and used to go out and fly all the time. So he's off flying and I'm looking at this joint. Oh my God, what's going to happen if I smoke this? You hear all this stuff about how you'll never come back. This was about 1965 or '66.

"I sat down on that very couch right there in front of the fireplace and I lit this joint. I smoked it. I remember looking at the fire and thinking that it was looking awfully beautiful. And then I fell asleep. The next morning I said, gee, I must not have done it right. Nothing happened.

"In the ensuing months, three young students got busted for marijuana and came to the office. I got to know them, and we started hanging out a little bit together. Here I am a housewife-secretary, dressed like a total asshole in my little outfit, and they had long hair, frizzed or braided, long skirts with big ruffles on the bottom. I had a car, and they did not. They were flat broke. My boss was going to represent them in trade for handmade ceramics, a string of beads. But they had a friend whose parents had a five-hundred-acre plot of land in the Santa Cruz mountains, and they were going to start a commune, whatever that meant.

"So they would come into the office along about quitting time and say, 'What are you doing tonight? Do you want to come up to the land and have dinner and hang out?' So I'd give them a ride up there. And the place was . . . they had wells tapped and you could take a shower on the side of the mountain and everybody ran around without any clothes on and nobody was nasty. It was just paradise. All the while I'm utterly miserable in my own house, wondering, What am I doing here?

"These kids were, of course, not only experimenting with marijuana, they were taking acid and anything else they could get their hands on. But I had much more in common with them than the people who were my friends. Up on the land we would talk about ideas and feelings, and it was like you could see who you were. You could express yourself, the part of you that nobody else wanted to hear.

"A few of them were talking about this new music thing that was going on up in San Francisco. Then one day I picked up a *Life* magazine, and there was this huge color spread of the Fillmore Auditorium. The smoke, the weirdos, the psychedelic images on the wall—it was like Halloween every night! My eyes were bulging. I said, omigod, I've got to go there. So I take this poor unsuspecting man that I'm married to, and I said, 'We've got to go up to the Fillmore Auditorium.' And he says, 'What's that?' He says, 'Okay.'

"The Fillmore Auditorium was on Fillmore Street, which was el sleazo. Bill* was panicked about parking the car there. So I'm driving up and down the street trying to find a place under a light, and I'm looking up at this brick building. The windows were open and there were freaks literally hanging out of the windows. We finally park and go up this long flight of stairs. There are all kinds of people lying around on the stairs stoned to the gills, begging for money to get in. There was some guy in a kamikaze outfit that got the outfit-of-the-year award. Goggles and this little head thing and a batman cape.

"Frank Zappa was playing that night, and *he* looked completely bizarre and weird. He came out and said, 'I'm going to do a new number for you now. It's called "The Electric Banana."' And I cracked up. He started jumping up and down with his guitar on the stage, and my life has never been the same! Talk about seeing the person you're married to in the most peculiar light: I was so anxious to find out what all this energy and excitement was about, and he was utterly repulsed by it. He was kind of hiding in a corner while I ran around looking at everybody.

"I left about six months later. On the surface, everything was just fine. We were paying a mortgage, we had a kid, a lawn, there were gardenias in the garden, a redwood deck was being built in the back. All things were progressing on all fronts the way they should be. I couldn't articulate what was wrong, because I didn't know. I thought that what was basically wrong was so solidly at the foundation of everything that nothing he could have done would have made any difference.

"I struggled and struggled and struggled with it, back and forth. Leaving him was not really the big hurdle, because I had already gone past that. But I had a child, and I didn't want to take her either. I knew the life I was going to seek out, and I didn't feel confident enough about my choice to drag her along and bring her up in that existence.

"When I finally left, I didn't know I was going to do it. Driving home from work one day, I drove by this apartment house with a sign outside that said 'Apartments for Rent.' I screeched to a stop. Jumped out of the car, ran in, and asked if they had a furnished one. The guy said yeah. 'Fine, I'll take it.' I gave him some money and I drove home and said, 'I'm leaving tomorrow.' He said, 'What are you talking about?' I said, 'I'm sorry, but I can't do this anymore.'

"I went to this place with my two suitcases, which was all I took with me. And looking at this ghastly furnished apartment, which backed up to the railroad tracks . . . it had that kind of stick furniture covered with lacquer, with the little legs that look like they're stuck on with glue and chewing gum. It looked like hell. I walked in there and all I saw was freedom." From the furnished room, Giannecchini moved up to the commune for four months, then went to Europe.

Giannecchini left in 1968, a forerunner of the unprecedented epidemic that would sweep the early Seventies: women leaving men. It wasn't only that women's new earning power freed them to opt out of marriages that weren't good. It was also that the definition of a "good" marriage was undergoing violent transformation. In place of the old bargain—security for her, superiority and comfort for him—women were beginning to demand equal respect and satisfaction. First-wave marriages were being challenged to evolve from a symbiosis of two unlike and unequal creatures to a partnership of equals with the same needs and rights.

DO YOU BELIEVE IN MAGIC?

Every marriage is unique, but first-wave marriages that failed to evolve seem to fall into certain patterns:

THE IDOLIZER AND THE FEET OF CLAY   "Once when I took acid, it became very clear to me that Jim didn't know who he was or what he was doing, and I'd thought that he did," Ananda Saha recalls. "His music was really a crutch to him rather than a clear statement of his inner voice, or at least it seemed that way to me. He's still doing his music. . . . So I took off my wedding ring and I said we're not married anymore."

CINDERELLA AND THE TRADITIONALIST   "I had to get married," says Los Angeles insurance agent Caroline Johnson. "I got out of high school in '67 and had a baby right away. So I was out of school for a couple of years. I got a job. And then, when my kid was young, I went back to school part-time, in '69. While I was in college the change happened to me. I had been extremely subordinate. Couldn't even write checks. And then I got out in the world and realized that I was very bright and very valuable to other people.

"So I got real angry and I tried to make some changes at home, and, y'know, they weren't going to happen. He was just very traditional. If I wanted to work or go to school it was, 'Make sure you finish all the housework, then you can go.' " Johnson left her husband at age twenty-two and threw herself into the anti-war and women's movements. "I went from being a very submissive female to Superwoman—single parent and independent head of a household. Of course it was a reaction."

THE RISING STAR AND THE PUT-DOWN ARTIST   "My husband was a graduate student," says Pittsburgh psychologist Marian Goodman. "I was working full-time, putting him through grad school. He worked part-time, but mine was the major salary. The women's movement had to be one of the influences as to why that marriage didn't last. Because as I grew stronger, it became more and more threatening to him. He was very opposed to my joining a women's group. He came right out and said, 'I don't think it will do you any good. I think it will do you harm.' That was when I started to realize that his head was not where my head was.

"He had problems in grad school. Flunked comps twice, which meant he couldn't finish his master's. When he finished, it was supposed to be my turn to go back to school and get a master's degree, but he couldn't get his. So I stopped working and entered the full-time program. Six weeks later I left him. He had been putting me down for a long time in order to move himself up. The day I finally walked out the door, there was a realization that I was starting to believe him. I came home with two A's in two courses, and he said, 'It's an easy program.' I said to him, 'You've said your last put-down to me,' and I walked out." Goodman had been married six years.

THE HANDMAIDEN AND THE NARCISSIST   "He's very self-centered, and that was just part of loving him, that came with the territory," says lawyer Carla Wilder* (1951) of her first husband, to whom she was married for seven years. "In a lot of ways he was incredibly dependent on me to baby him, to mother him. I was behind his going to law school. I did everything for him, the same as I saw my mother do for my father. This man was my world. It wasn't until I was about to start law school that he told me that he had been seeing this woman in his class. He declared his love for both of us and said he wasn't able to make a decision."

"I have never been so lonely as married," says airline purser Gloria Benedetta of her first marriage. "Because you keep trying to communicate with this individual, and there's nothing. I've never been a screamer or a yeller. I believe in mature, rational, adult discussion, where you sit down and say, 'Okay, here's the problem.' This man would get up and walk out of the room. When after eight years I decided I wanted a divorce, he said, 'I don't understand. I'm very happy with this relationship.' I said, 'I've spent the last three years telling you that I was very unhappy, and why, and you don't remember any of it?' He said, 'No.' I asked him, 'Are you willing to take care of any of *my* needs?' He got very huffy and said, 'I don't even know what your needs *are.*' I was just another one of his *things,* like his car and his clothes.''

As these stories show, both sexes had a hard time with the changing balance of power. Men were alarmed to feel their authority and superiority slipping away. But women weren't entirely rational, either. Why couldn't Ananda Saha forgive her musician husband for being merely human? Why did Marian Goodman start to believe her husband's slights? Why did Wilder and Benedetta serve incorrigible narcissists for so long? (''I spent two years in therapy asking myself that question,'' says Wilder ruefully.) The old hierarchy died hard. When Prometheus stole fire from the gods, though they dwindled in his eyes, he still feared retribution. As women began to reclaim some of the power we'd projected onto men, we became both contemptuous of their weaknesses and hypersensitive to their disapproval—symptoms of our own Promethean presumption and guilt. It would take time to see men in their true proportions, as humans no bigger than ourselves.

''He was hopeless at the time, but if I had stayed, the way he is now—he's okay,'' says Caroline Johnson, who has become friends with her son's father in the last five years and now sees their marriage differently. ''At the time, I thought it was all his fault. I didn't realize that I was just as angry at myself as I was at him. And I didn't appreciate that it was a very difficult time for him, too, being young and in school and having this family to support.'' She concludes with a fitting epitaph for many of our early marriages: ''We were both babies, and I was growing up faster than he was.''

Perhaps the first-wave couples that survived were those who were able to keep pace in their growth. (Another exception: many marriages of Vietnam vets, surprisingly tough compounds of terrible stress, compassion, and loyalty.) Most of us *were* wildly growing and changing, as if an entirely new, mutant biological stage had been added to the normal process of maturing. (Was it the strontium 90 in our childhood milk?) We plunged into this second adolescence—

and pushed each other in—not because we didn't want to grow up, but because we *did*. It had dawned on us that simply turning twenty-one, putting on the costume, and playing the role did not make an adult. Emotionally, many of our parents and politicians were big babies. So we rejected the costume and the role for the sham that they were, and we rejected relationships in which the partners were each other's mommy and daddy. We set out on the road toward a difficult new ideal: the marriage of grown-up friends.

Paradoxically, that road often began in solitude. "My big thing after I got divorced was, *What am I like? I don't remember anymore,*" says Marian Goodman. "I consciously wanted not to get too closely involved with anyone. I needed a good five or six months before I even wanted to start dating. One of the things I did that so many of us did was to take back my maiden name. It was an incredible feeling of identity." Gloria Benedetta was single for five years after her divorce: "I did not have one single romance. And I was never lonely. I loved it. I did everything that I ever wanted to do, just for me."

The period of solitude might begin in painful breakdown. Carla Wilder "went on a summer-long coke binge, where I got real crazy." Carl Nagin rented a sheep farmer's trailer on the Isle of Skye and spent two months alone, mourning the end of an intense relationship. "I went a little mad, I think. I heard voices, cried a lot. It was emotional turmoil and purging." And it became a rebirth: "When I left the island I felt a real strength in myself that I'd never felt before." After a time of healing, in the root sense of "making whole," we were ready to try again. "I spent a year by myself, finally living my own life," says Carla Wilder. "I discovered during that time what it was that I really wanted out of a relationship. And then I decided I was going to be open to it."

Open to love, that is, but slow to marry. To burned and wary first-wavers, as well as keep-your-options-open second-wavers, the new open-door institution of living together offered a way to test the waters and hedge the bets. "The trend toward living together has increased tenfold in the past decade," social-science writers Jacqueline Simenauer and David Carroll reported in 1982. "Approximately half of all single men and a third of all single women have at one time or another lived with a member of the opposite sex."[5] In the Seventies, living together became the laboratory of the new love, a halfway house to marriage or a semipermanent substitute for it. But there was less and less real difference between cohabitation and the marriage easily ended by no-fault, no-consent divorce—as witness the fact that some unmarried couples began to draw up legal contracts. (Probably the biggest difference was that living-together couples were less likely to have children, though some did.)

We had entered a middle phase with problems of its own. The old standard of a "good" relationship had been set by convention and sealed by dependency. Now convention had been blown to bits, personal independence was the ideal, and we needed new reasons to stay together, a new standard for the relationship worth saving. To what authority could we refer such judgments? (No wonder some people let their gurus pick their mates!) Many of us simply refused to decide, playing it one day at a time until the accumulated weight of good and bad days tipped the balance. The advantage of this method was that it gave the heart time to put down stealthy roots; the danger was inertia—and who could be sure of the difference? Others couldn't bear that much uncertainty, and plunged in and out of commitments based on romantic or political fantasies of what a relationship *should* be.

That was a common mistake. Rejecting inherited values, our generation tried to rethink all the basics of human life before we'd had time to re-feel them. In the vacuum left by the death of convention, all kinds of idealisms ran rampant, creating some relationships that could never survive and destroying some that probably could have. There was a lot of hurt. We chalked it up to spiritual growth. "You get into relationships you shouldn't be in from a certain point of view," says Sy Safransky. "Of course, you should be in whatever you're in, because that's where the teaching is. 'How did I end up with this person? Oh, yes. This is exactly what I need to learn.' " We all needed to learn that this least rational of realms would not submit to our ideas or our ideals. For instance:

THE IDEAL OF COMRADES IN THE STRUGGLE   Revolutionary politics were romantic. How many of us fell unforgettably in love at a demonstration or in a radical cell? Sexual and political passions fueled each other, and personality conflicts were submerged in a common purpose. Tina Ivans describes love affairs within the Socialist Workers Party as "ready-made," because you were never at a loss for something to talk about! But when the political winds changed, most such relationships lost their raison d'être. Joan Giannecchini left the filmmaker lover who'd been her political mentor when she realized that she "didn't like his point of view." Differences surfaced, and we discovered that we'd been in love with an idea more than with each other.

THE IDEAL OF THE OPPRESSED LIBERATOR   An upper-middle-class midwestern girl runs away to the West Coast with a poor black lover and has his baby. Eighteen months later, she wants to come home. Her father says, "I'll take you back if you leave the kid." She does. A WASP aristocrat has a love affair with a Hispanic junkie (both women). A Peace Corps volunteer marries an Ecuadorean Indian. A Marine photographer brings home a Vietnamese bride.

Love across race, class, and cultural lines was epidemic in our generation. Politics, travel, and the integration of school and work made such romances richly available. Qualities of the historical moment—the communications explosion, the fascination with other cultures, the feeling that it was time for old, false barriers to fall—made crossover couples feel like the advance guard of a new humanity. And in a sense they were—or their children are. My niece Paloma Nuñez (1978) is a Mexican-Jewish citizen of the world.

But again, many of us fell in love with an idea or a symbol (or a status symbol), not an individual. The fantasy that people of another race or class or nation were somehow superhuman—more radical, sensual, or mystical than thou—could pack an erotic and emotional wallop, but it was as prejudiced as its opposite. Intimate relationships were highly effective in curing people of that fantasy, and the disillusion probably did more for one world than the romance did. Discovering that one's exotic partner had a full set of human flaws, *plus* the psychological baggage of another culture, shipwrecked the majority of such relationships, including my sister's as well as the Marine photographer's (at high cost to the children). Those that survived should be studied as models of negotiation. (One definite finding: Class and culture are the tough differences, not race per se.)

THE IDEAL OF PERFECT EQUALITY   In the early days of feminism, housework and money were mine-field issues. To avoid any inequity, some couples, like English professor Sarah Weil and her ex-husband, a scientist, tried to run a household "quite theoretically, on those principles that we were equals, and that men and women shared everything. There was a rage for making contracts about sharing housework," says Weil. "I remember that we did that, and even wrote it down. When I look back I think that was extremely stupid. It just demonstrates our youthfulness and insensitivity to how people really work things out. We soon discovered that those new moral imperatives, like any others, could be used as weapons."

THE IDEAL OF ANDROGYNY   A major trend in our generation's thought has been that gender differences are creations of culture, and that the way to guarantee equality of the sexes is to make them as alike as possible. In the first wave, this required a kind of psychic sex-change surgery: women struggled to build up their own assertiveness and ambition while they *noodged* men to be more nurturing and open. Many women who hadn't had babies before feminism put them off indefinitely for fear of succumbing to traditional feminity. Second-wavers practiced a more androgynous style of adulthood from the start: Both sexes planned to devote their twenties to self, career, and relationship, and to become "parents" around thirty.

Despite professional rivalry and regressive yearnings for mother-hood or Monday night football, dedicated childless couples could approach the androgynous ideal. But the arrival of a baby blew it all to hell, bringing out differences deeply rooted in biology and child-hood. "Right after her birth, I was so aware of my physiology deter-mining my emotions," Lynne Burbridge said when her daughter was eight months old. "It was really striking. Feelings came out in me that men and women are very, very different. I'm supposed to have a career. I really should be working right now. We need the money. But it doesn't feel right to me. My mother enjoyed being at home, and I think I still have some of that in me." (But Lynne was back at work part-time four months later.)

Lynne's husband, Jay Newman, confesses to the complementary atavism. "It feels good for me to be the main breadwinner," he says. "My father was the breadwinner. I want to be. But then there's the undercurrent of, 'Wait a second. I'm also the New Age mensch here. I go shopping, do the wash, iron my clothes. Why shouldn't my wife be bringing home a lot of money and make my life easier?' So it's a conflict."

If Burbridge and Newman are a little sheepish about their post-partum semi-traditionalism, a couple on the borderline of the next generation, Stacey and Peter Meadows Adels, both attorneys, illus-trate the problems posed by a rigid androgynous ideal. During the six months Stacey stayed home to nurse Jonah, "I resented Peter, that he was out in the world. I was miserable with the traditional role. When you're a mother, you're not doing work that's recognized as productive, and that makes all the difference in your self-esteem. I wanted to tell people, 'Listen, I'm a lawyer. I'm not just a house-wife.' " "And I was very jealous of her," says Peter. "I hate my job right now. I would have loved to quit and stay home for a few months. But I'm still expected to be the one to bring home the bacon."

Stacey's return to work full-time "equalized our relationship a great deal," she says. "Now we both do all the chores, and we both take care of the food shopping and the child care. The resentments aren't there anymore. But we are completely strung out. When you have two parents working full-time, it's a scramble. The hardest thing is finding time for one another." At last, Peter says, he and Stacey have achieved equality: "Now that she's back at work, we are equally miserable." (By the fall of '86, though, Stacey described their lives as "hectic but fulfilling." Peter had left real-estate law for a lower-paying job with a non-profit agency, which he loves. Stacey had been promoted, and was enjoying her job with the City of Philadelphia. And she was pregnant with their second child: "I plan to be off for about three months.")

THE IDEAL OF TOTAL HONESTY   Particularly damaging to her marriage, Sarah Weil feels, "was the idea that you should *talk* about everything. You had to *deal* with everything. You had to be *up front* about everything. Confrontation, politics, was to go from the street into the bedroom. It was an agonizing demand."

Such grueling candor was often associated with the culture of group therapy, or with schools of spiritual growth where you were encouraged to let it all hang out so you could see what it was. "My second marriage ended partly because of the spiritual work we were doing with Ram Dass and Trungpa," says Ananda Saha. "It really did accelerate changes very fast, too fast to assimilate. It loosened up a lot of internal trauma without time or means at hand to process it. I could no longer pretend to be anyone but myself. I needed to be more involved with people, and he didn't want me to. I couldn't take that anymore. The marriage ended bitterly."

Janette Price got skewered on the crossing of two Sixties values: experience and honesty, "tasting everything" and telling the truth. "By basic nature I was never promiscuous," she says. "Still, I acquired a very long list. And here I am, thirty-six years old, and I'm in a relationship where the most important thing is honesty and knowing who you're with. He *asked,* and I openly told him, thinking, 'Well, you love me, so anything I've done you will accept.' And it tore him apart.

"He doesn't understand that it was not my choice. I didn't know sexual desire. I always felt awkward and inadequate. Now I'm in a situation where I love someone so completely that there's no effort. I *still* don't know what I'm doing, I just know I'm loving. And he interprets it as my being experienced. He imagines those thirty guys sweating on top of me. It's torturing us. We are two people who are intellectually, spiritually, psychically, in every way compatible, and yet this comes up every other day."

THE IDEAL OF NON-POSSESSIVE LOVE   Veterans of this one wince with pain recalling their bouts with that unenlightened emotion, jealousy. The open relationship is an ideal that makes sense in theory—who hasn't loved more than one person at a time?—but usually wreaks havoc in practice. A cautious assessment from Marc Sarkady:

"This blond woman . . . we met at the Newport Folk Festival in a very cosmic way. The next day she moved in with me. A week later she told me she didn't want to be monogamous but she still wanted to live with me. I remember trying to deal with that! That started a process of about ten years of experimenting with relationships and seeing what I thought was the right way for me to be. I've been through a lot trying to figure it out.

"What I think now is that there is no objective moral right way for everyone, but it works for most people to be one-to-one with each other. I've worked with jealousy over the course of almost twenty years. It does get less, but it doesn't go away. Given how painful it is, I don't want to live like that or impose it on others. But I do see that some other kind of life may be possible in a community setting, where people are really supporting each other and there's room for different lifestyles. It works at microcommunities like East Wind" (one of the Federation of Egalitarian Communities—Twin Oaks was the first—originally based on B. F. Skinner's *Walden Two*).

When I was in the Magick Land, a foxy lady with long red braids came into the yurt to discuss mermaids. After she left, Morning Glory surprised me by saying, "I try to be extra nice to her, because she's Otter's other woman." Her estimate of open marriage, "triads," and "expanded families": "There are times when I pull my hair out, but I am really glad I stuck by it all the way through, even when it hurts. We have for ten years now. It has to do with genuine freedoms, a genuine liberation of the spirit." On the other hand, in the communal Lyman Family it's just the opposite: most Family members have changed partners more than once in twenty years, but while paired, they are faithful. "Adultery, a serious social offense, is unheard of," marveled a newspaper reporter who visited the Lymans. "The singles among them are celibate."[6] Stephen Gaskin's Farm stressed an even more traditional monogamy.

THE IDEAL OF ROMANTIC LOVE   We didn't invent this one, but the collapse of practical grounds for marriage freed us to pursue it with a recklessness formerly reserved to movie stars. "I always made the woman into a goddess," says thrice-married Sy Safransky. "You project your own needs onto somebody else, not seeing who they are." Addicts of the infatuation high often marry the wrong person, or leave the right one when the magic fades, or turn down a perfectly sound possibility because it lacks that *je ne sais quoi.* "There's only one man that I in some ways would consider marrying," says thirty-nine-year-old social worker Ellen Herman. "He's an executive, and he was wonderful in a lot of ways. He never lost his manliness, and he also had a heart, he could cry. I did love him, and he did love me. But there just wasn't something right about it. I guess I wasn't *in* love with him in that most fundamental sense." (Hey Ellen, you jerk, what's his phone number?)

In short, we often demanded the impossible of a relationship: everything. It should be romantic, yet also comfortable. Egalitarian, but non-competitive. The man should be kind and sensitive, but also successful and brilliant. The woman should be bright and independent, but also beautiful and caring. Both should be deeply involved in work, yet spend quality time together. Each would give the other freedom, of course, but the relationship should be so perfect that neither is ever seriously attracted to anyone else.

It's all our ideals rolled into one, and it's a crock. Yet some of us continue to judge real relationships by this Olympian standard, and to find them subtly wanting. Others hold off on commitment because that magical woman or man might be just around the corner; what if she or he showed up and you'd already settled for less?! The pursuit of the unattainable is spurred by this ideal: if you never "get" someone, you can continue to believe that with him or her you could have had it all.

Are high ideals a block to the achievement of intimacy? Or are they really a cover for the fear of intimacy? Given what most of us have been through, that's not an unreasonable fear. But as we get older, loneliness can become more frightening, the lure of a port in the storm more compelling to the most inveterate free spirit. "Every single movie Paul Mazursky ever made is about finding a home," actor Joel Polis muses. "Everybody always ends up trying to go back to a home, a family, a wife or husband. Those are the things that are getting to me now. Food. Cooking. Peace. Families. But I love my life. The infinite variety of women is such a delight to me. I don't want to give anything up. When I'm ready to make that commitment, I will make it." As the Seventies turned into the Eighties, more and more of us felt ready—or woke in sudden panic to the departure of the boat.

Marian Goodman married her second husband in 1981, after dating him for a year and living together for four. Why so long? "I was afraid that marriage was going to destroy this good relationship"—a common fear, based on past experience or the dread of turning into those pumpkins, our parents. A year and a half before the wedding, Goodman and her partner bought a house together, a move that often precedes or replaces marriage, as if owning joint property were preferable to owning each other. Sarah Weil and her friend of seven years bought a house and moved in together as their act of commitment; two years later, they made an impulsive decision to marry. While Weil isn't sure she wants a child, it's significant that her decision to take the leap coincided with the biological clock. Other first-wave women have been able to fall in love—real, healthy, mutual love—for the first time in their lives as the deadline for babies approached. What's happening?

The end of childbearing is a limit—maybe the first unmistakable one our generation has encountered. We've always had a better sense of the planet's limits than of our own. The old cultural limits fell away as we came of age, creating a feeling of boundless possibility. Whenever we ran up against our own limitations, we worked on them in meditation, therapy, or est. The more we grew, the more "grown up" receded like a mirage. There was so much still to learn, so much to live! "We're not ready," editor Hugh O'Neill (1952) replied in 1979 when his father asked him why he and his roommate of four years didn't get married. "Hugh," his father said, *"nobody* is ever ready for *anything*!" It was a revelation. They got married.

For those who waited even longer, biology delivered the same message. Ready or not, we had to choose and act if we wanted to be fathers young enough to romp with a kid—or if we wanted to be mothers at all. And even those who didn't want kids were feeling the first humbling twinges of mortality. On the brink of middle age, we were realizing that discovering one's possibilities is only half the job of growing up. The other half is accepting one's limitations.

We would never be perfectly honest, or perfectly non-possessive, or perfectly egalitarian, or perfectly independent, or perfectly androgynous, or perfectly in love. We might be better, broader human beings—thanks in part to all our past relationships—but we were still human beings, with stubborn needs and flaws. Both love and enlightenment turned out to be (as we'd been told) not about getting rid of our imperfections, but about accepting them.

The surprise was that accepting limits brought a rush of liberation. Abandoning the vigil for the ideal partner released us to love someone real. And commitment supplied the missing ingredient: trust. With it came a feeling of freedom, not to "find oneself," but to be oneself. Tough old cynics and stoics found themselves deeply in love. *Yeah, but will it last?* said the little voice. And answered itself: *Hell, we don't know if the* planet *will last!* Our love, unlike our parents', is not "forever," but for now. Nonetheless, a grudging romanticism has crept into our hard-bitten style.

People tell little stories about how they met, giving it the retrospective burnish of destiny. "Stan and I met in the Spring Street Bar. It was just one of those things. You wander into some place and some funny guy comes up to you and offers you a light for your cigarette. And that was it. We always go back to the Spring Street Bar on our anniversary and argue about how we got together. Who exactly it was that asked for the light" (Joan Giannecchini).

"He came to me in a dream about two months before I met him. In the dream he gave me a mantra, *Om Va.* It was one of those clear, strong dreams. I wrote it down. We met later, and he started to talk about chanting and mantras, and all of a sudden I remembered that dream and told him about it. He said that he was aware of my presence for several years before that. The kind of energy. A certain light. He recognized me" (Ananda Saha on her life companion, a psychotherapist and piano tuner).

"He was a first-year law student, I was a third-year. I saw him. I saw him in the student lounge and decided I wanted to meet him. Then I saw him in the Giant one night, doing some grocery shopping. I tried to pick him up. He says he tried to pick me up. He was standing at some shelf and he was scowling. And I'd never seen him smile at school. I went up and I said, 'Don't you ever smile?' We spoke a few words, and then he went his way and I went mine.

"A few days later I approached him about going out dancing with a bunch of my friends and he did. Then we went to a party the following Friday night. He showed up at my apartment with a single flower, a poem, and a little bag of pot. I knew this man knows me. He had every single one of my weaknesses. From that time on we pretty much spent all of our time together" (Carla Wilder married Joel in 1981).

Note the mutuality in these stories, the egalitarian confusion over who picked up whom. Things *have* changed. And the change is manifest not only in recent relationships, but in long marriages that have gradually evolved, and in gay relationships, where fixed role-playing has largely faded from the scene. We have moved much closer to the partnership of equals. And we've found our persuasive new reason to stay together: "The best thing about being married," says Anne Strieber, "is you have a friend."

Not that friendship is a gilt-edged guarantee of permanence. Two men (both born in 1946) who told me that their wives were their best friends have since separated—at their best friends' instigation. The divorce rate remains high. It's still too soon to tell whether the high turnover in partners is a permanent cultural change or a peculiarity of our generation, which had such an explosion of new information to assimilate that many, like Ananda Saha, "have a feeling of having lived several lifetimes in one life." Men and women of the next generation, born after 1958, seem to arrive at adulthood more complete and self-aware, as if they effortlessly incorporated the lessons of our wanderings. In their twenties, they mate with their eyes open, with a blend of intention, romance, and realism that it has taken us twenty years to learn. Our new relationships are real. Whether they are also lasting will depend on whether—like other American pioneers—we can learn the art of growth within limits after the endless promise of the frontier.

Meanwhile, the lineaments of the new marriage of friends have come into focus:

Women have built strong independent identities, usually around the nucleus of work. (The older the woman, the longer it took: first-wavers spent our youth on this task, while women ten years younger entered adulthood fully fledged. "She was our ideal," Donna Henes says of a younger woman she met. "She was what we were fighting for. At thirteen she knew she could be anything she wanted to be: a fireman, an astronaut. And she took it completely for granted. I envied her, because she came out of college and she was ready. It took our whole twenties. We had so much anger and struggle and pain. But the ironic part is that she was jealous of me. She thought that the struggle gave us a depth and a beauty that you don't get easily. And you know, I think she was right.") Many men not only accept women's new strength, they have come to respect it and even to expect it. Actor Joel Polis is typical: "I would expect my wife to work, or to have something that passionately involved her, whether it was music, art, or business." Independence and competence have become part of a woman's appeal.

The older-woman/younger-man pairing is becoming increasingly common (a surprising 14 percent of all marriages in 1984)—a change that directly reflects the shifting balance of power. Fewer women need to look *up* to a man to love him; more men are willing to be women's political and emotional apprentices—in principle. In practice, the graciousness is sometimes undercut by resentment, but the admiration is sincere. "I have a feeling that women are going to turn this society around," David Banghart told me. "I learn from women, not from men," says Carl Nagin. And these are first-wavers. Many second-wave men have been feminists since puberty, and that makes them ideal partners for embattled first-wave women.

"It seems to me that women who were bitten by the feminism bug are very forceful women," says Lynne Burbridge, whose husband, Jay Newman, is three and a half years younger. "Some of them are used to getting their way, being very independent. They've been on their own for a long time, and they need a man who is flexible, not fixed and not set in his ways." Burbridge and Newman know at least six other couples in which the woman is two to ten years older than the man. "I don't know what happened to the men my age," Burbridge says. "I don't know any." For years, I hardly knew any either. My closest women friends have ended up either with younger men or (like me) with considerably older men, who've been married and divorced once or thrice and have mellowed into an appreciation of the headstrong woman. "I sometimes feel that it's partly because I can't stand some of the demands of my own generation," says Sarah Weil, whose partner is twelve years older.

First-wave lawyer Al Belasco would agree. After years of fleeing needy, angry contemporaries, he married a sane, sunny banker, eight years younger and much less conflicted about both love and work. Rather than a return to the old pattern, it's the exact equivalent of a first-wave woman being cooled out by a non-peer partner. I know another man born in 1946 who married a European woman ten years *older.*

All these combinations are ways of enjoying equality without rehashing the old battles for it—the same truce that long-married couples have had to come to. We've all become more tacit and tactful. Honesty and equality are as highly valued as ever, but we no longer measure our relationships with calipers, or dissect them with Texas chain saws. "What works for us now is taking a long time to be quiet, or to do a lot of adjusting, and not make a big verbal deal about it," says Sarah Weil. "Unless there's something really special that we need to work out, and then we do it as quickly as possible."

We've finally grown up enough, Weil says, "to understand that what you work with is the predilections and the strengths of each person, depending on who they are, not on some abstract model of how an ideal marriage ought to work. When we were young, we thought we could will a way." Now we feel our way, sharing housework and finances along lines of idiosyncrasy rather than ideology. No two couples have the same domestic or financial arrangements. There are joint checking accounts in which all money is heedlessly pooled, and scrupulously separate arrangements in which each partner pays for different expenses. The absence of codified gender roles frees both men and women to do whatever chores they're best at. In our household, for instance, I balance the checkbook and he cooks. (Were this reversed, we'd go broke and starve.) The most common phrase I hear about people's relationships is, "I don't know *how* it works, but it works."

One thing that helps make it work is flexibility—an ability to compromise and improvise, to trade roles back and forth as circumstances demand. "I don't see myself in many respects as a primary breadwinner," Lynne Burbridge said when she was at home with her daughter. "It's complex, though, because when he went back to graduate school, I *was* the breadwinner. And I can't predict what it's going to be like in the future, when our daughter is older. Probably whoever is able to do it, depending on the circumstances, will be the breadwinner. It's not even for us at all. It goes back and forth."

It's striking that this is a trait of Sixties-generation relationships *not* shared by the post-Sixties generation, who tend to be much more programmatically androgynous (like Stacey and Peter), or even to practice role reversal: ambitious woman/tender man. While our younger siblings were formed by feminist ideology, Sixties men and women have lived through so many metamorphoses—Fifties sex roles, Sixties androgyny, Seventies role reversal, Eighties return to gender—that we now have all these roles like costumes in our closets, to put on, take off, or mix and match. We are change artists. Younger people strive earnestly to "have it all"; our spiritual training taught us that you never and always have it all, so you might as well have as many versions as possible. Drugs, travel, and meditation gave us that little fillip of detachment that enables us to "play" all kinds of roles and enjoy them as adventures of consciousness.

"I was delighted to be at home with my children," says Ananda Saha. "I remember waking up in the morning and feeling so happy that I didn't have to go out to work. I had a garden, baked all our bread, canned all our food, had dinner ready. One man who had been in India with Maharaji [Ram Dass's guru] came and stayed overnight. There were babies and laundry and mushy food everywhere. He said, 'This is some *sadhana*, do you do this every day?' And here I'd thought I was just a housewife while they were off getting enlightened. I realized that I, too, had been doing spiritual practice. There are so many ways."

"We were talking about drugs earlier," says Jay Newman, "and you asked were drugs a waste of time or were they valuable. I said it's a combination of the two. And the way that it's valuable is that it was like some kind of yoga without knowing it, a subliminal teaching. It planted the seeds for realizing that a goal is not necessarily the important thing in life. It's learning to appreciate the process. So the payoff here will be when I really genuinely integrate it into myself to just enjoy ironing our clothes and helping raise our daughter."

Kids

The names any generation gives its children may be a clue to the particular gift and burden those parents lay on their young. The names most of our parents gave us were a hymn to the group, a paean to the norm: Patty, Barbara, Bobby, Bill. Our kids' names were solo flights into the stratosphere: Amara Sidra ("everlasting star"), Kamala ("white lotus"), Maya Leila ("her father wanted to name her Ramana, but it reminded me of Ramada Inn"), Terre Unité ("earth united"), Krishna, Gopal, Rainbow Harvest, Lovelady, Journey. We thought a name should make an individual stand out, not fit in, that it should connect a child to the earth or the sky, or history or myth, not to a docile little herd of Susans and Marks. So Daria and Saskia (after Rembrandt's wife), Abra and Petra, Clotilde and Cybele, Cato, Caitlin, Justine, Persephone, Paloma, Tiffany, Vanessa, Lorenzo Isaiah . . .

Even when vision subsided into taste, and we began to compile a ten-best list of our own, we chose earthy, sturdy, Biblical and Greek-myth names that smacked of pioneering and prophecy: Matthew, Sarah, Adam, Jonah, Jason, Rachel, Rebecca, Jeremiah, Joshua. And then there's our old standard, Dylan—a name that has increased in popularity since the Sixties. A sampling of states: two Dylans were born in Vermont in 1969, eight in 1984; four Dylans arrived in Missouri in 1974, thirteen in 1984; New York State bore fourteen Dylans in 1974—one a girl!—and at least thirty-six in 1984. (A friend of mine swears that his nephew, one of the thirty-six, isn't named after either Bob Dylan or Dylan Thomas, but after the Welsh for "wave.")

The names are rich with paradox. They say that we wanted our kids to conform to our ideas of originality and independence. Parents can't help imposing their world view on their children, even if that world view is Fritz Perls's Gestalt Prayer ("I do my thing,/And you do your thing . . ."). Perhaps what we imposed on ours was an exaggerated refusal to impose. "I always felt that I was more of a steward than an owner," says Marc Barasch of his daughter. "All the analogies of living lightly on the earth. Tread lightly on your child." Our parents had tried to make us in their own image; our children, by God, were going to be themselves. Our parents took too much anxious responsibility for the way we turned out. Our ideology may have allowed us to take too little responsibility for the way our turbulent lives, and our turbulent times, have affected our children.

"A bunch of kids came into the Riviera Café," Kathy Brimlow remembers. "And this one little girl had a doll. I call her a little girl, but she was about fifteen. And the doll was naked, and its hair was dyed with mercurochrome. And there was mercurochrome all over the doll, and Band-Aids. And I just wanted to cry for that little girl. We felt hurt, the flower children, but we had hope. These children's hope is in a Band-Aid and mercurochrome. They don't have any."

That fifteen-year-old could well have been one of our beautiful, "free," "natural" children. What happened? We tend to attribute the dissonance of punk to changes entirely beyond our control. "The world is less in tune," says Marc Barasch. "They see some real global entropy going on." Since World War II, as Margaret Mead pointed out, technology has replaced tradition as the matrix of human life, and accelerated change makes the culture of the parents irrelevant to the children. Having felt like a different species from our own parents, we look at our kids with apprehensive curiosity. Who *are* these green-haired teens and weirdly wise toddlers? Where did they come from? Surely not from us.

"I always saw her, not as coming from Roz and me, but as a person coming into the world with her own baggage and her own resources," says Marc Barasch. "I look at her and her friends as a generation to practice phrenology on, the same as we did on each other. It's interesting to see what their sense of mission is, what their point is going to be. There's some reason they're here. I look at them and I see interesting sociological, characterological, personality similarities in their generation. The way they play with each other. They are very compassionate. They seem to really care about each other, say if one were hurt. They don't fight over toys the way we did. There's a gentleness. That may be wishful thinking, but I don't think so.

"The other interesting thing is their sense of self-possession. That's been very striking. A lot of parents that I talk to notice it. I have terrible, adolescent table manners. My daughter was the one who specified that a fork be used. Just has this innate sense of propriety and decorum. Mind-blowing. Where does she get it? She didn't get it from me. I never said 'yes.' I always say 'yeah,' and my ex-wife says 'yeah,' and my friends say 'yeah.' The first time she ever heard the word 'yes' from somewhere, that became the word. Never 'yeah.'

"From the time she was two or three years old, she was very centered. She's a counselor. She's been counseling my friends about their love affairs since she was six or seven, and she's very smart about it. I don't know where she gets it. It's not TV precocity, because she's always had that quality. When I went to work on a job, we'd be separated a lot. And she would never throw a scene and say no, or whine, or cry and kick. It's always, 'Okay, go, Dad.' Don't stand around being sentimental. You have a job to do, don't worry about me."

We're surely right to emphasize the mysterious extent to which people come ready-made. But character is formed by the interplay of potential with environment. And many of the characteristics Marc Barasch describes in his daughter's generation are perfectly logical responses to the environment we made for them. What could be a more eloquent rebellion against a Sixties-generation parent than perfect table manners? "My daughter would come and visit me in a West Oakland ghetto in a warehouse full of rats," Joan Giannecchini recalls. "Here would be all these people running around Berkeley farting and smoking joints and fucking each other. Her little mind was just melted. I didn't see her for a stretch of about five years. We get along well now, in spite of the fact that she is straight and very conservative."

Some hippies' kids went Mohawk and black leather (expressing

"All that the hippies denied with 'Hey, man, Love and Peace,' " says one ex-punk, "the End, collapse, anarchy, Death. War. Hate."7). Others chose preppy clothes and frilly beds. Often the Wild Child with the one-of-a-kind name wanted nothing more than to fit in. I heard about a Krishna who changed his name to Christopher; my niece Paloma has been heard to introduce herself as "Kelly." Marc Barasch's daughter ran away from private school at age six, saying, "Daddy, I want to be with normal kids." We overturned our parents' ways. Our kids often set them upright again.

That's not to say that there has been no progress. On the positive side, our kids are mature because we never talked baby talk to them, or underestimated their capacity to understand. They are very much themselves because we've encouraged them to be: Leni Windle, whose mother always dressed her, lets her two small daughters pick their own clothes. Our kids are gentle with each other because we've rewarded their potential for compassion, not competition. They are independent and resourceful, in part, because we trusted them with responsibility. (We had to. We were at work.) They are wonderfully guiltless about their bodies because we let them see us nude, and never slapped their hands away from their pleasure. (A five-year-old niece of mine came running to her mother: "Mommy, can I have a flashlight? Danny [a four-year-old neighbor] and I are going in the closet and take off our clothes!" My sister gave her the flashlight.) And they are creative—the quality we value most—because, in Kathy Brimlow's words, they were never "squelched."

"I understood that I was in trouble because my spirit was squelched," says Brimlow. "I didn't want that to happen to my son. I wanted my child to be free. Some people would say that he was not well-behaved when he was three or four. But when my boy was four years old I saw him skipping, just freely skipping through a mall, because they play that music. And I saw other kids right next to their parents, and if the child went off—'GET OVER HERE!!' And I just looked at him and I went, 'Oh God, he's beautiful.' And then when he started writing, I was blown away. All children have that pure way of looking at the world. We're all trying to get back to it."

"The cult of the child was very big in the Sixties," comments Marc Barasch. "We became acutely aware of childlike wisdom. The little child shall lead, sort of thing. My parents always used to marvel at this reverence." "I did feel that in a lot of ways the kids were my teachers," says Ananda Saha. This metaphorical truth, when taken literally, became role reversal. The irony was that, aspiring to be childlike ourselves—and to treat our children as equals, so that they'd never hate us—we often abdicated the role of "parent," that is, protector, guide, and disciplinarian, and so forced our children to be premature adults. Wondering about his daughter's eerie wisdom and self-reliance, Marc Barasch says, "Families are archetypes, and certain roles have to be filled. There are adults and kids. My ex-wife and I were such children together. Maybe there was a vacuum." On the negative side, our kids are mature, independent, and resourceful —and depressed, nihilistic, stoned, and suicidal—in part because they couldn't count on us. Whether out of belief, irresponsibility, or preoccupation, we have often made them carry a burden of maturity beyond their years.

Part of it was just reaction to our own upbringing. Our parents were overprotective: "We had enormous security as kids," says Barasch, "we couldn't breathe." So we tried to suppress our instinctive protectiveness. "You get a little more anti-drug when you're a parent," says Barasch. "You don't want her exposed to sexuality too early. But in a way you discipline yourself, because you want your child to know the world." "The world" could include events as vital and frightening as childbirth. (If it's natural it's good, remember?) Prince Charles turned pale at the reality of his first son's arrival, yet Co-op America director Paul Freundlich (1936) had his fifteen-year-old son videotape the birth of a baby brother, and Francine Stone's daughter was only three when she assisted at her brother's home birth.

"It made a woman out of her," Stone says proudly, describing how her daughter sits in the tub and grunts, pretending to give birth. "My greatest memories of her are of her wiping my brow and holding me and patting me and massaging me, and also of her certain amount of dismay at the sheer messiness of it all, and I saw him being born in her eyes, 'cause I didn't watch. I was looking at her looking at him being born. And that was *great*! She was amazed. She couldn't wait to get her hands on him." Maybe it brands me as a prude of the old school, but I find this cruel. (It's revealing, I think, that Stone says, "I really wanted my mother there.") When I recounted it to a member of the Lyman Family commune, which is conservative on such matters, his response was surprising. He didn't mention trauma, but said, "They're trying to take the magic out of everything."

Not all our kids have seen birth, but they've all had to deal with death—not just pet death or grandparent death, but the concept of megadeath, planet death. "For weeks my son was preoccupied," says Kathy Brimlow. "He couldn't sleep at night. He was saying, 'I could just be lying here, Mommy, and my world could be destroyed.' He was eight years old." Psychiatrist Robert Coles says that such fears are rare among working-class and poor kids, whose family lives revolve around economic survival and basic pleasures. He has criticized middle-class, peace-movement parents for imposing their own obsession with nuclear holocaust on their children. But parents can hardly help transmitting their own preoccupations to their kids. When our parents tried to hide theirs, it only scared us worse. We prefer to tell our kids the truth. They'll hear it on TV or in school anyway. And they'll deal with it much as we do: nightmares, depression, denial.

Our children have not only had to deal with issues of life and death, but they have been intimate witnesses to our emotional and spiritual crises. "My daughter has seen every possible permutation of human interaction at this point in her life," Marc Barasch said of his nine-year-old. Our parents fought, loved, and discussed death and taxes behind closed doors; our kids have had near-total access to the adult world. As the price of that privilege, few have had the comforting illusion that life was under control, or that their parents were strong and sure. Instead of looking up to us as the confident masters of a culture, they've had to participate—often as full partners—in our confused struggle to create one. And they can be old and sad and wise. "My son writes about subjects a thirteen-year-old has no business writing about," says Kathy Brimlow.

> If life has no meaning,
> You make it so—
>
> Leaving not room
>   to live or grow—
>
> If that meaning is the fear of death,
> it reeks of life
> leaving nothing left—
>
> If that meaning is simply fun
> then you fool yourself
> more than anyone—
>
> If you seek to understand
> to find the truth
> to comprehend
>
> you could find yourself in a faraway land
>
> or deep within
>
> or as a speck of sand—

"I said, 'Jeremiah, where does that come from?' And he said, 'You!' I'm so sorry that he has that burden."

But probably the biggest burden our kids have had to carry is divorce. They were born of our experiments with new shapes of love and marriage, and half those experiments failed. "When we first broke up, the kids were with me for more than a year, but my ex-husband really wanted them," says Ananda Saha of her three daughters. "The conflict was terrible for us all. In a desperate hope of resolution, I left them to him. But he hasn't remarried, and his work commitments are often during the hours when the kids are home, so the three of them have bonded very close together and brought each other up. The oldest is fifteen. I'm very close with them now. I see them every other weekend, and they're here part of the summer for vacation. They are probably stronger than if I had protected them." So we hope. In my own family there are four children of divorce, whose visits back and forth between estranged parents are a chronic source of stress. No one has any idea of the long-range effects of divorce on the ability of these kids to bond and to trust.

We may be the first people who have ever allowed the emotional security of children to depend on the volatile sexual bond between a man and a woman. Every other culture has provided a safety net. In the old extended family, grandparents, aunts, and uncles were a strong presence in kids' lives. When the family shrank to its nucleus, marriage still had an economic and moral basis, so that parents stayed together after the fire went out. Having in some cases grown up in the ashes, we decided that aliveness and truth were more important than security. It was a decision that could only have been made by the very secure. And we underestimated our own kids' need for security in defense of our quest for fire.

We'll never go back to "staying together for the children's sake," and it's just as well. A bad marriage makes a rotten net. But we do owe our kids a net—a small constellation of still points in a whirling world. Some of us have begun to make the connection sensed by Marc Barasch: "Teenagers seem like they've lost hope because they weren't given security in any sense—material, sociological, geographic." Given the epidemic nature of divorce, we've begun to grope our way toward a new ethic: staying friends for the children's sake.

It's not easy, especially when the wounds are fresh. "My ex-wife and I have picked our way very gingerly through a field of broken glass," says Barasch. "But we've managed to develop a relationship which is fairly secure and amicable. We have joint custody, and when we first divorced, we tried to have our homes a couple of blocks apart. It was the closest thing to providing two parents for our child that we could do." The growing popularity of premarital agreements, joint custody, and divorce mediation—in place of adversarial proceedings aggravated by lawyers—suggests that more of us now recognize the existence and importance of a relationship beyond divorce.

Such relationships often improve when one or both ex-partners become attached to someone new. These links can then branch into "new extended families," with all the step-parents, in-laws, outlaws, and half-siblings getting together for holidays and longer visits. These patchwork clans have become so common that they're on the verge of being recognized as a genuine kinship structure, one that reconciles the new impermanence of marriage with the permanence of the bond that made a child. A commune that has deliberately gone further in this direction may shed some light on the path.

Most intentional communities promote either closed or open marriage, but the Lyman Family practices a kind of serial monogamy that is closer to the realities of life in our generation. Holding romantic love in high esteem as a means of spiritual growth—"You find a heart through heartbreak," one of them wrote in *U and I*—they regard the marriage bond as exclusive but probably not permanent. "We recognize that some relationships don't last forever," Family photographer George Peper (1945) told a Kansas reporter. "But it is the most unique thing in the world today that we have no divorce. When a relationship, for one reason or other, is over, it's painful, yet a living relationship continues."

The former couple can live in Family homes in different cities until the worst wounds heal, but they are expected to reconcile within the larger context of the Family. "They are bound together by the responsibility they feel toward their children," Peper says. "These children do not have divorced parents; they have parents. They don't lose one."[8] It can't be a coincidence that their children are strikingly calm, bright, and self-possessed.

Few of us would choose to live communally with an ex-spouse. What the Lymans' example suggests is that "staying friends for the children's sake"—when at all possible—is the discipline appropriate to this age, replacing the harsh old discipline of staying married no matter what. "Through it all, you have to find the love that brought you together in the first place," says Eve Lyman. "You are forced to a deeper place."[9] Letting go of the obsolete ideal of the nuclear family, defining divorce as a painful change in the form of a relationship, not the end, might make it less frightening for kids.

Still, it is bound to frighten. In a household of only two adults, the departure of one is a cataclysm. And so, in the wake of a bitter divorce, or in the interregnum between solid relationships, surprisingly many of us with children have found ourselves turning to . . . our parents. The very fixity that once made them so maddening becomes an anchor for us and our storm-tossed kids.

Parents (Coda)

In most families, in the natural course of things, some reconciliation had already taken place. "We just grew back toward each other," says Marc Sarkady. "Basically, it comes down to all three of us becoming more tolerant of each other." Our parents had reluctantly come to accept the farther shores of our lives: live-in lovers, multiple relationships, lovers of another color or the same sex, abortion, divorce. Embracing us had brought much more of the world into their lives. And we'd become more lenient toward some of their values. "There were a lot of outer steps in that process of getting back together," says Sarkady. "Part of it had to do with my becoming what their friends could label a success: making money, cutting my beard off, cutting my hair. What I realized later was that they were looking for a way to relate to me." Writer Carl Nagin was thirty-eight when he got his first major book contract; his father and long-time antagonist bought him a word processor. "And he said—and this was really significant to me—'Get whatever you want.' Not 'I'm a mathematician, I'm gonna tell you what kind to get.' "

But the change that did most to reconnect us to our parents was having kids of our own. With that act, we who had sought radical discontinuity were drawn into the continuity of life. It was both humbling and comforting to discover that we had not, after all, become "a new species," in Anne Strieber's words. Some constants survived all change. "On my daughter's fourth birthday, there I was, going to the day-care center with her birthday cake," says Grace Parker Sannino. "There are her and her pals. And here's Mommy with the birthday hats. And it was just the same, you know? So the fact is that our parents were not the cartoons we thought they were. They really aren't any different than we are."

More to the point, we've come to understand the differences that do exist as products of history rather than of willful obtuseness on our parents' part (or ours). "Their lives were shaped by different forces," Marc Sarkady says. "Their perception of life was shaped and molded by what they've gone through: the Depression, the Second World War, the Korean war." We are finally able to see some of what they learned and did as positive. "They saved us from Hitler's fascism—no small feat," says Sarkady. "I thank them for that, for myself and for my whole generation." "The challenges they had to face, the sacrifices they made . . ." says Carl Nagin. "I worry about my generation. Faced with similar situations, I don't know if we could do it."

Ironically, some of us also now wonder whether we can raise children as well. "Interestingly, you begin to see that your own parents are very competent," says Marc Barasch. "I see that my parents are rock solid in a way that I'm not. I'm much mushier. I don't always provide certainty for my kid. My life is more at loose ends. I'm divorced. My parents, oddly enough, are still married.

"Having rejected their model, we don't have any rules. We don't always know the right thing to do. Should you be an exemplar? A disciplinarian? A pal? In my parents, there's not a lot of doubt. Unlike us, they grew up in a society that had unity of purpose and vision. And they weren't raised to be as self-centered as we were. They handle my daughter with this sort of surety. She's watching a real pro take the bat, whoosh it in the air a few times, take the chalk and rub it in their hands. It's something they have that most of us don't."

And it's something they willingly share with us. "We're all trying to learn how to be certain, to be straight arrows in our own lives and in our work life and everything else we do," says Barasch. "We're accustomed to Talmudic reasoning: 'Maybe it's that, but then on the other hand . . .' Back and forth. But you can't do that to a child. You have to be a classic parent." After two decades of anti-authoritarianism and moral relativism, it's a role we wear awkwardly at best. Our parents serve as belated role models and as relief pitchers when the rookie needs a rest.

Mostly, though, they do it long distance, or on vacations and holidays. Most of us don't live near our parents. We left home to go to college, stayed far away during the years of rebellion, and had roots somewhere else by the time we had kids. Many now regret it. "Whitley and I live away from our families, and I think that's tragic," says New Yorker Anne Strieber, whose parents live in Michigan and whose mother-in-law lives in Texas. "When you have children, you start to see how the generations are intertwined. You see that that's important, and you've thrown it away all your life. But that was our style. 'My mother's always arguing with me. I can't be near her. I'd better move across the continent.' When you get a little older you realize how ridiculous that is. Maybe your parents drive you crazy, maybe you don't want to live in the same house with them, but they're still your family." And as they age and suffer illness, needing us, the natural bond contracts, and the distance hurts.

Yet the distance expresses something real. For all we've learned from each other, we remain denizens of different eras, our parents and we. Between us lies the iron curtain of August 6, 1945, the different meaning of the dollar, the freedom of the Pill, the nervous system of TV. We live in different worlds, with our heads if not our hearts, and the new relations between us have the strained graciousness of diplomacy. Most of us can respect each other's values from afar, or discuss them cordially for a weekend. But stay too close too long, and the fireworks start. The physical distance we maintain, crisscrossed with phone calls and visits, strikes a balance between cultural clash and emotional longing.

"I really wanted my mother there," Francine Stone says of her son's midwife-attended home birth. Knowing her relationship with her mother hasn't been the easiest, I asked whether that surprised her. "Yes, it certainly did! But I really knew that that was the nicest person to have around. And only because I knew she'd freak out at the way we chose to do it, I didn't. I called her about ten minutes after he was born, so I got as close to her as I could"—given that Stone was in London and her mother was in Pennsylvania.

In the Sixties, the tight old nuclear family exploded. But it didn't die. It slowly healed—in a looser, freer form, with more space and air and dissent in it. The boundaries of the new open family have never been clear. It has the capacity to extend itself indefinitely— even across oceans—by love, marriage, divorce, remarriage, friendship, adoption. The real social units many of us live in, and the real safety nets we give our children, are far-flung clans in which different kinds of bonds—blood relations, old and new friendships and passions—have equal status.

If we've tried to make friends with our mates, ex-mates, and families, we've succeeded in making families of our friends.

Friends

"It was a feast of friends," Carl Nagin says of his Sixties. "They were more important to me than job, career, family—anything." He speaks for us all, as Ringo Starr did when he sang in his innocent, off-key voice: "I'll get by with a little help from my friends."

"The journey we had taken was like finding our childhood friends who we really could trust," says Ananda Saha of the two men with whom she tripped across the country. "On our trip we had done important work on ourselves and for each other in a really childlike way. Everyone assumed that it had been a raunchy, sexual thing. There were perhaps overtones of that, but it was such a small part of it. We were like children. Pre-adolescent. Trying to understand who we were and how to live." "We suffered such horrendous confusion," says Jennifer Flinton Diener. "What actually saved me was the close friendships. The ability to just say how you felt about everything, without reserve and without any phoniness, for hours and hours and hours, was desperately necessary."

In the avalanche of change, they were the one thing you could hold on to. When the ship of the old world went down, they were the ones in the lifeboat with you. The stresses of the Sixties tore all other relationships apart—family ties, man-woman couplings. The bonds between friends grew stronger. Friendship was the form of love that survived the fire, and it is the basic unit of the new world. Even now, our friends from the Sixties are the core of our extended families.

How did we choose the friends with whom we shared so much? Often, by proximity. Adolescence is a "critical period" for forming friendships; a seventeen-year-old fresh from the nest will make friends with whoever is closest, the way newly hatched chicks follow the first object they see. Thrown together in college dorms or crash pads, we fell in with two or three or five or more people, of varied backgrounds but compatible attitudes, who were to become crucial to our lives.

"My group of people at Amherst, ten or fifteen of us, called ourselves the Yappies, the young apathetics," says Richmond physician Paul Monroe. "We thought the people in SDS were a little weird. They were too serious. We would go out on marches, but it was all in camp. I don't think we did anything significant. But we lived together every year. And we still get together, as recently as two years ago, when we all went down to Wilmington and stayed in a house on the beach. A very strange group."

In the Sixties, the painful social segregations of high school had broken down—in fact, we'd dismantled them. "No one was a loser," says Jennifer Diener. "You had this wonderful mixture and looseness; you'd just kind of hang out, and go to people's apartments, and it was cool if you smoked and it was cool if you didn't smoke. It was cool to treat everyone like they were cool, and so you couldn't distinguish the losers from the winners. It was uncool to really admit anybody was a loser; society had done it to them, or it didn't matter. Rich people ran around in torn-off blue jeans. Everyone was equal."

People who would never have met in another era—or had anything to say to each other if they did—became best friends in the Sixties.

Drugs helped break down barriers, revealing that you could love the essence of anyone. "My roommate my junior year of college was a person I didn't really feel that close to," says Jeff Maron. "We shared an apartment, and it wasn't going very successfully. Basically we were completely out of touch. Then we had a drug experience together, and we had this moment of complete lucidity with each other. We found such a dramatic bond during that one instant that we've never lost it to this day."

Shared political beliefs and activities often forged friendships that have outlived the politics. "I was sixteen or just seventeen when I went downstate to the University of Illinois for one year," says Tina Ivans, the daughter of a Jewish lawyer. "And there I met a person who is still probably my best friend today"—Berkeley disabled-rights activist Kitty Cone, who "comes from a ruling-class, Dixiecrat background. She was active in SNCC. I met her the night of the Johnson-Goldwater election. We had a lot of arch-conservative Goldwater supporters on our floor. She was arguing with them, and I was trying to study next door in the study room. I decided to go next door and get into the discussion. And Kitty and I got friendly, and we became best friends.

"I had to go back to Chicago the next year. Kitty had moved to Chicago and was very active in the Young Socialists Alliance and the anti-war movement, the Student Mobilization Committee. I really wanted to get involved. And the next thing I knew I was on staff, organizing demonstrations, negotiating with the cops." Though both Ivans and Cone eventually left the Socialist Workers Party and moved to opposite coasts, they remain in close touch with each other and with Ivans's ex-boyfriend, who comes from a working-class background and is still a dedicated socialist. "We went through a lot in Chicago," says Ivans. "It's forged solid, lifelong bonds, I think."

Sometimes the best friends met by cosmic chance. Panhandling, for instance. "There was a be-in in Central Park, and we were all going," Kathy Brimlow remembers. "And we didn't have the money for the subway. So this woman was coming up out of the subway, and I said, 'Hi, do you have any spare change?'

"She looked at me and said, 'I have nothing.'

" 'You have nothing? Then come with us!'

" 'Where do you live?'

" 'Nowhere . . .'

"She said, 'Oh, I have an apartment! I'll share that. If you'd like to come home with me, you're welcome.' And she was sincere. She was just so open and beautiful. So we went home with her to her apartment on 3rd Street in the East Village, and that was it. That was 1968. She was my tripping partner through all those years. And she is my dearest friend on the face of the earth to this day."

As soon as friends were made, it seemed natural to share everything: space, food, clothes, drugs, money, work, love. Having grown up in a world where material things separated people, we turned them into a medium of communion. "After I left school to live in New York, I was living in a hotel in the Village with a bunch of young kids, rock 'n' roll guys and girlfriends," says Zazel Lovén. "A bunch of us would drive to Boston for the weekend and we'd find through the network that there was an abandoned house where everyone stayed when they came to Boston. You'd knock a little code on the door and someone would open up. It was wonderful. Someone would buy a loaf of bread and a package of ham, and you shared and met new people. I met wonderful friends that I still have."

Groups of friends, especially those who lived together, were aware of being a kind of alternative family. Some named themselves accordingly. Carl Nagin and other dropouts sharing a Mulberry Street cold-water flat in the early Sixties—"six people and seven cats in two bedrooms the size of closets"—grandly called themselves "La Famille du Soleil," the Family of the Sun. Richard Leonard's Haight-Ashbury oil-and-perfume manufactory, Astral Industries, became "the Astral Family." And on Fort Hill in Boston was the Lyman Family. (Even the Brinks gang, that amalgam of black nationalists and underground Weatherpeople that surfaced with the bungled robbery of October 1981, called itself "the Family.")

"A lot of us were going through, 'Is the nuclear family the root of all these problems in society?'" says Marc Sarkady, who shared a house and published an underground paper with several friends from Brown. The new families of friends tried to be egalitarian and honest, mini-models of an ideal society. And most were deliberately open, extending friendship to "the community"—another charged Sixties word—and to the "family" of the planet. Sarkady and his house-mates worked with black, gay, women's, and neighborhood groups, "trying to create this family sense that we were all connected. And through the Underground Press Syndicate, we would hear from people all over the world: Cuba, Germany, Australia. You got a sense that you were part of this worldwide phenomenon. A larger family. You could feel it in your cells."

Many communes were originally "families" of friends that decided to make a conscious commitment to live together. Those that lasted didn't just exist to fulfill the needs or fantasies of their members, but took themselves seriously as laboratories of a new culture. That gave the motivation to face and deal with conflicts, instead of fleeing them. Friendships became the deliberate workshop of change. "We really worked at living," says Sarkady of the twenty adults and ten children at his conference center, Another Place (1974–80). "We did a pretty good job of practicing what we preached. And we learned some things that would, if people lived this way, change the world." Such experiments gave an early hint of the power of friendship, not just to console à la *Big Chill,* but to support life and actually engender new institutions—resilient, small-scale, tribal—in the cracks of the corporate world. Tiny mammals among the dinosaurs.

But while a small number of New Age pioneers refined the communal dream through the Seventies, most of us were yielding to centrifugal forces that gradually pulled us away from our friends. One was simply a need for solitude after a surfeit of group experience. "We got back from that trip in November or December," says Ananda Saha of her cross-country odyssey. "There was a party around the turn of the year which was really a low point for me and, I think, for everyone who had gone over that initial crest together. At the party, everyone seemed so unkind to each other and jaded. Horrible. I thought I needed to go someplace else fresh and try to live alone, get to know myself."

Another significant turning point in the Seventies was the rebirth of discrimination in our choice of friends. As some of us began to get our act together, to take a tentative shape and direction, we felt held back by friends still frolicking or floundering in the chaos. "For three years after college I had hung out with these messes," says Francine Stone. "People who were strung out on drugs, and sex, and just too much of everything. People I'd gone to India with, and just people who came to crash—you know, 'Hello, I'm a friend of so-and-so; can I crash with you?' And they'd practically get me thrown out of my apartment because of too much noise, or some indiscreet act.

"I remember the point at which I said, 'I'm not gonna give anymore. It's taking more out of me than it's giving me back.' I said, 'I'm fed up with fucked-up, unaware people, with neurotics who are about to commit suicide, and you spend all night with them to keep them from committing suicide, and the next day they go out and buy a new dress.' That sort of thing. It looks silly now, but it was dire at that time, and it was urgent that I stop associating with them. That was a step forward out of the problems of the Sixties. Shedding the dross."

For many, the separation was more ambivalent. The first runners to move away from the pack in the mass marathon of the generation felt disloyal and lonely. Those who stayed back, together, seemed to possess the pure revolutionary ideals, as well as the comfort of numbers. Individual achievement could be seen as a betrayal. This split was nowhere more painful than in the women's movement. "There's that myth that if you're successful you drop your old friends," says ritual artist Donna Henes. "It doesn't go that way. They drop you, which is a sad thing to know.

"I was in an early consciousness-raising group that changed my whole life. It was on the Lower East Side, in '67, '68, and it went on some three or four years. This group was wildly diverse. There was a black woman who grew up in the slums of Detroit. There was a woman who grew up in India of Mennonite missionary parents. There was a woman who grew up with Quaker Communists in Greenwich Village. Really different, different people. And we came together, and what was astounding was how much we had in common.

"We ultimately all did go out and do what we wanted to do. But that's when the support stopped, and that's what I found to be the problem with the women's movement. The more trouble you were in, the more victimized you were, the more support and affection and love you received. The minute you got your life together, then there's no support. It was the same old thing of nobody will love you if you're powerful. I know I personally had the experience of losing friends. It was real painful."

It wasn't always ambition that came between friends. As the economy shrank and we grew older, sheer survival began to separate the "grasshoppers" from the "ants." Catherine Banghart describes a second-wave couple she knows: "They're in their early, early thirties. John* is a mechanic, a welder, and a jeweler. Jean's* a masseuse. They were teenagers who got completely enchanted with the Sixties era and weren't old enough to participate in it, and so they were hippies after the fact, and became gypsies. They had little jobs here and there. They'd move into somebody's driveway while working on a job. They lived from day to day, week to week, in voluntary poverty. It's just in the past two years that they're starting to actually get their feet on the ground.

"They were feeling guilty about giving up the gypsy life, and last summer a good thing happened for them. Some old friends they used to caravan with were going up to the Rainbow Gathering, which is more of these after-the-fact hippies. John and Jean weren't going to go, because their life and jobs didn't give them that piece of time. But all these people stopped in and visited with them for two weeks before they headed on up. And John and Jean were completely dismayed by how flaky they were, how irresponsible, and how much they covered for that by abusing other people. They felt they were used the whole two weeks. They fixed their car for them, they fixed the meals, et cetera. That was a big turnaround for them. It made them sad."

Jennifer Diener puts it bluntly: "You can now identify the losers again. They've split. The people who were permanent losers have stayed kind of like that, and the other people have gone back into a more conventional life, outwardly, anyway. So you get the wheat and the chaff." Those who have struggled to stand on their own feet are no longer so willing to be leaned on by those who won't or can't. "It's a little reprehensible . . . I've kept track of the successes among my friends more than the failures," says former *New Age Journal* editor Marc Barasch. "They were visible. And some people you just don't want to carry anymore after they're wounded. That's a sad fact."

A note of guilty regret creeps into most such admissions. Partly, it's nostalgia for the generous spirit of community. (Some intentional communities, like East Wind in the Missouri Ozarks, still do take in a limited number of the wounded, on principle and because the communal structure distributes stresses that an individual friend couldn't bear.) Partly it's the apprehension that, in our new drive for survival and success, we've left deserving victims and dreamers behind with the self-indulgent fuck-ups (and drawn the line between them in a harsher, more self-serving place). "The Vietnam vets are still our wounded," says Marc Barasch. *"The Big Chill* wasn't a very positive movie, but the nice thing was that the outcast, the Vietnam vet, came to live with the achiever. I don't see that as much as I would like." Photographer Gail Kantor (1949) believes *The Big Chill* was unrealistic because, in her experience, the secure and the struggling envy each other. "I know a lawyer who wishes she were a photographer, but would she buy one of my photographs? No." The drifting apart of friends seems a microcosm of the loss of caring in society, which was, of course, the meaning of "the big chill."

But the main source of uneasiness about leaving the wounded and improvident behind is a sense of "There but for the grace of God go I." We took the same drugs. We shared the same ideals. What made some of us flourish, while others struggled and some sank? Better family relationships? Better brain chemistry? More selfishness? Less sensitivity? "Hard work," Donna Henes says firmly. "People who are successful are the ones who work the hardest." That may well be, but it was not a Sixties value, and a lingering allegiance to the ethic of Being, not Doing, is expressed as a wry affection for old friends who stayed true to it—our quixotic alter egos.

A Sixties-generation art form is what might be called "the litany of friends." We delight in telling what has become of each member of our "family"—a recitation sometimes accompanied by photographs. "The people in that picture will always be my family," Marc Sarkady told me, pointing to a snapshot of a bunch of hairy kids draped over a Volkswagen bug—the staff of his Sixties underground paper. "They're both whole-health chiropractors in the Northwest. He's an actor. He's a video producer creating innovative TV, including a documentary history of our paper and our subsequent lives. She lives in Atlanta, works with est, and is a construction worker." Kathy Brimlow showed me a picture of the fifteenth-year reunion of her far-flung flower-child "family," including a former Krishna devotee now working in textile sales "to slap some braces on the kids' teeth" and a tall crop of backpack babies. The yarns are always colorful; as Marc Barasch says, "All of my friends had these very circuitous paths." And by weaving the diverse destinies into a tapestry of the times, we reunite what time has put asunder. In a "litany of friends," there are no success stories or sad stories (for success, too, can be sad). There are only, as Steven Spielberg might say, "Amazing Stories."

It's a mysterious phenomenon, a sign of our revival, that in the last few years we've been reconnecting with old friends, reaffirming their importance in our lives. "I definitely built a cocoon around myself in the early-to-mid-Seventies," Liberation News Service founder Ray Mungo told old underground-press pal Abe Peck. "I felt there was no longer that society of brothers and sisters to sustain me. But in the early Eighties it changed again. Now I'm back in touch with hundreds of people I knew in the Sixties. The cocoon has blasted open."[10] And reuniting with old friends is only the beginning. We suddenly have the energy to make new friends again. Researching this book, I got in touch with people whose work I'd always admired.

I struck up conversations on buses, in health clubs, at parties. I went to visit friends of friends of friends. And I was received with an openness and eagerness that was the mirror image of my own.

Perhaps one reason for this expansion is that, after a period of focus on emotional and economic survival, we once again have something to share. Our values never really changed—"You can still stay at my house," says New York career counselor Andrea Gould (1950), "you can have anything I own"—but we got depleted, our energies scattered. We had to pull in, to collect and establish ourselves. The pleasure of sharing now is far greater than in the Sixties because we have created what we share, whether it's a spacious townhouse or a homestead, a professional contact or a loaf of bread.

We *have* become more selective about whom we share with. It's part of the shift from the "beautiful loser" to the competent yet compassionate survivor that we now make and keep friends we admire for some quality of being or doing. But because we recognize the power of vision and integrity, not only the power of success and money, our "families" still cross class lines. We expect our friends to be responsible, but we don't expect them to be rich. Or poor.

What do we share? Hospitality. I suspect the Sixties generation are wretched customers for hotels. Typically, we have standing invitations all over the country, welcomes we're careful not to wear out. I stay with my friend in California, she stays with me in New York. Friends who have summer houses invite friends who don't. Visiting, we merge easily into a friend's family, wash dishes, cook. Most of us are capable of resuming communal living at a moment's notice, and still spontaneous enough to sleep on a couch. Often we enjoy friends' visits so much that we ask ourselves why we don't live this way all the time, as we vowed to in the Sixties. Admittedly, an occasional weekend is the cream of commune-ism without the crunch. Still, I wouldn't be surprised to see a new wave of fortyish friends buying land together or near each other, embodying the bond. In August 1986, Kathy Brimlow moved in with her old "tripping partner," husband, and kids, re-creating their Sixties "extended family."

And we share children, as strange as that may sound. According to the Census Bureau, one in five of our generation's women will probably remain childless, by choice or not. Whether in instinctive compensation for our own numbers, or as a result of stresses we've lived through, quite a few men and women told me that they weren't going to have kids. "When I was about thirty, my IUD took off and tried to eat a hole in my tubes. If it's gonna involve major surgery, I'll just be a doting grandmother" (woman, born 1946, stepmother to a grown girl). "I never wanted to have a child until I had certainty about my job and my relationship with my wife. All of which are very good now, but it's just a little late" (man, born 1946, married to an older woman). "I love kids. But I don't want to raise a kid without a father. So I don't think about that" (woman, 1947). "I love kids, but my wife doesn't want them, and I kind of feel that it's her decision, 'cause her life would change a hell of a lot more than mine. I don't need to have a child to be remembered on the face of the earth. Because I'm coming back as a salami" (Alvin Cohan, 1945). "There's a definite tendency among certain pagans toward a sterility cult" (Otter). "It's called our dedication to the earth" (Morning Glory). "It is my duty to pervert as many minds and produce as few bodies as possible" (Lori Lobo).

Note that none of these childless people told me they hated kids. On the contrary. Obviously, we who don't have our own still need children in our lives. And parents, divorced, working, contented or lonely, need and want other adults around. Given the familial way we already feel about our friends, it's the most natural thing in the world to adopt their kids, becoming impromptu aunt, uncle, or godparent. I can hear friends from Mexico or Romania snickering at me. We've rediscovered a natural feature of village life, and we're exulting as if we had invented the wheel. But for the children of the nuclear family, tribal behavior is a conscious luxury—all the more so since our tribes are chosen, not given.

There's another important thing we're beginning to share, now that we're finally beginning to have it: power. Many of us have had the experience of finding a job or professional contact through—or for —a friend. Such acts are not only personally empowering; they also redistribute power in the world. Sixties friends didn't invent "networking"; the WASP "old boys" who run the country have been doing it forever. What's different, and subversive, about us is our wild diversity—and our still-smoldering ideals. Our networks of old and new friends are apt to link wealthy professionals and impoverished activists, entertainment stars and talented unknowns, overstressed administrators and mellow chiropractors, good news and media access. We are just beginning to glimpse the potential power of such links to yoke power to vision. Friendships made at Marc Sarkady's conference center, Another Place, led to the formation of the Calvert Social Investment Fund, which has one hundred twenty million dollars invested in socially and ecologically responsible businesses. Its parent company, the Calvert Group of Funds, is actually run by a network of friends in their thirties and forties; the whoops and hugs in its reception area would thaw the "big chill."

This new style of friendship—combining empowerment with empathy, the personal with the professional—is largely the creation of women and of women's influence on men. It's ironic when you consider that just twenty years ago, women were thought to be incapable of real friendship. But the women's movement outgrew its early phase of bonding as victims and sniping at stars, and women revealed such a genius for friendship that in the Seventies, *men* were thought to be incapable of it. Friends provided sustenance and inspiration as more and more of us learned to live on our own and make our way in the world of work. And women speak of each other with unstinting love and admiration.

"Between my first and second marriages, my woman friends became very important to me," says airline purser Gloria Benedetta. "Men come and go, but women friends stay." "My friends have given me so much," says social worker Ellen Herman. "We share a spiritual interconnectedness. They're alive, they're accomplished, they're vital people. And there's a way that they strive, not only for excellence, but to be kind." "I like friendship with women," says executive Jennifer Diener. "I just like women. They're so brave, so many of them. And feisty and scared."

To expand this quality of friendship and "heal some of the damage the early women's movement did," Donna Henes started a series of "networking rituals" she called "Elegant Evenings for Exceptional Women." The idea is "to have our own good girls', old, young girls' network, for women who are out there doing different things and still need support. Really nice things have come out of it. A designer I know met her gestalt therapist, and they've been working together for two years. The new director of Franklin Furnace [a New York art gallery and performance space] got her job there. All kinds of meetings. Business things, but also people who happened to go to camp together thirty years ago." Henes showed me a box full of women's business cards. Unlike men's—"all white cards with black type"— these were every imaginable size, shape, and color, as diverse as the women who'd made friends and connections there: bank managers, astrologers, film producers, artists, executives, printers, therapists, a veiled Black Muslim entrepreneur.

Our friends *are* our power, as we are just beginning to find out. But they're also our pleasure. And the ability to play together as well as be serious, to grow up and be childlike at the same time, is a distinguishing mark of the tribe. While we can now march around in power suits with attaché cases, like old-fashioned "adults," we are also expanding our "networks" in more informal ways. Like the Gallucci Family.

"It began by calling myself Marco Gallucci ten years ago," says Marc Sarkady. "The name just came to me, or maybe I came to the name. I had this whole language that I developed. A couple of years later, three brothers of mine decided they were Galluccis, too. So we formed a foursome. Friends. Over the course of the next year or two, lots and lots of other people decided that they were Galluccis. Then David, one of the four, went to a workshop with Marilyn Ferguson and told the people at the workshop about Gallucci, and they all decided they were Galluccis. Many of these people travel all over giving workshops, and they started telling everyone they were Galluccis, and they interested people all over the place.

"It was going out so far and wide, I decided something needed to be written about what a Gallucci was. So I wrote this statement called, 'What is a Gallucci?' Basically what it says is, Gallucci is an energy family. It's people who love to love. It's people who like to feel the ways of the universe and act in accordance. People know if they're Gallucci because you can feel it in yourself. It's a certain sense of being wild and crazy, but also clear and responsible. People care about the family and all life. The Galluccis want to make the world a good place for everybody and have a good time doing it. We want to love and be loved. And we don't mind laughing at ourselves, 'cause we know we all can make mistakes.''

Remember the Sixties dream of extending the family of friends around the globe? "There are Galluccis all over the world now: France, England, West Germany, the Soviet Union, Canada, Australia, New Zealand, Guatemala, Mexico, Japan, Korea, Brazil, South Africa, even China. Gallucci is really about working to form the families of the earth. And people in the family think there's a bit of Gallucci in everybody, so if people think they might be Gallucci, they probably are. It's not someone who knows the name, necessarily, but someone who knows the energy. There have been Galluccis by all kinds of names throughout history. So anybody can be a Gallucci who wants to be, and they can then initiate other Galluccis if they want to. It's very infectious." Sarkady initiated me by giving me a purple T-shirt with a rainbow heart on the front and THE GALLUCCI FAMILY on the back. "I didn't realize it when I took the name," he said, "but *gallo* means rooster. And the rooster is the awakener."

With a little help from our friends, we can be a generation of awakeners. In the coming decade, if our courage grows with our clout, creative investment and philanthropy (a fancy word for taking care of the wounded), political campaign financing and patronage of the arts, will flow along the lines of friendship. The romance of the Sixties was, "I have nothing." " Then come with us!" Our linked hands created the bare bones of a new world. Twenty years later, it's finally starting to have some muscle.

WORK

A quiz: Which of the following is *not* the résumé of a member of the Sixties generation?

- world traveler, traveling salesman, flamenco guitarist, high-steel worker, architectural innovator
- Asian-art student, bus driver, Peace Corps volunteer, high-school teacher, nomad, documentary filmmaker, corporate lawyer
- sculptor, astrologer, radio actress, psychotherapist, real-estate investor

- hippie, store clerk, mother, lay midwife, bookkeeper, restaurant manager, nursing student
- rich man, poor man, beggarman, thief, doctor, lawyer, merchant, chief
- textbook editor, fund raiser, business-school student, biker's old lady, junk-shop entrepreneur, temporary typist, rising manager, six-figure executive
- journalism student, reporter, traveler, ditchdigger, juice-bar operator, landscaper, pipefitter, small publisher
- student, communard, carpenter, weaver, anti-nuclear activist, political-science graduate student, mother, legislative facilitator, consultant, money-market fund manager (goal: country-and-western singer)

"**D**evious peregrinations," Marc Barasch calls them—these wildly winding paths through the worlds of art and ditch-digging, carpentry and corporation, panhandle and paycheck. "I've had three careers," says New Yorker Andrea Gould, whose current one is advising others about theirs. "I draw my career path on the blackboard, and it goes all over the place, and they get hysterical." It's no coincidence that "straight" was our favorite word of contempt.

The journey took some of us far in unexpected directions. "I was supposed to become a doctor or a lawyer," marvels artist Stan Kaplan. Others set out to be artists and are surprised to find themselves lawyers. Still others, like writer Carl Nagin and social worker Ellen Herman, are at last doing exactly what they wanted to do when they were fifteen—but what happened to all the years in between?

Class and gender boundaries got leaky in the Sixties, and we did a lot of "trading places." Some scions of the upper middle class are barely making it, while poor kids have become doctors and entrepreneurs; some men who fled the draft into teaching stayed there, while women became construction workers, executives, architects, and engineers. Some found their calling in the middle of the whirlwind and are now making organizational change, or wind rotors, or unicorns. Others got lost, and crawled into law school to rest. The journey may have left us supremely resourceful and versatile, or exhausted and broke. Or exhausted and rich.

One thing is certain: we cast a wide net, and pulled in a rich haul of experience. The question—the same one Kathy Brimlow asked about the magic of the Sixties—is, "Where's the practicality?" Where's the beef, the roof, the shoes and school for the kids? And if we master the practicality, where's the dream?

A Radical Education

Like every résumé, ours starts with our education. It was unprecedented: 85 percent of us finished high school, almost half of us enrolled in college, 25 percent graduated, and 7 percent went on to graduate school. (Slightly over half our parents were high-school graduates, and only about 10 percent finished college.) Perhaps the most common statement I heard in interviews (after "LSD changed my life") was, "Of course I went to college. That was assumed."

Once in college, the surprise was that we were ravenous to learn —not the skills to run the old society, as our elders had planned, but the ideas to create a new one. We devoured art and literature and philosophy courses literally as if there was no tomorrow. "I wasn't worried about what career I would be in," says lawyer Doug Weiner, Swarthmore class of 1972. Zazel Lovén, who attended Bard College in the same class as Chevy Chase and Blythe Danner, says, "You'd just study liberal arts till you were blue in the face, and then you'd get out into the world and not have either foot on the ground. It took a long time to realize that one worked for a living and not at theory and harmony of music."

But impracticality was not frivolity. We took our education very seriously, to the amazed delight of our professors, many of whom have never gotten over their nostalgia for the intellectual intensity of those times. (Sixties students were "more spiritual and certainly more philosophical than [those of] any previous time," says Wynston

Jones, who taught at Humboldt State University. "And they had a verbal facility, a clarity of thought.") The trouble was, we took our education so seriously that almost half of those who started college decided to transfer to the university of life.

According to the 1980 census, 24.6 percent of first-wavers (born 1946–50), or 4,363,360 of us, are college graduates. Another 3,904,938 have had "some college." (The most common time to drop out appears to have been after sophomore year, but these figures undoubtedly also include two-year junior college graduates.) More of the second wave (born 1951–55) have "some college" (4,570,615) than a bachelor's degree (4,294,575)! Some of the best minds of our generation are college dropouts. And there would have been even more of them if the war hadn't kept men in their 2-S foxholes. Drug casualties and nervous breakdowns accounted for some dropouts, but others left school because they felt they weren't learning *enough*.

"I decided to go to Brown University," says Marc Sarkady. "I went into a program that gave me a combined master's in biology and psychology. A very exclusive program, about a dozen people in the country got into it. I was very proud of it, and very happy to be going. After a few months I was very disillusioned, with the Brown lifestyle as well as with the content of my courses. Clothes were as important as grades. And here were these psychology courses, and professors talking about how people were, and it was obvious to me that they didn't *know* how people really were. I was doing some experimentation with meditation and different psychotropic substances, and all these things showed me that there was more to being a person than was being shown to me in class."

Sarkady soon left school, feeling that he could teach himself better than Brown could. (Twelve years later, he went back to school and got a master's degree from Harvard in counseling and consulting psychology, never having gotten a bachelor's degree.) Zazel Lovén left Bard to live in Greenwich Village. ("I wish my parents had put their feet down," she now says wistfully.) And Donna Henes dropped out of Ohio State to live in a radical commune. And Ron Bach dropped out of the University of Missouri: "Real life seemed a lot more exciting."

"The creature who grows in consciousness has as his supreme teacher Chance," wrote Louis-Ferdinand Céline. "Chance is the street . . . changing and multiplying truth into infinity, simpler than books."[1] And chance was the road. It's a cliché that "travel is the best education," but for many of us travel was *the* education, the world our university. Dropouts and graduates alike had the feeling that real learning began the day they left school. Francine Stone went to Poland to study theater with Jerzy Grotowski. Poet and journalist Roa Lynn visited Pablo Neruda in his home village in southern Chile. Ritual artist Donna Henes made a perilous journey up a Mexican mountain to find her spiritual mentor, Mazatec Indian "mushroom guide" Maria Sabina. Radical Kitty Cone went to see Peruvian guerrilla leader Ugo Blanco in the island prison of El Fronton, and brought back a carved wooden turtle he'd made. Eddie Lilburn, given a mysterious list of names by an English expatriate and psychic in Tangiers, embarked on a journey he compares to Gurdjieff's Meetings with Remarkable Men. Among other apprenticeships, he retraced explorer Sir Wilfred Thesiger's steps across Ethiopia, with Thesiger's blessing and his original maps ("I still have them"), and studied flamenco in a tiny Spanish village with gypsy master Diego Del Gastor.

Meanwhile, those who stayed in the academy might have the credentials, but in other ways, their education was becoming almost indistinguishable from that of dropouts. Strikes, takeovers, shutdowns, teach-ins, canceled classes and exams, buses to Washington, acid trips, experimental theater, intense all-night conversations, work-study and travel-study programs, "relevant" courses from history of imperialism to witchcraft and basketry—all made the boundary between "real life" and school fairly fuzzy. "My senior year at Notre Dame was the year of the Cambodian invasion," says Ken Guentert. "It ended on a strike. About half of the seniors showed up for a demonstration, and the other half went to the beach. Nobody went to class." "There was too much turmoil to sit in the ivory tower and study," says Marc Barasch, who majored in SDS before dropping out of Yale.

Richmond, Virginia, political scientist Deborah Coleman (1951), currently writing about U.S.-China relations, recalls both the political peer pressure and its easing in the second wave. "You remember that sense of obligation," she says. "The more you tore yourself apart, the better you were. It was a little easier being younger; my friends would dress up for Earth Day, but they didn't have this feeling of 'We've got to stop the war!' I had more peer support to cop out. Still, I feel it was only by the skin of my teeth that I got anywhere.

"I was a freshman at Colgate in upstate New York when Attica blew up. Kunstler came to talk. He said, 'I want every one of you on that bus tomorrow!' I had an exam the next day. I lay awake all night. 'What kind of person am I if I don't go?' But then I said, 'If every Bill Kunstler has a claim on my time, my thoughts, and my life, I just won't survive.' I stayed home and felt like the capitalist oppressor."

Within a few short years, such quiescent behavior would be the norm. "It happened in a two-year span of time, from '73 to '75," says a mystified Wynston Jones. "I started to notice this difference. Students would come into my office demanding to know what kind of grade they could expect. They said, 'What do I have to do to get an A?' I had never heard anything like this before."

At the time, we blamed the change on college admissions committees, cooling down the campuses by picking bland, short-haired freshmen. Astrologers point to the arrival of the cool, practical Pluto-in-Virgo generation (born after 1958) on the heels of its fiery Leo predecessor. But it seems likeliest that some survival instinct was triggered by the contraction of the economy just as the central bulge of the baby boom pushed into it (the boom peaked from 1957 to 1961, with about 4.3 million births a year). By the mid-Seventies the bachelor's degree had been devalued by oversupply, and students scrambled for the grades that would get them into law or business school. For our yuppie younger siblings, competition was not a cultural barbarism, it was an economic fact.

It was for the Sixties generation, too, but it would take time to clear the visionary smoke out of our eyes and see it. We rode out of college on the crest of an idealistic wave, scorning wealth and achievement, esteeming experience, creativity, compassion, and commitment. And we came, at first, into a society wealthy enough to extend indulgence to those values. For a few exhilarating years, we lived our ideals. It gave us time to deepen the changes in ourselves, but deluded us about the ease of changing the world.

Living the Pipedream

Business, law, engineering, and medicine, those favored Fifties professions, have made a strong comeback in the Eighties. But in the early Seventies, almost everyone wanted to be an activist, artist, musician, educator, therapist, craftsman, honest manual laborer, or some combination of the above. (Exceptions: the groundbreaking women in graduate schools—whose embattled professional ambitions counted as a kind of activism—and the hip capitalists, whose profits were somehow redeemed by their products, from dope to rock.) Except perhaps for therapy and carpentry—there were always cabinets and psyches that needed fixing—these were not occupations likely to flourish in the free marketplace. Most needed some kind of subsidy, and for a time the availability of such subsidies—from public and private sources—enabled us to do what we wanted.

"We called ourselves Street Revival," says Jeffrey Maron, who is nostalgic about the city-funded storefront organization he and other Washington University architecture students ran. "We did a lot of work in the community. We used to fix the parks, set up playgrounds. I invented the Mobile Hydro Pipedream, a jungle gym that you could put together and hook up to a fire hydrant and it sprayed an incredible spray. Kids could climb on it and get wet. The firemen asked us to do it. We renovated old storefronts and gave them to organizations like the Women's Coalition. I helped to rebuild an old-age center for some old ladies, reconverting two brownstones into a nice house for twenty residents."

John Niles graduated from Yale with a philosophy degree and started business school at the University of Indiana, but dropped out after two months. After "a nomadic time," he settled in Washington, D.C., and "took a serious approach. I became the coordinator for a technical-assistance program for early-childhood education. I had a large budget, a large salary, and total freedom. I chose child-care centers I liked and made sure they met standards for wholesome care facilities.

"While I was there, the budget for this child-development institute increased fourfold, with money from the Ford Foundation and other foundations. Child development was fashionable at the time. If you had plausible ideas and packaged them in an interesting way, you could get funding. But it was in a soft area, and it would go the way of Headstart when enthusiasm waned."

It's a misperception that the "Great Society" shut down with a crash when Lyndon Johnson left office. Actually, Richard Nixon spent more on social programs than any other president did; social spending was first slashed substantially under Jimmy Carter. In the early Seventies, government and foundations still had the money for store-front community centers and free clinics, early-childhood enrichment programs, breakfast programs, and experimental high schools. And we still had the time and energy for them. Some of us got modestly paid to be activists, helpers, or innovative educators. Others volunteered.

If you were in a "straight" job or in professional training, it was *de rigueur* to give some time to good works and to plan to devote your skills to the good of the community. Jeff Maron "wanted to build low-cost housing for poor people." Inclined toward scholarship, Sarah Weil got the message that "going into academics was definitely bad news. I felt that I should participate in this new life by going into education, either open-classroom education or teaching kids in the ghetto. So I went to the Harvard Ed School," where the master's program included a student-teaching stint in a Roxbury elementary school. Paul Monroe, a medical student at the University of Chicago, "got involved with the Medical Committee for Human Rights,

MCHR. We were the radical medical people in Chicago. I also got involved with the Young Patriots, a gang in an Appalachian neighborhood that had a free clinic. I spent a lot of time working on these little projects: social medicine, environmental medicine, occupational health."

While all these activist fires burned brightly, consuming the non-renewable fuels of public money and youthful energy, the radical arts flourished, too. Art and activism were not separate in the early Seventies. Street theater and experimental theater, the Mime Troupe and the Bread and Puppet, Third World poetry, feminist and gay publishing, little magazines, small presses, anti-war art, video art, all proliferated like colorful fungi on the log of public funding.

But tax dollars and foundation grants were not the only subsidies sustaining the counterculture. Considerable private resources of the middle to upper classes were invested in the bewildering transformation of their young, in the form of cash gifts for Christmas, interest-free loans that never got repaid, tuition and therapy money, and rent-free convalescence for the overwhelmed. Not all parents were generous enough to bankroll our inner-space explorations or let us start communes on their land. But everybody knew someone whose parents were—or someone who had a trust fund—and since we believed in redistributing wealth, a dozen artists, revolutionaries, and seekers could thrive off one such source, like palm trees around a desert spring.

Even when our parents did not support our activities, they had already contributed the most important subsidy: our childhood security, the psychic nest egg we lived on while we wrote poetry or ran our underground papers and food co-ops in the red. Children of the middle to upper classes could live on very little money with creativity in full flood and no sense of panic. Scraping by was even a stimulating adventure. "We all made twenty-five dollars a week and we shared two apartments that we all lived in," Marc Sarkady says of his underground paper in Providence.

And oh, those apartments—furnished with wooden milk crates, filched off the streets and stuffed with paperbacks and records (I still have mine, painted red and orange), five-dollar Indian-print bed-spreads, posters taped to the wall, and in the place of honor, like an altar, the stereo that kept getting stolen.

Living simply was another of those complex Sixties acts that made many statements in one stroke. It was defiant: it very effectively offended our elders. (My rich grandmother, an immigrant's daughter, visited me in a neighborhood too much like the one she'd clawed her way out of, and contemptuously ground out her cigarette on my floor.) It was righteous: it expressed solidarity with the poor (or so we thought: my Puerto Rican neighbors had much more furniture than I did) and unplugged us from the planet-eating American lifestyle. It was sensuously spiritual, spare as a Zen temple. ("There was a richness to the poverty," says Marc Barasch. "The texture was so wonderful. Brown rice was caviar. A delicacy, a novelty, a sacrament.") It was freeing: All those fat furnishings and appliances had suffocated us! And it was a key subsidy, diverting energy from acquisition to experimentation. We didn't need much to be happy.

Cultivating our disdain for possessions, we tried to be grateful to the junkies who broke in and unburdened us. "We'd always tell our kids the story about the monk who came home and saw that a burglar had taken all his possessions," says Kathy Brimlow. "And he shook his head and said, 'Foolish burglar! He took everything of no value and left the moon and the stars in the window.' We'd get robbed constantly out there. And if we didn't get robbed, we'd give things away. We never even owned a radio until our children were old enough to want them. We made our own music, or went to listen to the bands at free concerts."

Brimlow and her friends were unusual. There was one material thing that most of us couldn't shake our attachment to. We always replaced the stereo. This glaring flaw in our purity has earned us much ridicule. "I remember a guy telling me in college that he didn't care if the whole rotten capitalist society went to hell as long as he had electricity to run his stereo," says Stephen King. It wasn't a conscious hypocrisy; we simply did not see a stereo as a material thing. We still don't. Talking to Catherine Banghart about the appliances that could be run off solar panels, I mentioned the stereo. There was a pause, and she said coolly, "Is that an appliance?" We saw the stereo—like our books, records, and dope—as a *spiritual thing,* a source of experiences that were our necessities of life.

The seeds of yuppiedom were there: one day, we'd justify buying a BMW by its "spiritual" qualities of good design and engineering. But for the present, fashion dictated the VW bug, the People's Car. For the future, consciously we expected the Revolution; subconsciously, we expected our inheritance: a nice job and a decent standard of living whenever we were ready for it.

A cynical footnote to the subject of inheritance is Eddie Lilburn's tale of one wealthy family: "Their father was chairman of the board of a major bank. For years, the two middle sons just grew marijuana on the family land. If you asked them what they did, they'd say they were waiters. We'd say, 'What restaurant do you work in?' And they said, 'You don't understand. We're *waiters.*' 'What do you mean, waiters?' 'We're waiting for our parents to pass on.' " Did they hate their father? "No, they never saw him. He died while making love to one of his mistresses. Had a heart attack. They each got a cool million."

But there were a lot of the other kind of waiters, too. Many of us subsidized ourselves by working at odd jobs to support our politics, our travels, our inner-space missions—or our kids. We waited on tables, drove taxis, worked in construction, washed dishes, carried bedpans, picked fruit, baled hay, kept books, sold shoes, slung health-food hash. Landon Jones cites the statistic that of the eight million college graduates who entered the work force from 1969 to 1976—"twice the number of the preceding seven years"—27 percent, or 2.1 million, "were forced to take jobs they had not been trained for—whether clerical, blue collar, or agricultural—or were unable to find work at all" (compared to only 7 percent in the preceding seven years).[2]

Doug Weiner "applied for a position with an advertising agency and was told that the only position was in the mailroom. I said, 'I'll take it.' And they said, 'But you went to Swarthmore College!' That was the first time I'd ever heard the phrase 'overqualified.' " Weiner cheerfully went to work as a gypsy-cab driver, knowing full well that he wouldn't be doing it for the rest of his life. There was no stigma attached to taking a low-status job—on the contrary—and I wonder how many of those 2.1 million new graduates even tried to find "appropriate" work. Many of us were like Alex, the suicide in *The Big Chill*, who "turned his back on science and chose to experience life through a seemingly random series of occupations"—one of the lines in the movie that drew a knowing laugh.

In a boom economy, "little jobs" seemed to be in infinite supply. "I used to work two or three jobs at once," says Anne Strieber, who had dropped out of college because it was "not intellectually satisfying." "I tried being a bartender, a waitress, a clerk, a clerk-typist." This experience planted a permanent confidence in our subconscious that is utterly foreign to younger people. In lawyer Al Belasco's words: "You can always get another job. Shit, I've had so many already. There's more where those came from." It's the security at the root of our readiness for career change and our chronically cavalier attitude toward the future. "I frankly don't *want* to know what the future is," said Jennifer Diener, a senior vice president making a six-figure salary when I interviewed her. "I want it to unfold. I hate plans. Hate 'em. People say, 'What are you going to do five years from now?' And I say, 'Who knows?' " (In September 1986, Diener left her job, with no distinct plans for the future other than to learn to play the cello.)

More than just a convenience, humble work was an ideology. We were an elite that rejected elitism. To us, it was nobler to be a nurse than a doctor, a family practictioner than a hotshot heart surgeon. Sy Safransky quit his job as a newspaper reporter and "did a succession of odd jobs, just to learn what it was like to be ordinary." Driving a cab or digging a ditch allowed us to feel like "the People." It was also another adventure across boundaries, into forbidden worlds. "We would drive Harlem and the Bronx, because that's where the money was," Doug Weiner says of his gypsy-cab days. "We liked the money, sure. I was able to raise enough in five months to go to India.

But there was something about being a gypsy-cab driver, too. We had a sense of, 'Well, this is a discovery.' We were like always turning over rocks to see what was under there. And so we got lots of great stories."

Carl Nagin "went up to Brattleboro, Vermont, and got a construction job, working on a nuclear power plant with lower-middle-class French-Canadians. I had so little in common with those people, and I did it deliberately, to find out if I could make real friendships with them." Eddie Lilburn, between travels through North Africa and Spain, "spent six months in St. Louis working as a union ironworker up on the high steel, building high-rise office buildings. I managed to get right into the union, which was really dangerous, 'cause I didn't know anything. And the first day I was up six floors with no net.

"It was fascinating. I should have made a diary of all the things those ironworkers would say. A whole book could be written on that culture. They are the craziest and funniest people in our society. I never heard so many jokes. Part of it was just to allay the fear of being up there. But I was the new guy, so of course I was the brunt.

"They'd call me 'Ed.' 'Ed doesn't get afeared of heights. He can look up as high as anyone and not get afraid.' Everything you do they have a joke for it. I'd go to get a drink of water and they'd say, 'Ed, whatta you doing drinking that water? That water will tear your stomach out.' I'd say, 'What do you mean, guys?' And they'd pick up a rusty piece of iron. 'Look what that water did to this iron, Ed. Is your stomach stronger than iron?' There was a twist on everything. I'd be up on the high steel and I'd finish putting some girder together and they'd say, 'Looks fine. But don't step back to admire your work.' "

Construction, carpentry, and auto mechanics had a special place in our hearts, as did fine crafts like pottery and weaving that fused function and beauty. Never have so many college-educated people learned to work with their hands. For instance, in the 1980 census, there were 1,239,245 carpenters in the United States. Of those, 60,352 had four years of college or more; 170,593 had some college education. The college-educated carpenters came disproportionately from the Sixties generation. In the 25–34 age group (born 1946–55), there were 295,714 carpenters, or 24 percent of the national total, including 38,770 with four years of college or more (63 percent of the national total), and 95,492 with some college (56 percent of the national total).

Work with the hands combined the Buddhist tenet of "right livelihood" with the populist notion of "honest labor." Spiritual seekers found manual work more conducive to Zen clarity than mental work. Seekers of independence found manual skills liberating. "I made a decision back in school to acquire a skill which would be useful to personal choice," says David Banghart, who has made a good living as a construction superintendent and has also built his own house. Unlike many of our favored occupations, carpentry and construction didn't require outside subsidies. They were, and are, a rare blend of practicality and principle. Fine craftspeople eke out a more modest living by traveling to craft fairs around the country.

Of course, some of us spent stretches of the late Sixties and early Seventies not working at all. We were so overwhelmed by the changes we were going through that we couldn't work. Or we felt that the changes we were going through *were* our work. "I remember sitting in New Orleans, on acid, and feeling like we really had a mission, that what we were doing was not just for ourselves" says Ananda Saha. "I remember asking the others, 'What does this mean? We're doing this important thing.' And they said, 'We don't have to do anything but what we are doing. And witness it.' "

While busy witnessing, some of us subsisted on the kindness of strangers. "You could ask for spare change and people would think nothing of giving you fifty cents, a dollar, all the change in their pocket," says Kathy Brimlow. "I don't know if the flower children would have been able to exist if people weren't so generous." Others had an angry sense of entitlement to subsidy by the Establishment —parents, government, private enterprise—that makes them wince today. "I lived on a houseboat in Seattle on unemployment and food stamps," says TV producer Geraldine Hanon. "Who didn't? The government's sending us all off to war, we might as well get what we can from them. Now I'm appalled that I did that." "I could steal from A&P in 1971, because I felt that they were crooks and I deserved their hamburger meat because I was hungry," says photographer Jim Smith. "But I can't steal from anybody anymore, because stealing is stealing."

Perhaps the most unforgettable subsidy was the generosity of friends. "Karen subsidized my lifestyle quite a bit," says Ron Bach of his Seventies "sister" and landlord, St. Louis restaurateur Karen Duffy. "My rent was twenty dollars a week, and it was her couch that I slept on. She's a very giving person." Duffy's largess, plus his own minimal material needs, gave Bach the freedom to "just explore other worlds. The things that I was interested in didn't pay. If I lost free time just to make money, then I would rather not have the money."

He helped build and run Duff's Restaurant, "played meditative music to soothe the place down when it got crazy," went to therapy, studied Silva Mind Control as meditation, and "took care of plants. I'd ride my bike with my watering can and my hair flying in the wind." His goals were a little anthology of Sixties values: "to be as good a person as I could be, to do good work—work that was meaningful in terms of helping people—and to have a skill, my music. I had artistic statements that I wanted to make."

Today, Ron Bach is a computer programmer who recently finished his B.A. in management and is going on for a master's.

The Ax Falls

What happened?

The well ran dry. The price of oil skyrocketed in 1973; the inflation rate and the cost of living took off in hot pursuit. Only when it ended did we discover that the subsidy behind all the others had been the low cost of living. That had been the source of the sense of abundance. "I myself used to give out spare change to people," says Kathy Brimlow. "I'd give away my whole paycheck. It was okay, 'cause there was so much money. It's not even that, but everything was affordable." "How hard do you have to work to make one hundred thirty-five dollars?" asks Jeffrey Maron. "My apartment cost me sixty-five dollars a month. My food cost me another sixty dollars a month. And then I would buy gas. And occasionally I'd go to the thrift shop and buy a shirt. So if I had one hundred fifty dollars, I was covered—for a month! I can spend that in a day now."

When the economic ax fell, the generation fractured along class lines, but the deck had been shuffled; not everyone was where she or he had been before. The first inevitable split was that the educated middle class—including the minority middle class, newly expanded by college recruitment and affirmative action—began to pull away from its principled parity with the poor. Carl Nagin got a job teaching English at the New England Conservatory of Music and forced himself to write every day. College dropouts drifted back into school like children after recess; Donna Henes finished college at CCNY, while Tina Ivans, decompressing from the Socialist Workers Party, struggled toward a B.A. in history of race relations at Rutgers. Some college graduates decided to upgrade their education and shape a career. Caroline Johnson, who'd been supporting her son as a waitress and drugstore manager, got her master's in counseling psychology and a job as a prison drug counselor. "That's what I'd been doing as a volunteer all these years, and I thought I might as well get paid for it."

As the funding for community action and education slowly dried up, those with college degrees were able to retreat to higher ground in the helping professions, like Johnson, or to switch to another field, like John Niles, who entered law school when child development went out of fashion. The tragedies of the Seventies were self-educated minority activists and Vietnam vets who had been awakened by the great movements of the Sixties and now found themselves back on the streets, unable to get a job. They are among the bitterest members of our generation.

The Seventies shrinkage of funding in the arts, meanwhile, led to a harsh kind of survival of the fittest. "I used to know a *much* greater number of people who were artists or poets," says Anne Strieber.

"Many of them weren't very good, but *they* liked what they did, and they thought of themselves as having sacrificed the money part of life to dedicate themselves to it. I meet fewer and fewer people like that." Inevitably, standards rose, not only of talent—for talent alone has never guaranteed success or even survival in the arts—but of determination. Those whose calling was loud and clear found a way to subsidize their own art. Jeffrey Maron moved to New York and did construction contracting to pay for his power tools, steel, and bronze. Donna Henes taught art in the public schools.

And then there were the New Age visionaries, quietly experimenting with new social, economic, and technological forms. They subsidized themselves by holding conferences or selling handcrafts, and held the inflationary wolf at bay by continuing to share, Sixties-style. "Another Place was very communistic in the true sense of the word," says Marc Sarkady. "Not in the sense of the way Russia is. We all had our own houses, like a village. We all shared income. We all made the same amount: fifty dollars a week. It was a very rich, beautiful, wonderful life."

It was a quiet time, after the clamor of the Sixties. We worked, meditated, went to movies, smoked an occasional joint, tried to learn to love. On the whole, we felt we'd grown up but not sold out. (Not that anyone was buying.) Our adolescent fantasies of transforming the world now seemed grandiose, but we still wanted to do good, or at the very least—as in the Hippocratic oath—to do no harm. Our ambitions and tastes were modest, our principles high. We settled into our decent jobs and apartments and apprenticeships, no longer quite poor, but still comfortably far from power.

Meanwhile, a phenomenon had been building behind the scenes that was about to burst into the open and change the whole picture. In the late Seventies, our contemporaries who'd gone straight—into corporate law, business, and medicine—were finishing up their apprenticeships. And the next, even straighter generation was coming up fast behind them. We had never imagined, when we were all in the streets together, that someday some of us would be rich . . . and even worse, that the rest of us would envy them.

Superclass and the New Poverty

Landon Jones, in *Great Expectations,* called them the Superclass. "They are most visible on the two coasts—in New York and Boston and San Francisco and Los Angeles—and their capital is Washington, D.C. They are growing in power because they are socioeconomically distinct from most other Americans. They are the professional-managerial working couples who command more discretionary income than any other group."[3]

The key factor in the creation of the Superclass, according to Jones, was the influx of women into management, government, and the professions. The percentage of women in business, law, medical, and other professional schools has risen steeply and steadily since the Sixties. In 1960–61, women were 6 percent of medical students, 4 percent of law students, and 5 percent of architecture students. In 1966–67, the figures were not much higher: 7 percent, 4.3 percent, 7.4 percent. By 1975–76, the numbers had leaped to 20.5 percent of all medical students, 23 percent of law students, and 25 percent of architecture students. Today, 50 percent of law students, 60 percent of journalism students, and 33 percent of MBA candidates are women.

Unlike black students, most middle-class college women in the Sixties did not see professional ambition as a means of upward mobility. "Not one of over one hundred forty [Radcliffe] freshmen has ever mentioned money in discussing her future," wrote psychologist Dorothy Shore Zinberg in her 1962 Harvard Ph.D. thesis.[4] "This is relegated to the man she will marry. He will provide the status and the style of life." We never thought of ourselves as poor; we assumed we'd marry men of our own class and live at least as comfortably as our parents. Careers meant independence, self-respect, and identity, a way to prove that we were as good as men and could live without them in a pinch. In fact, however, professional women were not only climbing out of personal poverty—the hidden poverty of economic dependency—but were substantially elevating their future families' "status and style of life."

It is facetious, of course, to call a couple with an income of seventy-five thousand or even one hundred thousand dollars a year rich. After inflation, they are merely upper middle class. After taxes, they'll be lucky to have fifty thousand dollars in net income, and much of that will go for mortgage and maintenance payments, child care, and schools. Many Superclass members do not perceive themselves as being that much better off than they were in the Sixties.

"Back then, I was earning maybe one hundred dollars a week," says Washington mortgage banker Rob Jacoby. "Eve was a literal starving student, on scholarships, with no income. And we had separate apartments, all the food we wanted, all the records we wanted to buy, all the clothes we needed. Last year we made a hundred and ten thousand dollars. And we have *one* place to live, and all the food we want, and we don't buy records anymore—and it's the *same!*" "No, it's not the same, because the fringies aren't there," says Eve Mościcki, a U.S. Public Health Service epidemiologist. "How many times did we go to Europe in one year on student travel? I *love* to travel! Now, it's impossible to go anywhere, and in that sense we're much more restricted." Rob: "A big trip for us is our walk around the block after dinner with the kid."

Of course, the "one place to live" is a spacious, beautifully furnished, three-story townhouse, and Eve does her beloved traveling on an expense account. "Everywhere I go for my job, I take time off to look around." The point, however, is not whether Superclass members are better off than they were in the Sixties. It is how much better off they are than the rest of the Sixties generation. They (and "they" includes embarrassingly many younger people) can afford to live in houses, or to buy their apartments. They can have someone come in to clean. They can go to all the movies they want, or rent them for the VCR. They can get out of the city for weekends or summers. They can drive a nice car. They can pay off their credit-card bills. In short, they can live at least as comfortably as their parents. And someone with a gross household income of thirty thousand dollars a year—considered middle-class and taxed accordingly—cannot.

This is the new class split that has dealt such a stunning blow to the imagination of our generation. What's fascinating about it is how many members of the new educated lower middle class—the Toyota drivers and People Express fliers—are children of the upper middle class, and precisely those who took the Sixties most seriously. They are teachers, social workers, and legal-aid lawyers who held on to their compassion and now make less than bus drivers. They are artists and free-lancers who clung fiercely to their independence and still scramble from check to check, year to year. "We have a friend who got thirty thousand dollars in grants last year," says artist Stan Kaplan. "This year, she's looking for a job as a typist."

There's nothing wrong with idealistic life choices, but most of us did not realistically anticipate the price. We believed that a good society should support creativity and compassion, and, therefore, that ours would. We neglected to look out for ourselves, ostensibly because we believed achievement and money were oppressive, but perhaps because we secretly took them for granted. Our parents' generation had built the economic foundation for our youthful idealism, and it never occurred to many of us that someday we'd have to get down and build our own. The movie *Trading Places* presented as a cruel joke of the economy (embodied by the two old commodities traders) what was in fact a consequence of our own behavior: While we were sampling principled poverty, some of our poor contemporaries rode right past us into the Superclass.

"We *chose* poverty, because we felt guilty about not being poor," Kathy Brimlow said, looking around at the small Greenwich Village apartment she shared with her lover and their respective sons. "There were some black people at that time who made fun of us. They'd say, 'Who are you kidding? You're choosing to be poor. I have no choice.'" "We weren't really poor, just playing at it," another woman told me. When did the game turn real? When did we wake up and find ourselves trapped in an authentic, genteel but unromantic poverty?

Not, I would argue, until the emergence of the Superclass gave us a basis for comparison. But that phenomenon, coming around 1980, converged with another factor: fatigue. We'd been struggling for ten or fifteen years, and the normal rewards for years of effort had been swallowed by inflation and taxes. We were the ones who could *really* claim to be living just like we did in the Sixties, only worse. Back then, struggling on five thousand dollars a year had been novel and fun. In the Eighties, struggling on twenty-five thousand dollars a year was getting old—and so were we.

"I think you sort of lose a little of your stamina as you get older," Ron Bach said at thirty-four. "You don't want to have everything topsy-turvy all the time." Stan Kaplan agrees from a few years further on: "Forty is a very critical age. You just don't have the strength that you did even at thirty-four. If you ask me whether I can get up now with the same élan or the same optimism, no, I can't. And the reason I can't is not because I don't have the belief, but that I am tired of being poor. Five times in my life without a place to live, without a job, without a penny in the bank, and now that I am forty years old, I've got to say that, physically, it's just harder."

With fatigue came the first real awareness of mortality—and the first little chill of fear. "We've hit the age that I think every generation hits, where you're watching people die, or get old and not have any income potential, and realizing that you gotta get it together," says Catherine Banghart. Anne Strieber puts her finger on our worst fear: "I think we're realizing that those that don't have will be the virtual bag people of the future." For that matter, the future is here —we've all seen homeless, haunted men with beards and backpacks, Ancient Mariners from our own past. Lately I've taken, almost superstitiously, to giving them change . . . and homeless women, and anyone who says, "Sister, can you help out a Vietnam vet?"

The fear of poverty wakes ancestral echoes. "It wasn't just our war," Marc Barasch says. "It was our Depression." Suddenly we could better understand our parents' obsession with security. But an even more unexpected emotion, to the child of the upper middle class who was once ashamed of wealth, is the shame of poverty—the embarrassment of inviting a successful friend to a small apartment, or being aware of your cut-rate clothes when she takes you out to lunch. With the embarrassment comes envy of the friend's free, grand gestures, of a life as unbounded and full of possibility as our own used to be. We're ashamed of the shame and envy, because these emotions seem such a craven betrayal of our own values. We prefer to show indifference or contempt. But the values of the larger culture have shifted in favor of success. And what we're feeling now—we who were right at the center of the culture when we fancied ourselves the radical fringe—is the unheroic, cold and nasty sensation of being truly marginal.

And marginal not only economically, but morally. Americans never just cynically worship wealth, they find a quasi-religious justification for it. Around 1980, the moral center of our culture shifted from Jesus' "the last shall be first" to John Calvin's concept of the favored elect. The result was that those who were just doing good began to feel obscurely guilty, while those who were doing well began to feel great.

Marc Barasch was editor of *New Age Journal* when I interviewed him. He had spent much of the Seventies washing dishes and making jewelry as a meditation student of Tibetan teacher Chögyam Trungpa, Rinpoche, and he had written and published *The Little Black Book of Nuclear War* and edited other books before taking on the magazine. "We're Calvinists in our generation too," he told me. "If you are successful you must be doing something right. If you are not successful you must have done something wrong. That's deeply embedded in our psyches. I feel, too, if I'm so smart how come I'm not rich?

"I know some friends of mine think I'm quite successful. But I feel like what I'm doing at this magazine is social work. I'm horribly torn apart about money all the time. I don't have a penny in the bank. I'm living, in essence, the way I lived fifteen years ago. And every one of my friends is literally rich. It's funny to me how preyed upon I am by that."

Compare Paul Monroe, formerly one of the "radical medical people" in Chicago, now a Virginia gastroenterologist who can make
thirteen hundred dollars for a half-hour's specialized procedure and
has recently built a large new house. Monroe recalls that his radical
commitment "just sort of faded. In the third year of med school you
have to start working real hard, and from then on I worked too hard
till now.

"I really respect the people who have had the energy to commit
themselves to an ideal. There's no way not to respect them. But I
don't have the energy. There's things I could do, but I'm lazy. If there
was a war and everything got blown up, I could probably get off my
ass and get involved.

"What am I going to change? Seriously? I'm going to sell my
house and move out to Washington or Wyoming and be a small-town
country doctor and not make a lot of money? Live a good life? I'd
sort of like that, in a way. But I was doing some fancy stuff today that
I don't think anybody this side of New York City does. It's interesting
and exciting. I enjoy that kind of challenge. What am I going to do?
Leave an interesting practice of medicine and do boring medicine?
Am I going to leave my nice furniture? People try to satisfy themselves now." On a questionnaire handed out at Monroe's tenth Amherst reunion, he notes, "of the six people who considered themselves
unhappy, all were making less than median income."

What happened to put Marc Barasch on the fringe and Paul
Monroe at the center? Partly, it's that in hard times, the collective
fantasy turns to wealth. In the Depression Thirties, the Roosevelt
administration subsidized James Agee and Walker Evans's docu-
menting of poverty, but Hollywood, more attuned to the free-market
pulse of panic, churned out gilded Busby Berkeley movies. Photographer Jim Smith noticed a similar development between 1978 and
1981, years he spent studying metaphysics in the California desert.
"One of my first great insights on coming back to New York was that
two things had changed drastically while I was gone. Conspicuous
consumption had come out of the closet. There were more limousines
on the street. I'd hardly noticed them when I left, and they were

everywhere when I came back. And so were people living on the street."

But the main vehicle of the Eighties values shift has been the love affair between the Superclass and advertisers, who lavish approving feedback on the hectic, glamorous yuppie lifestyle. The media follow the money and flatter those who have it, with unknown but potent subliminal effects on those who don't. The baby boom, with its indulgent parents and huge collective allowance, has been accustomed from childhood to seeing its own face on the tube. A startling result of the class split in our generation is that those in the new lower middle class no longer see ourselves reflected in advertising or even programming, because we have so little "discretionary income" to spend. In a nation that virtually lives through television, this makes us feel invisible, if not non-existent—shut out of the warm limelight.

Advertising is the most insidious and powerful form of cultural peer pressure ever exerted on human beings. With the subtle shaming of have-nots, the message that *everyone who's anyone is making money,* came pleasures cunningly pitched to a generation bewildered by the ebbing of its own special pleasures: its collective sense of power, its sexual and spiritual thrills. The magic could not be commanded back, we knew, or bought, unless by suffering. But material pleasures could be. Making and spending money offered the devil's bait: control. If we were going to go through a dark night of the soul, by God, it was going to have track lighting.

Getting on the Gravy Train

It's a cliché of the Path that the dark night precedes the dawn. In a few more years, in the mid-Eighties, a late-blooming leadership class would begin to emerge, shaped by the utopian experiments of the Sixties *and* the hard practical lessons of the Seventies, able to fuse ideals and power. But in the early Eighties, all we knew was that we were poor and insecure, and our ideals were to blame.

"We were so naïve," was a common lament as we began to take stock of our choices and their prices. "The guys that set themselves up for life between '65 and '70 are the ones who went into the galleries and said, 'Hey, you want my stuff? Pay through the nose,' " a fellow artist ruefully told Stan Kaplan. "Me, I said, 'Gee, you want my stuff? I want to get it out. People should see it. I want to share it.' " "I feel like I'm at fault because I didn't make any easy money," says Marc Barasch. "I didn't write a screenplay that made me a million dollars. A lot of people got rich by taking counterculture themes and ideas and having the sense to make a product out of them. Like Trivial Pursuit, or *The Big Chill.*"

Some set out in belated pursuit of the bitch goddess or the block-buster. Others bailed out of the arts altogether. A common lifeboat was law school. "I know a woman who gave up being a concert violinist to be a lawyer," says Anne Strieber. Al Belasco, who'd scraped together funding for a film about the Hopi in the mid-Seventies and worn himself out trying to distribute it, consoled himself that law school was "just a phase. I'm taking a rest, letting the creative juices simmer for a while." Ron Bach's tentative ambitions as a standup comedian and singer got crushed between San Francisco's New Wave tastes and trendy prices. He went back to school in management.

The compassionate arts, too, saw their share of dropouts. The buzzword was *burnout;* the reality was that low-paid work with the poor and troubled, in a society that had turned its back, could make you feel like one of them. As an insurance salesperson, Caroline Johnson says with relief, "I don't have to deal with people who are stuck. And I don't have to be stuck anymore myself. I love psychology, and it's always going to be with me. But I didn't want to do it as a profession anymore. I got sick of talking about drugs, and seeing people who were whacked out. And I wanted to make more money."

Like many former activists, Johnson needs to convince herself that she is still being of service. "I'm going to be advising people about their insurance needs, which everybody has, and that makes me feel like I'm getting to stay in with my counseling somewhat. I have to feel like I'm contributing. But this is going to give me a chance to save money and plan for the future. And I like to be comfortable."

"I need to be comfortable to do my work in the world," psychologist Marcia Germaine Hutchinson (1941) told me in 1984, the year she began dabbling in real-estate investment. "You do have to be aware of the suffering in the world. You don't have to be immersed in it." Hutchinson had spent several years running a workshop to heal women's hatred of their bodies, a form of suffering that had been very personal to her. It was the subject of her Ph.D. thesis and of her book, *Transforming Body Image: Learning to Love the Body You Have* (Crossing Press). By the time the book was published, in 1985, Hutchinson was so engrossed in real estate that she didn't know how to talk about the book on TV.

Such stories have been legion lately, and they can give the impression that the whole generation, save a few stoned losers, has gotten on the gravy train. "If one job is fulfilling and one makes more money, people are going to go with the money," says Marc Barasch. "They've already *been* fulfilled. Nobody wants to live on bread and roses anymore." "What happened was, we got co-opted," sneers master cynic Stephen King. "You take your SDSers, and you give 'em a job where they can have a little discretionary income, and the first time they get one of those plastic cards, your rebel has joined the Establishment. On some level, most of us know that we copped out. Sure, there's a few people still out there on the communes. But mostly, we live in suburbia. We make guidance systems for Texas Instruments. And live in Plano. And our kids commit suicide."

But not everyone has gone where the money is. When a major national magazine ran a story on yuppies, the magazine got hundreds of angry letters saying, "I may fit the demographic profile of a 'Yuckie,' but count me out." A substantial number came from members of the "new lower middle class," including a new generation of teachers and social workers in their twenties, who had chosen service and satisfaction over income and consumption.

Such people may actually be our generation's "silent majority"— a majority because only 25 percent of us have household incomes over thirty-five thousand dollars, silent not because they have nothing to say, but because, in the Eighties, money does all the talking. In these letters, most of which were never printed, they expressed their contentment and resentment, doubt and pride, their balancing of spiritual and material pleasures.

> As an ex-hippie who chose a career in public service, I drive a serviceable old Chevy, enjoy home cooking and still believe in the ecology movement. I am proud to be a non-millionaire by choice. My last pair of jogging shoes were not Adidas and cost me only $12 at a local flea market. Maybe what we need is a 'supply-side' anthropology that accounts for what people contribute, not just what they consume.
>
> —Bart Brodsky, Community Resource Institute, Berkeley, CA

> As a 34-year-old graduate student living in a rural DMZ (downwardly mobile zone) where educated people who are downwardly mobile by choice have long been known for their community spirit, social conscience, sharp humor, alternative business skills, and high quality art and science, I look forward to future articles concerning intentional downward mobility.
>
> —Jeff Claus, Cornell Cornell University, Ithaca, NY
> (now an assistant professor at Mount Holyoke)

> My wife and I would dearly love to be yuppies. Yet with 13½ years of higher education between us, our combined teachers' salaries barely reach $35,000 a year. At least 10 percent of that we give away to social, political, and religious causes. . . . We drive two modest American cars, and our last vacation was to visit friends in Indianapolis. . . . We are both satisfied and happy with our laterally mobile lives.
>
> Mark Picus, Houston, TX

> There is an even larger group of Old Rural Fallbehinds (ORFIES) in North America than there are Yuppies. . . . Orfies earn less than $10,000 per year. They are the working poor who also depend upon welfare subsidies to survive. Because they are computer illiterates, they are often underemployed in low paying manual labor. Wearing second hand clothes, they drive a decade old car, and eat out of cans at home. . . .

The old rural finks (still ORFies) settle into an area intending to stay put and to cultivate neighbors. Slowing down enough to tune in to the plight of others around you, and then pitching in when a hand is needed is more vital than money. . . . When you chase after the dollar you . . . become too impatient to cook your own meal, or write a letter, or play with your child, or learn to listen to a musical instrument while playing it. . . .

It's tiring being poor, as well as seemingly not contributing significantly to society, yet the struggle is tempering, and may teach me values of worth to pass on through example to my children. . . . Remember you read it here first. Old Rural Failures are "Orfies."
—William M. Sweetman, Broadalbin, NY

I am a thirty-year-old unemployed social worker. Eventually I will be employed, but I'll never make any money at it. But then I guess I can content myself with knowing, as much as one can, that because I happened to be in a position to help, someone has a job, or has kept a job with my help, that someone else made it through a suicidal hour, or, less dramatically, someone was able to avoid hours of Public Aid red tape that I could cut through. . . . You can bet I wish I could earn a lot of money (like $20,000) at what I do, but until our culture values social work the way it values market work, I'll just have to console myself by thinking I can make a difference. I guess that's what happened to me and my fellow "flower children"—we're still looking for that balance between values and survival.
—Alisa Cohen, Chicago, IL

That statement is echoed in a letter from the other side of the new class divide. Of those making over forty thousand dollars, "many of us who are members of the late 1960's generation . . . are trying to reconcile our affluence with our social consciences," wrote Harvey E. Rich, professor of sociology at California State University, Northridge. In the early Eighties, some unease, of body or of spirit, seemed inevitable. If keeping the faith meant falling behind, keeping up seemed to mean leaving the best of oneself behind. "There's nothing wrong with being successful and comfortable" is an Eighties mantra Sixties people repeat so often that we're obviously trying to convince ourselves. And no one needed more convincing than late drop-ins like Ron Bach and Caroline Johnson, as they set off across the UMZ (upwardly mobile zone) between ORFism and the Super-class, clutching their endangered ideals.

Going into law or real estate was nothing as simple as "selling out." It was a Pilgrim's Progress, full of painful blessings and seductive traps. Could the Sixties survivor get through the labyrinth of the "real world" without losing his or her soul? (Is there a board game in it?)

In the Desert

First-wavers entering the Establishment went through a transformation almost as disorienting as that of the Marine recruit who gets his head shaved. It was necessary for those who hadn't yet to get rid of the long hair, beards, and scruffy clothes. It didn't feel bad, just weird. "My feet hurt all the time now, 'cause I wear heels during the day," Caroline Johnson says wonderingly. "I've never experienced it before. In college, nothing would I put on my feet but Earth Shoes. Now I really look conservative—the suit, silk blouse, the whole bit."

For a long time, the working uniform felt like a crafty lie. "The world has changed back, and now I have to pass," says Marcia Hutchinson. "A lot of us are trying to look a part, but still inside we're just as shiftless as ever." Marc Barasch calls it "feeling like a subversive, going into the 'straight' world in disguise. Most of the people who were part of the movement were middle class. It was easy to go back, but there was a sense of going as a bit of a fraud, smuggling the child all the way into adulthood. I'm in this corporation and they don't know what I'm thinking. I can fool them. I know how to hold a teacup. I can sit and take a belt of scotch and talk about football. People were trying it out." All of it—not just the costumes, but the structured rituals of this strange new world.

It came as a shock to self-styled savages whose days had been as unbound as their bodies. "So much of your life is eaten up working

full-time," Ron Bach says with genuine surprise, "compared to my
life before, when every day was very full." Marc Barasch fretted at
the constraints of working even at *New Age Journal:* "It's so ironic.
Being at this job, which should be compatible, I feel like I'm back
in high school. I'm in the office by nine. I'm punching a clock. I feel
like I'm not living up to my ideals. My ideals are personal also.
Personal joyfulness. Don't want to work myself to death. Want a
balanced life."

But the job, or the professional school, didn't care what we wanted.
Certain things had to get done in a certain time frame. And that,
finally, was what we were there for. Moses had kept his tribe in the
desert to shed the habits of slavery; many of us needed to shed the
slovenly habits of too much liberty. To accomplish anything, we had
to learn discipline, and skills, and deferral of gratification. Meet the
Reality Principle. It felt like punishment, but it would be essential
to real fulfillment.

"I studied all the alternative approaches to healing the body, but
I didn't know where your spleen was, or your gall bladder," Kathy
Brimlow admits. "I finally realized that if I'm really interested in the
healing arts, I have to find out what Western medicine has to offer.
I was born here; I should know this. The medical system is lacking
in some ways, but I'm not going to knock it. I'm going to become
practical so I can function within it doing something I believe in,
giving care. I'm not so naïve anymore. I realize that I need very real
skills to try to alleviate pain in some way."

For inner-space cadets, psychology and art and English majors
with moorings further frayed by drugs and meditation, this was a
grounding phase. "We're really getting a dose of the material life,"
says therapist-turned-real-estate-investor Marcia Hutchinson. (Her
husband, gentle Feldenkrais practictioner Bill Hutchinson (1938),
had been told that he was a monk in a former life.) "No more
protection, safety up on a mountain. Get out there and cope. It does
feel like very alien territory, and very dirty. At the same time there's
a fascination, and some sort of skill."

"People went in and paid their dues and learned their craft," Marc

Barasch says simply. "Competency wasn't required before, and I think that's why a lot of people left the counterculture. It was so incompetent. The code phrase of some friends of mine was, 'The domes leak!' Now there's a real emphasis on skill and craft. That's a little cruel next to the way a commune used to run, the brother/sister act: 'Sure, Trish, you can rebuild the carburetor.' Or Joe—I don't want to be sexist about it. But Joe's a painter, and then the car breaks down. I feel a little regretful, but you have to insist on competency and quality."

It was embarrassing to find our streamlined juniors so far ahead in this respect. Competing with them forced us to shape up, rather than romanticize our sensitivity and spontaneity. "The point of the next generation is utter competence," Barasch says with grudging admiration. " 'Okay, samurais. Go out and get this job done,' and they do it. A lot of my friends I can't ask to do the job. I know my peers. Their second wife and girlfriend will have a big blowout. They'll have a spiritual crisis. They'll drop the ball. These kids never even heard of dropping the ball." And some of their elders were belatedly learning to carry it. Getting hired by a corporate firm might not lead into the valley of love and delight, but it was one way of finding out that we could get the job done.

"After the second year of law school is when the important summer clerkships occur," says filmmaker-turned-corporate-lawyer Al Belasco. "I didn't seriously think I'd get an offer, because I've got a checkered background. Wandering around so much doesn't look good to these conservative types." To his surprise, he was offered a clerkship at a top West Coast corporate law firm. The clerkship was a success, and Belasco was hired out of law school in 1982.

I went out to visit him with some trepidation, unable to imagine this old Sixties nomad, whom I remembered with a guitar strapped to his back, as an officebound three-piece yuppie. It was a relief to find him tempered but not much changed. He showed me a piece of wood from the Hopi village of Old Oraibi, rubbed shiny from being his talisman all through law school, and spoke of his new work environment with respect, but little enthusiasm. "It's a wonderful firm in terms of standards and training and quality of work product," he said. "But I've been stuck on a humongous antitrust case that's going to go on for a long time: millions of documents, dozens of depositions. It's draining my energy as well as limiting the scope of my work."

My friend was doing his job well, outwardly fitting in, but inwardly feeling out of place. "There might be nothing wrong with doing the legal work I do, but it feels uncomfortable. You feel that it's not really you, that kind of thing. The job has made me very, very tense." Belasco consoled himself by doing *pro bono* work for a volunteer Lawyers for the Arts organization. "I get all kinds of strange stuff, which I actually prefer to what I'm doing for money." The Sunday I visited him, he drove over to talk to an angry black street performer in his early forties—perhaps a kind of alter ego—who'd been hassled by the police.

And yet, Al Belasco is no longer a pure product of the Sixties— as he discovered when he contrasted himself with one. "The person who was my secretary for a while—she and her husband were straight out of the Sixties. I met him once: long gray hair in a ponytail, wearing an old velvet Tibetan shirt, you know, washed a hundred times and never pressed. She's still contemptuous of anyone that leads a life she considers to be 'straight.' And I realized that we venerate the Sixties to the extent that we view them through a mist. Because there are people who weren't able or willing to make a transition out of there."

Only when we had made the transition could we evaluate what the Sixties had cost us—and what they gave us. What they'd cost us, in a word, was time. So many of us had dropped out of time, into the Dreamtime. Some stayed there, not just burnt-out meteors but new constellations, artists and mystics beaming back reminders of the cosmic depth behind our daily preoccupations. But most dropouts dropped back in, and found, like Rip Van Winkle, that we'd lost twenty years. We might have gained some unconventional wisdom, but professionally, we were just coming of age at forty. Al Belasco was a thirty-eight-year-old scutworker in his firm, and he found it galling.

"The apprenticeship is too long for someone that's coming in later in life," he said. "It's infinite shitwork and no substantial recognition, and it lasts until you're considered a partner. So it builds a frustration. I need to be in a working situation where I have an impact on the work, where I can carry a real share of the responsibility, not just be a grunt. It's *inappropriate* at this age." Ron Bach, four years younger, felt the same sting. "My company is run by the old guard. I'm still at the bottom, and it's a crummy place to be. I hate it. I know more about what's going on than these people, but I get no respect, as Rodney Dangerfield would say." Like a woman who enters the workforce after raising children, these men are feeling the incongruity of long life experience and low status. And it's happening because of what we called "the Grand Detour"—that period of revelation and disorder that produced such vast inner changes and so few concrete results. "It's like we're all out of phase," I said to Bach. "Our life cycles were so displaced by that time."

"But I wouldn't give it up," he said.

And that's the bottom line for most of the generation. We might wish that we'd been more practical, or smoked fewer joints for fewer years, but we wouldn't trade the visions or the values for all the respect in the world. The question was whether we would live the rest of our lives and go to our graves with all that treasure locked inside us, while the world rolled down an alien course. Outside of a few counterculture enclaves, the ideas of the Sixties survived only inside us. And we tended to keep them hidden, for in the slick, pragmatic Eighties, they seemed both quaint and dangerous, like loaded antique pistols likely to backfire on their owners. But many in mainstream jobs endured a nagging inner debate. Should I stay on in this job? Shouldn't I be grateful to have it? Is this all there is?

Al Belasco thought he might have found a way to reconcile himself to reality and corporate law. "This thing about what you do as an income-producing activity has been a barrier," he said. "So many people have either concentrated on resisting or trying to find the perfect thing to create the income. I know I've lost a lot of energy dealing with that aspect of life. There's a program now at the

Nyingma Institute in Berkeley called 'Skillful Means' that helps people to realize themselves in *whatever* work they do. What they're saying is, 'You've got to work for a living. You have a wife and kids, mortgage payments, car payments, insurance payments. You need income coming in. Why fight it? Find your realization through your work.' It releases a tremendous amount of energy that's been blocked."

You can hear, in his words, the struggle to soothe that unappeasable something that Sixties people have inside them, even those who have apparently reconciled themselves to the comforts of success. "The sad thing is all these doctors who feel that they have everything owed to them," says Paul Monroe. "It takes me a half-hour, so I should charge thirteen hundred dollars? It's crazy." Television director Mel Damski (1947) thinks it's crazy that you can make twenty thousand dollars teaching for a year—or directing a single episode of "Falcon Crest." And nearly everyone I interviewed said it drove them crazy to see homeless people. "I've been dragging this social conscience around for twenty years now," says Zazel Lovén. "The bums in the street, the people all over the world—I always think about it, I can't get it out of my mind. I don't know where it's gotten me or the world. I don't really do anything."

"I think the vast majority may still have the same ideals, but it doesn't become a big part of their life," muses Monroe. "Other things take precedence. The justification is that people say, 'Look, the system's out there. It's not right, necessarily, but it's how the world is. And I don't have the energy to change it.' "

But the gap between our ideals and our occupations would not be rationalized away. It has generated a constant little current of discomfort that has gradually built up a charge. That *is* energy, a spark longing to leap between old visions and new skills. "There is no energy crisis," Buckminster Fuller once said. "There's a design crisis." What was needed was *ideas,* new circuitry linking apparently opposite poles: compassion and competence, ethics and effectiveness.

That need was about to be filled. The world had turned. I would date the dawn of a new era from the 1982 publication of *The Fate of the Earth,* by Jonathan Schell (1944), a classic Sixties-generation product—and a best seller. It was the first time since the end of the Vietnam War that "our" vision—passionate, prophetic, apocalyptic —touched a nerve in mass consciousness. But it was not to be the last.

Successful Visionaries

By "successful visionaries," I don't mean the regulars on the New Age lecture circuit, but the people who are presenting new vision to the broadest public with the highest professionalism—in social service, business, and the arts. Bruce Springsteen is the best known, but they are not necessarily rich and famous, at least not yet. Few have been overnight successes.

Apart from the early rock stars, our visionaries tend to be late bloomers, like most of us. They went through the same transformative experiences—travel, odd jobs, drugs, relationships, communal living, spiritual training. They created their own life paths, feeling their way by chance and intuition rather than running a prescribed obstacle course. No wonder it took them at least five years longer to mature than it took the fast-track Superclass. It's a wonder that they arrived at all, when the journey unraveled so many.

But successful visionaries differ from the rest of us in one crucial respect. It's not that they are more energetic or idealistic. It's that they have found a focus for their idealism. Without a focus, you may care passionately about the state of the world, but that passion will diffuse ineffectually for lack of a channel of expression. Conversely, finding the right focus—a project, profession, or art that fits your talents and character—releases energy, integrity, ingenuity, discipline, and persistence. Most of us berate ourselves for our lack of those virtues. We miss the point that it's finding one's focus, like falling in love, that leads irresistibly to commitment and the creation of new form.

It was the exercise of creativity that enabled visionaries to integrate instead of disintegrating. Their first creations were what Marc

Sarkady calls "gut and visceral, not very intellectually worked out." In the Sixties, Marc Barasch says, "the vision came too fast to be embodied." Slapdash expression conveyed urgency and honesty; homemadeness was in style. But those who loved what they were doing soon began to care about doing it well—not out of an abstract concern for excellence, but out of a need to express vision more precisely, an instinctive sense of the power of quality. They became the exceptions to the incompetence of the counterculture.

Throughout the Seventies, while others lost their grip on the vision and splashed toward life rafts of established skill, successful visionaries were steadily refining their craft along with their vision. They got better and better at making songs or sculptures or organizations that brought people together for a purpose. They also managed to be self-sustaining—a point of pride, and part of the definition of the breed. But the reward was rarely wealth and fame. Mostly it was the pleasure of seeing one's vision realized, a pleasure so intense that it dulled the pangs of poverty the rest of us were starting to feel so sharply. "It might be hard to pay the rent," says ritual artist Donna Henes, "but it doesn't matter, because I get more and more reinforcement that, 'Yes, this is what you are supposed to do.' "

As the Eighties dawned, however, visionaries began to feel a frustration of their own. They felt constricted, not so much in their personal lives (though a little security and comfort wouldn't hurt) as in the scope of their work. They were no longer content to make waves in a small pond. They were ready to reach out to the general public, and to deal with the power, money, style, and standards that involved. Here's how some of them have made the transition, bringing vision into mainstream business and finance, arts and letters, and high technology.

OUT OF THE LABORATORY: MARC DAVID SARKADY ·

Most successful visionaries vividly remember a moment when they first understood what they were for. Marc Sarkady seems always to have known. He traces his talent for creative leadership back to his roots: "Learning and knowledge were always a strong tradition in my family. My grandfather was a classical American self-made man. He came over from the Ukraine when he was two, delivered milk with his father on a horse-drawn cart, then delivered oil. Went to Yale in 1915 with Dean Acheson and Archibald MacLeish. Worked his way through Yale doing vaudeville and song and dance. Started an insurance company and started the New Haven Arena, which was one of the first sports arenas in the country. His brother founded the National Basketball Association and was its first president. So that's the kind of crew that I came from.

"I was always an active person. In eighth grade, I ran for president of my junior high school on a platform that said we would get rid of the administrators and the principals, and the teachers and students would run the school together. When I was fifteen and working illegally in construction, I decided that the people who were working with me weren't getting paid fair wages, nor was I. So I tried to organize a union. My activity and activism didn't start with the Sixties. I was always like this."

In the Sixties, Sarkady started an underground newspaper, a church (the Kozmic Energy Church), and a community counseling center. In the Seventies, he founded a neighborhood block association in New York City, a series of food co-ops, a network of transportation linking farmers directly to the co-ops, and a holistic conference center. He was manager and drummer of Gallucci Brother Robbie Gass's band, Wings of Song. "Around 1979 I started saying to myself, 'Well, here we have this mountaintop heaven at Another Place. Yet if I want to change the world, if I want to make a real difference, I need to do more than this.' Maybe two or three thousand people would come to Another Place every year and be transformed by this experience. It was becoming time to take it from the mountaintop into the marketplace, from the retreat place into the mainstream. This challenge became more and more clear to me.

"Some people thought that the New Age culture was the solution. My view was becoming more that it was a laboratory, an experiment that people took to the fringes of civilization so that then it could be synthesized with the mainstream and create a new society. This synthesis is now ours to live and make. It's our responsibility to rejoin society and bring these discoveries in.

"I started thinking about leaving Another Place. About that time, a guy named Wayne Silby (1948) had come from Washington to a business conference that I put on. He asked me to come down and bring the kind of experience I'd been developing at Another Place to his business. It was a very young company starting a mutual fund, the first money market fund founded with the idea of variable interest rates, which not many people knew about at that point. It was called First Variable Rate Fund.

"Our first meeting was on Lafayette Square, right across from the White House. We made a circle on the lawn and sat down, and I asked people, 'How do you think things are going in your company?' We went around the circle and everybody said how they thought things were going. I said, 'What do you think we could do to improve things?' Everybody went around and said what they thought. Then I said, 'What is something in the company that you appreciate?' and people shared that. The meeting took about three hours, and it was a very positive experience for everybody. So Wayne asked me back a month later.

"Gradually, over a period of time, I began working with him regularly, and about 1980 or '81 I flew down to work with him two or three days a week. That was the beginning of my shift into the mainstream, getting involved in consulting work. A lot of things started to shift. For six years, I had made twenty-five hundred dollars a year. I remember my grandfather saying, 'Marc, just try to make ten thousand dollars.' And then the next year I made over twenty thousand. I had to get a car, and clothes. I had to be able to function in the world that I was entering. I cut my beard off and cut my hair. It was interesting to notice how counterculture people related to the style change. Sometimes they were offended by it. That made me laugh, but also get angry. It just further confirmed the idea that it wasn't the counterculture that was going to bring the change, but a synthesis."

Since then, Sarkady has become a sought-after consultant in "organization transformation"—the movement to create a responsible, responsive workplace by "embodying the principles of community and conflict resolution in the staff of a large company." By early 1986, he was working with the top managers of British Airways, as well as Digital Equipment Company and General Motors, to transform their corporate cultures and develop visionary leadership. But he still works with Wayne Silby in the investment group in Washington.

"It's called the Calvert Group of Funds now. There's about two billion dollars in the fund, and about two hundred people work there. One of the things we've done is develop a social investment fund to invest in socially beneficial companies around the country. We have one hundred twenty million dollars we invest in companies where people either produce a product that's ecologically beneficial or a service that's given and delivered in a way that's psychologically beneficial, where worker participation is encouraged, where women and minorities are encouraged to have positions of authority and responsibility, and where generally the milieu of the company engenders this new environment that we think is important. In addition, we don't invest in any weapons manufacturers, we don't invest in South Africa, we don't invest in nuclear energy. To me it's a perfect example of bringing ideals into the mainstream." (By early 1986, the Calvert Social Investment Fund was one of fourteen such funds, and a social-investment newsletter, *Catalyst*, tracked innovative investment opportunities and the political and environmental records of mainstream companies.)

"We're working on two practical levels, short term and long term. For instance, at one meeting we considered the issue of labor and management. The traditional approach is that there needs to be a strong union. One person in our group helps manage pension funds, and was involved in resolving the Eastern Airlines strike. Then another group of people on our advisory council said, 'If you have a union, haven't you already lost? Because you have an adversarial situation. Wouldn't it be better to have a new kind of company in which there didn't have to be a union, because everybody was working together, a community of workers?' Well, that's pretty innovative, but big companies aren't set up that way. So how do you look at the long term and also look at what needs to be done right now? One of the difficulties social-change groups always go through is being either too utopian or being too pragmatic too soon. The balance is really critical.

"The challenge is to run the world better. It means developing form. It means being good at something, not just running around with naïve or heartfelt beliefs. It's an ongoing challenge. But it can be done."

REALITY CREATION: GRACE PARKER SANNINO

Grace Parker Sannino, vice president and director of marketing for the Calvert Group of Funds, traces her playful, powerful creativity back to an experience at Barnard College. "I got involved in a scandal. I was living with a guy off campus. There was an article in the *Times* about unmarried couples living together, and they did an interview with us. The dowagers who were running Barnard said, 'Please tell us this person in this news story is not you, because the alumnae have been writing in.' But I couldn't do that. I said, 'It is.' "

Sannino was threatened with expulsion. "I knew a law student in the anti-war movement who said, 'This is in violation of your civil rights.' So we got a wonderful woman lawyer from Leonard Boudin's law firm, Joan Goldberg, and she said, 'It has to be public.' So it became big news. I walked onto the Broadway bus, and the *Daily News* had just come out for the day, and there's pictures of me all up and down the rows, on the front page. My name was Linda LeClair in those days. I changed it after this. And the headline says, 'Clerics Back Linda in Love Trial.'

"CBS, ABC, and NBC set up on the lawn at the campus. They interviewed my poor father at his New England bank. And my brother turned on the Johnny Carson show and the monologue was about me. I got burned out, I really did. I was just this farm kid from

New Hampshire. But what it did for my sense of reality was a gift. Things were never the same after that. Reality became much more pliable. All this media stuff is just made up, you know? It becomes real in the process of being communicated. That is how reality is created, by people's declaration. We say it and it becomes so.

"Something else I learned from that time is that there's always new, interesting things happening. The trick is to be able to notice which ones they are. Everything in my life has always been very magical. It's surprises and mystery, and things turn up in funny ways. Over the course of the last ten or fifteen years I was a carpenter; I built geodesic domes. I opened a restaurant. I was a weaver. I built looms. I was a founder of Clamshell Alliance, the New England anti-nuclear group. I did a slide show about development in the Third World and in New England, the mills moving away, farms becoming McDonald's. A lot of the time what I did was ancillary to some man or other, though I've started thinking maybe they were actually just as ancillary to me.

"I was in school in political science in Albany, pregnant, and married to a man who was working in the New York legislature. He was putting together a committee for a New York State food policy, with business people and farmers and food-stamp bureaucrats and poor people. He asked me to facilitate the meetings. And it was just a great privilege, because if you have people of such diverse backgrounds in the same room, you get down to the things that people really have in common, like children and food and survival. So there I was, pregnant. And then I had the baby, and I was chairing the meetings with the kid, changing diapers on the podium. I've been so lucky, that through my friendships I've gotten to do all this stuff."

Friendship led to Sannino's current position at the Calvert Fund. "Marc Sarkady was running Another Place with my friend Sydney [Morris, now a Unitarian woman minister], and I came and lived and worked there for a while. Marc and I put on a Right Livelihood conference in '77, and Wayne Silby came to that. That's how we met. He's the retired chairman of the Calvert Group now, and a dear old friend. He called and said, 'Could you be the marketing director of this new social investment fund?' I hardly had any knowledge in the area of finance. But there's nothing I can't learn. Money is interesting. And I know how to talk. So, of course, I was curious. I'll do this. Why not?

"We Sixties types had to sort of segment ourselves off in order to think. We had to make a lot of parts of life irrelevant because they were dangerous, or make ourselves safe by becoming irrelevant to them—like marketing, finance, mainstream politics. But what I'm doing here is the same thing I've done anywhere: reality creation. Using whatever it is as a context for a way of living that expresses relationships and responsibility and creation.

"I talk to press people on the phone. I've done over two hundred interviews in the last year. They like to talk to me because I'm real, you know? They call up and say, 'Well, that's fun that you're doing all this responsible stuff, but you're not making any money for people, are you?' And I say, 'Sure we are. We have great performance.' But the message behind the message, what I think they're really asking, is, 'Does anybody really care? Is it possible for the world to be a co-responsible place? Is it really true that I can have some concern about anyone besides myself? And are my kids going to live beyond tomorrow?' So that's really what my job is—blindly, out of nothing, to say, 'Yes, you can trust life.' Trust and hope, translated into net asset value, fluctuation, price per share, yield, and appreciation. It's been a tremendous opportunity to talk about the things I really care about.

"I won't stay here, though. The thing about me is that I love start-ups. As soon as it's actually created, it becomes a different job. I want to do something softer after three and a half years of this finance stuff. I'm getting an assistant that I can train and turn it over to after another year or so. I think I might start a country-and-western band. It's another opportunity to create a metacommunication about possibilities. I want to do a lot of neat music that says YES YES, instead of NO."

In mid-1986, however, Grace Parker Sannino was still with the Calvert Fund. I suspect that our generation's form of "mid-life crisis," as we finally begin to approach success in one field, may be the *fantasy* of drastic career change. That doesn't mean we won't actually do it. But whether we do or not, the fantasy is important. It doesn't just give us the illusion that we still have unlimited options. It keeps other sides of us alive. Grace Sannino is a better business-woman for the country-and-western singer in her.

ECONOMIC DEMOCRACY: MALON WILKUS

Second-waver Malon Wilkus (1951), former head of marketing for the Calvert Group, makes a straighter, more conventionally business-like impression than his elders. ("Grace works for me," he told me in 1984. "That's like saying a tornado works for the weather depart-ment," Sannino retorted.) Yet he spent nine years living on a com-mune. He moved to East Wind Community in the Missouri Ozarks after traveling and working in Latin America because "I liked the idea of a society that was based on cooperation, that believed in a more just and equitable distribution of wealth, and that didn't dis-criminate against minorities and women. East Wind had a very strong position on these issues."

Most progressives, Wilkus says, had humanities or social-science backgrounds and were lamentably naïve about business. Not so the inhabitants of East Wind. The community was (and is) self-support-ing, the largest customer of its county bank. One of Wilkus's under-takings was to start up and manage a collectively owned peanut butter plant that manufactured over a million pounds a year. He left East Wind for the Calvert Fund—and has now started his own company, American Capital Strategies, of which he is president—because he was "interested in trying to shape social structures" on a larger scale.

"I think that the liberal and progressive elements of this country have been as unsuccessful as they have been, particularly in recent years, due to the fact that they have very little capital," says Wilkus. "The right wing of the Republican Party has done an outstanding job of promoting its cause, mainly because they *do* have capital. If we are to defend ourselves, we have to get greater control over capital. How can we do that in a way that would cause fundamental social change? My belief is that we do it by using more cooperative structures— consumer and workers' co-ops, employee ownership.

"Today, such a small percentage of the population of this country controls such a large portion of the assets. And by the end of the century there'll be about thirty trillion *more* dollars' worth of capital wealth. That enormous amount of capital has got to be owned by somebody. Up until now, the way tax law and financing have been structured, the current owners would say, 'Okay, we're going to start a new division and produce a new product. We're not going to sell stock to raise the capital to finance it. We're going to borrow money from the bank and write off the interest payments, and once we have the division up and running it will produce an earnings stream and pay off the debt.' In the end, who owns it? The existing owners of the company in the first place—and their wealth has just increased. No new stockholders. That's how the U.S. will distribute its thirty-two trillion dollars of new wealth.

"But there are new laws now about employee stock ownership that reverse those advantages quite dramatically. Now there are tremendous tax incentives both for companies to include employees as owners and for banks to finance employee ownership plans. Under these new laws, if the owners decide to start a new division, they can borrow the money just like they normally would, but instead of the new wealth being accrued to the existing stockholders, it will go to the employees of the firm. The wealth is more equitably distributed."

Wilkus believes that employee ownership is an idea that could ultimately "align the interests of labor, management, and ownership. Organized labor has been very unreceptive to employee stock ownership plans (ESOPs) until the last few years, because they saw it as a management ploy to co-opt labor. ESOPs have been used in union-busting efforts, so labor never quite saw how it could be used for them. But today they're faced with a serious dilemma: an explosion of the workforce in the world that competes with jobs here. The only way I think they can really solve it is to adopt employee ownership as a major weapon to defend against having their jobs and income exported overseas. If twenty to thirty percent of the company's profits isn't going out to absentee owners as dividends, that money could be used instead to finance the company, or to buffer the fact that wages will have to drop. Then we're in a more competitive position."

Right and left, too, can find common ground, according to Wilkus: "The person who implemented this in Congress is no favorite of liberals and progressives—Russell Long! Reagan campaigned for years promoting employee stock ownership, though he hasn't supported it since he's been in office. It's an idea that both liberals and conservatives can adopt, because it's not suggesting that we do away with our ownership structures in this country, or with a free-market capitalist economy. It's well within our democratic tradition and our economic tradition. It's just basically saying that this is a decentralized alternative to both state socialism and monopoly or centralized control over ownership, which is what we have today."

According to Wilkus, employee stock ownership plans as they exist today are only an entering wedge—though an important one—toward actual employee ownership and control. "Six thousand companies in the country now have these plans," he said in 1984. "Chrysler— fifteen to twenty percent of the stock is owned by employees. Pan Am —around twenty percent. ConRail—about fifteen percent. There are a lot of examples you've never even heard of, like Raymond International, Boylan Steel. About five hundred companies are employee-owned or majority-owned by the employees. Of those five hundred, maybe fifty or a hundred pass through the vote to the employees. Most ESOPs still don't allow for employees to vote their stock. But that is changing and I think over time it will change significantly. As employees own more and more stock for many years, and an issue comes along that they feel very strongly about, they'll wonder why they don't have the vote, and they'll start lobbying.

"I think that economic democracy should be approached the same way as any other right to a franchise. The United States was the first place in the world where it was heavily promoted that the common man should have franchises. First it was only landowners. Then it slowly evolved to include non-landowners, and then blacks, and then women. It's sad that it took so long, but it's been a slow and constant evolution. I think that evolution should include not only your right to vote as a member of a county or city or state or country, but considering the fact that you spend seventy or eighty percent of your waking time in your workplace, you should also have the right to vote there. If absentee stockholders, who've never even set foot in the plants, have that right, why the hell shouldn't the workers?"

Since he left East Wind, Wilkus's visionary ambition has been "to create a company that could buy companies and sell them back to their employees. Actually, the process of making companies fully worker-owned is many years ahead; there are stages of getting there. Initially a company like that would merely sell a certain portion of their company to the employees, implementing employee stock ownership." In 1985, Wilkus left the Calvert Group to become president of Working Assets, another social investment fund based in San Francisco. And he founded American Capital Strategies, "the first full-service investment banking firm for labor." He is in the process of trying to develop a seventy-five-million-dollar ESOP leveraged-buyout fund to bring the missing equity to employee buyouts. The company has already enabled members of United Steelworkers to buy out ailing steel companies in West Virginia and Ohio.

The long-range view is another distinguishing mark of successful visionaries. Most of them have studied history and found roots in alternative traditions. (Wilkus gave me a brief history of the cooperative movement, from the mutual associations of the late 1800s and the employee-owned plywood factories of the early 1900s to the agricultural and electrical co-ops of the Twenties and Thirties and the food co-op movement of the Sixties.) The combination of perspective and practicality—knowing what has been done in the past, and knowing what can be done now—makes them uniquely able and willing to look into the future. Perhaps, today, the only way to see into the future is to be creating it.

RINGING OUT A WARNING: WHITLEY STRIEBER

Conceiver and co-author of two modern cautionary tales, the best-selling *Warday* and *Nature's End,* Whitley Strieber specializes in seeing into the future, trying both to head off its most catastrophic possibilities and to nurture a new, life-affirming culture. It is work that began, literally, in a vision. But the vision came late, in 1983. Like most successful visionaries, Strieber took fifteen or twenty years to put all the pieces together. And the pieces were an odd mix of the radical and the respectable.

After the death of John Kennedy, whom both he and his lawyer father had admired, Strieber "spent the Sixties in a rage of political dudgeon," infuriated by media co-optation of the Movement. "Once Abbie Hoffman got a lecture bureau, we were over." Strieber briefly attended law school at the University of Texas. "My idea was that I would use the System to work against itself. And I sat in those classes and the sheer weight of the thing . . . I realized that law is nothing more than a specialized language, full of trip wires to prevent the ordinary person from impinging upon the role of the professional. In the middle of a class one afternoon, I got up and walked out. Never even went back to pick up my sports jacket. I went and joined the film department. I had a wonderful year working under a brilliant man who later became Trevanian. He charged me up with the desire to create."

During a year in London, Strieber had a fertile and frightening encounter with his own imagination. "I fell into the hands of a certain rock star," he says. "A very evil man, and a very, very perceptive man. He proceeded to get me into a terrible state where I created a new image for him and his group that stayed with them for years. I gave them an idea for a record album, for songs, for a whole new view of themselves, and they proceeded to make themselves one of the greatest rock groups in the world—though they were already very big. I also wrote a fifty-page poem about the death of Nebuchadnezzar during this two-week period. That was my first inkling that I have a very creative mind. Because there was always this desire to straighten myself out, get a business suit on my body and on my soul, and get into politics, go to Congress or something. And live within the System."

Back in the U.S., Strieber worked as a film production assistant and began to write. During the Seventies he was a modestly successful, implicitly visionary horror novelist (two of his books, *The Wolfen* and *The Hunger,* have been made into films). He also had a long and ultimately disillusioning involvement with the Gurdjieff movement. Both lines of development had dead-ended when, in December 1983, "I had an experience that changed my life.

"It happened, oddly enough, on December twenty-first, which is the ancient festival of Yule, traditionally associated with rebirth, renewal, the return of the sun. I was sitting in my chair, and it was about two o'clock in the morning, and I had really reached the end of my rope. What I had accomplished in life was, I had a happy marriage and a beautiful child. My work was at nadir.

"I had written *The Wolfen,* which was a radicalizing book. It worked with a lot of ordinary people—they were really changed by reading it. That was a little political flicker. But then I got very bitter again. I wrote, sort of with the back of my hand, three more books: *The Hunger, Black Magic,* and *The Night Church. Black Magic* was written with what could be described as an informed imagination. Both sides are working very hard on psychic weapons, and that book is an example of what could happen if they amounted to something. But *The Night Church* was, to me, just a straight horror novel. It was a good novel, but it was the first one that I would have to say was just only that—an act of earning a living. I do earn one, because I have a family, but that's not why I'm alive.

"Anyway, I was visited by something. I suspect it came out of my own soul, or out of my essence. But it was a real, physical presence. Someone standing behind me in the room. And I turned around, and I looked up into what was like the face of Athena—the goddess

Athena, in the aspect of wisdom, and also in the guise of war. And in that moment I put everything aside except what had to be done.

"I identified two areas that I want to work in, to try to build sensitivity in. The two areas are, very simply, war and the environment. Those are the two problems we must solve if mankind is to have a future, if we're going to evolve, if these little evolutionary attempts that are being made are to flower. I'm not interested in telling anybody anything; I would like them to taste the experience, the emotional sense of a given experience. In *Warday,* the idea that we could, with regard to the Russians, adopt a non-threatening pose without endangering ourselves. In *Nature's End,* the real possibility that we could breathe up the air on this planet, or so alter the composition of the atmosphere that the planet becomes uninhabitable. In *Wolf of Shadows,* the cost of nuclear war to the rest of life. That book is about a wolf trying to survive in a nuclear winter, and having no idea what the hell it is or where it came from. I'll just write these books and put them out, and they're like seeds. Maybe they'll grow and maybe they won't."

They have grown—*Warday,* to the point of being a best seller. Despite his mistrust of the mass media, Strieber, like other successful visionaries, is willing to use them to reach "the ordinary individual," in whose awareness, he believes, the only true revolution will take place. "What I am doing, what my work is all about, is radicalizing Middle America," he says. "I'm a member of the radical fringe, but all I have to do is wear a suit from Paul Stuart, and I'm in!"

Otter G'Zell calls this being a "worldwalker": "One of the ideas of the shaman, or the true priest or priestess, is the one who can walk between the worlds and be a part of whatever world. Gwidion Pendderwen (1946–84), our bard, was really good at it. He could put on a business suit and go up to Sacramento and look like he belonged there, or he could be hanging out here playing music in cloaks or robes, or stark raving naked at the pond." Many Sixties visionaries are worldwalkers. Having been straight and stoned, high and low, East and West, they are at home in almost any company and costume, and can smuggle the vision in anywhere. Marc Sarkady's band, Wings of Song, played in the Pentagon.

URBAN RITUALS: DONNA HENES

And "urban shaman" Donna Henes performs solar-cycle ceremonies at the World Trade Center, a modern Stonehenge. Her work is part of the enlightened return to the "primitive" or primal that is turning out to be compatible with the highest technology.

"At this very moment we're on a planet, we're walking upside down, we're revolving and spinning through space at the same moment," says Henes. "How often does this enter your consciousness? We don't notice it, let alone notice the first day of the season, longest or shortest day of the year. Farmers notice, and at other times and in other cultures there have been people whose job it is to keep track of the seasons. So I guess that's my job, to point that out to us in the city and to create ways we can celebrate that are relevant and meaningful to us in modern times. Because the only thing that's going to save the planet is to start thinking of ourselves as a planet, realizing that we're all in it together."

Like Whitley Strieber, Henes got her "job" from a vision. "I've come to realize it was a vision. I didn't know what it was at the time. I was making webs. They were sculptures. And I was doing street events, communication pieces. It was the late Sixties, and who wants to sell pieces? You want to reach the people, free and non-elitist. Now, looking back, I realize the events were conceptual webs or networks, but I didn't have any of that down at the time.

"A woman I know moved out to Long Island, into a house that had been abandoned for a long time. In the attic she found a trunk that was the archives of a woman's life. This woman was the last surviving member of one of the Long Island Indian tribes. When she died, the tribe died. And in among her stuff were two silver webs. My friend sent them to me: 'These are obviously yours. They remind me of your work.'

"I had two friends sitting with me at the table, both men. One was a scientist, one was a painter. And both had exactly the same reaction: 'You should press it between Plexiglas so you could see both sides.' And I said, 'Shit.' I put it on as a veil, obviously. I put it on my face and I ran to the mirror and there was Spider Woman [a goddess in Native American mythology]. Not meaning that I saw . . . I didn't *see* anything, really. I didn't see a spider. I didn't see a woman. I didn't know about Spider Woman. I hadn't read *The Book of the Hopi*. But it was one of those gestalt-flash instant understandings. And it all came together. My life changed. Since then I've been directed on this path.

"All of a sudden I started making these webs, not as sculptures but outside, in nature. And I started making rituals, public and private, doing the solstice. And they were connected. All my work is about connecting: connecting us with the cosmos and with each other, even in a temporary community. And us with our past, our own personal rhythms and our primal past and our collective unconscious. I do a group ritual with knots. I've done it in a lot of countries. And at the Tel Aviv Museum I learned that in Hebrew the word for *knot* and the word for *connection* are the same. This whole ritual is to bring that home to us."

Henes's rituals, inspired by dreams, have involved chanting, fire, streamers inscribed with peace messages in many languages, and total personal commitment: she fasts to prepare, and may live on the site of an event for days or weeks. Performing in public places—parks, urban plazas, the United Nations, the grounds of the Manhattan Psychiatric Center on Ward's Island—she has found that people of all kinds are moved and drawn together. Her three-week healing ritual on Ward's Island created a new openness between patients and staff (documented in Henes's book, *Dressing Our Wounds in Warm Clothes*, published by Astro Artz in Los Angeles). A Halloween event at the New York City Municipal Building drew an international response.

"I made a big public altar called 'Esteemed Offerings for a Positive Public Spirit,' dedicated to the idea that we could all live together in peace. I lived outside for three days and two nights, tending the altar, tending the fires, keeping the incense lit. Each night I slept for an hour at the site in my car. And people came by and brought offerings: flowers and incense, lucky charms, seashells, locks of babies' hair. A lot of women who worked in the building really related to the idea. The Orientals, the Caribbeans, the Africans, all have these traditions. In the morning, on All Saints' Day, Latin people on the way to work were lighting candles and crossing themselves.

"Even the two types of people in New York that you never make contact with. . . . The old Chinese ladies in Chinatown never look at you, they never smile; they are completely in their own world. And this old Chinese lady, wearing her pajamas, looked at the altar, and she looked at me, and she looked at the altar, and finally she goes [nods her head]. And then a Hasidic Jewish man did the same thing. He didn't talk to me, but I said, 'This is dedicated to the idea that we can all live together,' and he goes [nods]. When have you ever made contact with a Hasidic man? Well, you know, there *is* a chance!"

By 1984, Henes felt restless, ready to expand. "For ten years I've been doing these things, and I think the people who come to them, or just happen by, really do feel transformed. But I don't want to spend the rest of my life going from park to park in New York City. This winter solstice is the tenth anniversary of my vision. A decade is finished. So this is a big transition point for me. I'm trying now to take all this out one further step, reach out through various media into the mainstream. I think that the time is right for that. I think people are ready to be shared with. And more than, let's say, a thousand people who happen to be at the World Trade Center at noon on the first day of spring.

"On the spring equinox, it's possible to take an egg and stand it up on its end. This is a miracle, you know? If you've done it then you're changed forever. Truly. I just happen to know about it and say, 'Look.' It's so simple, and it's such an extraordinary image that it has really caught the public's imagination, and it's been in the newspapers and on TV. Last year, Dan Rather ended his program with it.

And he didn't say, 'Well, look at this. In New York everything's weird.' He said, 'Frankly, I, for one, don't doubt it.' So how many millions of people have now seen this phenomenon? That's exciting.

"So I had a taste of mass media. And I saw that my whole vision was of webs and connecting and networking, and here were the networks —one hundred million people watching *Roots*! The infrastructure is right there. Even though it's satellites and computers and electromagnetic fields, it can enable us to do all this ritual ceremonial stuff. Daile Kaplan is producing a videotape based on my work. We want to interview Joseph Campbell on the importance of ritual and transition. We want to make it evocative, with the possibility of transformation, and try to deal with more ways of making TV interactive.

"So people could stand their egg up on their TV, or light a candle at the winter solstice, the darkest time, and be connected with millions of other people all over the planet. Like watching the ball come down on New Year's Eve—just like that, four times a year. Different countries could be connected by satellite. The clock time is different, but it's the same celestial time anywhere in the world." Having already had four "high mass" experiences of unison with millions through television—John F. Kennedy's funeral, the 1969 moonwalk, *The Day After,* and the opening ceremony of the 1984 Olympics— I, for one, don't doubt it.

ARCHITECTS OF THE NEW WORLD:
DONNA GOODMAN AND EDDIE LILBURN

Even in the Sixties, when so many of us recoiled from the destructive power of modern technology, a few young visionaries were becoming intrigued by the creative, life-serving potential of some of the most advanced technologies. Two whom I interviewed have since developed very different visions of future technology, incidentally confounding old stereotypes of how women and men think.

New York architect and philosopher Donna Goodman thinks big and urban: She has designed "offshore cities" that would also support underwater industry and aquaculture, anchored to the ocean floor like offshore oil rigs and powered by clean ocean thermal energy. Midwestern innovator Eddie Lilburn thinks small and decentralized: He uses lightweight space-age materials to construct completely self-contained little buildings that can "live" on sun and wind and rainwater anywhere on earth. Yet Goodman and Lilburn have a lot in common. Each is a boundary-crosser whose vision fuses the wisdoms of different worlds. Both illustrate the tenacity it takes to try to actualize new vision in the resistant "real world" of matter and money. And the lives of both were touched by one of the great transformers of the Sixties: Buckminster Fuller.

"I was very aware of injustice as a child," says Goodman, "of the differences between rich and poor. The opportunities given to boys and to girls." Her interest in athletics, tools, and building was not encouraged. "No girls allowed" was a boundary she was determined to violate. Briefly a high-school cheerleader and model, "I was primarily a tomboy. My friends were boys. I was always comfortable competing with men. And at Smith in the Sixties, I took a 'male' role; I was the resident radical, running things. I produced rock concerts and raised a few hundred thousand dollars a year for the anti-war movement, the black movement, the women's movement, the environmental movement. And I protested. I did it out of anger and determination to make a world that was better, so that other kids would not be raised with the same kind of frustration."

After spending graduation day in jail and a summer in silence, Goodman sought a positive expression for her anger. "I had begun to realize as an undergraduate that the only real protest is to work on the alternative." She decided to study architecture, "but I needed a year of technical preparation. I didn't have the tools. I'd been a philosophy student and an art student."

In grad school at Columbia, the outspoken Goodman, a rebel, found herself an embattled pioneer in a male world. "There was a lot of friction. I protested the reactionary way the profession of architecture was behaving—recycling the past, not looking at the current world. And my thesis project was more social and political than strictly architectural. So I got in trouble there and almost didn't graduate." But while she was there she met Buckminster Fuller, and he recognized a budding visionary.

"I was telling him about my interests, and he suggested that the ocean was really the next resource that we had to develop. I thought about that, and I also realized that I wanted to work in industry as part of my apprenticeship in architecture. So I went to work in a shipyard in Newport, Rhode Island—another very male world. Bucky helped to reinforce my getting the job. And I began to learn about new technology." While teaching architecture at RISD and working on the renovation of the shipyard, she began to set up an innovative educational program for shipyard workers. Goodman also visited and studied offshore oil rigs. She helped organize a local environmental movement, and planned "a floating museum showing some of the new ways that the ocean could be developed."

When a strike ended the educational experiment, Goodman moved to New York. She had passed her exams and become one of relatively few licensed women architects, but "I realized that it would take me five years to build one idea in the real world. And I had a lot of ideas, and I was anxious to express them. I've been thinking about what the ideal society would be since I was eighteen or twenty, and I decided to try to create this idea of a future city."

While supporting herself by teaching and practicing architecture, Goodman tried to write a novel about an offshore city called "Ocean Base One." After "a year and half of insomnia and real misery," she put aside the two thousand pages she had written. The problem, she realized, was that "I didn't have enough information. I was trying to write about a city that hadn't been designed." Slowly Goodman began work on a series of conceptual drawings of philosophical statements and architectural designs. The result is a grand and detailed vision, suggesting how a society could use high technology to nurture individual freedom and growth.

Goodman's utopian concept has a congress with two houses: one regional (like our Senate and House) and one technical house, to which representatives from every field—social sciences, the arts, business, industry, agriculture, public services, engineering—would be elected by their professional peers. Within each field, there would be seats for consumer activists and labor as well as management and technicians. Advantages: "You elect representatives in your own field, so we would all be much more intelligent voters. And it gets rid of the idea of the professional politician. You have people in government who *know* something, and who are more interested in problem-solving than in politics."

Several other features of Goodman's vision show how information technology could be used to enhance both international interchange and individual choice. There's a "School as Shopping Center," where children can go two afternoons a week "to see what they're naturally drawn to"; an "International Access System" linking developing countries' needs and opportunities with professionals in the developed world ("Let's say a small town in Mexico wants housing. They put that on the computer, and architects and contractors anywhere can bid on the job"); a modular system called "Kit-of-Parts Housing," in which plain, loft-like spaces can be inexpensively tailored to each tenant's preferred layout; and an information center for "Individualized Economic Planning," where one can go to define one's current needs and ambitions ("Struggle and Search"? "Balanced Life"? "Build an Empire"?) and be matched with an economic system that is communal or competitive, simple or fast-track. "No value judgments are imposed, except to say that there *are* no absolute values," says Goodman. "In a country with a disparate population, you have many kinds of people with different goals and needs. To try and impose one value system on them all is wrong. I think a society of multiple values is the only correct approach."

Goodman plans to write both the novel and a book of theory, which will include the drawings. She knows it is a life's work, and one that will proceed slowly through the interruptions of earning a living. But "I don't have anger any more," she says, "thanks to this project." And she fully expects to see parts of her vision realized in her lifetime, even within the next ten to twenty years. People at AT&T have expressed interest in the International Access System. And

Goodman thinks the Japanese will be the first to build an offshore city, park, or "multiport." "I showed my design to a man who will probably someday be president of Mitsubishi, just for the hell of it," she says. The man was impressed. He called her Madame Leonardo. (Leonardo da Vinci and Leo Tolstoy are Donna Goodman's "strongest influences.")

The boundaries Eddie Lilburn crossed in the Sixties were national and temporal as well as occupational. Traveling "back in time" to visit the nomadic tribes of North Africa, he saw a vision of the future. "I learned a tremendous amount about appropriate technology," he says. "Nomads are the ultimate in frugality. They do everything with nothing." Unlike most Sixties back-to-the-landers, however, who tried literally to climb back into the past, Lilburn wanted to translate that spirit of earth-sparing simplicity into twenty-first-century terms. His journeying included a chain of inspiring apprenticeships to an earlier generation of explorers, eccentrics, and visionaries; the final link in the chain was Buckminster Fuller, then teaching back home at Southern Illinois University. After studying with Fuller, Lilburn "traveled all around the country looking for somebody who was building a really new vision."

He found it in New Mexico at a place called ILS, for Integrated Life Support Systems Laboratories. "It was started by a guy named Robert Reines, whose father had been one of the key players on the Manhattan Project. He himself was trained as an atomic physicist. A young guy, my age, volatile, but brilliant. He'd been given grants by various people, including Bucky and Stewart Brand of the *Whole Earth Catalog.* And he had a little group on a mountaintop, just three or four people who were doing the best design thinking. Another key player there was a fellow named J. Baldwin. I ended up working with them, designing and building, and I learned a tremendous amount. They had access to NASA technology because Reines had grown up in Los Alamos. They were building with light, strong silo caps, buildings that were totally self-sufficient except for water. This was the leading edge of that technology, at least five years ahead of everybody else."

After a while, Lilburn felt the urge to start "taking it into the mainstream." He returned to Minneapolis and went to work for his realtor father, "trying to incorporate these ideas into the commercial business world" by designing and building solar office buildings and warehouses—and trying to rent them to wary, conservative clients. Meanwhile, he was acting on another personal principle: "You are where you live." Working on Paolo Soleri's Arcosanti, the futuristic city in the Arizona desert, he'd been disgusted to find the visionary architect living in a suburban ranch house. "How could he have any credibility?" A committed advocate of energy self-sufficient housing, he felt, should live in a self-sufficient house.

First in a warehouse, then in a mutated mobile home he called "the Pod," Lilburn created his own integrated life-support systems. In addition to solar cells, wind scoops, a composting toilet, rainwater collection and graywater recycling systems, the warehouse featured playful innovations like "Wear-a-Chair," a system of loose jumpsuits with rings that guests could put on, then snap themselves to cables suspended from the ceiling. When I visited Eddie in the Pod in 1984, he had equipped it with the latest space-age energy-savers: a high-pressure, fine-spray shower that could blast you clean with one gallon of water; a fold-up toilet; micropore filters for purifying water. Totally self-contained, unfettered by utility lines, the Pod *breathed,* organism and UFO in one. Inside, Mylar and sprayed foam coexisted with a hand-carved African bowl and the raw flamenco of Diego del Gastor.

But Lilburn wanted to move beyond one-of-a-kind demonstration projects to a modular design that he could manufacture and sell. Working with a partner who is a fellow Fuller alumnus, he took the next step. It is a building made of space-age materials that can be designed to any specifications, delivered to any site in a shipping container, and assembled out of identical three by three-foot pieces by two people with two wrenches in two days. It has adjustable legs that can be sited on uneven terrain or staked into swamp, sand, or snow; it is fireproof, and will withstand winds over 100 miles an hour. Once assembled, it is so well insulated that it will hold the heat or cool produced by tiny NASA units that use very little electricity.

Marine batteries charged by a wind rotor and a bank of solar panels provide ample power for the super-efficient lighting and appliances. State-of-the-art systems collect and recycle water and treat sewage.

Inside, Lilburn's modular pod is spacious, white and clean as a computer, with big bubble windows that bring the woods inside. Will people live in one? Lilburn, now struggling valiantly to raise more money for final tests and refinements of the design, thinks it will be years before his baby is widely accepted as a dwelling. "Most people think of home as a refuge from the future. They're out all day dealing with high tech; they want to come home to Tudor. So we're marketing it first as a research station that can be flown in and set up anywhere in the world—at the poles, in the jungle or the desert. We've already had strong interest from Arab countries." I'm not waiting. In a year or two, come see my house, the independent offspring of a moon module and a nomad's tent. Materials made for space may yet spare the earth.

A STUBBORN CONSCIENCE: SY SAFRANSKY

"I have a friend who is heavy into metaphysics," says mother and registered nurse Leni Windle. "She's into saving the earth now. She went to a reading and was told she's a healer of the earth. I listened to all that and I thought, I hope you are. But what about now? What about you? There's a lot of truth in the occult stuff, but it takes you away from the really important things. Who you are. Friendships and relationships and caring. Honesty, simple self-honesty.

"I've come full circle, from trying to clean up the world and not being able to do anything, to trying to keep my house neat, literally and figuratively. It takes all my energy. You have to really look at stuff you don't want to look at. But if we all clean our own little corners, everything will be clean." That point of view—that healing has to start in one's own heart and conscience, the hardest place— is represented by a magazine called *The Sun.*

Sy Safransky, *The Sun*'s creator and editor, remembers the origin of his vision—the moment when he knew what he could *not* do. He

had returned from his travels to a desk job at the *Long Island Press.*
"I wanted to save money so we could buy land. I didn't tell them my
agenda was to be out of there in a year.

"It was a little bit schizo, going in there with a pipe half-full of
tobacco and half-full of hash. I'd smoke all night as I edited wire
copy. Weekends, I'd do LSD. One day I had one of the half-dozen
or so really important trips of my life. I realized I was doing something wrong by trying to buy the future with the present, that I would
rather starve than be false to a growing sense of why I was in the
world. I quit the next day."

In 1974, after a move to Chapel Hill and a succession of odd jobs,
Safransky started *The Sun* with fifty dollars, which paid for paper. A
friend at the University of North Carolina with a Xerox machine in
his office ran off the first two issues at night for free. Thousands of
such little publications hatched and died like mayflies in the Sixties
and Seventies, but *The Sun* survived, evolving from a Xeroxed and
stapled pamphlet priced at twenty-five cents to a punctual, professional, yet very personal monthly, combining an undogmatic spiritual
awareness with the highest standards of style, content, and design.

In the process, Safransky has evolved from a romantic spirit seeking self-expression to a harried, responsible publisher who has to get
up at 4 A.M. to write. In 1984, feeling moved to contemplate his own
prejudice against the role of "businessman," he went to the local
thrift shop and bought himself a fifty-cent tie. ("I continued to wear
a tie for six months," he wrote me in 1986, "and then stopped,
because I felt I'd accomplished what I'd wanted to.") But the magazine has stayed true to his original vision: no to compromise, yes to
that exacting muse, the truth.

An almost painful integrity is both the form and content of *The
Sun.* Safransky will not accept advertising for products of dubious
value, or that he feels is deceptive or seductive. He will not rent the
mailing lists: "You get *The Sun,* and nothing else." He won't sell the
back cover or the inside cover for ads. "The conventional way to look
at a publication, even a New Age publication, is to accept the basically schizophrenic nature of it," he says. "The editorial department

may be made up of people who are well meaning and crusading but who don't really care what pays for it. On the business side, they probably care about the editorial policy, but not to the point where it's going to intrude on the bottom line.

"Magazines that think of themselves as 'spiritual' face a basic dilemma. The most spiritual approach to anything is not to manipulate people. And advertising by its very nature tends, if not to distort, at least to create a need, a desire, in subtle ways. A publisher needs to consider what's making up the whole book. I don't know that there's an answer, but I like to see people twisting in the wind on this one. I think it's healthy. I don't think it's good to be too peaceful."

How, then, does *The Sun* survive? "In conventional terms, barely. In non-conventional terms, sustained by miracle and a whole lot of hard work. If you've got enough passion and you're willing to bust ass, it can happen. Last year, the budget of this magazine for rent, salaries, printing, everything, was about forty thousand dollars. The money comes from twenty-five-dollar subscriptions, some ads. Last year we became tax-exempt and got a thousand-dollar grant from the Arts Council. That will probably increase. Gifts. Expenses are very low. My salary, for the first ten years, was a hundred dollars a week. But I live elegantly. Gary Snyder once said living elegantly does not necessarily mean living expensively. I've learned a lot of those tricks. Not being too proud to buy used things, getting my clothes from thrift shops. My diet is fairly simple, though it seems nice and varied to me."

Like many successful visionaries, Safransky ultimately attributes his survival to what might be called "the subsidy of grace" (as in an Italian proverb that Donna Henes would like: "For a web begun, God sends thread"). "I think less of it is being smart and figuring out ways to save money than that things come to me," he says. "Inexpensive places to live. This office, one hundred eighty dollars a month. And they come by virtue of my doing what I need to be doing. *The Sun* seems important to enough people, and I feel impassioned about it. There's nothing I would rather do. That's not to suggest that I'm above it all in terms of worrying. I have two children from a previous marriage. My wife just started medical school at twenty-nine, and she's had to borrow quite a bit of money. I wouldn't mind giving myself a raise. But if I was earning a thousand dollars a week, I have no way of assuming that I'd be any happier. This is heaven, including all the challenges."

Lately, though, Safransky has wrestled with his version of the question that troubles so many visionaries: "Why don't more people read it?" For this magazine, which publishes some of the best fiction, poetry, essays, and *pensées* in the country, has only fifteen hundred subscribers (many also contributors, for *The Sun* invites participatory readership). Another five hundred copies are sold through distributors. I told Sy that I'd never heard of the ten-year-old *Sun* until I happened to pick it up in a bookstore. "Right. We don't have money to promote it. And it's a difficult magazine. Not because it's intellectually intimidating; on the contrary, I try to concentrate on making it more accessible, more readable, less self-consciously spiritual. My intent is for as many people to be included as possible. But it doesn't indulge people in fictions about themselves. I like to provoke people about basic stuff, even if it's unsettling. It comes out of the spirit of compassion. But it means there are only a certain number of people out there who will read it."

Yes, but surely more than two thousand. *The Sun* could help light the way in the labyrinth of responsibility and power our generation is beginning to enter. "Basic stuff" considered in recent issues has included the ethics of a medical student (Safransky's wife) accepting the gift of a stethoscope from a drug company; the attraction of pornography; the dangers of guru- and hero-worship; the obligation to stay aware of hunger, injustice, and poverty; the death of a parent; the difficulty of keeping love alive. Not exactly fringe concerns. And so the editor wonders what to do. "Someone could no doubt sit down and make a very persuasive case: 'Look, Safransky, stop the bullshit. If you are really concerned about getting good articles across to people, be realistic. Roll up your sleeves. Print those ads. Run a little fluff.' "

Not a chance. Safransky won't "do anything that would compromise the intent of the magazine." He'll broaden his search for responsible advertisers; he has published a two-volume anthology, *A Bell Ringing in the Empty Sky: The Best of The Sun* (Mho & Mho Works, San Francisco), that should attract reviews and subscribers. And he'll continue to trust in the largess of the universe. "It's always taken a lot of faith to keep on. I don't think the faith gets justified by some payoff down the line. The faith is its own payoff. Nonetheless, partly as a result of that faith, the magazine builds up a certain strength, and is an example of something. Sooner or later, its effects will be felt, and there will be more readers."

In the new American and planetary culture, such innovators from the white American Sixties generation come together with their peers from allied subcultures, like the women novelists who have so enriched the American literary mainstream—Alice Walker, Gloria Naylor, Maxine Hong Kingston, Louise Erdrich—and contemporaries from other countries like German Green Party theoretician Petra Kelly, British rock philanthropist "Saint Bob" Geldof, Japanese Butoh dance group Sankai Juku, Israeli peace activist Shelley Elkayam, Australian director Peter Weir. All insist on the unaccidental nature of human beings, our meaningful kinship with each other, the earth, and the stars.

As the bearers of this vision come to the forefront, they are having two important effects. First, they are breaking the association of goodness with powerlessness and poverty that has been one of the most crippling legacies of the Sixties. "Most things you do for a lot of money do damage," says Seattle Legal Aid lawyer Laura Cargill. "If I made more than a certain amount of money, I'd be selling out." She needs to be proven wrong. "I'd like people to get paid well to do what they really want to do," says Marc Barasch. As more and more visionaries are acknowledged and rewarded for their excellence —largely through the influence of peers in positions of power—that will no longer be a pipe dream.

But that is actually the less important effect of this new breed. Most of us won't get rich from commitment. Teachers, for example, must be paid more, but they'll never make as much money as successful entrepreneurs and entertainers. They do, however, need rewards and motivation: hope, and a sense of belonging to the mainstream. And so the most important thing about celebrated visionaries is simply their visibility. The media show them to us. And what we see is not their wealth and luxury, but their heart and activity. The Boss is rich and famous, but I never hear people carping about his net worth, houses, cars, or clothes. They talk, instead, about the money he gives away to causes, and the totality with which he gives himself in his concerts. ("The guy'd punch a time clock before he went on stage if he could," says his friend Stephen King.) Springsteen affirms the values of people who will never see a fraction of his income. To factory workers, social workers, and struggling artists, he's not one of Them, he's one of us.

The potential is for a new alliance that cuts across class lines, linking the black, big-city real-estate developer who builds attractive, affordable housing to the small-town handyman who told me, as he put in a rock garden, "I'm trying to make the world better." Without scorning the material world, it's a shift of admiring attention away from what people get for themselves to what they do for others.

Visionary Successes

After successful visionaries, the most influential group in our generation, the "swing vote" that will change (or not change) the world, is —the Superclass. They're the ones who have recaptured the affluence that allowed us to be idealists in the first place. In effect, they've created a subsidy for themselves. ("Now that I'm rich, I can afford to be radical," writes a friend of mine who married an heir.) But will they use it? The media would have us believe that all their "discretionary income" goes into upscale consumption, and all their time into making more. But if the indignant response to that magazine article on yuppies is any indication, many Sixties successes still feel a strong connection to the less fortunate—and put their time and money where their mouth is.

"We are founding members of a lawyers' group working for Human Rights," said a typical letter, from Minneapolis attorney David M. Wheaton. "We sit on Boards of Directors of local arts organizations . . . we are volunteers in programs which provide legal aid to those who cannot afford it, and we stay up all night on Thanksgiving Eve mashing over a ton of potatoes so that 8,000 disadvantaged people in this community can have a complete turkey dinner delivered to them the next day." Such people have rediscovered that generosity is the ultimate luxury, rewarding long after acquisition palls.

Even those who are less active say they "care for people more than things," in psychologist Marian Goodman's words. "We are lucky that we don't have to worry about money," she says. "At the same time, it's not a major thing for us. During the Reagan-Mondale campaign, so many people said, 'But aren't you better off now than you were four years ago?' My husband's response was, 'That doesn't make any difference to me. There are more important things than how much money I have in my pocket.' We still have quite a bit of our idealism from the Sixties. It may not be the central part of our lives, the central path we're taking, but it's still with us, without a doubt."

The message is clear. The great majority of so-called yuppies need only to be inspired, emboldened—or, as a last resort, embarrassed —into putting their skills, position, or money to work for the world. "People would like to be awakened and alive again," says Marc Sarkady. "People who lived through that time were touched by a fire. More or less, but touched. And that exists in all of our hearts and cells. The dream needs to be fulfilled."

Now that the public success of many visionaries provides "a community of support," Sarkady says, "what I hope people will do is find a spark or kernel inside themselves and take responsibility for following it out." To be effective, this requires careful assessment of the match between one's own resources—time, money, interests, skills —and available needs. "We have to sharpen our aim," Sarkady said, actually drawing a bow and letting an arrow fly by way of illustration as he talked to me. "We have to figure out what we're aiming at. Choice is very important, because you can only do so many things. So we need to choose our arenas of action, evaluating leverage— *where* can you really change something?—and very clearly focus on that."

By focusing, we may avoid one of our worst Sixties mistakes: grandiosity—taking on everything in the whole world, so that you were paralyzed (or burned your brains out on acid in lieu of instant global revolution). "I thought I was responsible for everything, so I couldn't do anything," says Leni Windle. Small acts add up to much more than grand fantasies.

Another lingering error is accepting a narrow definition of "doing good." Many of us judge ourselves harshly for not having remained radical activists. Network TV director Mel Damski doesn't think he's true to his Sixties roots because he makes money, sometimes on sheer entertainment. As paragons, he points to old friends who make political documentaries on a shoestring—to whom he donates money. And he directed, at some personal risk, a hard-hitting prime-time docudrama on Synanon (he himself had lost a friend to the Moonies). Damski often uses his craft and clout to tell good stories about serious social issues. He *is* one of the people who are changing the world.

"I found teaching in the school system intolerable," admits English professor Sarah Weil of her brief stint in a ghetto classroom. "I felt that I *should* want to be a liberating reformer; it just went against the grain of my character. What I've now carried into my teaching from that time is talking about literature as social material. I talk about class conflict in nineteenth-century novels, and that indirectly forces the students to think about conflict and oppression, both between classes and between men and women. So it's become the content within a very conventional form." Some of us have the temperament and talent for activism or social service. Others can best contribute within "conventional forms" like business, law, medicine, or academics. All are needed. Knowing yourself is the key.

But when you know yourself, there's still the challenge to be yourself—to dare to stand out in a situation where you once had to struggle to fit in. A lot of us need to come out of the closet. For women in the professions and business, it takes courage to "act like a woman"—both on the job and in the balancing of job and family—yet that seems to be the source of our unique contributions, as well as, often, the key to success. "More women should get into business," says Grace Parker Sannino, who prefers to work four days a week to have more time with her daughters Terre Unité and Bess Lynn. "All it is is relationships. Now all these guys are discovering the importance of communication in the workplace. Women have been doing this for thousands of years." "I thought there were all these rules of the men's world that were the keys to success," says Jennifer Diener, who, in her rise to senior vice president at American Medical International, proved herself a gifted innovator in marketing and communications. "But I had no idea what the rules were, so I didn't know if I was breaking them. That's the great advantage women have. Don't learn the rules! As soon as I realized that, my career really took off."

Men can be even more intimidated by "the rules." "I talked with a guy who's become a big book company executive," says Marc Barasch. "He said, 'I don't feel like I have any power. I can't do anything.' I said, 'What do you mean? Now you've gotten there, don't you understand? You is them! You is the them that stopped you from being you! Now you can do some good. When are you going to stop camouflaging yourself?' People did it with a vengeance, and it worked and maybe they forgot why. You can't play at something without its beginning to seep into your skin. But now it's time to bring who we are fully into where we find ourselves. If you've become a lawyer or a businessman, there's a reason for it. You're supposed to do something with it, to help the world."

Our Sixties guilt at privilege has metamorphosed into a more constructive sense of responsibility. We *are* an elite, just by virtue of our education, and most of us no longer fight it. But we are something unique: an elite that has served a respectful apprenticeship to "the people"—and found them fundamentally no different from ourselves.

Unlike elites of the past, we have no illusions of innate superiority or divine election. We know that where you start is a throw of the dice. Those who've worked hard enjoy the fruits fairly guiltlessly. Guilt arises from a more intimate source: the family feeling for people outside our own class and culture (not to mention the debt to them) that we acquired in all our boundary-hopping. To Sixties veterans, the words "sisters and brothers" are more than just political rhetoric; they are a statement of real kinship that makes a moral claim. It is that felt bond between those in power and those out of it that is our hope.

"One interesting thing about being a real-estate developer is that you can, not always, but sometimes, do what you dream of," says John Niles, once a volunteer for the Black Panthers, still committed to community in his more "pragmatic" way. "You do have to make a profit. That's not disreputable, or contrary to principles. Income is necessary. But you *can* balance profitable developments with social objectives. They are *not* mutually exclusive." In the past three years, Niles has been able to realize a vision: planning and building "a new community that is as comfortable and attractive as a seasoned neighborhood."

His development company had won the contract for a major central-city site. Acting as a mediator between the demands of housing activists and the realities of financing, Niles persuaded the developer to make a commitment to a percentage of affordable housing. "They had to do something that was a gesture to the community. They could be dragged screaming into it, or they could take the high ground and say, 'We're good men of heart.' "

After putting together "a deal that worked on paper, to convince investors that I could pull it off," Niles chose a planner and architects who shared his vision: "Cities, I think, are works of art. We have to make them as sympathetic to human growth and development as possible. And communities are living entities. You need more than just a place to work. You need a park to go to, open space. You can plan certain cultural things like an outdoor performing facility, a museum. And a real community has an identity, a flavor. Corner stores."

Niles succeeded in giving his "new neighborhood" most of these features. "I lost on the cultural element. We ran out of space. You win some, you lose some. There's no magical way to effect change. It's a matter of pragmatism, what's actually feasible. I chose a rational, compassionate approach, not confrontation. Successful social activists are *activists.* Their stake isn't just verbal. They're *doing.* "

Many professionals our age, like Niles, have now earned enough clout and credibility to direct some of the resources of their firms toward visionary goals. They argue that corporations *can* be made socially responsible, by a combination of tax incentives and changing societal values. To skeptics like Jeremy Rifkin—who believes that the corporation is intrinsically utilitarian and profit-maximizing—the advocates of "organization transformation" reply that corporations are, in the last analysis, made up of human beings, and human beings can change.

Where organizational conservatism verges on inertia, however, it may be necessary to move on. "I'm getting out of my big corporate law firm," Al Belasco wrote me with relief. "It has served its purpose. Now it's time to use my skills for something useful." With his lifelong love of Asia, Belasco had recently become fascinated by the growing economic and cultural alliances of the Pacific Rim. He had tried in vain to interest his firm. "My immediate motivation for leaving is that nothing significant was happening in regard to the Pacific Rim," he wrote. "I lobbied hard to get the firm to send a representative on a major corporate trade mission to China. The amount of delay connected with this decision was shocking. These spiritual cigar smokers deliberated and they questioned and they deliberated. They believe the world is business as usual. They haven't figured out that the Chinese and Koreans don't belong to the cadaverous old-boys' network.

"One thing is clear to me. I must return to my efforts to synthesize East and West in some pragmatic way. I don't know exactly what I'm moving toward. It will unfold one step at a time. In the short term

I will stay formally in the legal profession—but I'm looking for an international business practice with a definite slant toward the Pacific Rim.

"This approach was corroborated by the *I Ching.* My inquiry was whether I should attempt to pursue international law. The answer was Ch'ien, the first hexagram. Each time I threw, the result was the same, a seven—no moving lines. I was startled. You know how rare this is. I have never had as clear an indication of the rightness of a pursuit since a dream I had before doing the Hopi film. In that dream, I found a gold ring in a swimming pool full of mud and junk, to the astonishment of the people around me, who had tried to dissuade me from jumping in.

"Recently, I've been reading Krishnamurti," Belasco ended his letter. "He has forced me back to basics. How easily we become sidetracked by what we are convinced by others to be real adult activities—professions, politics, investments, material accretions like cars and clothes. Unless we're careful and well-prepared, adulthood becomes a deviation from the path. Long live childhood!"

Of course he's being metaphorical. He isn't going to regrow his thinning hair, or give away his car and clothes. He hopes to become a father (long live childhood!), and will probably be more adult and responsible than before. What he is expressing is the feeling of being himself again, back on his own path, that comes from reconnecting with the vision. As more and more of us reconnect—through career change, volunteer work, social investment, or just living our beliefs in daily acts—we are finding it literally rejuvenating. Some of the joy and mystery have come back with the concern.

"There's a friskiness, a second adolescence stealing up on all of us," says Marc Barasch. "A feeling of wanting to show your colors. An urge to wear rainbow T-shirts." Kathy Brimlow and her best friend have begun making tie-dyed T-shirts and love beads under the name "Flower Child Emanations." The Gallucci Family, with its rainbow T-shirts, is "a context for people to have permission to feel that you can be boldly yourself in the world and still have a job and a family," Marc Sarkady says. "You can have values and still do everything you do." "The point," Barasch said of his vision for *New Age Journal*, "is to give people a context in which they feel they can be grownups, and responsible citizens, and sentimental idealists. It's not conflicting."

Under new editorship (Barasch had to leave for reasons of health), *New Age* became the slickest of several publications to expand that context by printing good, hard news of the new culture. Others include *The Utne Reader*, a superb "digest of the alternative press," and *New Options* newsletter. (See Access section for more information.) These highly professional, yet informal publications—factual, skeptical, hopeful, anything but flaky—are our generation's most characteristic creations right now, and the networks through which we talk to one another. Their "voice" could be your college roommate's. They are interactive, providing not only information, but access to the most effective people working on visionary change. These are the places to read about land trusts, revolving loan funds, worker-owned businesses, co-op health insurance, resource banks, bioregionalism, appropriate technology, flexitime, intrapreneurship, minority activism for self-reliance, Christian stewardship, "human economy," and every other dimension of the "sustainable" new world.

Lately, though, even the mainstream media have been celebrating compassion. "We Are the World," Live Aid, Farm Aid, and Hands Across America, with their sanguine suggestion that you can have your cake and share it too, have triggered a good-news trend. In its collector's issue on "The New Leadership Class," *Esquire*—as much a generation's as a men's magazine—profiled superstars and entrepreneurs, but also a small publisher, an innovative prison commissioner, a food-bank founder, two former VISTA volunteers who've stayed with their communities, and the black mayor of Bolton, Mississippi, a former Civil Rights activist. *Vogue* has been running articles on the turn toward the spiritual. Trendy *New York* magazine told readers where to volunteer to help the city's homeless.

The same trend is apparent on TV. Steven Spielberg has made *Trevor's World,* a TV-movie about the Philadelphia boy who insisted on taking clothes and food to the homeless, and later went to India to work with Mother Teresa. ABC's Brandon Stoddard (1937) and NBC's Brandon Tartikoff (1949), unabashedly commercial programmers, have been responsible for such powerful "television events" as *The Day After* and *Wallenberg: A Hero's Story.* The shift in the national mood is at least partly due to "visionary successes"—veterans of the Sixties coming into positions of power and being willing to "show their colors." "It's our time," says Marc Sarkady. "Our time to inherit the world."

Three minutes to midnight on the atomic clock.†

It often seems that what we've inherited is a big blue time bomb, and the task of defusing it before the ticking stops. Can we do that? Can anybody?

We're a strangely confident generation, for all the humbling setbacks we've had. For instance, many of us actually believe that, if we put our minds to it, we can end world hunger by the year 2000. (Laugh, but those who believe it do more than those who don't.) We have that latent Samson sense of power, even though our hair is shorn. "I still feel as if more is possible than people today ever conceive of," says Baltimore public defender Bob Waldman. He traces that feeling right back to 1968: "As people did more, more and more kept happening, until the entire borough of Manhattan was completely choked by anti-war demonstrations!" It's a theme that came up over and over: Nothing can stop us, because we stopped the war.

"All these years of floundering to find myself, to marshal my abilities," says playwright Francine Stone, "have been with the sense that I was doing something important, because I was a child of the Sixties. I had the power to stop wars." "My mother said, 'You can't fight city hall,' says Donna Henes. "And I said, 'Well, we did!' We did the Civil Rights movement, the women's movement, the environmental movement. We ended the war." "Toppling a president, end-

†The "atomic clock" is printed on the cover of every issue of *The Bulletin of Atomic Scientists.*

ing a war, when everything in the culture was against you, gives you a feeling of tremendous efficacy in the world," says artist Stan Kaplan. "You can do anything."

Call it confidence or arrogance—or faith—we need it now. Grant that we stopped a small war. Can we stop the big clock? This is the rendezvous we were born for, with the enemy we were born with. Boom meets bomb.

Conclusion: The Evolutionary War

I have set before you life and death,
blessing and cursing: therefore
choose life, that both thou and thy
seed may live.
—DEUTERONOMY 30:19

The end of this book begins with a story. It's the story of one of those poor kids who ended up in the Superclass: Los Angeles anesthesiologist Robert Murphy, the kind young doctor who tried to resuscitate E.T. in Spielberg's movie. He's been resurrected a few times himself, as he recounted with irresistible ebullience and comic energy one evening in late 1984.

"I was born in Chicago in 1948, in a real white ghetto," Murphy began (after warning me that "I have a real tendency to bullshit"— his wife, Marsha, says that his account of his drinking and drug use is wildly exaggerated). "I have very few impressions of it other than a lot of street violence and shootings. We moved then to the south-west far corner of Chicago—an incredibly lower white middle-class, blue-collar-worker area. Absolute ultra rednecks. It's the headquarters of the American Nazi Party—Marquette Park. There were no blacks, no Jewish people, education was frowned on, violence and alcoholism was rampant. I was a juvenile delinquent, stole cars and robbed taverns and was in jail.

"Grammar school was horrible. Really rigid, traditional, Catholic. Nuns. I was punished by my parents and the nuns and the neighbors. If you masturbate you're blind; you can't sit at a dinner table with a white tablecloth 'cause it reminds women of sheets and beds. I'm serious! Nobody ever heard that one. It blows away the patent-leather shoes. But y'know, you don't make that crap up! Everything from the waist down is bad; you're basically bad; you have to fight to be good. In eighth grade the entire class was thrown out of school 'cause somebody had a mixed party.

"All the kids were all screwed up. I was nuts; I broke all the rules. They used to send things home: 'We believe in corporal punishment. Can we beat your kid up?' My father would write, Yeah! Kick his ass! and sign the back of it. Y'know, it's fine. He's a rotten kid, he needs it. I stopped going to church, I lied about that. We drank heavily in seventh and eighth grade.

"Then high school starts. Three or four of my friends weren't going to high school. One of them was already in jail. I grew up in a very punk-oriented attitude. Flaunt authority; going to jail is cool; getting in fights is cool; getting drunk and drinking till unconsciousness is cool. Education is out, tattoos are in. Long, greasy hair is really cool; pointed shoes, white socks. My heroes were people a few years older than me who were drunker than me most of the time and had nice cars. That was success.

"We were totally paranoid of women, of relationships other than —nuts: no relationships. Nobody had relationships with women. They were over there, we were over here, we'd get drunk, grab each other, and run home. The adults in my life were the same way. They were drunk. They were fighting in the streets; we were fighting in the bowling alley. The police would come and take them away; the police would come and take us away. Just insanity.

"I got thrown out of the Irish Christian Brothers High School for smoking, cutting class, stealing cars, hanging around with bad people. Went to the local public school, where everybody was a punk, nobody went to school, we were all in trouble all the time. Nobody finished high school; nobody. I finished. My father said, 'I'll kill you.' Father says, 'If you don't go to college, you can't live in my house anymore.' I can't get into college. Father knows somebody at a little Catholic school in Dubuque, Iowa, and I get to school. The first time —I'm now seventeen—I'm away from home.

"Very strict place. Catholics again. Gotta sign in at night. All men's school, all women's school two miles away. I spend the first two semesters drunk almost daily, in trouble. Flunked almost all the courses, and had to go to summer school. Stayed out there all summer, flunking and getting drunk. Father pulls one more string, and I get to go back. The third semester ends in a disaster. I steal a car with a sixteen-year-old girl in it, cross the state line, and get picked up and have a lot of problems. I come back home, and Father says, 'You have two weeks to get a job and you're out.' I got a job with the phone company and moved in with some friends.

"They were living over in Hyde Park in a classic hippie pad. Everybody's got hair down to their waists. *Tons* of marijuana. *Tons* of hallucinogenics. Psilocybin, amphetamines. I loved it. I was stoned all the time. I had a reasonably good job with the phone company, AT&T, and I was responsible enough to go down there. I was on my own and I survived. That was a really nice time in my life.

"Meanwhile, the war's goin' hot and heavy. Daddy again pulls some strings. Daddy, with no money, has a lot of strings. I get into the Naval Reserves, which is, probably won't have to go to Vietnam, but I gotta go to meetings. I don't go to meetings, 'cause you can't go to meetings if you're stoned all the time, and all your friends are telling you you're a warmonger, don't go. I was a very uneducated person at this time. I didn't have *any* political savvy. All I was was some guy with a real religious Irish Catholic background, hanging around people in college who came from educated families and had different attitudes than mine. They all left the country, took over-doses of drugs, the draft board said they were homosexuals. I didn't have strong convictions either way.

"1968, the military says, You can't screw us over anymore; you're goin' in the service, bud. My hippie friends take me to the airport. I get on an airplane, first time in my life, stoned, scared. My hair's down to my butt. And I fly out to Treasure Island in San Francisco, freaked out of my mind. I get into this place, Berkeley, California, 1968. And nobody cares about me. All I have to do is stand in the square at six thirty in the morning, and the only time they want to see me again is in that square at six thirty the next morning. So I get into real heavy dope again.

"And then I get orders to go to Vietnam. And I go—Whoa! Life becomes intensely serious all at once. I run away; I go AWOL, live with a bunch of hippies in Oakland. One of them is a Marine who's just come back from Vietnam, who's willing to give me all his money and everything he owns to get me to Canada. Don't go; you're gonna get killed; it's terrible; you don't understand what's gonna happen.

"He was telling me the truth. But my attitude was, I don't really believe I'll die; I can't live in Canada; I can't live in Europe; I don't know how to speak the languages. I'm not so stupid through all this. I know my limitations. I also know I gotta be back at Camp Pendleton in twenty-nine days or I'm a deserter. So I hitchhike down twenty-eight days later. Try to turn myself in, but I've sold my uniform, I've sold my orders—I'm just some jerk who shows up in a pair of shorts. They don't believe me. But I have a number, my service number, B593576. This was ingrained in me from boot camp. They put me in jail for a week, and they slap my wrist and make me go through advanced infantry training. And I landed in Vietnam in September of 1968. Life turns to shit. Except, the drugs are great. Again, drugs permeate the whole thing.

"When I got there, I believed I would die. I was very frightened. I landed in Da Nang and then went very, very far north to a place called Dong Ha, which was a base camp of the Third Marine Division, and then went to smaller, little base camps, LZ7, Khe Sanh; nutty, crazy places that I don't remember that well. I was stoned immediately, and for an entire year. Took an enormous amount of amphetamines and barbiturates that the medics gave us. Here, take this, you gotta stay up all night; here, take this, you want to go to sleep. Marijuana you got from the people. Had hallucinogenics sent to us from overseas. There was a lot of drinking. Everybody was shootin' up. Not *everybody;* I exaggerate. A lot of everybodies and alwayses should be cut in half. But when you run in that sphere of people, you think it's everyone. I never shot up heroin; I did a lot of opium, soaked in marijuana. I think I was addicted to that at one time.

"I was not a front-line soldier. I didn't go out and shoot people. However, I was shot at very much. We lived in trenches and holes in a very remote area, and didn't have hot water or anything like that. We were support—the last point from the people that went into the field. And we were sapped a lot. It was very frightening and scary and nuts. I got a real good education about the world, and poverty and culture shock and insanity.

"I came home in 1969, 1970, and went back to my job at the phone company. I was doing drugs until the day I left Vietnam. I came home, smoked a little bit of street marijuana, and stopped. I don't know why. Drugs stop working for everybody after a while. When I got out I wanted to go to college. Vietnam was very impressive to me. I came out of there real frightened of my fallibility, and I didn't want to be a gofer; I didn't want to take orders. I wanted to have geographic mobility. I wanted to have good financial status; I wanted to have money, prestige, and power and all this bullshit. I was nuts. I'm still nuts. No, really, I'm a flamin' maniac. All I have now is, I've fooled a few people. [Laughs] That's how I feel.

"So I worked for the phone company at night and attended classes at Loyola University on a part-time basis. And I got all A's. I was also seeing a psychologist. Daily, 'cause I was nuts. Things about coming back after what I'd seen. My mind was blown. All this crazy bullshit. I hadn't eaten on plates for a year. I couldn't eat on plates. I couldn't sit in a restaurant. I didn't know how to *live* anymore. I got on a bus one day, and I couldn't get off. I didn't want anybody to look at me. I just rode the bus to the end. And I said, y'know, there's something the matter with me.

"So I went to this psychologist through school, and he helped an enormous amount. And he's saying, 'Why don't you go back to school full-time?' I'm saying, 'How can I pay for this?' He says, 'Well, the GI Bill.' It was like explosions in my head. Somebody was gonna *pay* me to go to school? I thought he was full of crap. I was making a thousand dollars a month at the phone company, which was a lot of money for me at that time. And I was frightened to quit, but I did. And I went back full-time and did marvelous.

"I went into a pre-med program and got a hundred and twenty hours of straight A, literally. And was a workaholic for three years —I finished school in three years. I would get up at seven in the morning and get home at midnight. I started off on a work-study program, cleaning chinchilla cages in a biomedical research lab for a dollar twenty an hour. At the end of the three years, I was running the lab and had eight people working for me. I wrote a book on hearing diseases and testified in front of the Illinois State Senate about noise pollution. I learned how to do an operation on the cochlea in chinchillas, which is a real good model for humans. And I still couldn't get into medical school, because of my old grades. Like an idiot, I was honest. I got ninety-seventh percentile on the medical school admissions test, and I got rejected by all these schools because my overall grade-point average was two-point-one or something.

"The man in the laboratory who I'm working with befriends me, is my father, my whatever. And he's just going on: I'm better than his graduate students—I'm a real Type A compulsive crazy. So, just by chance he becomes vice president of the university, takes my application to the Loyola University Medical School, and goes, 'Are you guys crazy? Take this kid.' So I got in.

"In medical school I did very well. I stopped going for grades and started to *learn*. I became a very, very good clinical physician—not somebody who had all of the answers to all the tiny, minute things, but someone who could look at a person and decide who was sick and who wasn't sick. I learned very quickly how to take care of a serious emergency. Somebody comes in and says, 'I got a stomach ache,' you can look it up and they're fine. But I didn't want to be uncomfortable around people whose heart stopped. And I learned that very much, and that tended to migrate me toward emergency situations, where I felt very good.

"I came to UCLA for my residency in surgery. I didn't like surgery 'cause I got lazy. I took a year out and worked in emergency rooms. Then I came back and did a three-year anesthesiology residency. In the last year of the residency, Steven Spielberg called UCLA and said, 'I want to talk to the doctor that runs the cardiac arrest team.' I was the chief resident in anesthesiology at the time and it was passed on to me. He says, 'You want to be in a movie?' I says, 'What do you mean? Of course I want to be in a movie!' And I was in *E.T.*, and it was very exciting. And from that, a man who was a stand-in doctor there, who was in private practice, needed an anesthesiologist in his hospital to do heart surgery, and I got a very, very good position in the community.

"Now, life is real nice. I have a lot of money. I did what people told me to do. They said put it in bonds, don't go out and buy a fancy car or a fancy house, and pay your taxes. I did all those things. I don't mind paying taxes. I don't get into tax dodges. I am a real right-wing person right now. I get frustrated seeing our country tear itself apart. I somehow think there's a certain amount of people that won't work for what they get, and I always refer back to myself, saying, 'If I can do it, they can do it.' Which is probably not justifiable, but it's how I feel. I don't know. A friend from high school is serving life in Arizona for rape and murder. Another one has been in jail all his life. They're all on welfare. I took care of two of them, dying from cirrhosis of the liver, when I was a medical student in Chicago."

Murphy had escaped with his life. I asked him if he felt twice-born; his seemed like a tale of rebirth. But the story wasn't over. He was beginning to realize that he still had a long way to go. "I'm financially successful. I don't know how emotionally successful—I'm changing a lot of that now," he said. "I'm starting to look at other things.

There's been this big grind all my life to be physically successful—money—and it really doesn't do it, because for a long time I wasn't real happy. Now I'm trying to learn and develop a program for living. I spent all these years getting successful, now I'm going to get in shape."

The first step in Murphy's "program for living" was getting off all the substances he'd abused on and off over the years. "In ten months I haven't had a drink, a pill, a snort—not even Sudafed, nothing—*nothing,*" he said. "When I stopped getting drunk and stoned all the time, I had all this free time with nothing to do. I'd go home and I'd start to wash the car, then I'd turn the record player on, then I would start to cook something, then I'd turn and I'd start to cut the front lawn. And then I'd take half a shower. Every day. There'd be eight books, on fifty different pages. I said, I gotta go back to drinkin' and usin' dope again. I didn't know how nuts I *was!*

"Then I meet this guy. He's not eating any meat; he wouldn't even eat bread if it was made with eggs. Something's around the guy. So I say, 'What the hell is this?' He says he's been meditating for twelve years. I say, 'What do you mean? *Tell me!* I want to know. I'm not gonna laugh at you.' I got to drag it out of him. He's not selling me anything; he's not Hollywood. He's just a guy from Milwaukee and he's serious. So he says, 'We started to meditate 'cause it helped us get our minds together. And organize our thoughts. And do one thing at a time. You know, if you controlled your body the way you control your mind, you couldn't get across the street.' And that's *true!* It *is* true! For me it was. It still is. But it's getting better slowly."

For Murphy, this dynamo of nervous energy, had begun to meditate. It was as if he'd raced through several lifetimes, three generations in one life, and was just now catching up to where his privileged peers had been in the Sixties. ("But they're all broke," he chortled. "They're all driving Toyotas. Oh, that's a terrible attitude. That's a shit attitude.") He told me that he could sit still, and keep his mind fairly still, for twenty minutes, as if that was a greater triumph than acing medical school—as in a sense it is. He had also become a vegetarian. "Eat like a gorilla," he urged. "I'm serious. Do gorillas have heart disease? Eat like a gorilla. You'll be fine."

With meditation, diet, and exercise replacing his frantic addictions to drugs and work, the world seemed new. "I'm trying to get my mind right," Murphy said. "That's gonna take *years*. Thirty-five years of insanity, and I want to reverse it in ten months? But I don't think too much ahead anymore. I just do what's in front of me right now. And it's real nice. 'Cause if you don't take any of this so seriously, you don't get crazy about it. You don't go to work to worry about your money; you go to work maybe to help the patients, maybe because it's a nice place to be. Maybe, after a while—which is coming into my head—maybe this isn't what I should be doing.

"If I wasn't such a coward, I'd go work for the Forest Service. Get out of the city. There's all these little communities that I could go live, work in, next to the Sierra Nevada mountains. So incredible. What do you do? You take care of the trees. It's pretty all the time and it smells good. That would be ideal. I just don't have the chutzpah yet. Yet. But it'll probably happen, 'cause I'll get crazy enough.

"It's really hard on your body, physically and mentally, to live in a city. It's fuckin' crazy. Living in an apartment, you get a little slot in the air. You get this little square. This is *my* little square!! You never get to see mountains. Y'know, human beings didn't evolve in New York City. We evolved in places like southern California, the Mediterranean, and that's where I think you're supposed to live. And you walked a lot, and you climbed trees, and you saw a lot of things, and you smelled a lot of good things. And you had a big, vast expanse of vision; you didn't just see across the street to another high-rise. I mean, everything is blunted in the cities! Plus the air is bad.

"It's all shit. Laser beams sound good, but they're not that big a deal. They're great, right, if you've gotta have something to shoot with. But if we never got into it we'd do fine without it. Get rid of water, you got a problem. Laser beams you can live without, but water, like, a real basic thing. H_2O: ya gotta have it, baby! Nobody's even found out how to make it yet, either. We can't *make* water. We can make laser beams. We can't make air. Only got so much. We can't make animals, and we're killing the ones we've got. Whales, gorillas; we're killing 'em left and right! We're chewing up the farmland. We're not doing a good job. And I only started thinking really serious like this when I started to meditate.

"I'm going to try to get out of *things* having value, and I'm looking at the things like—we're really fucking up! I'm part of it; I'm not trying to run away from it. A year ago, I believed in money. I believed in gold, silver, and diamonds, tax exemptions and sheltered annuities, trust funds, depreciation, and real-estate broker licenses, and all this shit! Aaaah! And you know what you got? A pile of this and a pile of that! Your lungs are shit, your heart's shit, your brain's *rrrr* —'Somebody took my pile! Where's my pile?? Aah!! The government took my pile!' Maybe, maybe—just maybe—I can live without the piles. I don't know yet, but we're gonna try."

If the story ended here, it would be "The Greening of Bob Murphy." A happy ending. But four days after pouring it out to my tape recorder, Murphy was in the hospital, deathly ill. At first they thought he had some kind of fungal pneumonia. It was worse. He had cancer, almost certainly caused by exposure to Agent Orange, and it had spread to his lungs.

"I was guarding a quarry for nine months that was sprayed daily with herbicides," he would recall later, after the news had sunk in. "They'd blow up the quarry, and the stuff would hang in the air. . . . This belongs in your book, too. Here's a guy who got out of it and did well, and eleven, twelve years later, Vietnam still cracks its whip."

But the story doesn't quite end here, either. Murphy pulled through that acute crisis, and as soon as he was strong enough, he began to fight. No way was life going to be over when it was just starting to get good. Chemotherapy, diet, visualization—he was willing to try them all. His lungs cleared; his tumor shrank; his hair fell out. He acquired a large wardrobe of funny hats.

In the good year that chemotherapy bought him, Murphy traveled with his wife and daughter to places he'd always wanted to see. He went back to work for a while. He was reconciled with his family. As the cancer gradually gained the upper hand, his two main emotions seem to have been a bottomless love for his wife and daughter and an inextinguishable anger at the theft of his life. He died on May 18, 1986, at the age of thirty-eight.

Bob Murphy fought a very private battle, but it is part of the evolutionary war. The combatants within him—the terminal toxicity of one culture, the life-giving dawn of a new—are the same ones that are contending for the planet. And though Murphy lost his life in that battle, he was so alive that he inspired everyone who knew him to love life more. We're all trying to stay alive long enough to evolve into love. And that hope, that possibility, is shining more brightly than ever just as dark tides are rising to blot it out. There has never been as much love in the world, or as much hate; as much abundance, or as much hunger; as much hope, or as much terror and danger. We are entering a time of extremes, of "mighty opposites." The Sixties were the vision; now, the reality. ("Now, the movie.") And the children of the vision are walking into it with eyes open, with a dire sense of coming home.

"We're in love with chaos," I'd told my father in 1980. Since then, a lot of us have learned to love security and comfort all too well. But it's always been with a certain mistrust, a sense of unreality. We knew the good times were a façade, a false calm between storms. In a country where most people happily have their heads in the sand or their Sony Walkmans, two generations—those reborn and those born in the Sixties—*know* that things will get worse, and that our sanity and integrity depend on not lying about it. The kids have a stony fatalism. Our feelings are more mixed. "When the dollar falls," people said to me, "when the oil runs out," and I heard in their voices, with the grim readiness, the anticipation. Chaos is, after all, our element—the stuff from which worlds are born.

Apocalyptic apprehensions are thick in the air as the year 2000 approaches. "Millennial hysteria" last convulsed the Christian world just before the year 1000; on a smaller scale, it has infected the turn of every century. It can be seen as an act of self-hypnosis, for the deadline is a human fabrication; time didn't begin with Jesus, and we count by tens only because of our endowment of fingers and toes. There is no year 2000 in nature. But so hypnotized are we by our own prophecy that we almost seem to have invented nuclear weapons just in time to fulfill it. We have also, however, invented planetary communications and travel just in time to transcend it. It's not the world that must end, just the Christian era (astrologers would say the Piscean Age). The only question is whether it is going to take the planet with it.

In this context, it's fascinating that the two groups of adults most obsessed with apocalypse are right-wing fundamentalists and the Sixties generation. Each group believes the other is the party of the Devil. Ronald Wilson Reagan sincerely expects Armageddon; Morning Glory G'Zell tells me that the letters of Reagan's name rearranged spell "Insane Anglo Warlord," and add up, numerologically, to 666. Born-again friends point out the many signs of the prophesied Last Days; Whitley Strieber, in *Nature's End*, calls these "the sunset years" before ecological or nuclear disaster. One faction speaks of "the Last Judgment," the other of "humanity's final exam." Christian fundamentalists have their Book of Revelations, the greatest disaster epic ever penned ("Now, the movie"—how about it, Irwin Allen?); our generation seems determined to rival it, for our most characteristic artifact is the apocalyptic fantasy. A short honor roll:

> *The Stand,* written by Stephen King (1947)
> *The Last Wave,* directed by Peter Weir (1944)
> *The Fate of the Earth,* written by Jonathan Schell (1944)
> *The Day After,* directed by Nicholas Meyer (1946)
> *The Road Warrior,* directed by George Miller (1945)
> *Koyaanisqatsi,* directed by Godfrey Reggio (1940), music by Philip
>   Glass (1940)
> *The Terminator,* directed by James Cameron (1954)
> *Warday* and *Nature's End,* written by Whitley Strieber (1945) and
>   James Kunetka (1944)
> *Wolf of Shadows,* written by Whitley Strieber
> *The Nuclear Age,* written by Tim O'Brien (1946)

Ghostbusters, directed by Ivan Reitman (1947), concept by Dan Aykroyd (1952)—a comic version, which also makes fun of our savethe-world fantasies.

And there's even a kiddie version: *The Care Bears Movie,* with its
endangered kingdom of Care-a-Lot.

The strange kinship between the visions of these two groups makes
sense as soon as you realize that they are looking at apocalypse from
opposite sides. Fundamentalists of every stripe (Christian, Islamic,
Orthodox Jewish) would rather see the world end than see it change;
in fact, change and diversity, the new global realities, *are* the end of
their world, of their identity and security and certainty. Their present
strength is the desperation of a last stand. If they cannot reimpose
their monolithic vision—and they can't—fundamentalists are not
afraid to die trying, for they believe that their unswerving faith will
reap a posthumous reward. Today, the fantasy of Heaven may be the
greatest single danger to the earth, for those who love this world—
be they atheists or neo-pagans—won't lightly risk destroying it.

Sixties survivors, by contrast, think the (old) world already ended,
and can't understand why it's still here. "At age eighteen or nineteen
or twenty, we looked into that crack between the worlds," says
Stephen King, "and we said, 'It's either all gonna end, or it's gonna
be transformed, and we're the lever and the fulcrum on which those
things are gonna move.' And *it didn't happen.*" The tenacity of old
institutions, old habits, dead gods, amazes and depresses us. The old
world view is like a bulldog that won't release its death grip on the
throat of the world, or the minds of men and women, even though
it's already dead itself. Our attraction to apocalypse—and it *is* an
attraction, almost as dangerous as that of the fundamentalists—stems
from the belief that only catastrophe can do what we've been too
impatient, or lazy, or just too small to do: finish off the old, clear the
way for the new. Or, as we said so graphically in the Sixties: "Burn
it down."

When Whitley Strieber published *Warday* with James Kunetka,
they were attacked by some in the peace movement for daring to

suggest that a nuclear war could be limited and survivable. (*Warday* was written before the release of findings about nuclear winter.) I suspect that the taboo that book violated was not survival per se, but the portrayal of some aspects of the postwar world as attractive— though bought at a hideous price. In *Warday*'s 1993, cancer was pandemic; six million had died in the 1988 half-hour war, millions more of lingering radiation sickness, and twenty-five million in the mutant Cincinnati flu. But the United States had been shorn of its imperial power, and had come apart into near-autonomous regions; there were fewer, simpler machines; true community had risen from the ashes of selfishness; midwifery, herbal healing, and other witch crafts were respected; people grew their own food; the embrace had replaced the handshake; a group called the Deconstructionists lived free of any institution larger than the family. All facets of the new world view.

"What there was and is in me," says Strieber, "is not a desire for a war to happen, but a very real desire for some of those attitudes to emerge. They emerge after the war because they emerge into a vacuum." He wrote *Warday* in the hope that if people tasted the terrors of the future in imagination, they might take up the spirit of community and simplicity and compassion as a preventive, not a consequence, of the worst.

The trouble is, those values require some sacrifice of the opulent pleasures of late industrial individualism. It's all very well to send checks to charity, but what if we actually had to (gasp!) *share a car*? So far, the majority of our generation has shown little inclination to make such sacrifices voluntarily, though they are small compared to those that may be forced on us. (A hopeful exception: the tendency to share with friends.) Paul Monroe was being more honest than most when he said, "If there was a war and everything got blown up, I could probably get off my ass and get involved."

Since the discovery of nuclear winter, however, we no longer have the grisly option of passing the buck to the Bomb. And accelerating environmental damage threatens effects hardly less devastating. The world has to be changed by human hands, or end indeed. That prospect can be either paralyzing or galvanizing. It's not grandiose to say that the fate of the earth may hinge on which effect is chosen by this large generation, now reaching the age of leadership planet-wide. I say "chosen" because we *can* at least choose hope or despair—and visionaries say that that choice could decide the outcome.

It's significant that while Christian fundamentalists' favorite apocalyptic prophecy is Revelations, which has one inexorable ending, our favorite—the Hopi prophecy—has (at least) two. This centuries-old prophecy foretold certain twentieth-century innovations—power lines, airplanes, "great roads like rivers"—as warning signs of a Great Purification if humanity did not return to the way of respect for the earth. "The petroglyph that represents the main symbol of the Hopi prophecy shows a path, a line that has its ups and downs," says Otter G'Zell. "And then there's a point where it branches. One branch continues on upwards, and the other one goes down and breaks apart and fades out."

"It's not decided, in other words," I said. "There are two possibilities."

"Right," said Otter. "A branching of the time lines, a branching of the universe."

"The one you believe in is the one you go with," said Morning Glory. "That's why the Christian prophecies are so important right now. We are living in those times when you must know your enemy."

The first enemy, then, is despair.

Stephen King believes that he is successful because his work is "a mirror that reflects the majority of my generation. None of it was ever serious line-for-line stuff about ghosts and goblins and ghoulies. It's about unease. It's about knowin' somethin's wrong somewhere. I think that I hold up the mirror and show people what they are." In the Eighties, that mirror has darkened. In *The Stand* (1978) and *The Dead Zone* (1979), and even in *Firestarter* (1980), the forces of good still had a fighting chance. In *Pet Sematary* (1983) and *Thinner* (1984), the protagonist is a normal moral weakling who sells out to the seductions of evil, as King thinks our generation has. "I'm not exactly pessimistic about the future," he told me at the end of 1984. "I just don't think it's there."

I told him about the Hopi prophecy. "I don't really think that there is any fork in the road," King said. "I think things have gone too far. If any of us are around to see 1990, I'll buy you a beer. Or we'll drop acid. You got it."

Sometimes I feel the way Stephen King does; I think most of us do. The process of evolution, like any creative process, must always be accompanied by doubt and despair. Will we pass the twentieth century? Or will we go down in the fossil record as one of nature's Edsels? There are gray days when the case against us seems overwhelming. Man is earth's cancer; the Bomb, a radical cure that may kill the patient. Then all we want to do is love our kids, enjoy our toys, and drug ourselves with entertainment, or entertain ourselves with drugs, as long as we can. This mood of evolutionary despair is eloquently expressed by movie monster Wynston Jones:

"I realize I don't even care if the world blows up. This is not out of despair or anything. It's just that I look around and see that, for some unknown reason, there are large groups of people in the world who *want* to blow each other up. I don't know why this is. I have no idea if it's because of what Ardrey says, because people are killer apes, or what. I don't know. It really doesn't interest me to try to find out. It just seems really bizarre to me. It isn't everybody, but there's enough of those people that there is nothing you can do about it. Even if you went around and personally assassinated all of them, I think it's something intrinsic to the human condition. I don't think it can be remedied.

"It's entirely possible that the world just may evaporate, and there will be nothing left except a ball of glassy slag. I think people will survive, like rats and mice survive, roaches. They live in the holes on what's available. If you bombard them with radioactivity, they will adapt. Okay, it's ten million years in the future. The human race has survived, and they are out in some distant galaxy on some planet, and some future anthropologist says, 'But where can it be that the human race originated? On what planet in this vast galaxy?' If I could be transported to that place, I could show them a way of finding where human beings came from. Just go from one gutted glassy slag planet to another, back through the galaxy, and when you find the first one —maybe it's reverted to green again—that's the earth.

"Either that or . . . even now I don't know what a dodo bird looks like, except in a drawing. It's no loss to me. No significant feeling of loss associated with a couple of lines scribbled on a piece of paper. A clear chance exists that future generations eighty years from now will not know what a deer is, what various forms of wildlife are, except as drawings in a book. It's entirely possible that they will go out of their houses in the morning and they will have to wear protective gear and breathing devices. And it will be normal. They won't say, like I say, 'What a horrible way to live.' They'll will say, 'I don't find that sad.' " Jones tries not to find it sad, either: "My survival strategy is just to laugh at stuff."

Wynston Jones's two bleak visions correspond closely to the ones Whitley Strieber portrayed in *Wolf of Shadows* and *Nature's End*. Apparently, these are two powerful possible futures, and we know it. But will knowing it prevent them or invoke them? "The one you believe in is the one you go with." You don't have to be a mystical believer in the power of creative visualization to understand why despair is a self-fulfilling prophecy, making inevitable what it believes to be inevitable. Despair breeds inaction, because it argues persuasively that action is futile. Therefore, whatever *could* be done is not done, and things get worse.

Those who despair act like bettors playing it safe. They want to be on the side of probability—rather than hope and lose—and so, they shift the odds. Hope isn't based on probability. It's based on that all-important crack of light between "probable" and "inevitable." It's the intention to shove a lever in that crack and widen it, shifting the odds the other way. It's not so much an act of faith—faith can be passive—as an act of will. But it's also a gift of grace, because those who have chosen to hope suddenly find that "the force" is with them. The force of evolution? The Holy Spirit? Goddess energy? Synchronicity? There are many ways to name it. Visionaries use magical, child-like imagery, because that force makes action not only possible but joyous, mysteriously guided, strangely lighthearted in the face of great discouragement. It can make the impossible actual —its symbol, the unicorn.

"Do you remember *Peter Pan?*" asks Donna Henes. "Do you remember when Mary Martin says to the audience, 'Don't let Tinker-bell die, everybody clap'? And everybody clapped. We were all clapping to save the life of, what? Hope, mystery, fantasy, magic." That scene was, of course, a childhood favorite of Steven Spielberg's, and a central image in *E.T.* But we're not children, and the healing magic isn't going to come from the sky. It comes through us or not at all. So clap if you believe in Murphy. "There's still a chance," Henes says. "And we *are* the chance. We can't leave it to Reagan, or to any country or government or corporation whatever."

But what can we *do?* Where to place the lever? Another way of asking the question is: After despair, what is the enemy? Until now, much of the peace movement has behaved as if the enemy were the Bomb itself. American nuclear-freeze advocates and European pro-testers have focused on halting the production and deployment of nuclear weapons—so far, without success. This has provoked some on the leading edge of the generation, like Whitley Strieber, to conclude that "the peace movement's usefulness and relevance is over."

"A bilateral nuclear freeze is just words on paper," Strieber says. "It has nothing to do with reality. If the United States declares itself ready for a nuclear freeze, then we still have to negotiate that with the Russians, and we're basically at ground zero [*sic*]. And a unilat-eral nuclear freeze is highly unlikely to be tried, although it would be a great experiment to try one for six months or a year. It's highly unlikely that that can be sold to the American people. So they have seized on an idea which must perpetuate itself and can never be realized. And I suspect that, unconsciously, that's what some of them want. Because they would become irrelevant if there was an outbreak of peace."

Clamshell Alliance founder Grace Parker Sannino has an even

more startling criticism. "The thing about the freeze movement and all that stuff is that it's deadly boring. And people would rather die than be bored. They would! Give me a bomb any day before this crap, you know? Hah! We are actually involved in the business of attempting to keep the world from destroying itself. But you cannot do that in all seriousness. I don't think there's any other way to get past all this than by creating something. And creation has got to be pleasurable. If it's not fun, it's not going to work. Forget it. I think the reason the Vietnam War movement was so successful is that it was a lot more fun than anything else going on. I was with the Workshop on Nonviolence in New York. We did yellow submarines in the East River, and we gave out fortune cookies to the soldiers, and flowers, and we were ridiculous."

In all seriousness, the peace movement—or its branches in the sciences and the arts—must be credited with one great lifesaving accomplishment: education. Thanks to Physicians for Social Responsibility, the discoverers of nuclear winter, and such media events as *The Day After*, politicians and the public now know enough about the medical and climatic effects of nuclear war to make it more than clear that these weapons must never be used. And yet, they continue to be built and, we sense, to strain at their leashes. If the Bomb *is* the enemy, it is a very sinister one.

"It's not for nothing that these weapons have a beautiful, terrifying phallic form," says Whitley Strieber. "I have stood in the presence of an H-bomb, a modern one; a relatively new one, which was maybe about seven feet tall and made of a carbon substance. And it was needle-nosed; it was a long, tall cone almost like a wizard's cap. It weighed maybe two or three tons. But it was not big; it was something you could put your arms around. But it was blacker than black, because of the carbon it was made of. It was like looking at a black hole; something that absorbed all light. It was almost so black that it had no real definition. I remember it more as a shadow. And I thought to myself that this is an expression of something unconscious. This is one of those unconscious forms that Jung talks about, an archetype.

"We have built an archetype of death. We have brought it into the material world. And all this human energy and resource, that could be used to save the forests or the lives of the Third World, is going into nothing, into the carbon body of the hydrogen bomb. What we're dealing with here is something much stranger than we think, and much more mysterious, and far more powerful. Very definitely capable of maneuvering us to its own ends. And its end is to blow up over a city of millions of people. That's what it's there for. And somewhere inside it, or inside the part of us that made it, is a great hunger for that to happen.

"That hunger resides in the consciousness of certain people. They appear in the world as senators and congressmen and presidents and military people, on both sides. They consider themselves devoted to peace and to defense, and they *are,* intellectually. But they're really out there to make a way for these weapons. In a sense they are the disciples of their own weapons. The president considers himself a man of peace, and he's not a hypocrite. He *genuinely* believes that, intellectually. But elsewhere in his spirit, something else is going on. It was expressed in that little sliver of reality that came out of him that afternoon when he said, 'The bombing starts in five minutes.' That came out of his mouth as a joke, because it was filtered through his personality. But you heard the truth in that voice. And the Russians heard it, too."

Is Ronald Reagan the enemy? And is voting the old world view out of power the thing we have to do? Like trying to reduce the number of nuclear weapons, it's one thing we have to do. But it's not the root of the problem, and like arms reduction, winning elections may prove impossible or futile unless we attack the root. The real enemy, every visionary has told me, is not a thing, the Bomb, or a person, the president. It's a mechanism in the human mind, and we won't be able to understand it, much less overcome it, until we acknowledge it in ourselves.

The Bomb can be seen as a very physical symbol of our desire to hurl all our darkness into the other and destroy it there. This mechanism of "projection" must once have been useful for group survival

—maybe that's why it's so ingrained—but now that the "group" is all humans, even all life, it is lethally obsolete. Yet it persists.

At its most obvious, it's the Rambo syndrome: I'm Good, you're Evil, so I can machine-gun you in all innocence. But this stance is hardly exclusive to our "enemies." It's right there in every marital quarrel. It's the demonstrator giving a cop the finger, the hippie sneering "Straaights!" at tourists in the Haight, the daughter saying "Fuck you!" to her father. And it's Morning Glory calling Reagan the Antichrist. It's a member of one surviving Sixties commune calling the leader of another an asshole—as silly as two sects of Orthodox Jews locking horns over a split hair. It's that which divides. It's diabolical—"dia-bollein," to throw apart—and it's in us, too.

You could put your arms around a modern nuclear missile, Whitley Strieber says. That chilling image—embracing the Bomb—could be a symbol ("syn-bollein," to throw together) of acknowledging our own complicity in that which divides and destroys. "I consider myself personally responsible for every atomic weapon that's there," says Strieber. "And I think every one of us should. Every time a person starves to death in the Third World or is killed because of some vicious, unjust government, supported by us *or* the Soviets, each of us is personally responsible. And we are responsible for the non-human, as well. Otherwise you can't really live. Otherwise you're not a whole human being." That may sound like an extreme statement, but it is the same as "We Are the World." In a way, we owe the Bomb a horrible gratitude. It has forced us, for the first time, to stop blindly firing off our hate and start understanding it. It is forcing us together. It is *forcing* us to evolve.

"Nuclear war is a metaphor," says Marc Barasch. "The gunman shoots both ways. It's our maturation as a species. The realization that you can't destroy the other. That other is you. You can't throw your garbage out without expecting it to wash up on Long Island again. In your immediate life, you can't decide that your ex-wife or husband can't be redeemed. Now there are friendships between ex-wives and husbands in a way that hadn't happened before." And, in our political life, there are human moments between enemies in a new way.

In nearly every hostage crisis, through all the jingoistic raging on both sides, there have been intimate, unmasked moments between hostages and captors, when they saw each other's human curiosity and pain. They talked about their wristwatches, or their children. "The Stockholm Syndrome," we belittlingly call it. Maybe it should be called "the Gaia Syndrome." Those moments aren't treason. They are our hope. They suggest that the new world might not come in fire, but as gently as Reagan's touch on Gorbachev's elbow.

The best thing we can do is to further what Whitley Strieber calls "the reconciling spirit"—between men and women, human and human, people and nature. The reconciling spirit is very different from both the self-righteous rage of the Sixties and the sappy peace-sign passivity. It is both tough and tender—and capable of laughter. Those who serve it don't deny the reality of injustice and evil, or hesitate to confront them. But they stay always open for that moment of connection, even—or especially—with the enemy. Vietnam veterans know that moment can happen in war. The goal is to have it happen *before* the war.

Between the U.S. and the U.S.S.R., this work is already under way. The 1985 Geneva summit has led to promises of increased cultural and business exchanges. But well before the summit, preparing the ground for it, American and Soviet doctors founded International Physicians for the Prevention of Nuclear War; Spacebridge, an interactive telecommunications event, linked children in Moscow and San Diego; Esalen founder Michael Murphy and members of the Association for Humanistic Psychology traveled to the Soviet Union to share findings on psychic and spiritual phenomena. "I was really moved by the experience," says Marc Sarkady, a participant in one AHP trip. He was moved to introduce Phil Donahue to Soviet spokesman Vladimir Posner, a meeting that led to "citizen summit" teleconferences between Seattle and Leningrad and Leningrad and Boston. "You know the Soviet people are people, but then you meet them and you *know* they're people," Sarkady says. "You can never go back to thinking that they're not."

For us, though, that's easy. The Sixties generation has always been quick to see humanity on the Left—and slow to see the human evil. That's what drives the Right crazy about us: they think we're dangerously naïve. But if we want to lessen the danger of war, maybe the real challenge for us is to see the humanity on the Right—in the defenders of the old world view, the people we love to hate. They seem so closed to us. Could it be because we're closed to them? We know their world is ending. Can we imagine how threatening that is? We can condemn them, and drive them into the arms of demagogues or the dream of omnipotent new arms, and fulfill the direst prophecies for sure. Or we can stay open to them, try to hear what they have to say, and invite them to bring their wisdom into the new world. After all, we've been "born again" ourselves. The old world died in us, and most of us lived to tell the tale, to swim like fish in a future more fluid and various, securely insecure. We know it can happen.

This work, too, is under way. In 1985 a former fundamentalist Christian, Richard Yao (1955), started a group called Fundamentalists Anonymous. Within a month of its founding, the organization was featured on the *Donahue* show—and over 4,000 people called seeking help. A year later, FA had worked with over 22,000. Congregational minister Leslye Faithfull (1957) has done Bible study with born-again Christians, and feels that a major attraction of this good-news religion is its denial of despair, fear, and pain. (Consumers of other opiates, including television, shouldn't throw stones.) Faithfull gives fundamentalists sound biblical grounds to face and feel their pain, reminding them that the Crucifixion necessarily preceded the Resurrection. When people are able to go through that process, they become more open. But she must first be open to them, and genuinely glad they're saved.

In the political realm, Marc Sarkady has been doing the same thing. "One of the things that's shifted for me is that I see everything as a two-way interaction," he says. "I think some of the people in our band, Wings of Song, thought that we went to the Pentagon to play to transform them. I think that too, but I also think that *we* were transformed.

"You have this image of the Pentagon as another *them.* Yet on the way to the concert, a little girl in our group said to one of my Gallucci brothers, 'Daddy, where are we going?'

" 'We're going to the Pentagon.'

" 'What's the Pentagon?'

" 'That's where all the armies are.'

"And she said, 'Does that mean we're going to have a war?' She started to get afraid.

"So this Gallucci brother told that story at the Pentagon. He said, 'I realize that all of you must be interested in peace, too. You have a different way, maybe, or different ways—not even one way—that you are thinking about doing this.' So it was a real reaching across: We're the same as you.

"There's a lot we don't understand. And it's very important at this time that we don't go around thinking we have the answers. There's a group in Washington called Search for Common Ground. They are doing great work in the field of national security, trying to develop a united American consensus about where we should be moving as a country, trying to bridge polarization between liberals and conservatives, hawks and doves, activists and military people. Great idea. But on some level the people who run that used to think that they were going to get people in there and tell them the truth. Subsequently, they realized the need to start from a more open perspective. They now co-host conferences with a conservative think tank.

"It's so easy to get caught in thinking you have the answer. I often think I have the answer. I think it's critical right now that we really begin to learn to work with people who are different from us, and not assume that they are wrong and we are right. At the same time, we need to own our power and our truth. There's a lot to do and be.

"During the last ten years I've become a specialist at resolving conflict. I've worked with the Harvard Program on Negotiation, authors of the book *Getting to Yes,* and with the Nuclear Negotiation Project, working to improve the hotline between Moscow and D.C. During this time I've worked very hard to learn to build off of different points of view to create a greater whole. But lately I've started to reinvestigate conflict and our generational relationship to it. I've been feeling that the task is to embrace conflict, but to embrace it in a different way, from this quality of love and care. Not to shy away from saying what needs to be said and doing what needs to be done."

We talked about conviction without arrogance, and conflict without hate, and about the evolution of the evolutionary war. It's no longer a war between one generation and another, or one race or nation and another. It never really was.

The image of the peace warrior comes up again and again. It was the name of Greenpeace's ship, the *Rainbow Warrior,* sunk by the French in an old-fashioned act of war. It's the mission of Turtle Heart (1949), a new-age Native American shaman, sent by Shinto priests in Japan to place a broken warrior's sword on the site of the first A-bomb blast in Alamogordo, New Mexico, and in Washington and Moscow. It was the theme of a global Gallucci Family festival:

"On June 6, 1984, which is also the Longest Day, we declared war against war," says Marc Sarkady. "All over the world, people gathered in great places of creation and destruction, adults and children, and fashioned their own rituals for a world without war. They gathered at the Eiffel Tower in Paris, and in Jerusalem, and in South Africa, and in Mexico and Guatemala, and in New Mexico near Los Alamos, and at Glastonbury in England, and Stonehenge, and in the Four Corners, where the Hopi are. In the Boston area we gathered at Walden Pond, and sat in a circle within the foundation stones of Thoreau's cabin, and shared our visions of a world without war and our personal commitments to make the world that way. That night people gathered around phones all over the world to report on their convocations and rituals.

"That began a two-month campaign called World War Four, so we wouldn't have to have a World War Three. Richie Havens wrote a song about it. We realized that this was only the beginning. We finished up the first phase with a radio broadcast on Hiroshima Day, where we had people connected all over the world, in the Soviet Union as well. Once again, people shared their personal commitments to work over the years to come to make the vision of a world without war a reality."

We are engaged in an urgent and joyous fight for our survival. The enemy is not "out there." It's that warmaking thing in the human spirit, fathered by fear.

"I think that we fought a war of love," Donna Henes says of the Sixties. We're still fighting. We can't lose.

NOTES

Writing a book, one draws not only on deliberate research, but on years of reading and on contemporary reading of newspapers and magazines. While I wrote, I continually checked my perceptions against facts and opinions appearing in current periodicals. I have not cited most such corroborative sources unless I drew specific facts or quotes from them. I list as "background sources" those books and articles I relied on to insure accuracy of fact and/or mood. Starred books are particularly recommended.

Three magazines have been indispensable over the years in keeping me abreast of my generation: *CoEvolution Quarterly* (now succeeded by *Whole Earth Review*), *New Age Journal,* and *Esquire.*

INTRODUCTION: EXILES IN TIME (1980–86)

Quotes from Dr. Sigmund Neumann are from "The Conflict of Generations in Contemporary Europe," in *Vital Speeches of the Day, V* (1939)—a source more briefly quoted by Landon Jones in *Great Expectations: America and the Baby Boom Generation,* Ballantine Books, New York, 1981.

PART ONE: RITES OF PASSAGE

Background sources:
Civil Rights: The 1960s Freedom Struggle, by Rhoda Lois Blumberg. South End Press, Boston, 1984.
Danse Macabre, by Stephen King. Everest House, New York, 1981.
The Feminine Mystique, by Betty Friedan. W. W. Norton, New York, 1963.
They Should Have Served That Cup of Coffee: Seven Radicals Remember the 60s, edited by Dick Cluster. South End Press, Boston, 1979.

Act I: 1945–63

1. The "white movement historian" is Rhoda Lois Blumberg in *Civil Rights,* p. 80.
2. John Lewis is quoted in *They Should Have Served That Cup of Coffee,* pp. 6–7: "Jim Zwerg was one of the most committed people. And I definitely believe it was not out of any social, do-good kind of feeling. It was out of deep religious conviction."

Act II: 1963–68

1. *Dispatches,* by Michael Herr. Avon, New York, 1984, p. 70.
2. *Home from the War: Vietnam Veterans: Neither Victims nor Executioners,* by Robert Jay Lifton. Basic Books, New York, 1973, p. 20.

3. Steve Rees interview in the essay "A Questioning Spirit: GIs Against the War" in *They Should Have Served That Cup of Coffee,* p. 158.

PART TWO: THE MOVEMENT
War

Background sources:

Healing from the War: Trauma and Transformation after Vietnam, by Arthur Egendorf. Houghton Mifflin, Boston, 1985.

Home from the War: Vietnam Veterans: Neither Victims nor Executioners, by Robert Jay Lifton. Basic Books, New York, 1973.

Long Time Passing: Vietnam and the Haunted Generation, by Myra MacPherson. Doubleday, New York, 1984.

Payback: Five Marines After Vietnam, by Joe Klein. Alfred A. Knopf, New York, 1984.

They Should Have Served That Cup of Coffee: Seven Radicals Remember the 60s, edited by Dick Cluster. South End Press, Boston, 1979.

Uncovering the Sixties: The Life and Times of the Underground Press, by Abe Peck. Pantheon Books, New York, 1985.

Vietnam: The War at Home. Vietnam and the American People 1964–1968, by Thomas Powers. G. K. Hall, Boston, 1984.

Vietnam Voices: Perspectives on the War Years, 1941–1982, compiled by John Clark Pratt. Viking, New York, 1984.

1. *Payback,* p. 42.
2. "Guerrilla War," from *To Those Who Have Gone Home Tired: New and Selected Poems,* by W. D. Ehrhart. Thunder's Mouth Press, New York, 1984.
3. Raymond Mungo on "the Americong" is quoted in *Uncovering the Sixties,* p. 72.
4. John Lewis's statement to reporters in Atlanta, January 6, 1966, is quoted in *Vietnam: The War at Home,* by Thomas Powers, p. 148. Martin Luther King's statement on "the greatest purveyor of violence," Riverside Church, New York City, April 4, 1967, is quoted in Powers, p. 161.

5. "Apocalypse Continued," by Edward Tick, About Men column, *The New York Times Magazine,* January 13, 1985.
6. Ray Mungo interview from *Uncovering the Sixties,* p. 315.
7. Mark Satin on "romanticizing the Sandinistas": *New Options* #11.
8. Milan Kundera, "the struggle of man against power," is quoted in *New Options* #9.
9. "to foster the democratization . . .": *New Options* #20.
10. "[T]he U.S. can't just 'get out' . . .": *New Options* #11.
11. "Why make ourselves temptingly vulnerable? . . . ": *New Options* #11.
12. "[N]eo-interventionism does not include military intervention . . . " and "[b]ut they share one core conviction . . .": *New Options* #20.
13. "Is there a vital . . . alternative . . .": *New Options* #11.
14. "If Benigno Aquino . . ." *New Options* #11.
15. "Literally millions of people . . . demonstrated for peace . . .": *New Options* #9.
16. "we want democratic governments . . .": *New Options* #20.
17. From "Ben Tre Suburb," by Michael Berkowitz, in *Demilitarized Zones: Veterans After Vietnam,* edited by Jan Barry and W. D. Ehrhart. East River Anthology, Montclair, New Jersey, 1976, p. 155.

Wanderlust

Background sources:
The Making of an Un-American: A Dialogue with Experience, by Paul Cowan. The Viking Press, New York, 1970.

1. "city-funded sleeping projects . . .": *Time,* July 19, 1971.

Revolution

Background sources:
Green Politics, by Charlene Spretnak and Fritjof Capra. E. P. Dutton, New York, 1984.
The Haight-Ashbury: A History, by Charles Perry. Random House/Rolling Stone Press, New York, 1984.

Kent State: What Happened and Why, by James A. Michener. Random House, New York, 1971; Fawcett Crest, New York, 1978.

★ *Power and Innocence: A Search for the Sources of Violence*, by Rollo May. W. W. Norton, New York, 1972.

They Should Have Served That Cup of Coffee: Seven Radicals Remember the 60s, edited by Dick Cluster. South End Press, Boston, 1979.

Uncovering the Sixties: The Life and Times of the Underground Press, by Abe Peck. Pantheon Books, New York, 1985.

Vietnam: The War at Home, by Thomas Powers. G. K. Hall, Boston, 1984.

1. Jane Alpert, "I wanted Apocalypse, Utopia": from *Uncovering the Sixties*, p. 202.
2. Abbie Hoffman, "the birth of FREE AMERICA . . .": from *Uncovering the Sixties*, p. 202.
3. Reggie Schell, "[W]hen [the Black Panthers] marched into Sacramento with guns": from an interview in the essay "A Way to Fight Back: The Black Panther Party" in *They Should Have Served That Cup of Coffee*.
4. Jerry Rubin, "I felt that America had to have on national TV a violent purge . . .": from *Uncovering the Sixties*, p. 118.
5. The National Guard sergeant's "I wouldn't dare to repeat what they said . . ." is from *Kent State*, Fawcett Crest, New York, 1978, p. 313.
6. From "Who's Speaking for the Baby Boomers?" by Horace Busby, an article constructed (with permission) from issues of *The Busby Papers* by the editors of the quarterly *Free Spirit: Resources for Personal and Social Transformation*, Brooklyn, New York, Winter '84–'85.
7. "Fifteen years ago . . ." from *New Options* #24.
8. "too counter-cultural": from *New Options* #25 (Editorial: "Top Political Consultants Say We Could Go Green").
9. Ralph Whitehead on "generational energies": *New Options* #25. In a letter in issue #28, Whitehead amended his original remarks, saying that after meeting with Missouri Representative Richard Gephardt and Arizona Representative Bruce Babbitt, he feels that these two members of the "new generation of Democrats" are "part of the solution, not part of the problem."

10. Owen DeLong's "Blue Party" statement is from *U and I*, no. 1.
11. John Sinclair, "Leaders suck": from *Uncovering the Sixties*, p. 173.

PART THREE: THE METAMORPHOSIS
D o p e

Background sources:
"Coping with Cocaine," by James Lieber, *The Atlantic Monthly*, January 1986, pp. 39–48.
"Crashing on Cocaine," *Time*, April 11, 1983.
Surveys done by the 800–COCAINE National Helpline
The Dog Is Us, and Other Observations, by Marcelle Clements. The Viking Press, New York, 1985.
The Haight-Ashbury: A History, by Charles Perry. Random House/Rolling Stone Press, New York, 1984.

1. *The Dog Is Us*, p. 49.
2. From "Coping with Cocaine," p. 42.
3. "The Agony of Ecstasy," by Kathryn Rose Gertz, *Science Digest*, February 1986.
4. "The Agony of Ecstasy."
5. "The Agony of Ecstasy."

S p i r i t

Background sources:
"A Faith of Our Own," by Norman Boucher, *New Age Journal*, April 1986, pp. 26–30, 75–79.
Books of Bhagwan Shree Rajneesh, *The Rajneesh Times*, *The Rajneesh Newsletter*, and *Bhagwan* magazine, published by the Rajneesh Foundation, Poona, India, and Rajneesh Foundation International, Rajneeshpuram, Oregon.
CoEvolution Quarterly, Winter 1983: "Special Section on the Politics of Religion," pp. 104ff. Articles on the financial and sexual abuses of two

prominent counterculture religious leaders: Swami Muktananda of the Siddha Meditation Movement and an American Zen master.

Divine Slave Gita: The Sacred and Foolish Song of the Hohm Community. Published bimonthly by the Hohm Community, Prescott Valley, Arizona.

★ *Drawing Down the Moon: Witches, Druids, Goddess-Worshippers, and Other Pagans in America Today,* by Margot Adler. Beacon Press, Boston, 1979.

★ *Dreaming the Dark: Magic, Sex & Politics,* by Starhawk. Beacon Press, Boston, 1982.

★ *Goddesses in Everywoman: A New Psychology of Women,* by Jean Shinoda Bolen, M.D. Harper Colophon Books, New York, 1984.

The Great Naropa Poetry Wars, by Tom Clark. Cadmus Editions, Santa Barbara, California, 1980.

★ *Inter Views: Conversations with Laura Pozzo on Psychotherapy, Biography, Love, Soul, Dreams, Work, Imagination, and the State of the Culture,* by James Hillman with Laura Pozzo. Harper & Row, New York, 1983.

"Peaks and Vales: The Soul/Spirit Distinction as Basis for the Differences Between Psychotherapy and Spiritual Discipline," by James Hillman. In *On the Way to Self Knowledge,* edited by Jacob Needleman and Dennis Levis. Alfred A. Knopf, New York, 1976.

★ *Shambhala: The Sacred Path of the Warrior,* by Chögyam Trungpa, Rinpoche. Shambhala Publications, Boston, 1984.

Tikkun: A Quarterly Jewish Critique of Politics, Culture, & Society, vol. 1, no. 1.

Womanspirit Rising: A Feminist Reader in Religion, edited by Carol P. Christ and Judith Plaskow. Harper Forum Books, San Francisco, 1979.

1. "Nothing to lose but your head": the title of one of the "Darshan Diaries" published by the Rajneesh Foundation, Poona, India.

2. "The heart is never untrue . . .": from *The Book: An Introduction to the Teachings of Bhagwan Shree Rajneesh,* Series I from A to H. Rajneesh Foundation International, Rajneeshpuram, Oregon, 1984. p. 633.

3. "If I am really a guide to you . . .": from *Won't You Join the Dance? Initiation Talks Between Master and Disciple,* Rajneesh Foundation International, Rajneeshpuram, Oregon, 1983.

4. "forever, so nothing can hold you back . . .": from *Won't You Join the Dance?*

5. "Now the time has come . . ." and "Each person is born to be a Buddha . . .": from *Philosophia Perennis: Bhagwan Shree Rajneesh Speaking on the Golden Verses of Pythagoras,* Rajneesh Foundation International, Antelope, Oregon, 1981, pp. 258, 47–49.

6. Lee Lozowick, "[T]his work . . . *has* to be done . . .": from an early 1986 issue of *Divine Slave Gita.*

7. "There will be wars . . .": from *The Book,* Rajneesh, Series I, pp. 650–51.

8. Lee Lozowick, "It just doesn't seem like life is that big a deal . . .": from the issue of *Divine Slave Gita* cited in note 4.

9. From "While There's Life, We Can Still Hope," by Robert Jay Lifton, *Vogue,* October 1984, pp. 210ff.

10. "A Faith of Our Own," pp. 29, 76.

11. "A Faith of Our Own," p. 77.

12. According to Otter G'Zell, the "Gaia Hypothesis"—that the earth can be viewed as a single living organism—was published (though not under that name) by the Ecosophical Research Association ("for research into philosophy, history, and theology"—Margot Adler, *Drawing Down the Moon*), of which Otter was a founder, three years before James Lovelock came to it. The name came from British novelist William Golding (author of *Lord of the Flies*).

13. "Reverence to Her": from *Tantric Art: Its Philosophy and Physics,* by Ajit Mookerjee. Ravi Kumar, 1971–72.

14. "The Callings," by David Black. *The New York Times Magazine,* May 11, 1986, pp. 30ff.

15. "A Faith of Our Own," p. 77.

16. "Dealing with Anger and Sexuality in the Parsonage," from an interview with Patricia Ferris McGinn, *Spice: The newsletter for women whose husbands are ministers,* edited by Laura Deming, vol. 3, no. 3.

17. The summary of Neo-Pagan values is from the pamphlet "What is Neopagan Druidism?" by Isaac Bonewits, published by Pentalpha: The Association for the Advancement of Aquarian Age Awareness, and the pamphlet "Neo-Paganism and the Church of All Worlds: Some

Questions & Answers," published by the Church of All Worlds, St. Louis (see Access section).

PART FOUR: BRINGING IT ALL BACK HOME
Love

Background sources:

Great Expectations: America and the Baby Boom Generation, by Landon Jones. Ballantine Books, New York, 1981.

The 1980 Census of Population, U.S. Department of Commerce, Bureau of the Census.

1. "And now we're being paid back for fucking in the streets": from Stephen Gaskin interview, *The Sun: A Magazine of Ideas,* no. 117.
2. "Children Having Children," *Time,* December 9, 1985, p. 89.
3. "Children Having Children," p. 90.
4. *Great Expectations,* p. 214.
5. *Singles: The New Americans,* by Jacqueline Simenauer and David Carroll. New American Library, New York, 1983, p. 267.
6. "Adultery . . . is unheard of": from "Once-Notorious '60s Commune Evolves into Respectability," by David Johnston. *The Los Angeles Times,* August 4, 1985, Part 6, pp. 1, 10–14.
7. "All that the hippies denied . . .": from an unsigned article beginning "Punk was something I did," in *U and I,* no. 1.
8. "We recognize that some relationships don't last . . ." and "They are bound together . . .": from "Family Portrait," by Diane Samms Rush, *The Wichita Eagle-Beacon,* September 22, 1985, pp. 1E–5E.
9. "Through it all, you have to find the love . . .": from "We *Still* Are Family: The Lymans of Fort Hill Then and Now," by Michael Matza, *The Boston Phoenix,* July 16, 1985, Section 2, pp. 1, 4–5, 11.
10. Ray Mungo interview in *Uncovering the Sixties,* p. 315.

Work

Background sources:

Great Expectations: America and the Baby Boom Generation, by Landon Jones. Ballantine Books, New York, 1981.

"Here Come the Baby-Boomers," *U.S. News & World Report* cover story, November 5, 1984, pp. 68–73.

1980 Census of Population: Detailed Population Characteristics: U.S. Summary, Volumes I and II. U.S. Department of Commerce, Bureau of the Census.

"What the Baby-Boomers Will Buy Next," *Fortune* cover story, October 15, 1984, pp. 28–34.

"The Year of the Yuppie," *Newsweek* cover story, December 31, 1984.

1. "The creature who grows in consciousness . . .": from *The Life and Work of Semmelweis,* by Louis-Ferdinand Céline. In *Mea Culpa & The Life of Semmelweis,* Little, Brown and Company, Boston, 1937, p. 54.
2. *Great Expectations,* p. 181.
3. "They are most visible . . .": from *Great Expectations,* p. 322.
4. "The Career Within a Career: The Freshman Year at Radcliffe," by Dorothy Shore Zinberg. Unpublished Ph.D. thesis, Harvard University, 1962.

ACCESS

This section tells how to find publications and organizations mentioned in the text, plus some that aren't mentioned but are closely allied in vision. This is far from a complete access guide to generational ideas and activism, but some of the sources listed here are gold mines of further information. I have marked those with a star. (Books starred in the Notes are also recommended.)

All-Purpose Periodicals

The following publications are the places where the conscience and culture of a generation are being forged. To subscribe to at least one is to experience the relief of rejoining community. Some may be the mainstream magazines of the future. Those that accept advertising do so selectively.

★ *The Utne Reader: The Best of the Alternative Press.* The best of the magazines. A bimonthly digest gleaned from scores of publications. Informative articles from different perspectives are grouped around a topic or theme: the farm and food crisis, worker ownership, "Vietnam: Can We Heal the Wounds?" "Kids: Should You Have One? Should Anybody?" "Between Idealism and Cynicism." Publisher/editor Eric Utne's name means "far out" in Norwegian. Six issues a year, $24. (Canada/Mexico, $29; elsewhere, $34.) From *The Utne Reader,* Box 1974, Marion, OH 43305. Editorial address: 2732 W. 43rd Street, Minneapolis, MN 55410. (612) 929-2670.

★ *New Options* Newsletter. (Described in the text.) Indispensable. Mark Satin, editor. Every four weeks except in August. $25 a year. (Canada and first class, $32; elsewhere, $39.) Back issues $2 each; $1.50 each for 5 or more; $1 each for 10 or more. New Options, Inc., 1701 K St. N.W., Suite 403, Washington, DC 20036. (202) 822-0929. (Through *New Options* you can also order recommended books and periodicals and a mailing list of 2,000 U.S. social-change periodicals.)

★ *Whole Earth Review.* Mildly mutated descendant of *CoEvolution Quarterly,* the offspring of *The Whole Earth Catalog.* "Access to tools and ideas." Cerebral, provocative, and addictive. Stewart Brand, publisher; Kevin Kelly, editor, 4 issues a year, $18; two years, $33. (Canadian and foreign surface mail, $22; U.S./Canada first class, $25; foreign airmail, $34.) Single issues $4.50. From *Whole Earth Review,* P.O. Box 15187, Santa Ana, CA 92705. Editorial address: 27 Gate Five Road, Sausalito, CA 94965.

★ *Mother Jones.* Muckraking from an intelligently paranoid little-guy's perspective. A working-class, leftish, big-is-bad, small-is-beautiful bias. Monthly (except for combined issues in Feb/Mar, Apr/May, and July/Aug), $24 a year. (Canada, $29/surface, $40/airmail; elsewhere, $30/surface, $60/airmail.) From *Mother Jones,* 1886 Haymarket Square, Marion,

OH 43306. Editorial address: 1663 Mission Street, Second Floor, San Francisco, CA 94103.

★ *In Context: A Quarterly of Humane Sustainable Culture.* The counterculture at its most mature and intelligent, with serious contributions to make in economics and politics, relationship and ritual. Some themes: "Living Business: Turning Work into a Positive Experience," "Play and Humor," "Governance: Power, Process, and New Options," "Living with the Land: Beyond Ownership, Sustainable Use." Robert Gilman, editor. 4 issues a year, $16; 2 years, $28. (Group rate: 3 or more subscriptions, $12/year each. Non-U.S.: surface mail, add $3.50/year, airmail, add $12/year.) Single issues: $4.50. From *In Context,* P.O. Box 2107, Sequim, WA 98382. Editorial address: P.O. Box 215, Sequim, WA 98382.

The Sun. (Described in the text.) Conscience and companion. Sy Safransky, editor. Monthly. One year, $28. Two years or more, $25/year. (Canada/Mexico, add $2/year; other countries, add $3/year.) Single issues: $2.75. From *The Sun,* 412 West Rosemary Street, Chapel Hill, NC 27514. (919) 942-5282.

War

★ *Healing from the War: Trauma and Transformation After Vietnam,* by Arthur Egendorf (coordinator of the first veteran rap groups). Houghton Mifflin, Boston, 1985. $15.95. "In the light of healing, warriorship is transformed, so that the spirit of service is renewed for causes beyond war." The best single book on acknowledging and transcending the pain of the Vietnam War—as individuals and nations, veterans and non-vets. Includes an appendix on "Suggestions for Healing Action," including a U.S. foreign policy of empowerment.

The Parable of the Tribes: The Problem of Power in Social Evolution, by Andrew Bard Schmookler. University of California Press, Berkeley, 1984; paperback edition: Houghton Mifflin, Boston, 1986. $9.95. Startling theory of how a power-hungry minority came to dictate the relations between (and within) nations—and how it might be possible to transcend this ancient bind. A great blend of intellect and personal passion.

Wanderlust

Mother Earth News. Six issues a year, $18; 2 years, $33; 3 years, $45. (Canada and foreign: $21/one year, $39/2 years, $54/3 years.) Single copy: $3. From *Mother Earth News,* P.O. Box 3122, Harlan, IA 51593-2188. Editorial address: P.O. Box 70, Hendersonville, NC 28793. (704) 693-0211.

Heart Politics, by Fran Peavey, with Myra Levy and Charles Varon. Comedienne/activist Peavey of the Atomic Comics writes of her travels around the country and the world: "I hold myself accountable to the people whose lives I have seen." Paperback, $11.50. New Society Publishers, 4722 Baltimore Avenue, Philadelphia, PA 19143.

"Alternatives to the Peace Corps: Gaining International Experience." $3 from Food First, 1885 Mission St., San Francisco, CA 94103.

Bioshelters, Ocean Arks, City Farming, by Nancy Jack Todd and John Todd (of the New Alchemy Institute, Falmouth, MA). Applying ecologically appropriate design to city and farm. Sierra Club Books, paperback, $11.

Ecology Action. Techniques for intensive small-scale agriculture developed by John Jeavons and others. 2225 El Camino Real, Palo Alto, CA 94306. Has published two books, *How to Grow More Vegetables* and *The Backyard Homestead Mini-Farm and Garden Log Book.*

Revolution

A Transformation Platform, by the New World Alliance. "First attempt to articulate what humanistic/ecological/'New Age' ideas look like when translated into a detailed, practical political platform"(*New Options*). $8 from New Options, Inc., P.O. Box 19324, Washington, DC 20036.

U and I. The magazine put out irregularly by the Lyman Family. Beautifully produced, mystifying, provocative. "You know, people might have wanted a New World, but no one was willing to pay for it." "Hope is another thing I hate. Acceptance—that life is as bad as you think—is better. Then you can start changing it." As of fall 1986, there had been two issues, both worth having. $5 each from *U and I,* P.O. Box 1886, Jamaica Plain, MA 02130.

Green Letter. The newsletter of the American Green movement, incorporating the COC (Committees of Correspondence) Newsletter. Supported by voluntary tax-deductible contributions. Make checks/money orders payable to Tides Foundation/Green Letter, P.O. Box 9242, Berkeley, CA 94709.

COC (Committees of Correspondence) Clearinghouse. Links Green groups across the U.S. and Canada. P.O. Box 30208, Kansas City, MO 64112. (816) 931-9366.

Free Spaces: The Sources of Democratic Change in America, by Harry C. Boyte and Sara E. Evans. Harper & Row, New York, 1986. An antidote to both "masses" socialism and excess counterculturalism. Argues that traditional voluntary organizations (church, PTA, neighborhood or ethnic organizations, clubs) can be important sources of empowerment, neglected by progressives.

Dope

Potsmokers Anonymous. 316 East 3rd Street, New York, NY 10003. (212) 254-1777.

Spirit

Divine Slave Gita: The Sacred and Foolish Song of the Hohm Community. An intimate inside look at life with a spiritual master. Six issues a year, $20. From Hohm, P.O. Box 25839, Prescott Valley, AZ 86312.

★ *Sojourners: An Independent Christian Monthly.* "Arising from a 40-member community in inner-city Washington . . . a meeting place for people . . . turning their lives toward the biblical vision of justice and peace." Monthly (except August/September), $18/year; $33/2 years. (Overseas surface: add $4/year. Overseas airmail: $33/year, $63/2 years.) From Sojourners, 1321 Otis St. N.E., Box 29272, Washington, DC 20017.

New Jewish Agenda. "A national progressive organization with chapters in over 40 cities working on nuclear disarmament, Israeli/Palestinian pece, peace in Central America, economic justice and feminism." Suite 1100, 64 Fulton St., NYC 10038.

Shalom Center. A Resource Center for Jewish Perspectives on Preventing Nuclear Holocaust. Arthur Waskow, Executive Director. At the Reconstructionist Rabbinical College, Church Road and Greenwood Avenue, Wyncote, PA 19095.

★ *Tikkun* ("to heal, repair and transform the world"). A Quarterly Jewish Critique of Politics, Culture, and Society. Four issues/year, $20. Single copy, $5. (Add $5/year for all foreign subscriptions including Canada.) From *Tikkun*, 5100 Leona Street, Oakland, CA 94619.

Declaration of a Heretic, by Jeremy Rifkin. Routledge & Kegan Paul, 9 Park Street, Boston, MA 02108. $8 paperback.

How Can I Help? Stories and Reflections on Service, by Ram Dass and Paul Gorman. Alfred A. Knopf, 201 East 50th St., New York, NY 10022. $5.95.

The National Havurah Committee. For referrals to and information about small Jewish faith communities. Publishes "Havurah" newsletter and *New Traditions* journal. 270 West 89th Street, New York, NY 10024.

★ *Festivals*. (Described in the text.) "Promotes the discovery of the sacred in ordinary life." Kenneth Guentert, editor. Six issues a year, $18; 2 years, $34; 3 years, $48. (Foreign subscriptions add $2.50/year.) Single copy $3. From Resource Publications Inc., 160 East Virginia Street #290, San Jose, CA 95112. (408) 286-8505.

Deep Ecology, by Bill Devall and George Sessions. Radical rejection of industrial/post-industrial civ for real reconciliation with nature. Peregrine Smith Books, P.O. Box 667, Layton, UT 84041. $24.50.

Deep Ecology, edited by Michael Tobias. Anthology of writings from the movement. Avant Books, 3719 Sixth Ave., San Diego, CA 92103. $13 paperback.

Earth First! Uses lawsuits and letter-writing but also "confrontation, direct action and civil disobedience to fight for wild places." Sample issue of journal free. Book *Ecodefense: A Guide to Strategic Monkeywrenching*, $10. P.O. Box 5871, Tucson, AZ 85703.

For a free catalog including books on Creation Spirituality by Matthew Fox and others, write to Autom, 2226 North 7th Street, Phoenix, AZ 85006.

The Emerging Order: God in the Age of Scarcity, by Jeremy Rifkin with Ted Howard. Random House/Ball, paperback, $2.95.

For a catalog of low-priced, high-quality pamphlets on Neo-Paganism, including "What is Neopagan Druidism," write to H.O.M.E., P.O. Box 982, Ukiah, CA 95482.

Love

The Gallucci Family Foundation: Route 11, Box 532, Plum Island, MA 01950.

★ The Networking Institute: a research and consulting organization on new communications possibilities in the electronic age. Connects social change networks and their members worldwide. Networking Newsletter, Networking Journal, and valuable Members Directory are included in annual membership, $75. P.O. Box 66, West Newton, MA 02165. (617) 891-4727. Founders Jessica Lipnack and Jeffrey Stamps have also published *The Networking Book,* Routledge Kegan Paul, 9 Park St., Boston, MA 02108, $12.95 paperback.

Work

Skillful Means. By Tarthang Tulku, Rinpoche. Dharma Publishing, 1978, 2425 Hillside Ave., Berkeley, CA 54704

The Calvert Social Investment Fund. 1700 Pennsylvania Ave. N.W., Washington, DC 20006. Toll free (800) 368-2748; (301) 951-4820.

Working Assets. "Tools for practical idealists" include a socially responsible money-market fund and a Visa card that charges lower interest than major banks and contributes five cents per transaction to a good cause. 230 California St., San Francisco, CA 94111. Toll free (800) 543-8800.

Catalyst. A newsletter on social investment that reviews the performance of individual companies as well as the social-investment funds. Write to 28 Main Street, Montpelier, VT 05602 for current subscription prices on *Catalyst* and two related publications, *Good Money* and *Netback Quarterly.* Also publishes book-length *Guide to Investing in Social Change.*

Co-Op America. "Building an alternative marketplace." A network of responsible businesses, co-ops and non-profit groups. Services include a catalog of humanely produced products, an information packet on socially responsible investment, and an innovative unisex health insurance plan provided by a worker-owned insurance company, CUIC, and covering alternative as well as traditional care. Membership dues begin at $15 (pay what you can). Co-op America, 2100 M St., N.W., Suite 605, Washington, DC 20063. (202) 872-5307.

The Evolutionary War

Fundamentalists Anonymous. P.O. Box 654, Wall St. Station, New York, NY 10005. (212) 696-0420.

Despair and Personal Power in the Nuclear Age, by Joanna Rogers Macy. "A groundbreaking work for overcoming the 'psychic numbing' which prevents us from coming to terms with the real threats of nuclear and ecological disaster." Paperback $8.95 from New Society Publishers, 4722 Baltimore Ave., Philadelphia, PA 19143.

Two organizations attempting to build bridges between doves and hawks, the longing for peace and the concern for security: Search for Common Ground, 1701 K St. N.W., #403, Washington, DC 20006; and Project Victory, P.O. Box 21146, Washington, DC 20009.

Citizen Summitry: Keeping the Peace When It Matters Too Much to Be Left to Politicians, edited by Don Carlson and Craig Comstock. Ark Communications Institute/Jeremy P. Tarcher, Inc. Distributed by St. Martin's Press. $10.95 paperback. To order toll free: (800) 453-5900; in Utah: (800) 662-2500).

Otter G'Zell plans a an essay contest for schoolchildren: *2020 Hindsight.* Topic: It is the year 2020. The world is at peace. The nuclear threat no longer exists. How did we do it?? Write to Otter at P.O. Box 982, Ukiah, CA 95482.

Addendum

★ *New Age Journal* is another "all-purpose" periodical whose existence was briefly in doubt when this section was being prepared. Now back on its feet, it's a good-news magazine, reporting on visionaries successfully infiltrating the worlds of business, religion, social service, and the arts. Heartening. David Thorne, editor and publisher. Bimonthly. $24 a year. From *New Age Journal,* P.O. Box 853, Farmingdale, NY 11737-9953 (800) 227-5782. Editorial address: 342 Western Ave., Brighton, MA 02135 (617) 787-2005.